# A Good Life

Human rights and encounters with modernity

# A Good Life

Human rights and encounters with modernity

Mary Edmunds

E PRESS

**ANU E PRESS**

Published by ANU E Press
The Australian National University
Canberra ACT 0200, Australia
Email: anuepress@anu.edu.au
This title is also available online at http://epress.anu.edu.au

National Library of Australia Cataloguing-in-Publication entry

Author:     Edmunds, Mary, 1943- author.

Title:      A good life : human rights and encounters with modernity / Mary Edmunds.

ISBN:       9781922144669 (paperback)  9781922144676 (ebook)

Notes:      Includes bibliographical references.

Subjects: Human beings--Social conditions--20th century.
          Human beings--Social conditions--21st century.
          Human Rights.
          Ethnology--Australia.
          Ethnology--Thailand.
          Ethnology--Spain.
          Social change.

Dewey Number:    909.82

Cover image: Photograph of Amanda Lempriere, Strathburn Station, Cape York, by Karen Leeman (nee Lempriere), 1998

Cover design and layout by ANU E Press

# Contents

## Introduction

## Part I. Tradition and transformation in a non-colonised state: Thailand

## Part II. Tradition and transformation in a non-colonised state: Spain

## Part III. Colonised people and the nation-state: Aboriginal Australia

## Part IV. Modernity and human rights

# Foreword

This is a book about hope, the hope that we have ways to live together in a rapidly changing world which will enable us to 'live a good life in the modern world'. It goes beyond hope and suggests how we may do this.

The how is a critical question at a time when rapid change is impacting on all societies. What will be the human outcomes of political turmoil in the Middle East and elsewhere? How will lives and societies be affected by the bewildering pace of economic change in places as disparate as China and the Pilbara region of Western Australia? How will we live together as the gap widens between those who rise in the new economies and those who through accident of birth, capacity or opportunities are unable to benefit? How will we manage the social impact of new media and invasive technologies that render privacy a distant memory? How do we live peacefully in a world where the race is to the swift and the appurtenances to modern life are so widely displayed and so unevenly available? How do we have a good society for all in the context of rising fundamentalism threatening violence and new despotisms? It is easy and even rational to be pessimistic when the race is to the swift, the strong overwhelm the weak, and unreason prevails.

The author draws her hope from her work as an anthropologist, staying true to her belief that 'examining the content and context of people's everyday lives' is at the heart of that discipline. Across 30 years, she draws on the experiences of three widely different groups caught up in very different ways in 'sweeping structural changes wrought by modernisation', each of whom has been able to craft their own answers to the questions she poses: what does it mean to be good and do good? What does it mean to have a good life? What sort of society do I want in order to have a good life?

In examining the disparate lives and circumstances of Spanish nuns affected by the Second Vatican Council, Thai factory workers at a time of political upheaval, and Aboriginal people in the Pilbara at a time of astounding economic and hence physical change, and their respective responses to change, a pattern emerges. The past cannot continue as it was. Modernity intrudes and is imposed in ways incompatible with the past. At the same time, the past as it was can have a role in shaping the future and be present in it in ways that are respectful of the past. A new order can emerge that enables each potentially conflicting element to construct a new future, which accords with autochthonous notions of what is a good life and a good society. And the enabling factor for all this to happen is a respect for human rights.

It might be otherwise expressed by those who are averse to the elevation of rights over responsibilities: that human beings in any society have the capacity to negotiate change and achieve ultimate harmony about how lives will be lived, as long as the position of each element in that society is accorded respect. Just call on everyone to act responsibly. But, as any practitioner who has worked at the interface between the powerful and the powerless knows, the reality is that respect can never be guaranteed by goodwill alone. In each of the studies presented an element of goodwill is present and acknowledged but it is difficult to imagine that the Thai factory workers could have organised as they did without the political and legal reforms of the day. In the same way, the nuns were faced with change by the Vatican Council, which then provided a legal framework for negotiating the tensions between modernity and earlier traditions. In the Pilbara, vague goodwill was overtaken by the emergence of native title, which at a minimum ensured that Aboriginals had a negotiating, rather than the earlier supplicant position.

Early in the life of the National Native Title Tribunal a seminar was held at the University of Western Australia on agreement-making between Indigenous people and, inter alia, mining companies. One of the speakers was a distinguished academic from the United States experienced in negotiations between Native Americans and miners. He gave some splendid best-practice examples of beneficial agreements. A shiny-eyed Australian, moved by these examples, asked why it was that miners in the United States were so positive as against the then generally negative attitude of prominent companies in Australia. His reply was that he got his best results from miners in the States by hitting them over the head with a piece of four-by-two timber. The recognition of native title in Australia, which gave Aboriginal people a legally backed place at the negotiating table, was the metaphorical piece of timber that transformed the mining interest into a leader in pursuing agreed rather than imposed outcomes.

For all of us who are involved in working with those who are threatened or ill served by externally imposed change this book is an important reminder that reasoned and reasonable outcomes are most likely where the rights of all parties are real and respected. We are reminded that respect for human rights is not some abstract academic folly but rather the best guarantee that we can each have an opportunity to create a society that works for us and enables us, and those with whom we share our place, to enjoy a good life.

Hon. Fred Chaney AO

October 2012

# Acknowledgments

When I took up my appointment at the Centre for Cross-Cultural Research at The Australian National University in 2003,[1] I thought I had died and gone to heaven. In times of great pressure on universities to adopt managerialist assumptions and organisation, not just to funding, but also to academic work, the Centre for Cross-Cultural Research was a haven of intellectual excitement and reflective space. I thank Professor Howard Morphy and Dr Mandy Thomas for making my time there possible, and my colleagues and postdoctoral students for challenging and enriching my intellectual imagination. In particular, Dr Monique Skidmore stretched my thinking by being much more academically modern than I, and suggesting the possibility that my original more modest proposal could usefully encompass the sweep of my previous research. This book is the result.

In the process, I also received invaluable support from the Centre's Executive Director, Anne-Maree O'Brien, and her administrative colleagues, especially Alan Wyburn and Suzanne Groves. Glenn Schultz and Anna Foxcroft provided timely and always helpful technical support.

My thanks go also to the many people with whom I have shared my research journey over the past 30 years. My former husband, Brendan Doran, was the reason that I found myself in Bangkok and Madrid; his support was strong and unstinting, even in the face of some disapproval from his diplomatic superiors. Without that support, I would have found it much more difficult to turn his overseas postings into research projects of my own. The late Professor Anthony Forge accepted my unorthodox proposals to undertake, first a Master's degree and then a PhD, while on overseas postings, and assisted me in negotiating the necessary approvals from The Australian National University. The Australian Institute of Aboriginal Studies—now the Australian Institute of Aboriginal and Torres Strait Islander Studies—provided me with the opportunity to carry out the first Roebourne research. I have engaged in an ongoing dialogue with Diane Smith since we were undergraduates together at the University of Queensland; I value greatly her extensive knowledge and experience, anthropological and practical, and always deep insight. And of course there are the people in the book, who allowed me into their lives and enriched mine in the process.

My friends at the Human Rights Council of Australia never allowed me to shelter from the demands of human rights advocacy even when I wanted to. Patrick Earle and others did much of the difficult work that resulted finally

---

1   The Centre for Cross-Cultural Research has now been subsumed into the Research School of Humanities and the Arts and no longer exists as a separate centre.

in the inquest into the deaths of Nurjan Husseini and Fatimeh Husseini, who drowned while seeking the better life that they thought would be offered in Australia. Julian Burnside, Catherine Crawford and Lisa Roche provided legal representation pro bono for the families of the two women. Leith Maddock, of the Fremantle asylum-seeker support group, gave generously of her time and heart to those family members and to other asylum-seekers in Perth. Angela and Fred Chaney offered me a haven, friendship and support during the demanding days of the inquest, and since.

A number of people have read and commented on the draft manuscript for this book—in particular, Professor Howard Morphy and Dr Monique Skidmore. Michael Robinson and Yindjibarndi leader Michael Woodley provided initial responses to the draft of the Pilbara chapters. Anne McMillan read each chapter as I anxiously produced it, and gave me the encouragement and courage to continue. I could not have sustained my focus without her. Kitty Eggerking provided early editorial assistance, as well as new insights through her own doctoral research. Dr Adam Chapman kindly read the Thai chapters in order to update my rusty Thai orthography. Carolyn Nagy gave an overview of the whole book by reading the complete manuscript in final draft form. Dr Debjani Ganguly took precious time from her own writing to give me advice when the time came for revision. Karen Leeman kindly gave me permission to use the photo of her daughter, Amanda, on the front cover. Karen took it, as she said, 'with love', on Strathburn Station in Cape York in 1998. Clive Hilliker produced the maps. The Australian National University provided a welcome publication subsidy. Jan Borrie undertook the intensive task of copyediting and completed it expeditiously and comprehensively. My thanks go to all of them.

A book is never completed outside the context of family and friends. This one has been accompanied by the joy of my grandchildren, Fin, Tilly, Charlotte, and Miles. I hope that their life journeys will be as serendipitous, enthralling, loved and loving, as mine has proved to be.

# Notes on names and spellings

## Note on names

In the different ethnographies, I have changed some names and not others. I have done this taking into account that some names are in the public domain, or sufficiently in the distant past, and therefore do not need to be disguised. Others—and the nuns in particular—would still be identifiable and I have not been in a position to ask their permission to do so. I have therefore changed them.

For Aboriginal people, I have checked whether there is an issue in the Pilbara, as there is in some other parts of Australia, when I make reference to those who are deceased. In general, there is no formal customary suppression of these names, although there is some avoidance in practice. For those still living, I have again checked with them or with family members to ensure that there is no concern about naming them. Where there appears to be a problem, I have not used the names of individuals. Where the text refers to 'Roebourne people' the reference is to residents of the town and surrounding small communities, regardless of tribal or linguistic affiliation. Any reference to Pilbara native title groups includes those living in the Pilbara and elsewhere.

For referencing Thai individuals or material, I have followed the Thai custom of referring to people's given names rather than their surnames. Prime Minister Kukrit Pramoj is referred to as Prime Minister Kukrit; the scholar Thongchai Winichakul is referred to as Thongchai. In the list of references and the index, Thai writers are listed according to their given names followed by the surnames, for example, Chai-Anan Samudavanija 1992.

## Note on spellings

Thai spellings are largely based on the *Thai-English Student's Dictionary*.[1] Although other dictionaries are more recent, Haas's work remains a standard text. Thai proper names and the names of festivals have been spelt using a system that preserves Thai orthography. As a result, the pronunciation cannot always be guessed—for example, Winichakul is pronounced with a final 'n' rather than

---

1 Haas (1964).

'l'; in Pramoj, the final 'j' is pronounced as a 't'. Other words—for example, the names of political parties—are romanised using a phonemic system. With these, I have chosen the form that seems to have most common usage.[2]

Spanish spellings are unproblematic.

For Pilbara Aboriginal groups, I have generally kept those used at the time, except where spelling through the native title process has become current. Ngarluma and Yindjibarndi, for example, have changed and come into accepted use; for Panyjima I have used the spelling Bunjima, which appears in native title applications. Others—for example, Innawonga/Yinhawanga or Marthuthunera/Mardudhunera—use different spellings in different situations.

---

2   I am indebted to Dr Adam Chapman for checking and updating as necessary my spelling of Thai words.

# List of maps

# Introduction

# Introduction

This book is a story. It's a story about ordinary people in very different parts of the world dealing with rapid change in the late twentieth and early twenty-first centuries. It's about times of turbulent and violent social upheaval and rupture with the past. It's about modern times. It's also about being human: what it is to be human in a modernising and globalising world; how, in responding to the circumstances of their times, different groups define, redefine, and attempt to put into practice their understandings of the good and of what constitutes a good life. And it's about how human rights have come to be a key principle in those understandings and practices.

My approach to the story is an ethnographic one, examining different groups over the last three decades of the twentieth century and the first years of the twenty-first. My main focus is on three groups: Thai factory workers over a period of two coups in the 1970s; Spanish nuns in the 1980s, in the aftermath of the Second Vatican Council and the end of the Franco dictatorship; Aboriginal people in the remote Pilbara region of Western Australia dealing with the impact of late colonialism and moves towards self-determination, from the 1980s to the present. Each of these groups has its own stories, illuminating ways in which, despite the assault of modernisation on deeply held traditional beliefs and practices, particular cultural understandings and practices continue to shape people's responses to their novel circumstances.

At the same time, the stories throw light on the intimate connectedness between a good life and a good society. They demonstrate that modernity does not permit an unquestioning acceptance of 'the way it has always been', but demands an active response to the question of what constitutes a good society. In so doing, the stories make clear that there is not just one idea of the good or of a good society within any community. The concepts themselves and their appropriate practices are the subject of intense, often savage, conflict. At stake is a contested foundation on which each of the proponents bases their judgements of what is good, for themselves and for others. As modernisation fractures the familiarity of traditional ways, calling into often anxious question the continuities between the present and the past, so it also ruptures the possibility of a unitary moral source.

The people in these studies make choices that were not traditionally available. Some of those choices are willingly embraced; others are forced on them by circumstances. Some are an invocation of past certainties, where the moral source was external and based in a religious interpretation of the world. Others reflect the shift to a secular, humanist understanding wrought by modernity. For the people in these studies, the distinction between the religious and the secular humanist conceptions of the world is not, as is generally proposed, a stark opposition. Rather, their moral framework is distilled, more or less consciously and deliberately, from their experiences of the past and the present in ways that accommodate both.

The direction mapped out in very different ways by the different groups suggests that one of the key possibilities offered by modernity is not necessarily, despite ongoing tensions, the displacement of a religious view of the world by a secular, humanist understanding, but rather the possibility of forging links between the two. The studies show that the vehicle that offers a dynamic relationship between them is the principle of human rights.

Emerging in the shadow of two world wars, the articulation of human rights marks a critical shift in the twentieth century from the earlier modern concept of natural rights and the Rights of Man as citizen, to civil rights, also as citizen, and then to rights based in the fact of being human and pertaining to all humans. In this book, I trace these shifts over time and place: in the faltering development of labour rights in Thailand in the brief democratic period between 1973 and 1976; in the ways in which the nuns in Spain, after the Second Vatican Council, moved from their cloistered separation from the world to being in a world where they saw the fight for human rights and social justice as an essential part of their vocation and Christian commitment; in the impact for Pilbara Aboriginal people of the expanding application of human rights, from their struggle to protect cultural heritage and identity to the legal and political recognition of their native title rights. In all three instances, the invocation of human rights is connected to, even pivotal for, and certainly not in opposition to, the group's religious beliefs.

This ethnographic insight offers a compellingly different view of how people can live in the modern world, not as a clash of civilisations, in conflict over religious differences or over religious and humanist oppositions. Rather, these studies show people drawing on a variety of sources, both religious and secular, in transforming their moral frameworks in order to live a good life in the modern world.

At the same time, the stories also show how deeply divided communities can become when the adaptation of their moral source compromises or denies the universal application of human rights; where evil—itself a moral choice—is chosen; where the urge to power privileges one interpretation of the good and the good society over others; where that interpretation is made singular and dominant. This is the true divide: not necessarily between religious and secular moralities, but between fundamentalist certainties, whether religious or secular, and humanist moralities. The studies indicate that the Buddhism of the Thai factory workers, the Christianity of the Spanish nuns, the creation and Christian beliefs of Pilbara Aboriginal people can all be fundamentalist, professing as absolute their versions of the truth. They can also all be profoundly humanistic. The recognition and acceptance of the role of human rights, through the experience of modernity, have come to play a central part in making the distinction.

Modernity has challenged the role of religion as arbiter of truth to being one of framing moral choices with reference to humanity. In so doing, it has universalised the notion of the good by drawing it into the discourse of human rights. The principal vehicle for developing a formal discourse has been the United Nations. At the same time, the story demonstrates that the notion of human rights itself is always in a process of becoming, always in need of further reflection, differentiation, negotiation. The idea of human rights can fail with the failure of moral imagination.[1] It can also fail when national and international institutions neglect to entrench adequate human rights standards and practices, or renege on their universal application in the name of national interest, security, or a 'war on terror'. The history of the late twentieth and early twenty-first centuries—an age that 'has witnessed more violations of their principles than any of the less "enlightened" epochs'[2]—is as much about the flight from human rights as it is about their implementation.

The studies show that the acceptance of human rights can never be taken for granted, that their practical meaning is itself contested when captured by sectional interests—whether national, ideological or religious—or subjected to a struggle for power. The dialectic between human rights implementation and its distortion or rejection is present in Thailand, in Spain, and in Australia. It was also present in the United Nations World Conference against Racism in Durban in 2001, and in the Non-Government Organisations (NGO) Forum that preceded the Conference. In Durban, both national governments and NGOs, on the basis of bitterly different interpretations of human rights, challenged the international standards agreed to in and since the 1948 United Nations *Universal Declaration of Human Rights*.[3]

The Conference demonstrated that the notion of the universal is itself contingent, subject to historical and social conditions and to cultural meanings. Nevertheless, despite its faltering, and the attempts to impose the simplicity of binary oppositions rather than to work towards the complexity of consensus, the Durban World Conference maintained the universality and indivisibility of human rights principles as the basis for the idea of the good and of the good society. Durban also provided a strong signal that understandings based on

---

1   Grayling (2003: 166).
2   Douzinas (2000: 2).
3   <http://www.un.org/en/documents/udhr/index.shtml>

human rights principles of the good, of a good life, and of a good society, do not come at the cost of diversity. It reaffirmed, often uncomfortably, that a moral order centred on human rights is not abstract or ideal, but relational; that it demands dialogue and openness to the other; that the negotiation of tensions in those relationships is never binary and never total but interdependent, contradictory, ambivalent: 'making possible and making trouble, both at once'.[4]

In the story that I set out to tell in this book, Durban provides both a climax and a denouement. The story is one of how human rights provides pathways for each of the groups included in this study to engage in their own culturally shaped dialogue with modernity. It is also my story. I encountered these groups as an anthropologist, examining the content and context of people's everyday lives. But I also encountered them, to some extent accidentally, as a result of life choices that involved family and a husband's career, and participation in human rights advocacy, as much as my own academic interests.

Like the people in these stories, I am also a product of modernity, someone who has moved from finding my moral source in a traditional religious interpretation of the world to finding it in a secular humanist one. My experience of this personal transformation, and my own human rights journey, provides its own thread, linking these apparently diverse stories; it constitutes the background to an understanding that a religious interpretation of the world does not have to be either anti-secular or anti-humanist. For me, as for the nuns in Spain, a pivotal experience was that of the Second Vatican Council and the opening of the Roman Catholic Church to the world and to those previously defined—and officially condemned over centuries—as Other. The radical nature of this shift was embodied for me in a moment when the then pope, John XXIII—Angelo Giuseppe (Joseph) Roncalli—came down from the papal throne to greet a Jewish delegation during the Vatican Council and embraced them, saying, 'I am Joseph, your brother'.[5] In that moment, and throughout Vatican II, the Roman Church placed humanity at its centre and challenged the authoritarian and hierarchical moral framework that had been its hallmark since the Reformation. As the story demonstrates and the nuns experienced, that shift was too radical to be sustained, as were the Thai 'democratic experiment' and moves by Aboriginal people to true self-determination. Nevertheless, the axis of tradition wobbled, and human rights principles have maintained it with some, if not all, of that tilt.

The structure of this story, then, is personal as well as conceptual; if, indeed, those two things are different. They are combined, at least, in my decision to situate my analysis within an enlightenment tradition, necessarily modified but not invalidated by more recent critiques. Anthropology over the period

---

4    Bhabha in Mitchell (1995: 9).

5    Genesis 45: 3–4.

covered by this book—that is, over the past 30 years—has gone from the self-assurance of structuralist-functionalist or Marxist theory through the self-doubt and often navel-gazing of reflexivity. I have gone some way with it, though I parted theoretical company in its period of postmodernism and cultural relativism. Along the way, the discipline has, quite properly, further dethroned the anthropologist as the authoritative voice speaking for others; it has responded—sometimes cleverly, sometimes not—to the challenges of new approaches brought by feminist, subaltern, post-colonial, critical and other perspectives and by the increasingly active involvement of anthropological subjects in speaking for themselves. Despite the upheavals, ethnography— analysis based on the intimate observation of and participation in the daily lives of a particular group of people—has remained the heart of the discipline.

It is through the ethnographies presented in this book, and through the multiplicity of voices and experiences, that I examine how those people who are its subjects have responded to the questions: what does it mean to have a good life? What does it mean to be good and to do good? What kind of society do I want in order to have a good life? Each group, as it has been caught up in the sweeping structural changes wrought by modernisation, has crafted its own answers. No one set of answers is complete, and the story suggests that, in the sequel, people will continue to confront moral choices that either centre or marginalise human rights. Their experience of a good life, and a good society, will depend on those choices.

# 1. Culture, morality, modernity, and the transformation of social imaginaries

There is no single notion of a good life, or of a good society; or, indeed, of how they are connected. This proposition holds at the philosophical, moral and political levels of theorising, discussion and debate. It is also true of the people in this book, all of whom have striven, in widely differing circumstances, to forge for themselves what they interpret as a good life. In each case, the interpretation was generated by specific experiences of both tradition and modernisation, and by the particular circumstances in which they found themselves. To that extent, this book offers no single interpretation either. By exploring a variety of ways in which different groups of people have sought to achieve a good life, however, the book identifies some central commonalities clustered around emerging notions of rights.

The two vignettes sketched in this chapter provide an introduction to the three more detailed case studies and indicate the fraught and contested character of these key concepts. In the first, a group of Hazara refugees fled the absolutist and oppressive Taliban regime in Afghanistan to seek a better life in Australia, only to be confronted by the limits imposed on their personal desires by an exercise of territory/nation/state[1] sovereignty that defined a good society in terms that sought to exclude them. The second vignette foreshadows the longer analysis in Chapter 8 of the 2001 Durban UN Conference against Racism. It relates the very minor incident of a press conference and information session organised during the Non-Governmental Organisations (NGO) Forum in the wake of the Australian Government's refusal to accept asylum-seekers who had been rescued by the Norwegian ship *Tampa*. The session's degeneration into an unseemly competition between the different civil-society representatives mirrored the central issues that bedevilled the Forum and the Conference itself: that is, incommensurate understandings of the practical meaning of human rights, and of what constitutes a good society. On these issues, and their very specific expression in strident anti-Semitism, the Forum and Conference foundered. In the view of many, both were entirely wrecked. My conclusions, based on the ethnographic studies presented in this book, are at odds with this view. They suggest rather that, despite such dramatic dissensions, human rights, and the principles that underlie them, remain a generative source for ordinary people's understanding of both a good life and a good society.

---

1   Zygmunt Bauman (2002: 287), echoing Agamben (1995: 117), refers to this combination of territory/nation/state as 'the (un)holy trinity'.

# Vignette 1

On 7 November 2002, two unrelated Hazara farmers from Afghanistan, Musa Husseini and Sayed Husseini, sat in the dock in the Magistrates' Court in Fremantle in Western Australia. They were in the dock, not accused of any crime, but because they were asylum-seekers who had the misfortune to collide with the Australian Government's year-old refusal to accept refugees attempting to arrive in the country outside the UN refugee system. They were there to attend the coronial inquest into the deaths of Musa's mother, Nurjan Husseini, and Sayed's wife, Fatimeh Husseini, who had drowned when the boat in which both families were trying to reach Australia sank. The Muslim fast of Ramadan began on the second day of the inquest, so that Musa and Sayed were fasting on four of the intense five days. I was in the body of the court, observing the process for the Human Rights Council of Australia, an NGO that had lobbied persistently over the intervening year to have an inquest held.

The men had fled civil war and the Taliban regime. Musa left because of fighting between Pashtuns and Hazaras in his village. His son was less than fifteen years old and was likely to be taken to fight. In fear of this possibility, Musa decided to try to come to Australia with his mother, his wife, his five children and his brother-in-law. They went first to Iran, where they lived for three to four months. They left when they heard that the son of fellow Hazara refugees had been sent back to Afghanistan and was killed on his return. Their journey took them first to Malaysia and then to Indonesia. Sayed, who had been married to Fatimeh for about a year and a half, was persuaded by her to leave their village. As Hazara, they were persecuted by the Taliban, and the regional political party wanted Sayed to go to fight the Taliban. This was something that neither Sayed nor Fatimeh wanted. Their route was through Pakistan to Malaysia and then Indonesia over some two months. The families met for the first time when the people smugglers whom they had paid to find them a passage got them a place on the *Sumber Lestari*,[2] a small coastal trader-type vessel. By then, Sayed and Fatimeh thought that she was pregnant with their first child. The boat left Surabaya, Indonesia, on Friday, 2 November 2001. Crowded on board were a crew of four Indonesians and 160 mostly Afghan asylum-seekers.

Their journey into the unknown was made in order to find a better life for themselves and their families than the one they were experiencing under the Taliban. They believed that they would find greater freedom and security in Australia and were prepared to pay the price and undertake the risks necessary to achieve that. They were among a number of people who, increasingly since late 1999, had been making their way from oppressive regimes in Afghanistan,

---

2    Officially referred to by the Australian Government as SIEV 10. See Footnote 4.

Iraq and Iran to Indonesia, and from there to Australian territory or territorial waters in small, overcrowded and usually unsafe boats. They were not to know that, two and a half months earlier, another group of 433 asylum-seekers, whose wooden boat had been badly damaged in a storm after six days at sea, had been rescued close to the Australian territory of Christmas Island by a Norwegian cargo ship, *Tampa*. When its Captain, Arne Rinnan, had changed course in order to reach the nearest port on Christmas Island, the Australian Government breached the most basic conventions of international maritime custom and the law of the sea and refused him entry. For five days, the *Tampa* waited. Its crew of 27 was swelled to 460 people, on a ship licensed to carry only 40 people, with only 40 life jackets on board, and with a number of people needing medical assistance, some urgently. It was only after the Government had finalised a comprehensive policy of rejection of boat people, and announced what it called the 'Pacific solution' to prevent them reaching Australian territory or waters, that the *Tampa* asylum-seekers were transferred to an Australian Navy ship. From there, they were taken to a hastily organised detention camp in the small neighbouring Pacific island country of Nauru.

A few days later, the Government launched 'Operation Relex'. This was a military operation involving both Navy and Customs ships. It was designed to block entry to Australia of asylum-seekers arriving on boats officially categorised as illegal. A few weeks later, in an exercise of superlative casuistry, the Government passed a package of laws and amendments to the *Migration Act (1958)* that designated a number of offshore Australian islands as 'excised offshore places'. The effect of this 'excision' was to remove those islands from the Australian migration zone and therefore to prevent asylum-seekers who managed to arrive successfully at those places from having any right to make a visa application to enter Australia. Both Christmas and Ashmore Island were included in the excised offshore places.

The impact of Operation Relex became clear throughout October. Two main incidents received extensive media coverage. The first was when the Navy ship HMAS *Adelaide* became embroiled in a highly politicised process of, first, attempting to turn back a boat with 233 Iraqi asylum-seekers aboard, and then, when the damaged vessel sank, managing to rescue them and bring them aboard the *Adelaide*. The invidious position of the Navy personnel involved was lost in the accusation—later proved false[3]—that the asylum-seekers had threatened to throw children overboard if they were prevented from reaching Christmas Island. This group of asylum-seekers was finally taken to a detention centre on Manus Island in Papua New Guinea. For most of those on another boat a fortnight later, the tragic SIEV X, rescue came too late. The overloaded

---

3   Commonwealth of Australia (2002).

boat capsized in heavy seas and 353 men, women and children drowned. An Indonesian fishing vessel rescued the 46 survivors—33 men, nine women and four children—more than 12 hours later. They were taken back to Indonesia.[4]

The *Sumber Lestari*, too, was confronted under Operation Relex. On 8 November 2001, the Australian Customs vessel *Arnhem Bay* intercepted the boat, possibly just outside the Australian contiguous zone off the coast of Ashmore Reef.[5] The Indonesian vessel was ordered to stop. This did not happen. Instead, there was an attempt to speed up. Nearby was an Australian Navy ship, HMAS *Wollongong*. Crew from the *Wollongong* boarded the Indonesian boat shortly afterwards. While the Navy personnel were on board, there was an explosion and a fire began in the engine room. In panic, those on the boat jumped overboard. Because there was an accusation that the asylum-seekers had sabotaged the *Sumber Lestari*, much of the questioning in the inquest focused on the state of the boat before it left Indonesia. Sayed was asked, 'Was the boat safe?' He replied, 'I am not sure what a boat is supposed to look like, so I don't know.' Nevertheless, in the chaos that followed the explosion, Sayed tried to persuade Fatimeh to jump with him into the water but she was frightened. Sayed described to the Coroner what happened: 'But when the Australians told us to jump, we held hands and jumped. That was the last time when we were together. Then we were separated. I couldn't see my wife'. Musa had his whole family—his wife and five children as well as his mother—to protect.

> First my wife jumped, then one of my daughters. I held my other daughter and jumped, then my sons. My brother-in-law jumped with my mother. I saw my wife with too much water in her trousers, she couldn't get her balance and would have drowned. I had to help her. I couldn't see my mother because of the waves. The last time I saw my mother was on the boat.

Most, if not all, of the asylum-seekers were wearing life jackets but of substandard quality. The crews of the two Australian ships managed to rescue alive all but two of the asylum-seekers and the Indonesian crew. The two who did not survive were Musa's mother, Nurjan Husseini, approximately fifty-five years old, and Sayed's wife, Fatimeh Husseini, twenty-one years old. Much of the incident was videoed by one of the Customs crew, up to the point of the

---

4   Under Operation Relex, the boats coming from Indonesia were labelled and numbered. The label was 'Suspected Illegal Entry Vessel' or SIEV. The *Olong*, the boat confronted by the *Adelaide*, became SIEV 4. The name of SIEV X, the boat that capsized, is not known. The *Sumber Lestari* became SIEV 10.

5   Under international law, the contiguous zone refers to an area of 12 nautical miles beyond Australia's territorial waters. Article 24 of the UN *Convention on the Territorial Sea and the Contiguous Zone, 1958* sets out that a state may exercise some control related to necessary protection of its territory. Less than two months before the *Sumber Lestari* incident, Ashmore Reef had been excised from Australia's migration zone as part of a suite of eight bills 'rushed into law' as part of the so-called 'Pacific solution' (Mares 2002: 167 ff.).

explosion and when people started leaping overboard. At that point, the video ceased, with a startled exclamation from one of the Australian crew of, 'The motherfuckers are jumping!'

A year later, the rest of the story was told from its different perspectives to the Coroner in the Fremantle court. The video footage was shown on the first day. It was the first time that Musa and Sayed had seen it. After the Navy and Customs personnel had given their evidence, Sayed told his story through an interpreter.

> We started our journey on a Thursday evening, and then the next Thursday all these things happened. I was sitting with my wife and I heard from others that a ship was coming. Then we saw the other boat coming, but we didn't know it was the Navy. We weren't concentrating on the boats. I was paying attention to my wife, and my wife was paying attention to me. We were caring for each other.

After they jumped into the water and were separated, 'one of the rubber boats saved me'. He was taken to the *Arnhem Bay*.

> After I was saved, I was asking about my wife. They didn't know. Then they told me she was on the other boat. I asked to be taken to her. That took quite some time. They told me there was one deceased lady on the ship. I went to her and saw that it was Musa's mother. So I asked again. But I wasn't informed about my wife.

In fact, Fatimeh was already dead. According to the Navy evidence, there may have been a very faint indication of life after she was taken out of the water, but she failed to respond to attempts to resuscitate her both then and later on board the *Wollongong*. Sayed did not find out until the following morning.

> In the morning, they took me to the other ship. They were having their breakfast. Another man knew some English and asked for me. They told us to sit down and have breakfast, they told me my wife is sick and a doctor is attending her, and I should sit here and eat my breakfast.

At this point in his story, Sayed wept. When he could go on, he told how one of the officers came out: 'I could tell from his face that it was very severe. They whispered to me that my wife had died'. Sayed then apologised to the Coroner and to the court for his emotion: 'I am very sorry if I have upset anyone today.'

The account of Nurjan Husseini's death was given mainly by the sixteen-year-old boy who had tried to save her. Ali Reza Sadiqi had left Afghanistan because of trouble with the Taliban. One older brother had been killed by the Taliban. Another had escaped three years previously and for most of that time the family did not know where he was. In the end, he had arrived in Australia and was living in Perth on a temporary protection visa. Their father was a blacksmith and, as Reza told his story: 'The Taliban used to come and take things without paying. Once I refused to serve them, and they stabbed me'. He still did not have the full use of his right hand and it continued to trouble him. He had tried to get to a UN doctor, but was introduced to a people smuggler and travelled to Pakistan, Iran, Malaysia and Indonesia. Overall, his journey took nearly a year. His attempt to reach Australia on the *Sumber Lestari* was the third time he had tried to do so. The first boat proved unseaworthy, the second one sank. As a result, Reza had bought his own life jacket before he left Indonesia. He was wearing it at the time of the explosion.

> I threw my bag with my birth certificate and clothes, and a piece of [loose] wood into the water. Then I jumped…I had my bag for a few minutes but then I saw a person without a life jacket and gave it to him. I was having a problem with my right hand, but I tried my best. I can swim a little. I gave the piece of wood to another man who had been in the villa in Indonesia. I saw a tube in the water, I put a child in the tube and told the man to help. Then I saw Musa's mother. What I saw first was another person with her face down in the water. She had a life jacket on. She was not moving and her arms were down in the water. I did not recognise her. I pulled her face out of the water. She wasn't breathing. I pushed her chest and tummy and foam came out and she started breathing. I took her and tried to swim towards the Australian ship but the waves kept pushing me away…I was struggling to hold Musa's mother's head above water.

Reza and Mrs Husseini were finally taken on board the *Arnhem Bay*. Attempts to resuscitate Mrs Husseini failed.

The next morning, the bodies of both Nurjan and Fatimeh were transferred to another Navy ship for burial on Christmas Island. Instead of asylum, those who had survived were split into two groups and confined in detention centres for the next two and a half years. Sayed was with the group who were detained on Christmas Island. There he was able to make regular visits to his wife's grave until he was removed to Nauru, at three o'clock in the morning and with almost no warning, in March 2004. Musa and his family and Reza were taken to the detention centre on Nauru. After a year there, Reza spent the year that followed the inquest under guard in a solitary motel room in Perth. He was still a minor and the Perth detention centre was not authorised to house minors. Nor would the Commonwealth Department of Immigration and Multicultural and Indigenous Affairs (DIMIA) allow him to be released into the care of his older brother.

Sitting every day in the court in Fremantle, I watched the impact on these men as the interpreter—a gentle Iranian Bah'ai woman—translated what was being asked and said about the events that had changed their lives. Although I had gone to the Perth detention centre to meet them, although I was representing the NGO that had been actively instrumental in getting the inquest held at all, and which was providing the interpreter after the refusal by the Commonwealth to do so, I was not permitted to approach or speak to the men in the court. They were treated as prisoners and kept separate and under guard. We felt the full force of this on the final day, which was also the first anniversary of the deaths of Nurjan and Fatimeh. A number of local refugee support groups had organised a small memorial vigil to be held outside the courthouse half an hour before the inquest was due to begin. I sought and gained permission from the Perth detention centre manager and from the Coroner for Musa and Sayed to attend. Minutes before the vigil was to begin, this permission was personally overridden from Canberra by the Federal Minister for Immigration, Phillip Ruddock. As we joined in commemoration and prayer on a grassy area adjoining the courthouse, Musa and Sayed waited inside under the usual guard, forbidden to share this moment that touched them so deeply.

These circumstances of fear, insecurity, loss, imprisonment did not constitute the better life in Australia that these families, and several thousand other asylum-seekers over the same period, were seeking. Musa's teenage daughter Amina wrote from Nauru to Bishop Brian Kyme of the Anglican Church in Perth:

> The situation of the camp is not good. Here is very hot. There isn't enough water. I hate it. We are fed up with this situation. I always pray for everybody. I pray for my parents because they don't feel happy in here, my mother always has headache and she's ill. My father too. My father can't eat anything due to he hasn't got any teeth. I worry for them…I don't like to lose my mother due to she really is ill and here hasn't got good doctor. Please you help us…I request you from the bottom of my heart that you help us to get free from this camp as soon as possible…Please help, help, help. Perhaps you can't believe if I tell you now that in writing the letter I'm crying…
>
> * hope
>
> Hope here dies, as long as hope lives
>
> life thrives on hope, hope keeps me alive.
>
> Amina
>
> your friend

Whatever expectations these families had in leaving the familiarity of their traditional village lives as farmers, they did not include a hazardous journey by sea and long-term detention at the end of it. Sayed commented, 'As soon as I saw the sea, I was frightened. The smugglers told us that the boat would be quite safe. If I knew it was this kind of boat, I wouldn't have come.' Musa talked of the drought and the lack of wood in his village and very much about the fighting and his fear for his fifteen-year-old son. Life was very difficult. After they left Iran, they intended to come to Australia, because 'we had heard that human rights people were very active and that there would be a place for us there'. The first part of Musa's statement was borne out. The second was frustrated by their encounter with a government whose idea of the good was dictated by narrow political rather than humanitarian concerns. The families' experiences, in both Afghanistan and Australia, make clear that the idea of the good, and of a good society, is not a matter of consensus but of intense conflict. This is a theme that will be central to this book.

The men's accounts also give brief glimpses of the lives of Hazara villagers in central Afghanistan at a time of intense and immediate internal conflict. Traditional ways continued, but already disrupted by decades of war. Things had got worse under the Taliban, especially for women, as Musa reluctantly responded when questioned: 'I cannot really tell because it is dishonouring for me, but they were raping women and girls. It was very bad for them.' The context for both families had become the immediate threat and the reality of violence and death. Their choice to escape, despite its own dangers, reflects the families' recognition that, under these conditions, they could not succeed in 'the struggle to be ordinary'.[6] For them, the local of their village and region was subsumed by the larger regional and national conflicts. In embarking on the journey to Australia, they entered the alien worlds of, first, people smugglers, temporary sojourns in strange countries, and the fear and discomfort—with insufficient food, no bedding and extreme overcrowding—of the long days and nights on the *Sumber Lestari*. They also entered a world in which the familiarity of traditional ways was fractured by the new, where the ways they had taken for granted were reduced, and each day required new decisions and new choices. In the process, and without actively seeking it, they also came to confront the ambiguities of modernity, as well as entering a globalised world in which borders are open to trade but not to people.

## Vignette 2

A year before the inquest, I was in Durban, South Africa, again representing the Human Rights Council, this time as part of an Australian delegation to the NGO Forum that preceded the United Nations' overly ambitious World Conference against Racism, Racial Discrimination, Xenophobia and Related Intolerances. On Wednesday, 29 August 2001, the day after the opening of the Forum, news from

---

6    Ross (2003b: 6), discussing the South African Truth and Reconciliation Commission.

Australia reached us of the *Tampa* stand-off. We learnt by short-wave radio, fax, phone, and email from other delegates that the Australian Government was refusing to accept asylum-seekers arriving by boat from Indonesia; even refusing, to the Norwegian ship that had rescued them, entry to Australian waters and to Christmas Island, and rejecting requests for assistance from the *Tampa*'s Captain Arne Rinnan. The details were incomplete and frustrating. The thousands of delegates were spread across multiple locations at the Kingsmead Cricket Stadium and beyond. Different people had sporadic access to different communication media. The queues were long for terminals in the internet room that the Forum organisers, the South African Non-Government Organisations Coalition (SANGOCO), had set up. By the next day, the situation had become clear enough for Australian delegates from a range of organisations to have set up an NGO Working Group and to have circulated, as did Amnesty International and Human Rights Watch, a media release, outlining the situation and condemning the Australian Government.

Subsequent events could be seen as a microcosm of the dissension with which the whole Forum and then the Conference was riven. Our response began as a cooperative effort to organise a joint NGO position with a view to mobilising international pressure on the Australian Government. Despite our shock that Australia could so rapidly jettison its commitment to the principles fundamental to good international citizenship—the Refugee Convention and international law more generally, especially the law of the sea, and humanitarian obligations— we felt that we could use our presence at a world conference against racism to shame the Government. Instead, we shamed ourselves. The press conference and information session that the working group organised a few days later mirrored the tensions that had plagued the Forum and were to overshadow the Conference itself.

A little before 8 am, we gathered in the Forum media tent. Despite some activity around other tents, there was an early morning calm instead of the usual dust and noise. The ugly confrontation between Palestinians and Jews, which every day throughout the Forum defined the entrance strip close to the media tent, had not yet got under way. It was another beautiful early spring day and the final day of the Forum. The official Conference had begun the previous day in the splendid Durban International Convention Centre some blocks away from the Kingsmead Stadium. Our information session was small but well organised. We had chosen a panel, including a representative of the Norwegian Red Cross, who could speak with knowledge and authority about refugee issues. The names had been suggested and agreed to at earlier, well-attended meetings of the Australian NGOs. We thought the focus was *Tampa* and collective action. We found that, like much of the Forum itself, this degenerated into a competition of victims. In this case, some Indigenous Australians, aggressively supported by a small group from an NGO representing one of the Australian Ethnic Communities Councils, asserted prior unresolved injustices as against those of the *Tampa* asylum-seekers. The point of the Australian Government's decisions about *Tampa* was lost as the shouting from the floor escalated in accusations about us as organisers not representing Indigenous people or issues and having set up an 'all-white Australian' panel. The Norwegian representative looked bemused at being lumped in as a 'white Australian'. The failure of the press conference and information session was a very minor preliminary to the defeat of the hope for a more humane government response to the terrible predicament of persecuted people seeking safety and shelter in Australia.

In the heat and disappointment of the incident, I could not see that what I was witnessing was, as Canadian philosopher Charles Taylor was later to put it in a different discussion, a clash of divergent modern social imaginaries.[7] Importantly, that clash was not just at the level that we had anticipated of a national government and its own civil society but also of groups within civil society who are defined differently by colonisation and modernisation within that nation. At issue were different understandings of what constitutes a good society. At stake was a common understanding of the good. At risk was a vision of a modern international order, represented by the United Nations, based on a recognition of the bond of common humanity, and a willingness by all member nations to work together towards common understandings and actions. UN processes like the Durban NGO Forum and the World Conference are predicated on the possibility of negotiating agreement about principles and issues that touch all people and all nations—in this case, about finding ways to eliminate racism throughout the world. No-one expected that to be easy. No-one expected it to come so close to collapsing in a morass of vituperation and overt mutual hostility. The shock for many NGO delegates was that this was not confined to a confrontation between the sectional interests of governments in the official Conference, but that it also contaminated the NGO Forum. As Myrna Cunningham, one of the members of the NGO International Steering Committee, commented in a striking understatement, 'It was not a conference of happiness, but a conference of pain'. She was referring to the key issues—the Israeli–Palestinian conflict, the question of reparations for slavery, the multiplicity of victims' voices—that dominated the proceedings. Had she been at our modest *Tampa* press conference, she might have used a similar description.

The divisions among Australian NGOs receded as the Forum gave way to the Conference. However, the broader NGO dissensions and issues were not resolved in Durban, as they were overtaken by the more public and dramatic dissensions of the Conference itself; as, indeed, the significant actual achievements of the Conference were largely overtaken and overwhelmed three days after its close

---

7 Taylor (2004).

by the events of 11 September and the attack on the twin towers in New York.[8] And the three incidents—*Tampa*, the confrontations in Durban, and the attack on the twin towers and its aftermath—are not unrelated in their demonstration of the fragility of the achievements of modernity and the malaise, disaffection, and violence that are their dark side. The modern forms of racism, so closely linked to colonialism, which Durban was established to defeat are themselves part of that malaise.

Durban, like its other World Conferences, also embodied the United Nations' struggle to maintain the ideal of its Charter 'to save succeeding generations from the scourge of war', 'to practise tolerance and live together in peace with one another as good neighbours'.[9] But *Tampa*, the confrontations in Durban, the attack on the Twin towers—all in their own way threatened the 'friendly relations among nations based on respect for the principle of equal rights and self-determination of peoples'[10] that was the basis of the United Nations' establishment and of the international order the United Nations was designed to represent. The three different events underline that the greatest challenge to the effectiveness of the United Nations and the international cooperation that it was set up to foster comes from the sectional interests and power struggles of its own member states and from groups that those interests exclude. The global village has given way to globalisation; modernity carries the seeds of its own potential destruction.

# Culture and modernity

These two different sketches illuminate the dilemmas and contradictions that lie at the heart of globalisation and of modernity. They throw into relief the main propositions that I address through more detailed ethnographies in this book. In the following chapters, I offer a multi-sited, comparative analysis of three different societies struggling to come to grips with the assault of modernisation on traditionally held beliefs and practices. My interest has always been social change, since the moment as an undergraduate student in anthropology at the University of Queensland when we moved from structural-functionalist presentations of what appeared to be static traditional societies to Edmund Leach's study of the Kachin in his *Political Systems of Highland Burma*.[11] Suddenly, in that hot lecture theatre, anthropology came alive for me. I understood that all societies, even the most traditional, are dynamic, that they are about change, not equilibrium, that culture is a frame of reference, not a

---

8   I will look at the Conference in more detail in Chapter 8.
9   *Charter of the United Nations 1945*, Preamble.
10  ibid., cl. 2.
11  Leach (1954).

straitjacket, that people respond to the historical and political conditions—of continuity or of rapid change—in which they find themselves. The common thread in all my subsequent research has been the impact of social change, in the form of modernisation, on traditional groups. The questions have focused on the meaning of people's everyday lives, how ordinary people experience the often extraordinary events of their time, what human groups have in common, but also, and crucially, how culture shapes but does not determine the ways in which people respond to change.

My assumption is that, by examining the various ways in which different groups respond to and invest meaning in their new situations, we can learn something important, not just about each particular group, but about what humans have in common and about the human condition. More immediately, one of my aims in this book is, by looking at a range of different social groups in the process of encountering modernity, to throw some light on the urgent social issues of the early twenty-first century. Many of the issues arising from globalisation that we now confront can be better understood through the lens of the modernising processes that have taken place in the second half of the twentieth century.

In order to canvass these issues, the book draws on anthropological research that I have undertaken at different times and in diverse regions of the world: Thailand (1975–77), Spain (1981–84), and Aboriginal Australia (1987 to the present). It also follows the personal journey that took me, and often my family, to spend some years in each of these places, providing a context of daily familiarity with not just the subjects of the study but also with the broader conditions in which they lived. They also gave me the ethnographic orientation that has informed my briefer encounters in other situations—the inquest in Fremantle and the Durban World Conference—and confirmed my view that, despite enormous diversity, postmodern or cultural relativism collapses in the face of demonstrated human universals.

In drawing on this material, my aim is to explore what it is that humans see as having a good life. On the basis of this deceptively simple premise, the book examines a range of traditional societies and the variety of ways in which modernisation, through its fracturing of the past, has demarcated particular notions of the good and of a good life as key to the continuity of a culture. At the same time, the case studies make clear that culture, with its 'unyielding ambiguity',[12] is a protean frame of reference, offering differing facets to its constituent groups in forms that depend on the social and economic circumstances through which they are experienced. The book also examines, therefore, what alternative notions, distinct or oppositional, are held within as well as between groups who identify themselves as part of the same cultural tradition.

---

12   Bauman (1973: 1).

I examine the extent to which differing notions of the good may be essentially incompatible and what means—formal or informal, institutional or violent—are used to impose or resist certain notions of the good. And I analyse how these contradictions and struggles are played out in particular circumstances. The ethnographies identify at which points traditional notions may be open to expansion and transformation and where these notions are unable to withstand the assault of modernisation and result in conflict. Finally, I examine some of the consequences of these divergent understandings and experiences in order to understand the extent to which violence emerges from the clash between modernity and tradition, or is spawned by modernity itself.

My interest in exploring commonalities as well as difference has led me to a number of propositions that the book examines. These propositions are, firstly, and drawing again on Charles Taylor, that the concepts of the good and of a good life are human universals and that moral evaluation—morality—and the concept of the good are at the centre of human agency.[13]

Secondly, one of the characteristics of modernity is the struggle to identify agreed fundamental aspects of these human universals. Modernity places secular humanity rather than religious beliefs at the centre of moral evaluation and action, giving rise to a new moral source. This new moral source is the key moral principle of respect for the bond of common humanity. In our modern—globalising—world, the principle of respect for the bond of common humanity links all humans across cultures, underpinning notions of personhood, equality, freedom, justice, and rights. Its primary source of articulation is the United Nations. And, like all moral principles, it is honoured as much, perhaps more, in the breach than in the observance as self-interest, national interest, the thirst for power, even the rejection of universality, combine to resist its application.

Thirdly, despite this commonality, different human groups understand and experience these concepts differently, and the variety of ways in which they understand them are culturally and historically constructed and contingent. Even where the moral source may be shared, particular understandings of the good and the moral frameworks arising from those meanings are culturally negotiated. As morality is about choice and reason is about order, culture is about framing those choices and giving meaning to them and to the particular order that prevails. Culture mediates and makes meaningful the relationship between reason and morality. And culture may also be seen as

> a *permanent revolution* of sorts. To say 'culture' is to make another attempt to account for the fact that the human world (the world

---

13  Taylor (2003).

moulded by the humans and the world which moulds the humans) is perpetually, unavoidably and unremediably *noch nicht gewroden* (not-yet-accomplished), as Ernst Bloch beautifully put it.[14]

This view of culture challenges, as Bauman means it to do, a totalising notion of culture as an instrument of 'continuity, reproduction of sameness and resistance to change…culture as a "preservative"',[15] or even as resistance. Instead, culture is about creating, modifying and reproducing meaning, those 'webs of significance that [man] himself has spun'.[16] Such 'webs of significance' may be more or less generalised in any particular society. Inherent in the notion of a 'traditional' or 'pre-modern' society is a comprehensive and stable set of meanings that infers the world as complete rather than as 'not-yet-accomplished'. These meanings include a customary order and moral framework that, in turn, reinforce those meanings that underpin particular notions of the good and of the good life. Nevertheless, as these studies will show, there is not a single notion of the good even within as well as between societies. Conflict, often violent, is generated by opposing and sometimes incompatible differences in meaning and in practices designed to implement particular notions of a good life and a good society. This is so in the confrontation between different social groups and cultures, and can be so even within the same social group where there are differing interpretations arising from the same moral source.

Both the agreed articulation and the culturally specific understandings of these concepts, and the principles that underlie them, are subject to the 'compromised pragmatics' of people's daily lives,[17] as well as to the possibility of transgression. They are also subject to the struggle between opposing interests, whether of individuals or of nations, to impose one totalising view and suppress others.

Finally, the possibilities of a good life and a good society are essentially related; one is not possible without the other.

## Reason and morality

This book's theoretical framework emerges particularly from the work of Charles Taylor and Jürgen Habermas. Taylor and Habermas have engaged with and critiqued each other. At the same time, the early thinking of both was shaped by Marx as well as Hegel and, despite their divergent paths, both continue in the tradition of Marx's moral, as well as practical and political, core. Just as importantly, they offer cogent, constructive alternatives to contemporary social

---

14   Bauman in Bauman and Tester (2001: 32).
15   Bauman in ibid., p. 32.
16   Geertz (1975: 5).
17   Miller (1995: 322).

theories focused principally on deconstruction and on the exclusive predominance of relations of power. Both seek—and offer—a theory of the self and of society and social action that addresses and takes issue with the contemporary position, theoretical and practical, of desolation. Neither dismisses the insights gained in the examination of relations of power, but both look to go beyond a defining notion of power to the effectiveness of human agency and, indeed, freedom. In *Sources of the Self*, Taylor asserts the fundamental importance of morality: that 'selfhood and the good, or in another way selfhood and morality, turn out to be inextricably intertwined themes'.[18] Morality, in turn, implies choices made freely by human agents, even within the limits imposed by external conditions, and not necessarily in pursuit of the good.

In *The Theory of Communicative Action*, and throughout his work, Habermas places reason, and rationality—'a disposition of speaking or acting subjects that is expressed in modes of behaviour for which there are good reasons or grounds'[19]—at the centre. His analysis challenges the notion of the amorality of reason argued by writers such as John Ralston Saul because, in Habermas's view, reason is not divorced from, and therefore is not in imbalance with, 'the other more or less recognised human characteristics: spirit, appetite, faith and emotion, but also intuition, will, and, most important, experience'.[20] On the contrary, 'reason is, by its very nature, incarnated in contexts of communicative action and in structures of the lifeworld'.[21] Habermas rejects the nihilism of Nietzsche and the position taken by Max Horkheimer and Theodor Adorno in the *Dialectic of Enlightenment*: that 'reason itself destroys the humanity it first made possible'.[22] He sees this analysis as 'mutilating' reason, 'because it lays claim to it only in the form of a purposive-rational master of nature and instinct—precisely as instrumental reason'.[23] Habermas's work is an ongoing investigation of the proposition that only in a society in which a richer, more complex, notion of reason can be invoked can we hope to sustain a good society[24] or, indeed, a good life. In Habermas, reason is redeemed, as morality is re-centred in Taylor, and the essential relationship between reason and morality is affirmed.

In this book, I build on Taylor's argument that moral evaluation—morality— and the concept of the good are at the centre of human agency. Through the examination of different groups subject to rapid social change, I also develop the links between Taylor's propositions and Habermas's analysis of communicative

---

18    Taylor (2003: 3).
19    Habermas (1984:22).
20    Saul (1993: 15).
21    Habermas (1987: 322).
22    Habermas (2002: 110).
23    ibid., p. 111.
24    Seidman (1989: 1).

action. In communicative action, human action is oriented towards reaching understanding[25] and is essentially interactive and intersubjective—that is, relational—invoking a moral as well as a normative dimension. A communicatively achieved agreement, he suggests, 'must be based *in the end* on reasons',[26] and the structures of rationality are embedded in everyday life.[27] Communicative action represents for Habermas the utopian potential of modernity.

The particular theoretical contribution of this book begins at the juncture of the works of Taylor and Habermas. From that point of critical convergence, my analysis moves to a series of further propositions emerging from the book's ethnographies. The first is that people's experience of modernity is inevitably partial because the processes of modernisation are regulated and to varying extents limited by historical and institutional structures. People respond to modernisation from within their cultural frameworks. They respond as individuals and as members of social groups. Their responses involve rational and moral choices. Where reason and morality combine to generate action that is oriented towards reaching a common understanding of the good, different groups also develop ideas about what constitutes a good society. Modernity assesses and universalises key aspects of these ideas through the discourse of human rights. The practical application of these ideas requires the active support of institutional structures, at local, national and international levels. Conflict arises within and between societies when there is no common understanding of the good or of what constitutes a good society; when communicative action collapses.

Habermas recognises that communicative action is only one among the possibilities for human action. Not all are based on reaching understanding. Strategic action, for example, arises from interests and distorts rationality. The result is one of the central paradoxes of modernity: that the search for freedom, meaning and a good life can lead equally to the loss of meaning and of the moral framework that sustains particular understandings of the good: of what it is good to be—of wellbeing—and of what it is good to do; and of what constitutes a good life.[28]

This paradox becomes most acute in the processes of modernisation:

> 'Being modern' means to be in a state of perpetual modernization: modernity is, so to speak, the time of 'new beginnings' and of forever new 'new beginnings', of dismantling old structures and building new ones from scratch.[29]

---

25  Habermas (1982: 234).
26  Habermas (1984: 17).
27  Seidman (1989: 2).
28  Taylor (2003).
29  Bauman in Bauman and Tester (2001: 72).

The notion of modernity is one generated by and rooted in European history and in the Western imagination. Among the many available descriptions, Taylor offers one that has the merit of being succinct:[30]

> By *modernity* I mean that historically unprecedented amalgam of new practices and institutional forms (science, technology, industrial production, urbanization), of new ways of living (individualism, secularization, instrumental rationality), and of new forms of malaise (alienation, meaninglessness, a sense of impending social dissolution).

Modernisation, whether through colonialism, industrialisation, or globalisation, has drawn, often forced, the rest of the world into grappling with this originally European paradigm. Modernisation fractures the continuity between the present and the past, and looks instead to the future:

> Because the new, the modern world is distinguished from the old by the fact that it opens itself to the future, the epochal new beginning is rendered constant with each moment that gives birth to the new…A present that understands itself from the horizon of the modern age as the actuality of the most recent period has to recapitulate the break brought about with the past as a *continuous renewal*.[31]

For asylum-seekers like Musa and Sayed and their families, however, for Durban delegates focused on reasserting the validity of claims based in the past, for the different groups in the case studies, the break with the past is not, cannot, be absolute. The past may no longer be the primary source of either meaning or legitimacy, but it remains a potent one, and one that is essential to making sense not only of the present but also of the future. Culture, like history, is grounded in the past, and continues to inform and shape the ways in which these different groups develop new meanings out of their changed situations, giving rise to 'multiple modernities'.[32] Inevitable in modernisation, too, as the case studies in this book make clear, are encounters or clashes between different ways of defining the good and the good life. With modernisation have gone its ancillary experiences of rapid and drastic, indeed often violent, social change; and the many equally violent reactions, like that of the Taliban in Afghanistan. Ordinary people, like Musa and Sayed and their families, are caught up in the ensuing conflicts.

In struggling for new meanings, all the groups in this book offer a further challenge to one of the key characteristics of modernity: the replacement of religion with secular humanism as the fundamental moral source. For none

---

30   Taylor (2002: 91).
31   Habermas (2002: 6–7).
32   Comaroff and Comaroff (1993: 1).

of these groups has religion been replaced; God is far from dead. At the same time, religion is no longer the sole moral source or source of meaning. In fleeing Afghanistan, Musa and his family, Sayed and Fatimeh, Ali Reza and his brother did not make a choice in terms of modernity. Their choice was made to avoid the consequences of the Taliban's rejection of modernity. But in so doing, they laid claim to sources of meaning and morality other than religious belief, or at least the religious belief expounded by the Taliban. They did not reject religious belief; on the contrary. But their action put them in opposition to the Taliban's orthodox expression of religious belief and to religious authority as the sole imposed moral framework.

The case studies will make clear that this is the situation for other groups. Religious belief is not in necessary opposition to an assertion of common humanity based in the secular humanism of modernity; the two can coexist and indeed complement each other. But religious belief does not, of itself, provide a sufficient moral framework to encompass the multiplicity of belief systems and cultures in the modern world. Modernity displaces the hegemony of religious belief with a privileged role for reason and, by extension, for rationality in engaging with the world; humans knowingly reliant on their own devices and meanings. Only where religious orthodoxy asserts itself as the sole moral source and framework does it become anti-modern and deny in practice that human agency, not divine or preordained order, is at the centre of the human world in the making both of history and of meaning.

In examining what it is that humans in different societies see as having a good life, the case studies identify the connection between those notions of a good life and particular ideas of the good; how different groups attempt to put those ideas into practice; and what happens when those ideas and practices are confronted by modernisation. A key and generally radical impact of modernisation on traditional communities is, indeed, to challenge, override, or shatter the accepted order and its moral framework; and hence different notions of the good and practices tied to particular understandings of a good life. Modernisation relativises or fractures also the traditional moral sources from which people derive their legitimating frameworks, and gives rise to one of the other key characteristics of modernity, that is, uncertainty. This may result in a purposeful agency or, as Camus argued, in absurdity.[33] The case studies make clear that the result is turbulent, often violent, social upheaval and change as different groups struggle to come to grips with, and react to, the assault of modernisation and modernity on deeply held beliefs and practices.

In the societies under review, the responses are chaotic, coherent; pragmatic, ideological; violent, confused; self-interested, altruistic; idealistic, mundane.

---

33   Camus (2000).

In each case, the ways in which these particular groups have responded to modernisation are culturally shaped, though not culturally bounded. The moments of acceptance or rejection of themselves indicate the permeability of cultural boundaries, suggesting some areas of existing or possible common understanding, while areas of conflict identify points of greater or lesser contradiction or incompatibility. Within this range of differences, I include an examination of attempts by these various groups to accommodate and, in some instances, appropriate the new. At the same time, they continue to retain, assert, or transform their own notions of the good and the practices associated with the good life. These dialectically related movements occur in the face of challenge, from within their communities as well as from without. Nevertheless, the different responses share a common striving to make sense of these experiences and to maintain or reconstruct a good life, for themselves and others, and for the next generations, under the circumstances in which they find themselves.

The case studies analysed in the book also provide the material for a comparative analysis that looks not only at cultural specificities. On the basis of this material, it becomes clear also that it is possible for different groups—within the same society and between societies—to reach, out of their particular experiences, consensus about what constitute universal moral principles and about some of the ways in which those universal principles are to be implemented. Implementation takes place in the modern world particularly through the articulation of rights, which have 'become central to our legal systems' but, in an analogous way, have also 'become central to our moral thinking'.[34] Such consensus may be achieved because of the pervasiveness of 'the medium of action orientated to reaching understanding'[35] and of the centrality to human agency of morality; of the relatedness of morality and reason; and of the idea of the good itself. This is so, whatever the varying meanings attached to that idea of the good may be.

The ethnographies demonstrate that individual societies stand in different, and often contradictory, relationships to modernity's placing of secular humanity at the centre of the vision of rational order. Nevertheless, despite these complexities and contradictions, the material shows that all are required to engage with the concept of rights—the practical expression of secular universal moral norms— and with the legal formulations of and safeguards for those rights. The Durban World Conference against Racism indicated the moral as well as political pressures on nations and on civil society to participate, however rancorously or unwillingly, in the discussion of rights, even where this discussion was hijacked by a power struggle between sectional interests asserting incompatible interests against one another.

---

34    Taylor (2003: 11).
35    Habermas (1982: 227).

# Structure of the book

The book is divided into four sections. Parts I and II examine the impacts of modernisation in two non-colonised countries, Thailand in the period 1975–77 and Spain in the period 1981–84, keeping in mind Spain's earlier role as itself a major colonising power. Nevertheless, both countries in the periods dealt with here were still in the process of formation as modern nation-states. The material demonstrates that the impact of modernisation has been radical for both societies, despite the absence of military or settler colonisation, or the heritage of Spanish colonialism. The analysis makes clear, that is to say, that colonisation is not a necessary vehicle of modernisation. Nor is the imposition of a colonising power or culture a prerequisite for the effects of modernisation to be felt as radical disruption within particular societies and social groups. Both case studies analyse the differing but deeply cultural—and gendered— understandings of the good within each particular society and the ways in which people with different notions experienced and responded to change, including conflict.

## Part I. Tradition and transformation in a non-colonised state: Thailand

The Thai material in Chapters 2 and 3 deals with workers in a Bangkok factory over the latter period of the 'democratic experiment' (1973–76), the incipient development of labour unions, the violent end to that experiment in the coup of 1976, and the re-establishment of military rule. At this time of transition in Thailand, from a primarily peasant to an industrialising economy, most of the workers were drawn from rural Buddhist families, with a small minority from the Muslim south. The factory was a co-owned Japanese–Thai enterprise under a Japanese parent company. The analysis will demonstrate that the workers' experience of urban factory work was, because of the implementation of Japanese rather than Thai industrial practices, a relatively benign one, with the factory management attempting to incorporate or accommodate as many aspects of traditional social relations and practices as possible. The context, however, was the ultimately violent clashes experienced in the broader Thai society, as traditional hegemonic notions of the good were rearticulated around the triadic invocation of Nation–Religion–King. This was in opposition not only to the modernising tendencies that escalated after 1973 but also, though in much milder form, to the changing notions about a good life developing among the workers themselves. This occurred as they embraced many aspects of what they saw as the better conditions offered them by urban factory rather than by rural agricultural employment.

## Part II. Tradition and transformation in a non-colonised state: Spain

The Spanish study in Chapters 4 and 5 deals with an order of Catholic teaching nuns in the aftermath of the changes initiated by the Roman Catholic Church's Second Vatican Council (1962–65) and by the political and social changes leading up to and following the death of General Francisco Franco in 1975. All the nuns articulated their choice of the religious life in terms of 'vocation', the calling by God, not just to a good life, but to a better life. Many of the older nuns had lived through the attacks on religion and religious orders during the period of the Republic (1931–36) and the Civil War (1936–39) and had retained the meaning of religious life as separate, sacred, and hierarchical.

These were the notions challenged most directly by the Second Vatican Council, with its emphasis on the sacredness of ordinary life and the fellowship of hierarchy and laity within a pilgrim, not triumphant, Church. Coinciding as it did with the opening of Spain to the influences of modernisation, also in the decade of the 1960s, Vatican II led to a radical re-evaluation by many of the nuns of the meaning of the good and of a good life and to the collapse of the distinction between a 'good' and a 'better' life. These new meanings mirrored in important ways the shift at the time of the Protestant Reformation from the imposition of orthodox dogma to the priority of individual conscience. They also reconstituted the relationship between the nuns and the laity and took many of the nuns out of their enclosed convents and into the community. Some left completely. Others remained committed to the religious life and the vows of poverty, chastity, and obedience, but initiated much closer involvements with the lay community and changes to their own interpretation of Christian belief, leading to a dramatic shift in their practices as well as in their values.

## Part III. Colonised people and the nation-state: Aboriginal Australia

Part III—Chapters 6 and 7—looks at some of the ways in which Aboriginal people in Australia have experienced and responded to modernisation through the experience of colonisation. Beginning in 1788, colonisation occurred in different stages and different forms in the various regions of the continent, setting the stage for modernisation but not always bringing it immediately in its wake. It would be difficult to claim, for example, that Aboriginal groups on the pastoral frontier were exposed to many facets of modernisation, although they were certainly subject to colonisation. In areas that were settled earlier or more closely, where colonisation resulted rapidly in the displacement and dispossession of Aboriginal landowners, and where major economic developments such as mining occurred, colonisation became the instrument of modernisation, fragmenting the relationship between the present of Aboriginal Australians and their past. Colonisation resulted also in a dislocation of Aboriginal people from the source of their social and moral vision and practice, that is, the land. In so doing, it led to a consequent distortion of the coherent connection between moral evaluation of the good and the social practices designed to express and promote a good life. Colonisation robs people of their past.

The book focuses on the remote Pilbara region of Western Australia, examining changes since the 1960s, and specifically the complexities of modernisation over that time. I examine a number of the ways in which, despite and in response to their experience of modernisation, these groups have shared a discourse developed with other Aboriginal Australians that affirms certain core notions about the meaning of the good and of what constitutes a good life for them. While the practices of daily life may be more diffuse, ambivalent, or downright contradictory, foremost among the values that have come to be publicly articulated are those of the primacy of kinship or relationships, of the generative power of the sacred, and of the intimate relationship, founded in the land, between the two. The analysis will demonstrate that the articulation of these values has come to constitute a central element of identity within Aboriginal groups themselves, as well as in their interaction with non-Indigenous people and institutions. The chapters also show that these values are often precisely those that are invoked in the interaction, often conflictive, among different Aboriginal groups.

The symbolic and practical power of these values has been enhanced through the translation of indigenous rights into a land rights discourse: the Commonwealth's *Aboriginal Land Rights (Northern Territory) Act 1976*, the High Court's recognition of the continuing existence of native title in the *Mabo* case (1992),[36] the Commonwealth's *Native Title Act 1993*, the participation of Australian Indigenous groups in discussion and exchange with Indigenous groups from other countries and in the international arena, have all contributed to a central emphasis on land and land rights. Within these processes, Indigenous Australians have themselves appropriated the discourse and practice of land and rights as a way of reaffirming the legitimacy of their understandings of the good, and of repositioning these understandings and their related practices in an active dialogue with modernity.

This dialogue with modernity is an uneven and unequal one. Nevertheless, it takes place in the context of a modern, liberal-democratic nation-state and of an increasingly accessible international and globalising arena. Indigenous Australians now therefore can, and do, draw from this wider context in order

---

36    *Mabo v Queensland* [No. 2] (1992) 175 CLR 1.

to position their moral vision as a legitimate interpretation of the good. This interpretation interrogates and calls to account various notions of the good proffered as characteristic of modernity. The distinction is not absolute, nor the webs of significance associated principally with Indigenous or non-Indigenous Australians bounded and separate. At the same time, disjunctions between Indigenous and non-Indigenous understandings of what constitutes a good life and its sources, and resources, remain, and the engagement with modernity generates often stark contradictions, both internal and external.

I will examine a number of key aspects of this engagement and these contradictions in repositioning Aboriginal and non-Aboriginal notions of the good in relation to each other within the parameters of modernity. I will cover some of the more broadly institutional or informal processes of encounter since the 1960s. A major part of this section will focus on the native title processes since 1993. It will draw especially on a particular case study from the Pilbara, permitting a narrative that traces the complex layers of meanings of the good for Pilbara Aboriginal people. The chapters will do this from the first major impact of mining developments in the mid 1960s, through one of the most widely publicised deaths in custody dealt with by the Royal Commission into Aboriginal Deaths in Custody, to a successful native title claim under the *Native Title Act 1993* and an ongoing engagement and tough agreement negotiations between native title groups and resource companies through the resource boom of the early twenty-first century.

## Part IV. Modernity and human rights

The analysis of the impacts of modernisation in particular societies is the grounding from which Chapter 8 then moves to the broader international arena, to test the proposition about the universality of the human activity of moral evaluation and of agreed notions of the good. Elaborating the comments in this Chapter about the Durban World Conference against Racism, Chapter 8 examines the role of the United Nations in struggling to realise and maintain international agreement about the principle of respect for the bond of common humanity and the essential conditions for a good life. The chapter looks specifically at how these have been articulated through the paradoxical discourse of human rights that attempts to encompass the contradictory principles of the rights of individuals and the sovereignty of states. Drawing on Habermas's theory of communicative action and Bhabha's concept of the Third Space, I examine the new articulation of a universal secular moral order and framework, through the agreement of nation-states, in the UN Charter, the *Universal Declaration of Human Rights*, and the international human rights conventions.

The analysis focuses on the UN World Conference against Racism (Durban, 2001), a key process in attempting to maintain international agreement about a universal notion of the good. The World Conference demonstrates the contradictions and clashes inherent in an international forum aimed at achieving international consensus, where the often opposing principles of human rights and the rights of nation-states vie with each other,[37] and where separate nation-states are committed to protecting their own sovereignty and promoting their own national interests. In such a context, where strategic action vies with communicative action,[38] the pressure for fragmentation and isolation is great, and I will look at the extent to which and the conditions under which delegations are prepared or not prepared to subordinate strategic to communicative action. Despite these pressures, the World Conference achieved final agreement. This was by consensus but in the absence of the United States and Israel, whose delegations walked out of the Conference on its third day, and with reservations being made by representatives of a number of countries, including Australia. The section will argue that this agreement, nevertheless, and the common meanings finally formally subscribed to were possible only because of the acceptance, through the fraught process of agreement itself, of respect for the bond of common humanity as a universal moral principle.[39]

Finally, I draw on the themes elaborated throughout the book to suggest that modernisation effects a radical transformation of traditional social imaginaries. I reflect on the relevance of these transformations to the proposition that moral evaluation is at the centre of human agency and is an essential universal principle in the different ways in which human groups define their meaning of the good and of a good life. At the same time, I stress, on the basis of the material, that there is not one notion of the good across any society or between societies, and that conflict, often violent, is generated by opposing and sometimes incompatible differences in meaning and in practices designed to implement particular notions of a good life. Nevertheless, there can also be consent to the universal principle of respect for the bond of common humanity, and agreed interpretations, based on this principle, about the essential conditions that constitute a good life.

Based as the book is on ethnographic material, I also reflect on the relevance of anthropology to, and for anthropology of, a comparative analysis that interrogates the concept of a humanity that is equal while culturally diverse.

---

37  Douzinas (2000: 118).
38  Habermas (1984, 1987).
39  The deep flaws demonstrated in the Durban conference were further exacerbated by the Durban Review Conference (Durban II), held in Geneva in 2009, again overshadowing any achievements. Australia was one of a number of countries which chose not to participate, on the basis that the Australian Government could not support a document reaffirming the 2001 Durban documents in their entirety, that is, the 2001 Declaration that singled out Israel and the Middle East (The Hon. Stephen Smith MP, Media release, 19 April 2009).

# The book as anthropological reflection

In neither of the situations that I sketched at the beginning of this chapter—the inquest for Nurjan Husseini and Fatimeh Husseini in Fremantle and the UN World Conference against Racism in Durban—was I carrying out fieldwork as an anthropologist. But the anthropologist, like Nanki-Poo in Gilbert and Sullivan's *The Mikado*, is in many ways 'a thing of shreds and patches'. So too is the material that is available. A further element of this book is the exploration of the different and always partial ways in which the anthropologist builds an understanding of culture and social relations. This can be done not only through the longer-term ethnographic involvement demonstrated in the case studies. It can be done also by drawing on the practical and conceptual frameworks derived from this ethnographic experience, from more fleeting encounters, such as the earlier vignettes, that evoke rather than describe the workings and effects of power on particular social and institutional relations. It is the specific task of anthropology to gain an intimate knowledge and understanding of the local and, on that basis, to draw the connections between the subjective experiences of ordinary people and the objective conditions—social, cultural, increasingly global—that shape both them and their way of experiencing and engaging with the world. In undertaking this study, I examine the complexities, ambiguities and contradictions of modernisation through the diversity and concreteness of particular societies and particular groups; trusting to do so, to borrow Said's comments about philology, in 'a profound humanistic spirit deployed with generosity and, if I may use the word, hospitality'.[40] For all of the material I have used for this book, I have drawn, as anthropologists need to draw, on the fragmented range of sources—secondary as well as primary, global and institutional as well as local and familial—that increasingly constitutes the complexity of social life.

At the same time, if the anthropologist's access to the world of others is never complete, neither is that of those whose world it is. As Bourdieu observed, 'native experience of the social world never apprehends the system of objective relations other than *in profiles*'.[41] Modernity has, however, transformed the profiles that he described as 'relations which present themselves only one by one, and hence successively, in the emergency situations of everyday life'.[42] Modernity replaces the sense of manageable predictability that he invokes for the Kabyle of Algeria with a superfluity of influences and an ever increasing rapidity of change. This is one of the key aspects of modernisation experienced by the people whose stories form the content of this book. It is my task as an

---

40  Said (2003: xix).
41  Bourdieu (1979: 18).
42  ibid.

anthropologist to examine the commonalities and the differences in the ways in which they experience it. It is in attending to the changing situations in which we find people today that we can hope to understand both the pervasiveness and the contingency of culture, together with its inherent contradictions and conflicts. In this way, too, we can explore what it means to be human in the contemporary world and engage more fully with 'the potency and grandeur as well as with the terror of the modern age'.[43]

In undertaking the anthropological task, I cannot ignore the question, most eloquently posed by Said in *Orientalism*,[44] of the representation of the Other. Nor can I ignore the accusation, reinforced most strongly by writers in subaltern and postcolonial studies, of anthropology's complicity in the colonial enterprise: what Said calls 'the insinuations, the imbrications of power into even the most recondite of studies'.[45] My study is not an apologia in reply to these accusations. Nevertheless, I want to draw attention also to Said's further comments in his added 2003 Preface: 'There is, after all, a profound difference between the will to understand for purposes of co-existence and humanistic enlargement of horizons, and the will to dominate for the purposes of control and external domination.'[46]

I would suggest that much anthropology belongs in that first category, and attempts its role—even if it does not always succeed—not as an orientalising or objectification of the Other, but as an openness to the ways in which the Other calls into question the Same.[47] Part of this openness demands a capacity to imagine the Other and, in so doing, to ask the further question about what kind of act such imagining may be. The answer is to be found only in the experience of encounter—Buber's dialogue between *Ich und Du*: I and Thou[48]— and in acknowledging that 'the self only exists in relation to other selves':[49] that is, in relation to the Other. There is no self except in relation to the Other, and the moral choices of the self are ineluctably framed in relation to others. When the imagining of the Other takes place from a position of power and a will to dominate, the Other is indeed objectified and diminished. But it is possible to imagine—and recognise—the Other on the basis of 'knowledge of other peoples and other times that is the result of understanding, compassion, careful study and analysis for their own sakes'.[50] This kind of recognition is key to the recognition of a common humanity and to the anthropological enterprise that I undertake in this book.

---

43   Taylor (2003: x).
44   Said (2003: xxii).
45   ibid.
46   ibid., p. xiv.
47   Levinas (1979).
48   Buber (1970).
49   Taylor (2003: 35).
50   Said (2003: xiv).

In most instances, I did not undertake the studies dealt with here in the role purely as researcher. All reflect a multi-layered experience that started with being in particular places at particular times largely because of family, not academic, reasons and with forging my own place, and a place for our family, within terms set out by others. I was in Bangkok and Madrid because of my husband's work. Not wishing to play the role of an incorporated wife,[51] I spent a year in Bangkok getting to know the country, learning Thai, meeting people, and looking after my daughter who was born two months after we arrived there. In the second year, I was able to spend much of my time at the factory compound where I undertook my ethnography.

My research in Madrid was made very easy because of friendships I had already made with a group of the Spanish nuns a decade earlier when, as a member of the same religious order, I had shared several intense months with them at the order's central governing convent in Rome. Although we had not stayed in touch in the intervening years, they made me and my family very welcome and we enjoyed many informal times together. My knowledge of the order went back even further, to my eight years as a pupil in their boarding school in Brisbane. My eldest daughter's early experience of school was attending one of the order's schools in Madrid. These broader experiences provided a background of mundane familiarity to my research and enriched my understanding of the women with whom I was working and the context in which they were living and acting.

Western Australia's Pilbara was different. My first time there constituted regular fieldwork over several months in Roebourne as an academic anthropologist carrying out ethnographic research for the Australian Institute of Aboriginal Studies,[52] and then a brief review for the Royal Commission into Aboriginal Deaths in Custody. My children attended the Roebourne Primary School. But Roebourne people have changed in many ways over the nearly 20 years since I first went there, drawn increasingly beyond the local into regional and global arenas. Their daily lives involve meetings with lawyers and with mining companies, negotiating agreements, and participating in native title processes. I have needed different forms of ethnography in order to match these changes.

When I returned several years later, it was not as a researcher but as a member of the National Native Title Tribunal, with responsibility for co-mediating the Ngarluma/Yindjibarndi native title claim. Over the next eight years, I continued to mediate other claims in the central and west Pilbara. The meetings held as part of the mediations were confidential so I have not used any of that material. Nevertheless, they gave me deeper insight into the social and cultural relations

---

51  Callan (1977); Callan and Ardener (1984).
52  Now the Australian Institute of Aboriginal and Torres Strait Islander Studies (AIATSIS).

of people in the area. The Ngarluma/Yindjibarndi claim finally went to trial in the Federal Court. The evidence given there, as well as the Court's judgement, is on the public record and forms part of the different kind of ethnography needed in contemporary representations of Indigenous people. In 2006 I returned to Western Australia to take up the role of lead negotiator in developing agreements between Rio Tinto and central and west Pilbara native title groups. Over the next two and a half years, I was involved in regular meetings, formal and informal, with the groups and their representatives. As with Native Title Tribunal mediations, the formal meetings were confidential, but there were many exchanges outside those meetings that have enriched my analysis.

In many ways, therefore, the subjects of my research did not present as Other, but as other players with whom I was involved in particular moments. These case studies show also the fluidity and permeability of the cultural boundaries across which we were able to meet. I experienced my own foreignness more acutely in some contexts than in others, but perhaps nowhere more sharply than in Durban, and subsequently back in Australia, in the face of the actions of my own country's government. Perhaps otherness, like beauty, is in the eye of the beholder, or at least in the face of choices and actions derived from a moral source that seems alien. At the same time, the case studies demonstrate that one of the impacts of modernisation is to exacerbate the potential for very different, often violently conflicting, responses to arise from the same moral source. More radically, modernisation fractures the moral source itself, creating, as Miller suggests, 'a new fragility in which people become much more conscious of the processes of self-creation and the creation of the principles by which they judge themselves',[53] and, I would add, to do so in relation to the Other. By bringing together very different groups at different moments in time, I hope that the material presented in this book, and the people whose lives are its content, offer insights into the act of imagining and recognising the Other; but, even more, into the commonality of our humanity and the multiplicity of relations that bind as well as differentiate us.

---

53   Miller (1995: 16).

# Part I. Tradition and transformation in a non-colonised state: Thailand

**Map 1. Thailand**

# 2. Continuities and crisis

Each country, and each group within a country, has undergone its own experience of modernisation. In Thailand, the beginning of this process can be dated to the middle of the nineteenth century and the reign of King Mongkut, followed by that of his son, King Chulalongkorn. Despite turbulent political events over the subsequent century, including the end of constitutional monarchy in 1932 and the growing dominance of rule by the military, the resistance of the country to European colonisation resulted in a totalising discourse privileging continuity and tradition. At the heart of this interpretation were the Thai monarchy and Thai Buddhism.[1] Buddhism, the Buddhist concept of the good (*bun*), and traditional relations and practices, became the prism through which most ordinary Thai people saw their own lives and their society. These accepted views were challenged by the advent of the 'democratic experiment' in 1973 and its brutal end in 1976.

## View from a Bangkok factory

At around lunchtime on Wednesday, 6 October 1976, I was sitting on the common verandah area of the women's dormitory of a Bangkok factory, talking to Nopawan about her family, her growing up, and her school and work experiences in Korat before coming to Bangkok. It was the late monsoon season, still humid, and with the oncoming afternoon downpour remaining fairly predictable. The long verandah area, with the shop at one end, a common TV room at the other, and staircases going up to the sleeping areas on the two floors above, caught what breeze there was. Near us, other young women relaxed and chatted between shifts, prepared food or caught up on their laundry. Khun Phadungcit, the dormitory supervisor—the *mee baan*—came back and forth from discussing shop business with Lek, who ran it. This largely domestic scene was suddenly interrupted by Ratana, who came running out from the TV room, calling to everyone to come quickly. Something big was happening at Thammasat University.

As we looked at the black-and-white television images, it wasn't clear that what we were seeing was part of a massacre. But it was more than apparent that what was happening was terrible. There were pictures of police with machine guns standing over dozens of students who were lying on the ground, stripped to the waist, with their hands behind their heads. Police were shouting, students

---

1   The privileging of Buddhism as a key component of national identity ignored, and therefore excluded, non-Buddhists, especially those in the largely Muslim south.

were crying out, there was the sound of bullets in the background. Other cameras picked up an individual student being attacked by an angry mob in the Pramane Ground opposite the university. There was mention of other attacks and deaths. The commentary was along the lines that there must have been Vietnamese infiltrators among the students, because dog meat had been found. The commentary seemed to be offered as an excuse for the mob's behaviour. The factory women watching did not appear to be persuaded, or at least did not indicate agreement, although my attention was not really on them but on what we were seeing.

In memory, that moment and those images are overlaid with later knowledge of the extent of the violence and cruelty of that day, and with other images that were smuggled out of the country before the military, yet again, took over the Government in the evening and suppressed all further reporting. As a result, only one afternoon newspaper, *Sayamrat*, managed to carry photos before they were banned: among others, of a crowd of spectators around several burning bodies; a dead man—later identified as student leader Jaruphong Thongsindhu—being dragged across the soccer field by a piece of cloth around his neck; rows of anonymous corpses. 'It was a Wednesday morning in which the deaths by gunshot seemed to be the least painful and most civilised of murders'.[2] Coverage of the day's events on the evening television news gave no indication at all of the sadistic horror of what had actually occurred, beyond reporting that there had been 'further' incidents at Thammasat University. Nevertheless, as a result of these events, the new National Administrative Reform Council (NARC) had taken control in place of the elected government. Their reason was 'in order to restore stability and law and order to the kingdom'.[3]

At the factory, or among its workforce, there was no particular sense of instability or of disorder. The factory was part-owned by a Japanese parent company and run by a Japanese manager along largely Japanese organisational lines. The wages and conditions for its employees were significantly better than in wholly owned Thai factories. Its workforce had not felt the need to participate in any of the many strikes since the beginning of the 'democratic experiment' in October 1973. This included a major strike by workers in the textile industry of which they were a part. The factory's location in the suburb of Bang Khen, away from the centre of Bangkok, was not a reason for this lack of involvement. Textile workers in other areas of Bangkok and in neighbouring provinces to the west and south were actively engaged in the labour movement. In Omnoy, an industrial area in Nakhon Pathom Province west of Bangkok, five unionists had been arrested and imprisoned in March 1976, along with two students and two young graduates. They were charged with being Communists, undermining

2   Thongchai (2002: 244).
3   Morell and Chai-anan (1981: 275).

national security, and the illegal possession of firearms. The evidence was so slight that the Public Prosecutor had to keep deferring their trial, and they were still in jail at the time of the coup on 6 October.

There was none of this political drama at the Bang Khen factory. Many of the employees had chosen to leave provincial areas to take jobs in the factory. They made this choice because they preferred it to domestic or rural work. For them, becoming industrial workers under the particular conditions established at the factory was not an alienating experience, but one that offered them a better life than they thought was available at home. Nevertheless, this personal choice was made at a time in Thai history that brought starkly into question the relationship between a good life and a good society and challenged any assumption that one was possible without the other.

# Bang Khen workers and the brush with the new

These chapters explore the essential connection but also the distinction between a good life and a good society. The employees' experience with conditions in the Bang Khen factory provided them with many of the elements—social, cultural, religious, as well as material—that they saw as constituting a good life. Even work was not excluded from this view. For shopfloor operators in particular, the routine time spent in the repetitive interface with noisy machines was not of itself desirable. Nor was it repugnant. They saw it as a condition of their freedom because it was better than the alternatives, including equally monotonous and more arduous rural work or other work in the provinces. They valued the possibility—offered by modernity—of a freedom to choose something beyond the confines of family and family locality, even in contrast to the expressed wishes of their parents and the Buddhist norm of filial obedience.

At the same time, the experience of the workers illustrates the difficulties of maintaining or developing a good life without its being grounded in a good society. In the Thailand of the period under review, the processes of modernisation were giving rise to changing and contested meanings about what constitutes a good society. It is easy, and tempting, to dichotomise these differing views as either based in the past or oriented to the future. The experience of the factory workers suggests that this is not a dichotomy in people's mundane experience. The employees drew meaning and legitimacy from both sources; more even from the past in terms of how they explained their lives. Nor did they see the two as in contradiction, but as ordinary. Their work was for them not a rupture with the past but a present that provided wider possibilities than had been available for their parents. The contradictions inherent in their position as urban industrial workers in a partially modern society were buffered by the conditions provided by the factory. Although these conditions arose from principles based in Japanese rather than in Thai industrial experience, they allowed for—indeed encouraged—a sense of personal continuities.

Nevertheless, the factory and its workers were living through a pivotal moment in Thailand, in which the period from October 1973 to October 1976 constitutes Act One of an ongoing and not yet completed crisis in the process of Thai modernisation. The workers' responses, muted though they were in comparison with others', show that they, too, were brushed by the dilemmas of the new. Their responses need to be understood in the context of what was happening more broadly in Thailand at that critical time, but also in relation to the particular history of modernisation in the country.

## Monarchy and modernisation: The Chakri kings and the building of a nation

Since the reign of the scholar-king Mongkut (Rama IV),[4] from 1851 to 1868, a national discourse has developed around the Thai experience of modernisation that links a very particular set of concepts and gives these concepts meaning, and consequent value, in relation to each other. These are summarised by Thongchai as 'continuity, homogeneity, and the persistence of traditions, especially Thai Buddhism and Thai monarchy'.[5]

History regards Siam's struggles against European imperialism in the nineteenth century, as with those of other nations outside Europe, as the advent of the modern nation. Unlike others, however, Siam was never formally colonised, a distinctive phenomenon of which Thai people are always very proud. Therefore, Siam has been regarded as a traditional state that transformed itself into a modern nation, thanks to the intelligence of the monarchs who responded wisely and timely to the threats of the European powers by modernising the country in the right direction at the right time. Thus continuity, homogeneity, and the persistence of traditions, especially Thai Buddhism and the Thai monarchy, have been the distinct characteristics, or even the unique features, of modern Siam.

Mongkut and his son Chulalongkorn (Rama V), who reigned from 1868 to 1910, are central to this discourse as the historical heroes of the Chakri Dynasty and the kings who 'wisely and timely' resisted colonisation and chose the path of modernisation. Mongkut, who spent 27 years as a Buddhist monk before

---

4   Mongkut remains revered in Thailand as scholar, religious leader and king. Hollywood did his image no favours when it made him the subject of the film *The King and I*.
5   Thongchai (1994: 13).

becoming king,[6] is credited with a major reform of Buddhism and the Buddhist *sangha* (community or monastic order) as well as with the introduction of modern science into Siam.[7] His foreign policy was directed towards the maintenance of Siamese sovereignty, no longer only against the incursions of neighbouring kingdoms such as Burma and Cambodia, but also against the imperial expansion of the British and the French. The process resulted in a forced delineation of Siam's boundaries in order to satisfy the territorial demands of these two European colonial powers.[8] It also resulted in the signing of a treaty with Great Britain in 1855, named for Queen Victoria's representative, Sir John Bowring, who is quoted as having coined 'the immortal axiom': 'Free trade is Jesus Christ and Jesus Christ is free trade'.[9] The Bowring Treaty conceded effective control over the country's foreign trade to Great Britain.[10] By the end of the nineteenth century, some 90 per cent of the total value of Siamese trade was in British hands.[11]

By the end of the nineteenth century also, the identity of the amorphous Kingdom of Siam had been transformed into that of a nation.[12] Together with this transformation was an appropriation of Buddhism to the discourse of nationhood, providing the foundation for the enduringly powerful mantra: 'Nation, Religion, King' (*chaat, saatsanaa, phra mahaa kasat*).

# Early twentieth-century stirrings of democracy and the failure of the Great Revolution of 1932

The mantra was first coined by Chulalongkorn's son, King Vajiravudh (Rama VI, r. 1910–25), and embodied in his redesigned national flag with its stripes of red for Nation, white for Religion, and blue for King.[13] Buddhism thus gave the nation its moral dimension; the Buddhist concept of 'good' became the prism through which modernisation could be separated into identifiable components, each of which could then be assessed in terms of its suitability or otherwise for Siam. This was expressed as what was good or not good for the nation, allowing King Chulalongkorn to declare that 'the concepts of political party and

---

6   Rong (1973: 118).
7   Thongchai (1994: 38–9).
8   ibid.
9   Anderson (1998: 175).
10   Bello et al. (1998: 1).
11   Turton (1978: 105).
12   Thongchai (1994: 16, 134–5).
13   Bowie (1997: 50).

parliamentary system were not appropriate to the Siamese political tradition'.[14] On the same basis, King Vajiravudh banned the first text on economics in Thai because

> apart from the monarch...Thai people were all equal under him. Thus economics might cause disunity or disruption because it concerns social strata of rich and poor. Instead, he proposed his own economic philosophy based on a Buddhist precept that one should be satisfied with what one has.[15]

The central place of Buddhism within national discourse has made it available to be invoked by all subsequent political groups in their struggle to normalise their particular version of national identity.

At the same time, there has been a tension between democratic movements and the specific invocation of Buddhism as a source of legitimacy. The Democracy Monument in Bangkok, for example, is a secular memorial, built in 1939 to commemorate the Great Revolution of 1932, which marks the end of the absolute monarchy and the initiation of constitutional government. It involved civilians as well as the military and was the first major attempt to modernise the political system. A copy of the original constitution is enshrined in the Democracy Monument. Despite the practical failure to establish democracy, the potent symbolism of the Monument was made apparent when it became a key rallying point for the demonstrations in both 1973 and 1976; in 1992's Black May, the time of a third protest and massacre; and again in 2010, the most recent in this quartet of popular uprisings against the continuing dominance of the military. Thammasat University, which played such a central role in 1973 and especially in 1976, is also linked directly, as well as spatially and symbolically, to the Democracy Monument and to the events of 1932; it was founded in 1934 by Dr Pridi Phanomyong, the leader of the civilian group in the People's Party that staged the coup. He was also the drafter of the first constitution. He established the university, originally named the University of Moral and Political Sciences, as an institution, independent of government, to promote academic freedom and to foster the principles of democracy. He was its first rector.

The coup of 1932 was, in a sense, the ironic culmination of the efforts of the Chakri kings to modernise the state, but to do so without breaking with what they saw as traditional Siamese political culture and values.[16] Instead, they created a system that resulted in limiting the power of the monarchy, while failing to establish the foundations for strong democratic institutions. Their failure continues to bedevil the state. In particular, by reforming and strengthening the military, they allowed it to grow into the powerful institution

---

14   Thongchai (1994: 4).
15   ibid.
**44**   16   Likhit (1985: 264).

that effectively controlled government for most of the twentieth century and continues to influence events in the early twenty-first. The military thwarted the modernising and democratic energy of the Great Revolution and beyond.

## Monarchy and military: The ascendancy of the Generals

The year 1932 was followed by two and a half decades (1932–57) that included 10 coups, nine elections and six constitutions.[17] Even with elections, there were civilian prime ministers for a total of less than two and a half years of that period. The reference to politics was removed from the name of Pridi's University of Moral and Political Sciences, which became the University of Moral Sciences or *Thammasat*, 'Wisdom of the [Buddhist] Dharma'. And in 1939, the name of the country was changed from Siam to Thailand: *muang thai* or 'land of the free'. This was effected by Phibul Songkram, whose military government first (1938–44) took Thailand into active collaboration with Japan during the war years and after the war (1948–57), to atone for the country's lapse from grace, into a fundamental change in the nature of Thailand's treaties with the West. Before 1941, these had been confined mainly to the commercial sphere. The postwar era saw the first political and military agreements. With a military assistance agreement with the United States in 1950, and by joining the South-East Asia Treaty Organisation (SEATO) alliance in 1954, Thailand became officially aligned with the Western bloc, an alignment ratified by the establishment of the SEATO headquarters in Bangkok.

The ascendancy of the military after 1932 occurred in the face of the weakness of other balancing institutions, including the monarchy. The limitations set on the monarchy by the Constitution did not bring about a revolution in the modern political sense. Instead, the leadership of the People's Party allowed the monarchy to 'exercise sanctioning prerogatives of legitimisation. The constitution became not the work and toil of the people but a royal gift from a benevolent king.'[18] At the same time, the role of 'benevolent king' was rapidly left vacant after the abdication of King Prajadhipok (Rama VII) in 1935 and remained in the hands of Regents for 15 years. The new king, Prajadhipok's nephew Ananda Mahidol, was a boy of ten and living in Switzerland. Apart from a brief visit in 1938, he did not return to Thailand until after the end of World War II in 1945. In 1946 he was found shot dead in his bedroom, in a mystery that has never been solved.[19] He was succeeded by his brother, Bhumiphol Adulyadej, who did not himself

---

17   ibid., p. 266.
18   Thak (1979: xiii).
19   Kruger (2009); Rong (1973: 166, 178).

finally return to live in Thailand until 1950, when he was crowned as Rama IX. Bhumiphol's reign has continued for 60 years, reinforcing the development of a 'selective and elite narrative of security [that] asserts that the king is the pre-eminent site of virtuous and disinterested power'.[20]

The failure of political modernisation was matched over this period by a failure of economic modernisation. Outside the region of Greater Bangkok, Thailand remained an essentially rural economy. In 1960, of the total economically active population, more than 80 per cent was in the rural sector.[21] The rural sector was not isolated from change, including the stirring of a Communist insurgency, mainly in the north-east, but in many ways it continued to operate within systems of traditional hierarchical relations. For the Thai Buddhist majority in this sector, this included different forms of patron–client relations. They were little affected by the constant political changes in Bangkok, which did not, in practice, lead to the development of repressive internal security or to instability. On the contrary, the military had achieved its own internal mechanisms for stability: coup, election, a semi-democratic government, internal coup.[22] Nor did these processes usually produce violence, even in the case of failed coup attempts, such as that by naval officers against Phibul in 1951 (the Manhattan revolt). Perpetrators were imprisoned or forced into exile but rarely executed.

## Dictatorship of Field Marshall Sarit

Much of this changed after the coup led by Field Marshall Sarit Thanarat in 1957. Sarit had been involved in an earlier successful coup against Pridi in 1947 but had arranged the reinstallation of Phibul as Prime Minister. Even after the 1957 coup, he did not immediately take on the role of prime minister but briefly installed first a civilian and then one of his coup cronies, General Thanom Kittikachorn, for nearly a year. At the end of that time, he executed a further internal coup, and seized power himself. In this sense, Sarit was Thailand's first true military dictator. Although he was in power for less than five years, dying of cirrhosis of the liver at the end of 1963, his impact on Thai politics and development was extensive. He abolished the Constitution, banned all political parties and trade unions, suppressed the opposition, and censored the press. His autocratic personal style was demonstrated by his solution to the spate of fires that regularly broke out at Chinese New Year and which he saw as an insurance scam. It was popular belief that he acted personally on his declaration that he

---

20   Walker (2010: 1).
21   Silcock (1970: 15).
22   Chai-anan (1992: 1).

would shoot the owner of the first building to burn down at the next New Year, regardless of the cause of the fire. It was also popular belief that the number of fires dropped dramatically subsequent to this execution.

Sarit was aggressively anti-Communist. His abolition of labour unions was for two main reasons: that they were, in his own words, the 'main obstacles to economic development' and 'gateways for communism to enter Thailand'.[23] As well as his support for the growing US involvement in South Vietnam, his establishment of the Department of Community Development in 1962 was in response to the threat of insurgency.[24] At the same time, but not unrelated to his counter-insurgency policies, Sarit gave firm support to the monarchy, aligning himself with the King, reinforcing his own legitimacy and that of the military as protectors of the monarchy,[25] and encouraging the revival of traditional symbols, especially the triad of the three pillars (*lak*): Nation (*chaat*), Religion (*saatsanaa*), King (*phra mahaa kasat*).[26] For the first time, King Bhumiphol emerged from the shadow of the military and began to define his role as an active social participant in national life and not merely a figurehead and source of legitimacy for whatever government was currently in power. At the same time, this alliance can be seen as the beginning of a symbiotic relationship between the army and the monarchy that has not yet been severed.[27]

Sarit's approaches were hardly triumphs for modernisation, but he was also determined to encourage foreign investment in industry and achieve economic development. Indeed, his overriding national policy was national economic development and social improvement.[28] He launched a first five-year National Development Program in 1961, reinforced by financial support from the United States and other foreign investment, such as Japanese.[29] Industrialisation expanded rapidly, but in an environment still constrained by authoritarian rule.

## Sarit's successors: The 'three tyrants'—Thanom, Prapass and Narong—and the war on Communism

Sarit's policies were continued after his death by his successors, Field Marshalls Thanom Kittikachorn and Prapass Charusathira, together with Thanom's son

---

23    Morell and Chai-anan (1981: 184).
24    Bowie (1997: 73).
25    Keyes (2006: 14).
26    Morell and Chai-anan (1981: 64 ff.); Thak (1979: 312 ff.); Turton (1978: 128).
27    Reynolds (2010: 5).
28    Likhit (1985: 308).
29    ibid., p. 298.

and Prapass's son-in-law, Lieutenant Colonel Narong Kittikachorn. Under their ongoing military regime, the encouragement of industrialisation and foreign investment was reinforced, leading to unprecedented economic growth throughout the 1960s.[30] The mechanisms for counter-insurgency, financed largely by the United States, were strengthened, including the establishment in 1965 of the Communist Suppression Operations Command, renamed 10 years later the Internal Security Operations Command (ISOC).[31] The fact that Thanom and Praphass succeeded to government at almost the exact time of US President Lyndon Johnson's escalation of the Vietnam War added a practical intimacy to this alliance. Commitment to the ongoing role of the United States in Vietnam led to a massive increase in the number of US military in Thailand. Figures for the number of US servicemen increased over a three-year period, from 6500 in 1966 to 47 600 in 1969.[32] These servicemen operated from at least eight major bases and from dozens of minor installations. The figures do not, moreover, include troops on rest and recreation—R&R—from Vietnam, who were estimated to number at least 5000 a month in the peak years of 1968–69.[33] Anderson suggests that, over this period, Washington treated Thailand, and was encouraged to do so, as 'a sort of gigantic immobile aircraft carrier'.[34]

At the same time, Thanom attempted to distance himself and his government from the scandals that followed the death of Sarit by reframing his own public image. His central message was that his government was an honest one, and that it was committed to the development of a good society. The official slogan became 'Do good, do good, do good'.[35] The popular uprising against him and his military colleagues in 1973 made clear that his government's model for a good society was actively opposed by others.

The first decade of the Bang Khen factory spanned almost exactly the period of the Thanom–Prapass regime. The factory was established at the end of 1963, as a joint Thai–Japanese venture to produce nylon and polyester thread. It was part of the push to industrialisation under Sarit, with the 1960s seeing 'extraordinarily rapid industrial expansion, particularly in the textile and food processing industries'.[36] It began production in 1967 and was fully operational at the time of the 1973 overthrow of the Thanom–Prapass government and establishment of a civilian government. In accordance with the foreign investment laws of the period, the company had to be at least 51 per cent Thai owned. As it was part of a Japanese corporation, this meant that the company president was

---

30   Thak (1979: 342–3).
31   Bowie (1997: 73, 105).
32   Elliott (1978: 42).
33   ibid., pp. 15, 26.
34   Anderson (1977: 15).
35   Thak (1979: 342).
36   Morell and Chai-anan (1981: 185).

president of the corporation and based in Japan. The vice-president was the Thai majority owner, referred to by the workers with the polite but not overly formal honorific of '*Khun*' Iid. He shared full and final power with the Japanese factory manager, Mr Suzuka, in all matters concerning the factory. Khun Iid was not based at the factory but had an office in the company's Thai headquarters in the city. He was also on the board of a number of other Japanese companies in Thailand. Mr Suzuka dealt with all the day-to-day decision-making, the running of the factory and its production, the development of factory policies, and the maintenance of links with the Japanese parent corporation.

# The Bang Khen factory world

Sarit's drive to industrialise may have resulted in a notable increase in the number of factories and urban workers, but it had done little to ensure adequate conditions for those workers. This was left to the discretion of the private owners and managers. In wholly Thai-owned enterprises in particular, conditions and pay were miserable, and often dangerous—a state of affairs that continued beyond the political changes of 1973. For that reason, such factories did not welcome external scrutiny. Even after approval by the National Research Council and accompanied by an official from the Labour Department, I needed some months and visits to a number of different factories before I found one where I could undertake long-term ethnography. When I was accepted as a researcher at the Bang Khen factory, it was clear that the company was satisfied that the conditions that it offered its employees would bear scrutiny. This was in addition to the reason stated by Mr Suzuka that the company valued education and was willing to encourage it.

This approach to education was reflected in the company's recruitment practices, which required that applicants undergo an examination as part of a selection process even for operator positions. In order to attract employees in its early years, the company undertook a recruiting drive through the Labour Department. Among other strategies, advertisements were broadcast from time to time over the wireless in provincial towns. Nopawan heard this in Korat (another name for Nakhon Ratchasima) in 1972. She had left her job at a hairdresser's when the owner, her friend, got married. She had been in this job for almost four years and earned good money. Most of this she had been able to save, as she lived at home. If she had to work late, she stayed overnight with her friend, as her parents did not want her out after dark. Sometimes she went home only at the end of the week, as there were many bars and clubs in Korat catering to the American soldiers, and the salon was constantly busy with its regular clientele of girls who worked in the bars and clubs. Many of these came to the salon every day to have their hair and nails done. They were mostly from the poorer region of the north-east provinces that stretch beyond Korat to the border with Laos. They had come to Korat because, with the Americans there, there was work, even though it was work that they said they disliked. At the time of the company recruitment drive, Nopawan was living at home again, with her parents and the three youngest of her seven brothers and sisters. She was without regular work although she had done a dressmaking course and was often employed by the wives of Thai soldiers, friends of her mother's, to sew for them. Before special occasions, this kept her very busy. She had looked for other work in Korat that would be like her previous work in the salon where she could live with her friend as well as work and be not like an employee but a friend. None of the jobs that she checked was like this. When she heard the Bang Khen advertisement, she hesitated because Bangkok was a long way away and she was reluctant to go so far. But she wanted work and wanted to see what it was like. First, she spoke to her mother and father. They were not willing for her to go but finally gave their permission for her to apply. Then things happened very quickly. She sat the exam in the morning and heard in the afternoon that she had passed. Two days later, the company sent a bus to bring the successful applicants to Bangkok. With Nopawan, there were altogether 20 from Korat on that trip: 14 men and six women. Nopawan was twenty-two years old.

The bus trip was down Highway 2—the Friendship Highway, built with US aid—dropping down through rocky hills from the Korat plateau to the central plains. They reached Bang Khen in the late afternoon. The group of young women was introduced to the *mee baan*, the women's dormitory supervisor, Khun Phadungcit, who allocated them together to one of the dormitory rooms. That evening, they began to meet their co-workers. Most of these were also young and, since the dormitory was for single employees, all except for Khun Phadungcit were unmarried. The majority also came from or had been born in provincial areas. For Nopawan, the factory met her desire for a workplace that also offered companionable living arrangements. These were provided within the factory compound where more than half the employees lived as well as worked. Most were accommodated in dormitories within the walled factory compound, though separated from the work areas: for unmarried workers, a men's dormitory, with a separate foremen's wing, and a women's dormitory. Many married salaried staff lived in an apartment building, with family quarters and an adjacent building with maids' rooms.

Nopawan, like the other women employees, spent much of her spare time in and around the dormitory area, with her work mates becoming also her principal social circle. Friendships were expressed by choosing to go out together, to shop or go to a movie, in free time between shifts or on days off. Those who had come to the factory from the provinces had little occasion to meet other new people. Even for the minority with families in Bangkok, few lived close by, and visits home were infrequent, with the daunting combination of distance and Bangkok traffic. The men tended to spend less time in the dormitory area, making greater use of the sporting facilities, including the football field, and also leaving the factory more frequently between shifts to *paj thiaw* (go somewhere for a good time). Nevertheless, the dormitory provided their home base. Even the police regarded the dormitory areas as domestic space, refusing to intervene in cases where serious assault resulted from the frequent quarrels in the men's dormitory. When a fight broke out in the early hours of the morning between Patana and Veera, Patana grabbed an iron pipe and hit Veera over the head with it, causing him extensive injuries. The police made no arrest on the grounds that 'the dormitory is like home'. This view was not shared by the management, who immediately gave Patana the sack.

Men living in the foremen's wing either had their own room or shared with no more than two others. In the men's and women's dormitories, the rooms were built to be shared by eight people, though there were often only six or seven in each. For new groups, as with the Korat group when Nopawan first arrived, the dormitory supervisors decided the allocation. Once people had been there for some time, they were allowed to choose their room and with whom they would share it. This was normally once people had established friendships and was then approved by the dormitory supervisor. There were occasional exceptions. One concerned Vicien and Nipaphorn, a gay couple who were in the same room for some time. Because they quarrelled a lot, and loudly, no-one else was prepared to share with them. Khun Phadungcit therefore separated them, a decision that was supported by the respective heads of the two rooms. In one sense, of which this incident is an example, the factory shared some of the characteristics of a total institution for those who lived in the dormitories, with the factory operating as an institution 'purportedly established the better to pursue some worklike tasks and justifying themselves only on these instrumental grounds'.[37] Goffman's examples include army barracks, ships, boarding schools and work camps. The factory, however, lacked the collective regimentation that Goffman identifies as one of the characteristics of a total institution. Outside the shift arrangements, employees were free to pursue their own activities, as long as they stayed within the limits, legal and social, set for behaviour. Men were not allowed to go into the women's rooms, nor women into the men's, though they could visit each other in the open dormitory areas.

All employees had access to sports facilities within the factory compound: a football ground, a swimming pool, a golf practice area, and a volleyball and *ta-kraw* court (*ta-kraw* being a kind of foot volleyball, in which the players are not allowed to touch the ball with their forearms or their hands). Between shifts, or on their days off, workers relaxed in the television rooms provided in each

37   Goffman (1962: xx).

dormitory and made use of the basic cooking and laundry facilities. Many of the women used the sewing-room from time to time, with its number of sewing machines provided by the management. Both men and women regularly used the shop to buy toiletries, washing powders and other small items provided by the company at cost price. For meals, they sometimes used the company food coupons to eat at the factory canteen, though they also took advantage of food stalls set up outside the factory. Here they mingled with workers from the next-door factory.

In addition, the employees saw themselves as much better off financially in the Bang Khen factory than workers in many other factories. Workers who began in 1972, like Nopawan and the group from Korat, started on a base wage of 17 baht a day, with a day measured as one eight-hour shift out of three. After six months, this went up to 18.50 baht, and 20 baht after one year. At the same time, the average wage for comparable workers in other factories, particularly in the textile industry, was only 10–12 baht for a day of up to 18 hours, with no official minimum wage and no provision for increments.[38] In 1976, when a legal minimum wage had been set at 25 baht a day, the lowest starting wage for workers at the Bang Khen factory was 36 baht a day. With the Bang Khen company also covering many daily living costs, Nopawan and others were able to send money back to their families, often for the education of younger siblings, and still save a little each month. Niroot, a foreman, supported his younger sister for three years through university and, after she graduated, did the same for a younger brother. The employees were also given opportunities to study, to improve their position within the factory but also more generally. Nopawan had been studying for 18 months, with another six months to go for her to be eligible to sit the exam for a further promotion. During the time that I was there, I was asked if I would give English classes; these were attended by junior as well as senior employees.

As a result of these conditions, the factory enjoyed a relatively stable workforce, with a majority of employees having been there between three and six years. At the celebrations for the factory's tenth anniversary in 1977, bonuses were given on the basis of the number of consecutive years of full attendance. Sixty-nine employees received the bonus for three years, 31 for four, and 17 for five. A number of the original group from Korat were still working at the factory in 1977. Nopawan's view was that she might leave in another two years when her younger siblings had finished studying, but she had made no definite decision.

The work itself was not attractive but was not a cause of special complaint. Onsaeng pointed out that she preferred it to getting up at three in the morning to tap rubber trees: work that she hated and which is what she would have

---

38   Morell and Chai-anan (1981: 194–5).

been doing if she had stayed with her family in the south. Even Nopawan's experience in the salon in Korat made the factory job preferable. In the salon, she had to wake up really early and did not get home—on the nights that she went home—till eight or nine o'clock. As well, she would often be standing all day. In comparison, her job at the factory meant that she had much more time to herself; 'it's more important to have time to yourself than to have interesting work'.

At the same time, routine practices in the factory to some extent cushioned the shift from a rural social world with its focus on family and traditional relations and obligations to instrumental work relationships. Rather than regarding the factory as a total institution, the employees used familiar family terms to address many of the people with whom they worked: *Khun* as the impersonal honorific of courtesy but *phii*, older brother or sister, for respectful familiarity towards those older or more senior. Nopawan addressed and referred to Khun Phadungcit as *Phii* Dung, and to her popular section chief as *Phii* Supachai. She retained *Khun* for more senior Thai management and the Thai version of the Japanese *san* for Mr Suzuka. In turn, she was referred to as *phii* by the younger women in the dormitory. Niroot addressed his dormitory supervisor to whom he was very close as *Lung*, uncle. To some extent, these practices reflect the voluntary character of kin relationships in Thai society generally, which individuals can activate for particular purposes at particular times while leaving others dormant.[39] It also reflects the broadly asymmetrical character of Thai social relationships in general between the *phuu yaj*, the superordinate senior generation, and the *phuu nooj*, the subordinate junior generation.[40] In the expression of these asymmetrical relationships, respect is the most significant element.

In the factory, the meaning invested in these practices varied from person to person and individuals exercised choice about how they referred to different people, though all agreed that the management constituted *phuu yaj*. The wedding of Khun Supachai, Nopawan's section chief, illustrated the extent to which these naming practices operated as a network of personal, kinship-like bonds, reflecting the asymmetrical character of relationships in a context of both respect and reciprocity. The wedding took place in the bride's home. I had been invited to attend with a group of the *phuu yaj* from the factory. We arrived about mid-morning. A saffron line of monks was coming across the verandah and down the shallow front steps, having completed their chanting to bless the couple. Some family and guests waited respectfully in the garden. The bridal couple was in the front room of the house, kneeling on prie-dieux in front of a decorated altar. We filed past them, sprinkling lustral water as we did

---

39   Piker (1969: 64).
40   Tambiah (1970: 23).

so over the hands of each, first the bride and then the groom. Khun Supachai's assistant section chief acted as master of ceremonies and stayed for the party afterwards. Several days after this ceremony, Khun Supachai and his wife put on a party especially for the factory personnel. The company provided buses to take employees to the hotel. Nopawan and almost all the staff of Supachai's own section joined several hundred other workers. This was their opportunity as individuals to express their own feelings, and many did so by giving a personal gift in addition to the group offerings. I cannot describe these gifts, as it is impolite in Thailand to open a gift in the presence of the giver; the fact of the gift is sufficient. This kind of party, given by a *phuu yaj* for the people from his workplace for an occasion such as his wedding, was not unusual. On this occasion, the workers enjoyed it as a special event, and one that expressed the nature of their relationship with *Phii* Supachai in a peculiarly appropriate way.

At one level, these practices and relationships are no more than a personalising of the work place, the establishment through communication of a shared sense of meaning and value and a combining of labour and language that Habermas suggests is fundamental to being human.[41] They allowed the employees to invest the mundane world of work and domesticity with moral as well as rational and emotional meaning. At another level, their practices were profoundly cultural, providing continuity between the industrial present and the rural past by expressing and enhancing a moral order, grounded in traditional Thai social and religious discourse, of reciprocal relations between the self and the other. This discourse integrated notions of merit (*bun*), obligations, gratitude and doing good. The same discourse was to infuse the events leading up to 6 October 1976 and to be invoked by the main protagonists.

For the Bang Khen employees, it was a taken-for-granted way of framing their world even though they recognised that they paid it little active attention. Niroot certainly saw his contributions to the education of his younger siblings as his obligation as an elder brother with a job. It was something he had done since he completed his own studies. As he saw it, his father had helped him and his brother with everything they needed while they were studying; in return they had to help the younger ones. He did not give it a religious meaning or relate it to the making of merit. Nor did he think that because you did good things in a previous life that you would do well in this life, though he acknowledged that other people did believe this. He thought that things had changed for the younger generation and that only old people thought like that any more. Dirake believed in *bun* when he was young, as he also believed in ghosts. That, he said, was before he learnt to reason. When he went to school, he learnt about science and since then he had applied reason to these things. As far as he was

---

41    Habermas (1984, 1987); Ingram (1987: 12).

concerned, believing in ghosts was for children. But both Niroot and Dirake considered the possibility of taking the time allowed by the factory for men employees to become monks for a short period, to make merit for their parents.

Neither did Nopawan give much thought to any relationship between her present life and either a past or a future one, about which she was agnostic. Although she used to go to the temple regularly when she was younger, in Bangkok she had little time to do so, but thought that she would go again often when she was old, as her mother did. In her current circumstances, she thought about work, 'work only, not about merit. They're two different things'. Making merit was not about any future life, but about feeling good. 'Making merit gives happiness. Sometimes if I'm not happy, I make merit and that makes me happy'. Occasionally, if she felt unhappy and unsure about things, she went to see her uncle who was a monk in a Bangkok temple, and from time to time she would go to the temple near the factory. When she gave alms to monks (*saj baat*), she did it for her relatives who had died, so that the merit could go to them. 'This is part of Buddhist religion; not a matter of being useful but a belief, a custom of Buddhist religion.' As for others being wealthy, she saw that not as the result of having made merit in a previous life but as a matter of luck (*chok dii*).

The exception to this way of thinking for the employees was Khun Iid, the Thai majority owner and vice-president of the company. I had not met him when I was negotiating permission to carry out my research, but I encountered him frequently on my own visits to the factory. This happened both on routine workdays and at times for particular festivals and celebrations organised by the factory. While I always addressed him as *Khun*, all the employees spoke and referred to him as *Phii*, a practice that he had himself initiated. When they talked about him, it was with warmth as well as respect. As a foreman, Niroot was sometimes part of a group that played golf with him; afterwards they had the chance to talk. Niroot's comment was that 'Phii Iid is a very good and kind person. He likes helping staff and always understands'. He added that it was also Phii Iid's duty to help staff.

Employees' respect for Khun Iid was not confined to words. When a few years previously news spread at the factory that his wife was ill with cancer and needed a blood transfusion, a number of the employees donated blood. This was a gesture of gratitude, 'because Phii Iid has always been very kind and very helpful to the workers'. It was also a gift steeped in morality, as Mauss suggests,[42] with the giving providing an opportunity for the employees to reciprocate the largesse received from Khun Iid, reinforcing the moral bond created between them that drew its meaning from a traditional patron–client relationship.

---

42   Mauss (1970).

Thai anthropologist Prudisan defines the patron–client relationship as[43] 'a more or less personalised and reciprocal relationship between actors or sets of actors, commanding unequal resources, and involving mutually beneficial transactions that have ramifications beyond the immediate sphere of dyadic relationships'.

In the absence of either formal kin groups or traditional formal groups of any kind,[44] van Roy identifies patron–client ties as the institutional base of Thai life in the lowlands.[45] Hanks links the asymmetrical character of Thai society with the Buddhist doctrine of merit (*bun*), in which the onus is on the superior to aid those below him in the hierarchy in order to increase his own merit.[46] In so doing, he acts as a patron, utilising his greater resources in favour of his inferior, who reciprocates out of gratitude with such services as are at his disposal. The patron bestows favour (*bun khun*), which demands reciprocity (*katanyuu* and *kataweethii*). The gift from the patron is also laden with power,[47] constituting as clients those who receive the gift and those related to them by family or other ties. The gift from the client, as in the donations of blood to Khun Iid's wife, acknowledges the power—personal, practical, social, moral—of the bond. In the social world established by the factory, Khun Iid acted as the practical and symbolic expression of the moral dimension of the principle of reciprocity.

This moral bond, and the asymmetrical reciprocity that it entailed, was reinforced in many other ways. Somthuwin, a member of the Culture Committee, was enthusiastic about the preparations for the party they would give Phii Iid, as they did each year, on the evening of his birthday. She was also involved with the rest of the Culture Committee and the Staff Committee in helping to organise a special event to assist a rural school in a tiny outlying village in a neighbouring province. Viboon's father was the school principal and his mother was also a teacher there. Viboon approached Mr Suzuka to ask for help in the building of a reading room. After consultation with Khun Iid, it was agreed that the factory would give a donation of 20 000 baht. Khun Iid added a personal— and powerful—donation of 20 000 baht. To celebrate the occasion, everyone was invited to the school for an overnight party, and the committees organised participation in a monastery benefit (*thoot phaa paa*) being held for the monks at the temple adjoining the school. About 100 people set out on the Saturday afternoon, first in buses provided by the factory, and then in long-tailed boats along the *khloong* (canal) that was the school's easiest access. The factory band played into the small hours of Sunday morning while people ate, drank, sang and danced. On Sunday morning, the monks came to the school to accept the *phaa paa* tree—with gifts of money and goods attached—that the employees

43    Prudisan (1973: 2).
44    Wijewardene (1967: 83).
45    van Roy (1971: 114).
46    Hanks (1975: 198 ff.).
47    Mauss (1970).

had prepared for them. Not all the partygoers made it to the ceremony, but Khun Iid did. He was accompanied by his brother, Khun Adunsak, a retired major who held the position of assistant manager in the administration section of the factory, and was addressed and referred to by most workers as *Khun*, not *Phii*. After the ceremony, Khun Iid invited my husband and me, with our baby daughter, to join the other official guests for refreshments in a separate room. There we exchanged courtesies and general pleasantries about the school and its work until we returned to the rest of the employees for yet more music and dancing before the regular afternoon downpour and the *khloong* trip back to the buses and home. Viboon and his parents waved us all off from the school's landing stage.

Unknown until a few days later, Chuusak, one of the workers, was killed in a motorbike accident that same day. Because his family was poor, the company played a leading role in his cremation, with unforeseen consequences that I will discuss in the next chapter. The school party and *thoot phaa paa* also took place in the final few days before the 6 October massacre. Although the events that precipitated the massacre had been the major news items for weeks—since the return to the country of, first, Field Marshall Prapass and then Field Marshall Thanom—there had been no reference to them among the official reception guests. Politics was not an appropriate or seemly topic for discussion at a celebration designed to demonstrate the ongoing vitality of the patron–client relationship operating between Khun Iid and the factory employees.

Nevertheless, events outside the factory formed the background to all these activities, and employees had access to the full range of media available in Bangkok. As well as radio, and television in the dormitories, each section had daily deliveries of two newspapers, *Thai Rath* and *Dao Siam*. Like most of the Thai newspapers, they were sensationalist rather than informative, with their main focus on crime and scandals. The presence in Thailand in 1974 of Roger Moore and his co-stars for the filming of the latest James Bond film, *The Man with the Golden Gun*, received as much coverage as the emergence of a swathe of recently permitted political parties in preparation for the first general elections scheduled for January 1975. Even with that tendency, the media was provided with enough sensation by political events from late 1972 to ensure ongoing and sweeping coverage. University students figured very prominently in those reports.

# Monarchy and democracy: The uprising of 14 October 1973 and the beginning of the 'democratic experiment'

Students had not been politically active during the Sarit regime or in the early years of the Thanom–Prapass period. In 1965, they founded the National Student Centre of Thailand (NSCT), mainly to make contact with foreign university students. In 1969, they transformed their desultory activities in relation to foreign exchange programs into fledgling political activity at home. In November 1972, they organised an anti-Japanese goods campaign over 10 days. Their strongly nationalistic protests received maximum, and largely approving, coverage in newspapers and on television.[48] After that, students remained in the news and student activities continued to be reported, as did their critique of the increasingly aggressive actions of the third member of the Thanom–Prapass triumvirate, Colonel Narong Kittikachorn. Narong was Thanom's son and Prapass's son-in-law and extremely unpopular. Then came the massive anti-government demonstrations from 6 October to 14 October 1973. They involved university and vocational students, workers and farmers. Bang Khen employees watching TV between shifts over the whole week, or reading newspapers, saw images of up to 500 000 demonstrators filling the whole area around the Democracy Monument and surrounding streets, carrying pictures of the King and Queen and waving Thai flags. On 13 October, the images turned violent; the Government had ordered the military to suppress the demonstrations. In the subsequent clashes on that and the next day, demonstrators burnt down a number of government buildings, including the police headquarters, but a number were killed: at least 70, with some estimates much higher. Unlike the Thammasat massacre three years later, these pictures of police killings of unarmed demonstrators were not censored in the press. On 14 October, the King intervened publicly, an act that was unprecedented, and announced the resignation of the Thanom government. That night, the 'three tyrants'—Thanom, Prapass and Narong—went into exile. The King appointed the Rector of Thammasat University, Professor Sanya Thammasughdi, as provisional Prime Minister. It appeared that the rule of the Generals had ended.

The experience of civilian and later democratic government that followed the 1973 uprising—the 'democratic experiment'—was new for everyone in the country, including the Bang Khen employees. In the weeks and months following 14 October, the students continued to provide the media with plenty of material. Still in October, there was a successful student demonstration in the north, from where Niroot and many of the other Bang Khen employees

---

48   Morell and Chai-an (1981: 141–3).

came. Students in Lamphun Province accused the Governor of corruption in administering funds allocated for local school projects. They demanded and obtained his resignation. In November, they forced the resignation of the Dean and Rector of the School of Public Administration at the National Institute of Development Administration. The Dean had been an advisor to the National Executive Council of the Thanom–Prapass government. Also in November, the independent Chulalongkorn Student Group launched a city-wide protest against the newly appointed US Ambassador, William R. Kintner, a former US Army colonel who had also worked for the Central Intelligence Agency (CIA). Newspapers carried anti-CIA editorials and cartoons. By January 1974, this campaign, assisted by the accidental exposure of CIA clandestine activity in the north-east, culminated in a public apology to the Thai Government by the Ambassador, and a statement from the embassy that the CIA would be told to close its field posts in Thailand. In the same month, the Japanese Prime Minister, Kakuei Tanaka, visited Bangkok and was met with large, hostile demonstrations.[49]

In spite of the new freedom in reporting, the students did not spare the press itself in these early days:

> During the months following the student revolt, a major student protest was also launched against Thailand's most influential Thai language newspaper, *Siam Rath*, because of a letter critical of King Bhumiphol. At a student rally the newspaper was publicly burned as a symbol of the students' discontent with the letter and determination to censor the editor from further publication. Shortly thereafter, the Thai police suspended the editor's license indefinitely for publishing the article by two Thais in Sweden criticising the King for not controlling troops and police during the student revolt in October, 1973. The newspaper's editor, Nopporn Boonyarit, hopelessly attempted to defend himself by asserting that the paper was simply trying to expose attempts to undermine the monarchy.[50]

Student activities were not the only topic for news reports. Two other sectors also became a major focus: labour and farmers. The 14 October uprising and subsequent killings had included workers as well as students. Without unions or other official forms of labour organisation, worker involvement in these events had been haphazard. Their response to the situation was, nevertheless, seen as newsworthy. Strikes had occurred previously, even under the Sarit regime, but unions had remained banned. Legislation in 1972 provided for employees' associations to be formed; with workers deeply suspicious of government and

---

49  Prizzia and Narong (1974: 157–61).
50  ibid., pp. 161–2.

of potential repercussions, this had led to only some 15 such associations being registered up to June 1972.[51] In the period 1963 to 1972 of the Thanom–Prapass government, the average number of strikes per year was 16, with the lowest number being two in 1967 and the highest number, 34, in 1972. In 1973, there were 501 strikes.[52]

This situation was exacerbated in 1974 with the impact of the 1973 international oil crisis being felt in many Thai industries. The impact was particularly strong in the textile industry. Like the Bang Khen factory, most textile factories were jointly owned with Japanese or Taiwanese companies. The Bang Khen factory had only just begun processing its own industrial chips, which it had previously bought from Japan and Singapore. With the rise in the price of oil, the price of chemicals necessary for production also rose, and the company ran into temporary difficulties. A general response from employers across the sector was to announce production cutbacks, wage reductions and worker lay-offs.[53] In response, workers from about 600 factories went on strike in June 1974. The strike was led by the newly formed Samut Sakon Textile Workers Union and supported by the National Students Centre.

Again, the Bang Khen workers did not participate. Contrary to the general response from other employers, the Bang Khen management did not impose redundancies. Instead, they indirectly invoked the patron–client relationship that was focused in the person of Khun Iid but was also fostered by management. Without making any direct reference to gratitude or obligation, they asked the single shift workers to volunteer to take up to a month's leave, during which they would receive 70 per cent of their normal wages. Niroot stopped working for 15 days and went back to Chiang Mai. Nopawan stopped work for a month and also took the opportunity to go home. They agreed that many of the other employees accepted the proposal, pointing out that all those involved were young and unmarried. Some who did not take advantage of the time to go home took casual work. They ended up with more pay for that period than they would have had if they had stayed working at the factory. Still others saw it as an opportunity to *paj thiaw*. The general attitude was that, with the problem of rising unemployment, they valued their jobs, and were glad to receive less money for a month rather than be laid off like so many other workers. Normal shifts resumed after three months. Niroot commented that the factory had been good (*bun khun*) to him and to the other employees. He was grateful and felt positive towards the company. At the same time, his attitude reflected the impact of the modernisation process in which he was participating and the increasingly

---

51    Mabry (1977: 935).
52    Supachai (1976: Appendix II).
53    Morell and Chai-anan (1981: 189).

conscious discourse of student and labour activists. He did not feel that he owed *bun khun* to the factory, because he worked for them and was paid in return; in his own words, 'I exchange my labour for money'.

# The move to democratic labour and agricultural worker institutions

Despite the increasing profile being given to strikes and labour disputes, this basically conservative attitude among the Bang Khen workers was not atypical of the labour sector in general. In some ways, it was more representative of the pragmatic rather than ideological approach taken by the leaders of the main labour organisation that emerged in early 1976.[54] This was the Federation of Labour Unions of Thailand, reorganised after May 1976 as the National Labour Council. Its foundation was in response to the rapid growth of labour organisations after 14 October 1973. From some 15 associations in June 1973, these had increased to about 80 in late 1974 and to 153 in July 1976. Almost 90 per cent of these were found in the Greater Bangkok region and most were located in manufacturing. About 25 of these were located in foreign-owned firms; 23 were in textiles and clothing.[55]

In 1975, the newly formed coalition government of the remarkable Kukrit Pramoj passed the *Labour Relations Act*. Supachai Manusphaibool, the Chulalongkorn political scientist best known for his study of the Thai industrial relations system, suggested before the coup in 1976 that the *Labour Relations Act 1975* became 'the most important impetus to the development of [a] modern industrial relations system in Thailand'.[56] Although it was amended in significant ways after the coup—most importantly in removing the right to strike—the Act itself was not abrogated. It provided for the formation and registration of trade unions and for the amalgamation and federation of a national trade union congress.[57]

The National Labour Council grew initially out of the public utilities sector, where unions had been government endorsed since the 1972 legislation had permitted the formation of labour associations. It was led by Paisal Thavatchainant, President of the Metropolitan Electricity Authority Workers Union. By October 1976, the Council's membership had reached around 300 000 workers, 200 000 in public utility enterprises and around 100 000 in other sectors.[58] The Council deliberately chose to develop an image of conservative

54   Mabry (1977: 935).
55   ibid., pp. 935–8.
56   Supachai (1976: 17).
57   ibid., p. 18.
58   Morell and Chai-anan (1981: 201).

responsibility, discouraging its members from identifying with the radical student movement or more radical labour groups.[59] I first met with the acting president and secretary of the Council in June 1976, soon after the Council's formation and while working to establish my research. My project nearly came to an abrupt end when I made the mistake of assuming their support for student collaboration with the labour movement and telling them about my involvement with a group of student activists and factory workers at Thammasat. Their displeasure, and my mistake, was exacerbated when I mentioned the factory to which one of the workers had asked me to go; its union was not a member of the Council and had worked actively with students in a strike and confrontation with the Prime Minister earlier in the year. Fortunately for my research, I did not go so far as to tell them that, a week later, I was due to accompany a group of the Thammasat students and workers on a visit to the Lard Yao prison to see the unionists from the Omnoy textile factory and the students who had been arrested on charges of Communism.

The caution of the National Labour Council was understandable in the context of the long suppression of unions and freedom of association in Thailand, but also in view of the eruption of labour disputes and strikes after October 1973. Of the 501 strikes in 1973, 73 per cent occurred after the October uprising.[60] This dropped to 357 in 1974 but included some spectacularly newsworthy ones, such as the June textile workers' strike and one by the hotel employees at the five-star Dusit Thani, then one of the best-known hotels in Bangkok.[61] In 1975, the number of strikes dropped again, to 241; and in the first year after the introduction of the *Labour Relations Act 1975*, and before the coup, the number of work stoppages dropped by almost 30 per cent;[62] however, by 1976 both the labour and the student movements had fragmented.

The June 1974 textile workers' strike had led the Government to increase the minimum wage for all industrial workers in the Bangkok and surrounding industrial areas to 20 baht a day. This was the second rise in the minimum wage by the new Government.[63] It did not affect the majority of the Bang Khen workers, who were already receiving this amount or higher. The Government also agreed that all textile workers should be paid for the week during which they were out on strike. More significantly in the longer term, however, the strike led to a split in the labour movement between the more moderate and broadly representative National Labour Council and politically radical leaders such as those in the Samut Sakon Textile Workers Union.[64] As a result, the latter

---

59   Mabry (1977: 939–40).
60   Morell and Chai-anan (1981: 187).
61   ibid., pp. 196–7.
62   Supachai (1976: 17).
63   ibid., p. 27.
64   Morell and Chai-anan (1981: 190).

groups joined to form the well-organised but short-lived Labour Coordination Centre of Thailand (LCCT) as an organisation distinct from the National Labour Council. The imprisoned Omnoy unionists were affiliated with the LCCT. An important part of the LCCT approach was ongoing cooperative action with student activists and with the recently mobilised farmer groups.

Like the labour movement, farmers and agricultural workers had mobilised rapidly after October 1973 and had been actively encouraged and supported by student groups. Debt had long been a serious problem for Thai farmers. As early as 1931, rural debt had been estimated at 143 million baht, with the most critical problems around Chiang Mai and the Central Plains. In the following four decades, not only debt but also rural tenancy and landlessness in those regions rose to around 50 per cent.[65] After October 1973 it was possible to articulate these grievances publicly for the first time. The first large farmers' protest was held in March 1974 to demand higher paddy-rice prices.[66] In May, hundreds more demonstrated to protest the dispossession of their lands by moneylenders.[67] In June, more than 2000 staged a week-long sit-in in Bangkok, with Thammasat students providing temporary lodging for them.[68] In the same month, some 20 000 farmers were reported to have marched on Bangkok in sympathy with the textile workers' strike.[69] June also saw the Government respond to farmers' protests with the establishment of a committee empowered to investigate grievances. In the first month of its operations, the committee received 10 999 petitions from six provinces. In December, the National Assembly passed the *Land Rent Control Act*.[70]

In the same month, the Farmers Federation of Thailand was established. Its headquarters in Chiang Mai were organised under its Vice-President, Intha Sribunruang, former village headman, farmer and storekeeper from that province.[71] It was the first farmers' organisation to be independent of government supervision and grew rapidly, setting up provincial branches in all of the northern and upper central provinces.[72] One estimate was that by mid 1975, 100 000 farm families in Chiang Mai Province alone had joined the Federation.[73]

---

65  ibid., pp. 208–9.
66  ibid., p. 214.
67  Bowie (1997: 102).
68  Morell and Chai-anan (1981: 217).
69  Turton (1978: 129).
70  Morell and Chai-anan (1981: 215–16, 221).
71  ibid., p. 222.
72  Bowie (1997: 102).
73  Morell and Chai-anan (1981: 222, 225).

# The hardening of positions and the challenges to democracy

By early 1975, therefore, the labour movement and issues were centred in Bangkok, the farmers' movement in Chiang Mai, and students remained active in both. Thammasat students provided a busy office, Room 426, at the university, where workers came and went freely, using facilities, meeting and planning. Students from all the Bangkok universities continued their program of political education and activities in rural areas. But by early 1975 also, divisions between moderates and radicals within each of these movements were becoming clearly demarcated. At the same time, although the rhetoric and methods of each of the movements increasingly differed, their principal objectives remained the same: that is, improvement in conditions for both urban and rural workers. Unfortunately, radical methods and rhetoric are newsworthy. The media focus throughout this period was on strikes, demonstrations and increasingly extreme statements. The media also made much of the proliferation of political parties in the lead-up to the elections of January 1975.

Once a government had been settled under the prime ministership of Kukrit Pramoj, media focus was on the fragile stability of the Government, with its difficult and shifting coalition of eight parties. Reporting about Kukrit himself reflected the general respect for his eminent reputation and many previous achievements. Among these were his founding of Thailand's first political party, the Progress Party, in 1945–46, his establishment of the paper *Siam Rath*, to which he contributed for many years, and his many other literary and artistic accomplishments. Not least among these in popular esteem was his appearance in 1963 with Marlon Brando in *The Ugly American* as Prime Minister Kwen Sai, a role perilously close to his actual prime ministership in 1975–76.

Over these two years, the general perception of barely contained chaos and potential disaster was exacerbated by ongoing coverage also of the war in neighbouring Vietnam, Laos and Cambodia, and the continuing Communist insurgency in the north-east and in other border areas. External events combined to inflame this perception. In March 1975, in the midst of a high-profile anti-United States campaign and massive demonstrations in Bangkok orchestrated by student leaders, Prime Minister Kukrit implemented one of his election promises and requested the withdrawal of US troops. In April, the Vietnam War came to an end with the capture of Saigon by North Vietnamese troops, and the Khmer Rouge under Pol Pot declared the Democratic Republic of Kampuchea. Rumours began to circulate almost immediately in Bangkok about executions and the forced removal and hard labour imposed by the Khmer Rouge on the people of the new Democratic Republic. In July, Kukrit led a Thai delegation to Beijing and established diplomatic relations with the communist Chinese

Government. In December, the new communist Lao Government abolished the Lao monarchy. On 11 January 1976, with alarm at these developments and in the face of growing instability in the government coalition, a number of military leaders called on Kukrit in order to deliver an ultimatum. The Prime Minister should either dissolve the House of Representatives and call new elections or allow the military to return to the administration of the country.[74] Faced also with a no-confidence vote in his government scheduled for 14 January, Kukrit dissolved the parliament and set an election date for 14 April 1976.

The election campaign was defined by violence. More than 30 people were killed and dozens more injured. Grenades were thrown into crowds gathered to listen to political speeches.[75] The violence was perpetrated almost exclusively against socialist or leftist candidates or organisations. The most prominent assassination was that of Dr Boonsanong Punyodyana, Secretary-General of the Socialist Party, who was shot in his car near his home on the night of 28 February. Boonsanong was a well-known and popular former lecturer in sociology at Thammasat University. Another party identified as left-wing because of its social reform policies was the New Force (*Palang Maj*) party, led by the urbane and highly respected medical practitioner Dr Krasae Chanawongse. Dr Krasae was the holder of the Magsaysay Award for his long-term medical work in rural areas of the north-east and had represented his north-east electorate of Khon Kaen since 1973. During the election campaign, the party's headquarters in Bangkok were attacked with firebombs and partially burned down, and a New Force Member of Parliament from Lopburi was assassinated.[76] On 21 March, 10 people died when a grenade was thrown into a New Force party rally in Chainat Province.[77]

The violence and intimidation enacted during the election campaign were just another step in the ubiquitous violence of the previous two years, most notably against members of the Farmers Federation. Guns and other weapons were plentiful as a result of US aid to the military and police and its secret war in Laos.[78] Between March 1974 and August 1975, at least 21 Farmers Federation leaders were assassinated. These included the Chiang Mai leader, Intha, who was shot in front of his house in August 1975.[79] In Bangkok, there had been a number of incidents of serious injury and death as a result of grenades being thrown into demonstrations. This violence was no longer carried out by the military, as it had been in October 1973, but by increasingly radical right-wing organisations. These professed to be civilian organisations but were in fact supported by and closely related to sections of the military and the police.

---

74   ibid., p. 262.
75   ibid., pp. 262–3.
76   ibid., p. 263.
77   Tienchai (1993: 263).
78   Anderson (1998: 179).
79   Morell and Chai-anan (1981: 225).

The three most visible groups were the Red Gaurs (*Krathin Daeng*), Nawaphol and the Village Scouts. The Red Gaurs, confined primarily to the Bangkok area, quickly became notorious and were responsible for much of the violence leading up to the 1976 massacre, including strikebreaking. They were a combination of former mercenaries, unemployed young men, petty criminals and disaffected vocational students who, having played a significant role with university students in the 1973 uprising, saw themselves as excluded from any subsequent benefits. The organisation was set up by a leader in the Internal Security Operations Command (ISOC), Colonel Sudsai Hasadin,[80] and maintained its direct links with that section of the military. Nawaphol—referring to the 'ninth power' or 'nine strengths'—was set up as an ultra-nationalist organisation to operate mainly in provincial and district towns rather than in villages. It was supported, though indirectly, by ISOC and provided with a form of legitimacy by the endorsement of the well-known anti-Communist Buddhist monk Kittiwutho Bhikku, who stated publicly that to kill a Communist was not an act of demerit (*baap*).[81] Nawaphol's program to preserve Thai nationalism contained nine themes.[82] Its rallies were whipped into a fever by challenges of 'Do you love your king? Do you love Thailand? Do you hate communism?'[83] The Village Scouts were established in 1971 specifically as part of the Thai counterinsurgency strategy. Their founder was Major-General Somkhuan Harikul, an officer of the Border Patrol Police,[84] itself a paramilitary organisation developed as an internal security force in the 1950s with support from the CIA. Although technically located within the Thai National Police Department, the Border Patrol Police maintained direct links with the military. Its main area of activities was, as its name suggests, along the borders with Laos and Cambodia, covering both Thai village areas and hill-tribe settlements. The Village Scouts, modelled on the Boy Scouts, was designed specifically to involve villagers as an active element in the Government's anti-Communist strategy. Critically, they enjoyed royal patronage and became closely identified with the royal family.[85] One comment made in retrospect was that 1973 and 1974 were 'the years of the students, workers, and farmers', whereas 1975 and 1976 were 'the years of the Village Scouts'.[86]

---

80   Bowie (1997: 106).

81   ibid., p. 319 n. 42.

82   Morell and Chai-anan (1981: 252 fn. 7).

83   ibid., pp. 238–40.

84   Bowie (1997: 55).

85   ibid., pp. 81 ff. Bowie highlights the role of the royal family in the success of the Village Scouts (p. 82): 'The ambiguity in the symbolic meaning of the royal family is a crucial factor in explaining the dramatic success of the Village Scout movement in the mid-1970s. To the extent that the king symbolized hope among his poorer subjects, his involvement with the Village Scouts attracted the lower classes to the movement. To the extent that the king was transformed into a symbol of conservative reaction against progressive reform, he catalysed the financial contributions of the upper classes and conservative elements in the middle classes. Thus the king played an important role in the expansion of the Village Scouts, initially as a powerful symbol of unity and later as a multivocal political symbol motivating an intricate fusion of class fractions and state factions.'

86   Morell and Chai-anan (1981: 245).

Together, the three organisations of the Red Gaurs, Nawaphol and the Village Scouts covered all the main population centres of Thailand: Bangkok, provincial and district towns, and villages. All three took as their principal slogan the mantra of 'Nation, Religion, King'. All three—Nawaphol and the Village Scouts ideologically and the Red Gaurs pragmatically—were passionately opposed to Communism. In the volatile politics of the region, as well as in the country in the three years of the 'democratic experiment', these factors merged into an explosive mixture. The victory of Communism in the neighbouring countries in 1975 was the element that provided the trigger for the explosion.

# The destabilising of democracy: Return of the Generals

The fuse was set by the return to Bangkok of the previous dictators. Their return to the country from exile, having been ousted by the uprising in 1973, was seen as a direct challenge to Thailand's fledgling democracy. Field Marshall Prapass arrived first, on 15 August 1976. Field Marshall Thanom came secretly into the country a month later, on 19 September. Prapass's return was short-lived, with the National Student Centre threatening mass demonstrations. During his fortnight in the country, however, he was granted an audience with the King, a public gesture of recognition from the King that signalled a withdrawal of the monarchy from its support for a democratic system.

The King, without consultation with the Government, also gave personal approval to the return of Thanom, who was taken immediately on his arrival to Wat Boworniwet, the principal royal monastery, not far from Thammasat University. There he was ordained as a Buddhist monk. The King, as well as the Crown Prince who had returned from his military studies in Australia just a few days earlier on 1 October, paid him visits, providing a further provocative legitimacy to a potential overturning of the Government. Others were quick to declare political support. Nawaphol leaders went publicly to pay Thanom their respects, and Red Gaur members were posted in the temple grounds to ensure his safety.[87] When the Government tried to persuade him to leave the country and the students again threatened demonstrations to force him to go, Thanom refused on the grounds that he was following tradition in making merit for his father who was old and ill. This claim made it difficult for his opponents to sustain their demand for his expulsion. It also threw the Government—again a coalition, this time once more led by Kukrit's older brother, Seni Pramoj—into crisis, reflecting the sense of impending crisis that gripped the country.

---

87   ibid., pp. 270–3.

Despite the fissuring of support, however, major non-violent protests were held. Even some 40 affiliates of the moderate National Labour Council called for a protest general strike for 12 October.[88] In Nakhon Pathom Province, where the Omnoy unionists and students were still in prison and 18 more key LCCT members had been recently arrested,[89] two activists—Chumporn Thommai and Vichai Ketsripongsa—were murdered by police while they were distributing anti-Thanom posters. On 5 October, Prime Minister Seni announced his new Cabinet, but they had still to be sworn in, a ceremony that never took place.

On the same day, photos appeared in the press of a mock hanging of the two Nakhon Pathom students, staged on the previous day by student protestors at Thammasat. The English-language daily, the *Bangkok Post*, published the photo over the caption:

> It was just a mock hanging but the effect was such that it created an eerie atmosphere at the Thammasat University campus to kick off another anti-Thanom protest…A student acting as one of the two garrotted victims was 'hanged' from a tree in front of the Dome while another student dressed in robes and carrying a gun, depicting Phra [Monk] Thanom, walked around. Nearby several dozen students lay 'dead' on the ground.

The photo adjoined the front-page main headline, 'Srisuk admits police behind garrottings'. As I read the paper over breakfast on a humid morning, the relevance of the dramatised hanging to the Nakhom Pathom killings seemed clear. It was not until I got to the factory a couple of hours later and saw the same photo as published in *Dao Siam* that I could make sense of the outrage that was being expressed. The *Dao Siam* photo—and its reproduction the same day in some other Thai-language newspapers such as *Banmuang*—made the hanged student, Apinant Buahapakdi, look very much like the Crown Prince. This was the spark that ignited the madness and grief of 6 October.

# Marked with blood: The forgotten coup of 6 October 1976

It was established later that the main perpetrators of the violence on that day were neither the army nor the police, though there may have been some involvement, but rather the civilian Red Gaurs and the Village Scouts, with support from Nawaphol and the Border Patrol Police. No-one was ever charged with the killings or assaults. Apart from the students who were killed, and

88    Mabry (1977: 940).
89    Tienchai (1993: 264).

no longer just playing 'dead', around 1300 others were arrested at Thammasat and taken away in buses. Another 1700 people were arrested elsewhere in the city.[90] In the aftermath of the massacre, many fled to the jungle and joined the Communist insurgency. Despite a number of attempts, I was never able to find out what happened to Nittaya Maphungphong from Thammasat, Prudhisan Tumbala from Chulalongkorn, or the other students with whom I had been working over the previous months, or what became of their idealism and energy. Thammasat, along with all the other universities, was closed down for some time. It reopened with a striking symbolic statement about the powerful re-emergence of tradition in opposition to modernity; those students who returned wore, for the first time, the uniform that was common to other Thai universities.

On the night of 6 October, the rule of the Generals returned in the guise of the National Administrative Reform Council (NARC). The constitution, parliament, and all political parties were banned.[91] Martial law was proclaimed, with political gatherings made illegal and a nightly curfew imposed. The establishment of press censorship was immediate, newspapers suspended for several days, and liberal magazines such as *Prachachat* that had flourished in the democratic period were closed down and its editor arrested. When newspapers were permitted to resume publication on Saturday, 9 October, the *Bangkok Post* reported the appointment by the King of Supreme Court Judge Thanin Kraivichien as Prime Minister. The *Post* also reported that the NARC had had 'a one-and-a-half hour audience with His Majesty the King' and that

> in its Announcement No. 3, the public was asked to place their reliance and trust in the NARC which will do its best to maintain peace and order. The NARC assured the public that it will not seize control of anything more than is necessary for the welfare of the country.

Announcement No. 3 identified clearly that what had been at stake over the period 1973–76 were contested notions about what constituted 'the welfare of the country'; in other words, contested notions about what constitutes a good society. The notions were played out against the background of a war in Vietnam, and in neighbouring Laos and Cambodia, which itself crystallised conflicting ideologies about what constitutes a good society. The predominance of the military over four decades, together with the push to rapid industrialisation under the dictatorship of Field Marshall Sarit, left Thailand with a limited range of possibilities.

The uprising of October 1973 had been an expression of desire for a differently imagined possibility, that of a socially just response to modernisation, including land reform and increased wages, and a strong democratic participation of all

---

90   Morell and Chai-anan (1981: 275).
91   ibid., p. 275.

sectors in society in order to achieve it. Time and deep vested interests did not allow that to be achieved. The institutions established in the wake of October 1973 were too weak and were not given time to strengthen. Without the superlative political skills of Kukrit Pramoj and his own richly imagined vision of the meeting of the old and the new in a modern Thailand, the 'democratic experiment' would have been terminated even more abruptly. Under the historical circumstances, not even a Kukrit could defy the power of the past. The decision of the newly formed and necessarily inexperienced progressive parties, like the Socialist and New Force parties, not to join with him in the coalition government in January 1975 betrayed the possibility of implementing their policies both for him and for them. They forced the response to modernisation into an opposition between the past and present without addressing the question about whose past was being privileged. The result was the terrible bloodletting, both metaphorical and actual, that was played out in increasingly stark and violent ways between 1973 and 1976: exactly three years bracketed by two late rainy seasons but increasingly marked by blood. There was a seasonal downpour on the afternoon of 6 October. The areas in and around Thammasat literally ran with blood.

# 3. Dictatorship and democracy: Competing social imaginaries

In making a choice to move from their hometowns and villages to Bangkok and to take on factory work, the Bang Khen workers had already shifted outside their accepted traditional roles. Modernisation had made that choice available to them and they saw it as an opportunity for achieving a better life, principally for themselves as individuals but also in relation to the greater assistance they could provide for their families. Their new experiences were what expanded this understanding and forged the link for them between their desire for a good life and the broader need for a good society. Despite their relative distance from the immediacy of political upheavals, and an environment within the factory that drew on traditional relations and practices, their encounter with the emerging language of rights led them to a modest engagement with the political and legal reforms of the time. The establishment of their own labour union was based in a growing awareness of their place in a wider world and of the necessity of developing a good society in order to have a good life.

## Dictatorship and the return to traditionalism

The events of 6 October 1976 constituted a fulcrum in Thailand's faltering attempt to incorporate modernisation. On that day, it appeared that the conservatism of many elements of Thai society had triumphed in recasting modernisation, and the model of a good society, in terms of a social and political past. However, if the period 1973–76 can rightly be seen as a crisis of modernity, then the return of dictatorship in October 1976 compels an answer to the question of whose past was reinstated. There arises also the question about whose or what modernity we are referring to. For the student and farmer activists, their experience of the changing world allowed them to imagine a good society as a just society in which hierarchy no longer privileged an elite over the masses, and certainly one that demanded democratic participation and in which authoritarian military rule had no place. Their experience also led them to believe that, in the Thailand of the 1970s, this was possible.

They plundered the rhetoric of Marxism in order to express this vision, though it was in practice a socialist rather than a communist one. They also seized the opportunity to republish the banned radical text of one of the local heroes of the student movement, Jit Poumisak. *The Real Face of Thai Feudalism [Saktina] Today* was first published in 1957, and then banned under Field Marshall Sarit. Jit was imprisoned and kept without trial for eight years. Ten months later, he was shot as an outlaw. *The Real Face* broke completely with the tradition of Thai historical writing and presented a graphic critique of Thai society, not as one of harmony, equilibrium and mutual respect, but as one of feudal domination and conflict.

> They eat and sleep on that pile of silver
>
> They take from the excess value of my labour.
>
> My wife and children have nothing,
>
> Who knows if they'll starve.
>
> The state's not there to look after them
>
> But rather to serve the capitalist pack...
>
> The bunch of us will starve for sure
>
> There's no way out of this dark mess
>
> As long as those greedy men
>
> Reap profit by ploughing on our backs.[1]

*The Real Face* was republished after 14 October 1973, 'in another euphoric moment', and became, along with the writings of Che Guevara and other Marxist revolutionaries, a regular text for the student movement. It was banned again after 6 October 1976.[2]

For farmers and agricultural workers, the changes after 1973 provided their first opportunity to make a collective challenge to growing levels of debt, tenancy and landlessness. There was also the critical issue of the falling price for paddy rice at the same time as the price of purchased rice was rising. These were for them the main impacts of modernisation. A contemporary economic study identified the 'concern that agrarian conditions are deteriorating, and that fragmentation of holdings into smaller, less economic, units is occurring, together with increasing tenancy', and that 'peasants are losing their land to landowners'.[3] A recent land boom had spawned a rich agribusiness, which operated wholly on wage labour. Associated with this was a new class of entrepreneurial small farmers whose position had been strengthened, not only by the acquisition of larger landholdings, but also by government-sponsored farmers' groups.[4] The interlocking of such projects with American strategic schemes was instanced by programs such as the Accelerated Rural Development (ARD) program, which was initiated in 1965 with large-scale US backing. The program was concentrated in the north-east, the focus of the insurgency, to which some 70 per cent of US

---

1   *To Labour*. Written in the mid 1950s. Quoted in Morell and Chai-anan (1981: 181).
2   Reynolds (1987: 11, 13).
3   Ho and Chapman (1973: 28, 29).
4   Turton (1978: 116–18).

aid to Thailand was directed.[5] Farmers demonstrated their resistance to these changes with the high number of petitions—10 999—received in its first month (June 1974) by the national committee set up to investigate grievances. These came from six provinces only. The committee found that most of these farmers had been cheated of their land. Over the next three months, the number of petitions averaged more than 14 000 per month, and by the end of September 1974, the number had reached 53 650.[6] The farmers received support not only from students but, to the astonishment of all sectors, also from members of the Young Buddhist Monks group of Thailand. This was the first time that monks had ever participated publicly in a political process, though not, as the monks themselves pointed out, in public life. Their justification was that 'monks should help people rather than serving the rich and powerful'.[7]

For workers in the growing industrial sector, too, the advent of democracy was full of the promise of urgent improvement in pay and conditions. They had some opportunity to assess these against international standards, as Thailand had continued its membership of the International Labour Organisation (ILO) over the period from 1958 and sent delegates to annual conventions. The ILO had equally regularly criticised Thailand for its refusal to allow a free labour movement.[8] The explosion of strikes after October 1973 and the rapid growth of trade unions were indications of the frustration of workers and their desire for a better deal. They were given practical assistance in developing their unions by volunteer university staff. The staff set up weekend labour education programs at the three Bangkok universities, Chulalongkorn, Thammasat and Kasetsart.[9] It was at one of these courses run by the Chulalongkorn Faculty of Economics in August 1976 that I was introduced to Khun Thongying, the deputy personnel manager of the Bang Khen factory. The meeting had been generously arranged by Supachai Manusphaibool as a way of breaking my impasse of locating a factory that would allow my research.

Even the anxiety of the reactionary opposition reflected a particular view of the meaning of modernity that grew out of nostalgia for the stability of the past. The trajectory of opposition to the introduction of democracy, with violence as its method, was propelled by the incantation of the three heavily mythologised pillars of Thai tradition and identity: Nation, Religion, King. But traditionalism, as Morris suggests, is itself a discourse, elaborated around the fear of tradition's loss.[10] Rather than being an alternative to modernity, it is in fact its effect. For the Village Scouts, the political good was defined by an authoritarian government

---

5   ibid., p. 107.
6   Morell and Chai-anan (1981: 216).
7   ibid., pp. 220–1.
8   Mabry (1977: 934).
9   ibid., p. 941.
10  Morris (2002: 71).

that promised the old stability. Bowie reports a chant during a Scout initiation ritual in 1977, after the re-establishment of military rule, of 'I will do good things, things that the government wants. Whoooooo'.[11]

The Bang Khen employees felt the effects of these external contests over the nature of the good society, though their experience of the democratic years was much less turbulent than that of many others, even in response to 6 October. With the suppression of details, and especially the banning of photographs, only those who happened to have been watching television during the day or thought to buy the afternoon's edition of *Siam Rath* were exposed to the extent of the morning's brutality. Those who did have an inkling saw it initially as one more episode in the series of violent political incidents that had been constantly reported, especially since 1973, and to which they had access through the media and through memory. Violence itself was a daily part of the image politics of media representation and unnervingly graphic images of violence were commonplace.[12] In a country that, at that time, had one of the highest homicide rates in the world,[13] and lethal road rage was often practised long before the invention of the term, violence was not of itself shocking or sensational. Klima argues that critical meanings[14]

> can develop in the interstice between the politics of graphic sensationalism in the public sphere and reclusive Buddhist visualization of the body in death and decay…Like the image of the cadaver in the public sphere, this [Buddhist] work with images of death can be chaotic and dangerous, though not hopelessly so…What Buddhist meditation lacks in explicit political intent it gains in its unsettling and counterintuitive deconstruction of the human being through vision.

The employees were, therefore, very familiar with images of violence. Moreover, whatever their backgrounds, even the youngest had grown up under military dictatorships. Older employees remembered Sarit's five spectacular years (1959–63). Some of them spoke admiringly of him, not because of his political reputation as a strong man, but with reference to the number and quality of his mistresses. Khun Phadungcit, the dormitory supervisor, explained that magazines of photographs of his more than 100 mistresses used to be available, in the same way as they were for beauty queens or movie stars, and were equally popular. She was also less interested in the corruption exposed after Sarit's death than in the story of the fight over his wealth between his wife, his minor wives and mistresses, his brothers and the Government.

---

11    Bowie (1997: 209).
12    Klima (2002: 11).
13    Turton (1978: 108).
14    Klima (2002: 11).

The Bang Khen employees viewed the last years of the Thanom–Prapass regime, and the minimal easing of the Government's anti-union policy in 1972, as workers in the industrial sector. As in most other places, they made no move to set up an association. For most, indeed, there was little interest in politics before 1973. The Generals had always been in charge, and the regime was not obviously repressive in ways that affected their ordinary lives. As the factory workers saw it, politics was a patchwork of inadequate government responses to rising prices, active government support for the United States in the Vietnam War, or occasional scandals, sexual and financial. The period after October 1973 was novel, and interesting, but potentially anomalous. Very few, if any, employees voted in the first general election in January 1975. This was consistent with the low voter turnout in Bangkok, where only 34 per cent of eligible voters went to the polls.[15] They were interested in the royal family, but saw the members of the royal family as separate from and above politics. As with their experience of military dictatorships, for them the only king they had known was King Bhumiphol. His wife, Queen Sirikit, was much admired for her beauty. The royal family was very visible and very popular, with constant and widely read and viewed reports of their activities. These reports were necessarily always very positive, with the criminal charge of lèse-majesté, with its heavy penalties, as an active reality. The reports covered travels inside and outside Thailand, participation in religious and secular ceremonies, and active involvement in welfare, charities and rural development projects. When I started regular visits to the factory, people were interested that I was from Australia because, apart from knowing that that was the home of kangaroos, they also knew that Australia was where Crown Prince Maha Vajiralongkorn had been studying and doing military training (at the Royal Military College Duntroon). Exchanging gossip around the communal table on the women's dormitory verandah, I was let into the public secret about the eldest daughter of the King and Queen, former Princess Ubol Ratana Rajakanya, and how she had given up her royal privileges for love. She had married an American whom she had met while studying in the United States and had gone to live there. She was no longer included in official reports about the royal family but the women remembered her with a touch of envy and romantic regret.[16]

The daily routine of work and leisure activities enhanced this dislocation of politics from everyday life. So too did the annual cycle of festivals and commemorative events, cultural and religious, actively incorporated by the company into factory life. These effected a perception of continuity between

---

15    Morell and Chai-anan (1981: 114).

16    In 1998, the Princess and her husband were divorced. In 2001, she returned to Thailand with her children and began to act in a semi-official capacity. In 2004, her son was drowned in the 26 December tsunami.

the factory environment and that of Thai customary practices. At the same time, their mode of celebration also signified yet another transformation of traditional practices wrought by urbanisation and industrialisation.

# The factory and continuities with the past

Loy Krathong, the Festival of Lights and Water, is one of the country's most cherished, and most beautiful, festivals. The *krathong* is a small float, traditionally made of banana leaves, although now any material is used. It contains a candle, and often money as well. Its symbolism has differing interpretations. Nopawan explained that it is a gesture offered to the waters—*klongs*, streams and rivers—asking forgiveness for all the acts of pollution with which each person inevitably fouls them during the year. At the same time, the *krathong* carries all the sins of the individual out to sea, where they are lost, so that the person is left cleansed. She was happy with the grand celebrations at the factory but commented on the loss of meaning when a swimming pool became the medium of offerings. The moment of collective ritual purification was emptied of the very content of tradition that it sought to embody. Sacrament became show.

But it was a good show, and everyone had a good time. The Dormitory and Culture Committees had hired a band and the company provided plenty of food and drink, including beer and Mekhong whisky. Each section had spent weeks preparing its own *krathong* and these were judged by the *phuu yaj*, with a prize for the best. There were around 30 of them, from a peacock with a spray of candles for its tail to a tiered platform with a copy of the Emerald Buddha enthroned. A month after the 6 October coup, Dirake's section braved an oblique political reference, with a model of the Democracy Monument. Its lights were very dim. When the array of *krathong* was floated, the Democracy Monument tilted and was in danger of catching alight; Wongkot and his mates joked about democracy going up in flames.

With the midnight curfew still in place a month after the coup, the band was not able to keep the party going until the usual small hours and my family and I had to leave in plenty of time to get home before midnight, but there was time for a beauty contest, with the prize decided for the best traditional Thai dress. Khomkaay had kept Nopawan very busy in the preceding weeks helping to make hers. Tradition was the note of the evening. Most of the other women wore simpler Thai dress and the wives of the Japanese staff came in kimono. Once the judging for the section *krathong* was over, other employees floated their own.

Songkran, the Thai New Year or Water Festival in April, was a less elaborate but nonetheless festive affair. The home of the most spectacular Songkran celebrations is Chiang Mai, Khun Phadungcit's family home. She organised a group of the women to prepare a *Khan Toke* feast, a traditional northern Thai meal served with sticky rice and accompanied with a deceptively potent rice wine. We sipped this tentatively, with much false bravado and giggling from the women. Enough food had been prepared to feed the hundreds of staff. Again, the setting was the swimming pool; again, there was a hired band and a beauty contest, with girls from different sections representing various styles of traditional dress.

Other annual events celebrated the monarchy. The Culture Committee looked after the design and preparation of the wreath for King Chulalongkorn Day. This contained a model of the mounted figure of Chulalongkorn, done in coins and outlined in flowers. Less than three weeks after the coup, as soon in the early morning as the curfew allowed, Somthuwin went with the rest of the Culture Committee to place the wreath by the King's statue in the square outside the Throne Hall and the old parliament, not far from the Democracy Monument. Here it joined massed wreaths from other institutions.

After the coup, the factory carried on. On 8 October, two days after the coup, there was a holiday for the end of Buddhist Lent (*ook phansaa*). Two days after that, the factory formally participated in the *Kathin* ceremony at the neighbouring monastery: the presentation of new robes and gifts to the monks. A number of the workers joined in the festivities with other people from the surrounding district, and Mr Suzuka and Khun Adunsak presented a gift of 10 000 baht on behalf of the company and its staff. This was to go towards the building of a new pavilion (*saalaa*) and, since Mr Suzuka performed the act in his official capacity, merit was seen to accrue to all. On 5 December, two months after the coup, the Culture Committee monitored the lights and other ornaments used to decorate the main gates for the King's birthday. Under Prime Minister Thanin and the NARC, the new government took advantage of the birthday to promote further their nationalist agenda of a beautiful Thailand. Their call was to celebrate the birthday by cleaning up the country. Mr Suzuka applied this to a clean-up day for the factory.

Religious rituals were woven into the secular world of work itself. Monks came to bless the dormitories at New Year. Morning almsgiving ceremonies (*kaan liang phra*) were held to mark a change in Khun Supachai's section from three teams of shiftworkers to four, to celebrate the factory's tenth birthday in January, and to launch the new company credit union. The company made time available to the men employees to enter the monkhood (*buat pen phra maj*) for a period of up to three months. Niroot and Dirake were part of the group of around half the men who thought they might do so. Thongkam was among the more than one-third who had already done so. Because he had worked at the factory for more than three years, he received 45 days' pay for his three months in the monastery.

The value afforded to this religious practice for men was in contrast with the company's maternity leave provisions. These consisted of one month's leave on full pay and the possibility of a second month's leave without pay. Further leave was at the discretion of the personnel section.

Focus in the factory, then, was obviously primarily on work and production. But it was also on reproducing as far as possible the social, cultural and religious habitus that anchored the life of the factory into a local community and into the broader communities from which its employees were drawn. The mundane routines of work and leisure, with study for some, and interspersed with sponsored regular special events both secular and religious, offer an image of a Thai branch grafted onto a Japanese stem, resulting in a peculiarly Thai hybrid of patronage by the company and employee satisfaction as both workers and clients. Parallel developments among the employees suggest that this hybrid had another branch located at a fork of what Bhabha calls domains of difference, where the intersubjective and collective experiences of cultural value are negotiated.[17] These developments also indicate that the employees were negotiating their own place at this moment of historical rupture.

# The factory and new directions: Development of the trade union

The employees responded in their own way to the social conditions in which they found themselves. They did not reject the traditional hierarchies of respect and reciprocity that they brought to the factory and that continued to link them with their own families and communities. But their move into an urban industrial environment altered the basis of those relationships and gave them a modest place in the secular world, which Said defines as the world of history as made by human beings.[18] In the secular world, hierarchies are made, not preordained, and can be changed. Politics therefore shifts from the wings and plays a central, if not an all encompassing, role. The establishment of a trade union by the Bang Khen employees was a small but radical act that gave them a bit part in those larger events, which, whatever else the democratic experiment did or did not achieve, fractured irrevocably what Thongchai refers to as the master narrative of Thai history.[19]

In February 1975, the Government announced the new *Labour Relations Act*, to be effective the following month. The law recognised the right of workers to

---

17   Bhabha (1994: 2).
18   Said (2003: xxii).
19   Thongchai (2000: 3–5).

organise and bargain collectively. Union membership was to be either plant or industry based, meaning that any factory workforce could set up its own union. The law also provided for amalgamation and federation and the organisation of a national trade union congress. Unions had to be registered with the Director General of the Labour Department. The objectives of the unions were to be twofold: to maintain or advance the interests of members and to promote the peaceful settlement of industrial disputes. Management was required to recognise the representativeness of a union that had more than 20 per cent of employees as its members. Strikes were made legal, as long as the established procedures had been exhausted.[20] The provisions of the new law did not change immediately the prevailing practices in industry but it provided legal avenues to address the concerns of workers. As a result, not only did the number of work stoppages drop by almost 30 per cent after the new law was in place;[21] very few of those strikes that did take place occurred in registered unions in 1975–76 and none in early 1977.[22]

Niroot talked about the setting up of the trade union at Bang Khen. A group of 15 men—five more than required under the Act—got together in the later months of 1975 to undertake the preliminary steps necessary under the new law. This involved approaching the Labour Department to apply for a certificate of registration and to undertake some basic training. Mongkolchai, Wongkot and Chingchai were the principal organisers. Importantly, they did this without seeking the approval of the factory management and, indeed, without their knowledge. By January 1976, they had met the legal requirements. On 28 January, the Labour Department registered the union. Only then did the organisers inform the management. They did this in order to set in place the union elections, which could not be held until three months after registration.

The process of organising a trade union redefined the relationships between the employees and the management. No longer was management solely the *phuu yay* nor was the interaction between the two groups primarily that of patron and client. These relations remained active and continued to call into operation the moral bonds of reciprocal obligation. But the fact of the trade union unsettled the comfortable legitimacy of *bun khun*, of the expectation by both employers and employees of employer benevolence as the underlying principle of their interaction. The establishment of the union in the factory community brought into play what Habermas identifies as one of the key criteria of modernity— that 'modernity can and will no longer borrow the criteria by which it takes its orientation from the models supplied by another epoch; *it has to create*

---

20   Supachai (1976: 18 ff.).
21   ibid., p. 17.
22   Mabry (1977: 942).

*its normativity out of itself*.[23] This, as Miller recognises, is an ambivalent achievement, requiring humanity 'to forge for itself the criteria by which it will live'.[24] Reliance on custom is inadequate.

At the same time, modernity's 'crushing burden' of moral creativity is not usually how people experience their everyday lives. Certainly this was not the case for the Bang Khen employees. They retained a rich connection with the sources of customary morality, which continued to shape their attitudes and their actions. Nevertheless, they were willing to explore an alternative framework, in which the union rationalised moral obligation into legal obligation. Nopawan did not find the two frameworks to be in opposition and found it generally easy to operate with both. She, along with half the employees, joined the union as soon as it was available to do so. Having done so, she paid her monthly fees of 5 baht but did not attend meetings or engage in any other union activities. In practice, she combined the emerging language of rights with the old discourse of *bun khun* when discussing what she saw as appropriate standards for the employees. The men had had new dormitory quarters for some time, but the women had moved to a new building only a few months earlier. The women's old dormitory had been adjacent to the work areas; this was bad in a number of ways, not least because proximity to the machines meant that washing always got dirty again. But it was also 'wrong' for the dormitory to be in the same area as the workplace and was against the labour law. It was necessary for the company to be 'fair'; at the same time it was also their duty to 'look after' their workers. In return, the employees owed honesty (*seusat*), not loyalty (*congrak phakdii*), to the company. Loyalty was reserved for the King, the Lord of the Land (*phra mahaa kasat*).

Khun Phadungcit, a former teacher, was not altogether approving of the union, but was also a member. She saw the union as the recourse for any employee who did not get fair treatment from the company, thus acknowledging the possibility of this. She also saw it as involving the Labour Department directly with the factory to monitor that things were fair. At that moment, she did not need any help from the union, but some staff did and had been assisted. She too would ask for union help if she was treated badly by the company, for example, if she were to lose her job for no fault of her own and was not paid her six months' severance pay.

Niroot, who was on the union committee, also employed the language of fairness: if there was a problem between an employee and the management, it was the responsibility of the union to ensure that its members received fair treatment. But the union's role was broader than this: as well as taking good care of its members, its duty was to educate them about their rights.

---

23   Habermas (2002: 7).
24   Miller (1995: 62).

The establishment of the union hinted at the fault lines in the fusion of rights and *bun khun*. It forced management to move from its position as the gracious dispenser of benefits to one of entering into dialogue with the union. The company's initial response was reluctant and designed to lessen the impact of the union on the other employees. Within days of being notified by the union committee of the union's registration, management announced the establishment of an Employees Committee. The *Labour Relations Act* provided for such a committee to operate until more than half the employees were members of the union. Until it reached that level of membership, the union was not legally regarded as representing the workers and had very few rights, beyond the right to actually exist. The company presented the Employees Committee as an interim organisation, to give employees practice in negotiating while the union was developing experience. Management also argued that, while for the union no-one above the level of assistant section chief was eligible to be a member, the Employees Committee was open to all personnel, of whatever rank. All staff were automatically members of the Committee, without the requirement for any fees. In addition, the law did not set any interval between the announcement of an Employees' Committee and its elections. While the union elections could not be held until April, elections for the Committee were held in February. The administration supported the elections with full publicity and about two-thirds of the total number of employees voted. Afterwards, Mr Suzuka personally donated 1000 baht towards the opening of the Committee's office. The Committee used this for an almsgiving ceremony for the monks and for a modest party.

By the time of the union elections, the Employees Committee was firmly established. Fewer employees voted in the union elections but there was still a turnout of almost 50 per cent. Thereafter the two executives worked in conjunction. Boongsongse was a member of both. Niroot made an unsuccessful attempt to become a Committee member, wanting to know for himself how the Employees Committee worked. He also wanted all the staff to understand the union's purposes and how they worked, that if the union was strong, it would 'stand forever'. He also commented that the factory did not accept the union and gave it a difficult time. The view around the verandah table in the women's dormitory, put forward without rancour, was that the Employees Committee was on the side of the management. The only dissenting voices from this were from Khun Phadungcit and the members of the Committee itself.

Even though it remained nervous about the union, however, the company acknowledged both organisations. It made a room in the men's dormitory available as a union office though there was no ceremony attached to its opening. Charat, one of the section heads and a *phuu yaj*, explained the management's concerns: 'At the beginning, the union committee was rebellious, like teenagers. The first union president worked in our section and I had troubles with the union. The members were all very young and new, and wanted to exercise their rights too much'. In order to deal with the problem, Charat invited the president to come and talk things over with him. Since then, things had settled down, with the union establishing a schedule of two meetings a month. Nevertheless, the company kept a careful eye on the union and took an active role in managing its impact. For the union's second monthly meeting, its executive and the Employees Committee met collectively with the administration, including Khun Iid's brother, Khun Adunsak. Khun Iid personally attended the meetings, which were cancelled if he was not available. These meetings gave rise to a number of changes in the first year of the union's operation. The employees saw the union as acting for them, despite the presence also of the Employees Committee. The first change was an increase in the monthly food allowance, from 160 to 250 baht. The second was a change from the use of food coupons to cash, allowing employees a choice of where to eat. The third was the establishment of a credit union. The company donated 200 000 baht to set it up. It started with more than half the employees as members and provided borrowing facilities with an interest rate of 10 per cent.

An important element in the company's strategy to manage the union was the Workers Agreement. The *Labour Relations Act* provided for collective bargaining, with the onus on management to enter into negotiation with the union within three days of receiving written demands.[25] At the factory, the company pre-empted this process; as soon as the Employees Committee was set up, management drafted an agreement, with the Committee as the official staff representative. In April, the draft was presented to the newly established union and signed three days later. The employees, including the union, were satisfied that it was a good agreement, incorporating as it did a further management initiative for significantly improved health benefits for the employees.

Over the following months, the union made progress in gaining acceptance as part of the overall functioning of the factory. They were also exploring the process of affiliation with one of the national labour federations. They had been approached by the Samut Sakon Textile Workers Union to join the Labour Coordination Centre of Thailand (LCCT), but were unsure about whether to align themselves with so radical an organisation. While they were still considering this option, they also requested information from the National Labour Council about possible membership and attended a couple of their meetings. Then, in September, the executive surprised everyone by resigning. They explained the reason as concern about the effective functioning of the executive, as well as their relationship with the rank-and-file members. Niroot complained that only three of them—he, Mongkolchai and Chingchai—ever turned up for meetings. They wanted to give the employees the opportunity to choose again, after having

25  Supachai (1976: 19).

had some experience as trade union members. An election committee of five was set up, and a new election scheduled. The date for this event was to have been 14 October, to coincide with the anniversary of the 1973 uprising. The coup intervened on 6 October, forcing the deferral of the election and denuding it of its democratic symbolism.

## Death and the medium

Death also intruded into these mundane arrangements. On 10 October, the police informed management of a motorbike accident that had happened the previous Sunday, on the day of *thoot phaa paa* for Vibun's father's school. The dead man was Chuusak, one of the factory workers. He had been knocked off his motorbike by a car. Identification of the body had been slow, as Chuusak was carrying no personal papers. He was eighteen and had been at the factory for only a year. His older brother had been an employee for three years. Their mother was dead and their father lived up-country. The company offered to take responsibility for the funeral arrangements and for the cremation. In assuming this responsibility, the company was not so much acting in the place of Chuusak's family as fulfilling the role of the householder of high rank who customarily should give generously to his subordinates and dependants. The employees contributed 5 baht each, in their turn meeting the expectation that the donation by individuals is small when the funeral ceremonies (*ngaan*) are sponsored by their superiors.[26]

Chuusak's funeral ceremonies made clear that the rites surrounding death and cremation are, on the whole, simpler and more standardised in modern Bangkok than in rural areas. It also demonstrated the ongoing power of traditional rituals. Mortuary rituals are amongst the most elaborate of Buddhist ceremonies.[27] In rural areas, there is a marked difference between the treatment accorded to the corpse of a person who has died of natural causes in the fullness of time and that meted out to the victim of an accident or other violent or sudden death. Although customs are changing, even in rural areas, a common practice still is for the corpse of a person who has died of natural causes to be brought home and kept there from the time of death until cremation. The family quickly brings others to join in a funeral wake, so that the dead person will not be lonely.[28]

In contrast, the victim of sudden or violent death is traditionally buried with great haste, and often with little ceremony, the religious rites being performed only

---

26  Bunnag (1973: 164).
27  Klima (2002); Tambiah (1968: 88).
28  Klima (2002: 247).

after burial (not necessarily cremation) has taken place.[29] The body, moreover, is not kept at home, even for the short time before burial, since it is believed that the spirit of the dead person may become a malevolent ghost (*phii*) and haunt or harm the living. According to Tambiah, this fear arises from the belief that such spirits hover on earth because of an attachment to worldly interests, from which they have been untimely snatched. This also partly explains the element of haste; although another aspect to this is that, by releasing the spirit of the deceased without delay, it may be reborn as quickly as possible, thus allowing it the opportunity to compensate for the time so rudely denied it in this life.

Some of the abiding grief attached to the massacre of the Thammasat demonstrators was the non-performance of funeral rites for the murdered. In October 1974, a year after the 1973 uprising, the King and Queen had presided in a state ceremony over the cremations of the 'October 14 martyrs' and their families were publicly honoured. In 1976, of the 43 deaths officially recorded, and taking no count of the many more unrecorded, only half a dozen corpses were claimed by their families for cremations.[30] Thongchai, now an academic staff member at the Center for South-East Asian Studies at the University of Wisconsin–Madison, was himself one of the student leaders of that day and was imprisoned for two years afterwards. He points out that the rest of those murdered on 6 October had never received any kind of cremation and still nobody knows what happened to their remains.

On the anniversary morning of 6 October 1996, as 'the most memorable activity' of the first ever series of commemorations for the 1976 event, a symbolic cremation was held at the soccer field where the massacre had taken place. It was performed by Buddhist monks and spiritual leaders of other religions. 'Twenty years later, in my opinion, former radicals of the 1970s had accomplished one of the most important missions in their lives: to publicly cremate and say farewell to friends who had forfeited their lives in the event that shaped thousands of lives of their whole generation forever.'[31] Twenty years later, those former radicals reclaimed the past, engaging in a reflective dialogue between what had been local events and what had become history.[32]

In the death of Chuusak, coinciding as it did with the massacre and its aftermath, the Company ensured that proper mortuary rites were carried out. A fortnight after the death, they organised for the corpse to be brought to the neighbouring monastery, which acted in this instance, as in many others, as the local temple for the factory. Here the monks prepared the body and set up an altar in the *saalaa* where the ceremonies prior to the burning (*phaw*) were to be held. Three

---

29  Kaufman (1960: 157); Kingshill (1960: 164–5); Tambiah (1968: 98).
30  Thongchai (2002: 266, 275).
31  ibid., pp. 275–6.
32  I am indebted to Professor Howard Morphy for this comment.

nights of chanting followed, each night with its own host, a role that was a rich source of merit: the factory administration on the first night, the trade union and Employees Committee on the second, and Chuusak's work section on the third. The chanting preceded a wake which, on the second night, produced 'a community of gamblers [and drinkers] for the sake of the dead'.[33] It was not the elaborate funeral casino of Klima's description, and participants had to conform to the curfew, but it did constitute a similar illicit act. Gambling was then, and remained, illegal, though the police tended to turn a blind eye for funerals, even one so soon after the imposition of martial law.

On the morning of the burning, there was an almsgiving ceremony of the family and close friends. In the afternoon, I went with Khun Phadungcit and a group of other women to the crematorium. We were among several hundred employees and a number of the *phuu yaj*, including Khun Adunsak, Khun Iid's brother. Khun Iid did not attend, though this was not unusual for a cremation where the patron who has given generously to the ceremonies is not required to attend in person.[34] The chanting of the monks combined with the soberly dressed mourners to produce an emotional solemnity around the open oven. Because Chuusak's corpse was already starting to decompose, it was not on display for these urban participants. His brother gave a short eulogy, lamenting the sudden and early death, and distributed to each of us a small memento from the family, a symbolic but eminently practical Vicks inhaler, with thanks for our attendance. Once the fire was lit, and the monks and family had filed past the oven's open door, we each cast in our own gifts to the dead: an incense stick, a candle and a flower. Some of the mourners added coins as an additional offering of merit for the dead boy. Khun Phadungcit also explained that attending the burning was an opportunity to settle any outstanding personal accounts, both offering forgiveness to and seeking forgiveness of the dead.

The unsettling potency of death extended beyond the funeral ceremonies. On the way back from the cremation, Khun Phadungcit invited me to go with her and a small group of the other mourners to access the power of a local spirit medium. We entered a world eerily distinct from the formal Buddhist rituals to which I had become accustomed at the factory. The opaque darkness that absorbed us as we walked from the lighted compound of the monastery into the semi-rural surroundings of the medium's house signalled more than a movement in space. Together with the spirit possession of the medium herself, it signified a repossession of urban modernity by village atavism. The sense of descent into a different world was reinforced by the disembodied sounds of night creatures as we crossed the provisional and not very reassuring planks sunk into the swampy approach to the house.

---

33 Klima (2002: 251).
34 Bunnag (1973: 164).

In contrast, the room where the medium sat enthroned was comfortingly familiar. There was an altar crowded with flowers and ornaments and with a Buddha image presiding. The smoke from burning incense sticks was thick and stifling. The electric candles threw shadows across the stuffy room where already around a dozen visitors sat at the medium's feet. We had missed the beginning of the session but were permitted to interrupt to place money in the box on the altar before retiring to sit in an empty floor space. The questions, including ours, were banal: if my birth date and time was this, what did my future hold? Would I be happy? Would I have good luck? Would my son/daughter succeed? The medium had answers, with occasional supplementary clarifying questions, to all. She was not disconcerted to find a foreigner in her audience and replied to the questions that I was urged by Khun Phadungcit to pose. As I did not know the time of my birth, and had to make it up, I was not able to put much faith in her answers, but that could be attributed as much to my false information as to her insights. My friends were satisfied that she had predicted more children, wealth, and a happy future for me. As we once more navigated our way across the planks, we heard, but did not feel, a loud rush of wind. Khun Phadungcit identified it as the spirit leaving its medium.

In her study of mediums in northern Thailand, Morris argues that spirit possession is less a return to the past than 'part of a heroically translational effort to mobilize the manifold possibilities of being in the place of origins', where 'place' connotes both location and relationship.[35] She also suggests that the varying manifestations of mediumship are an outcome of, as well as a response to, modernity. With no more than one short exposure to a Bangkok medium, I cannot confirm her analysis in relation to the medium herself. But it does throw light on the way in which the women employees approached the medium. Drawn mostly from rural backgrounds, they paid occasional visits to her in moments of uncertainty. The visit on the night of Chuusak's cremation expressed the unarticulated anomalies produced by their position at a point of juncture between a remembered past and an undefined future. It helped to close the uncertain space that his death had opened up between the domains of the supernatural and the mundane, literally embodying in the person of the medium the inseparable intertwining of the one with the other.

The funeral rites for Chuusak also produced repercussions in the wholly secular domain, revealing the tensions between the reciprocal and the contractual.

35   Morris (2000: 15–16).

# A clash of old and new

It was perhaps the permissive environment of the second night's wake coupled with copious tumblers of whisky that enticed Chingchai, the union secretary, to go beyond the trade union role of host for the evening and to stray into unwise comments about Chuusak's death. He was discussing with his friends the fact that the driver of the car that killed Chuusak was a doctor—*dokter*, an academic, not medical, title—and a friend of one of the senior staff members who worked in the head office. According to Chingchai, rumour had it that the 'doctor' had made use of his company contact, and that there would be no prosecution. He went on to accuse the company of being on the side of the doctor, and not on the side of the workers. This ill-fated statement, made only in conversation with friends, was overheard by Khun Adunsak, who subsequently reported it to Khun Iid. Not surprisingly, Khun Iid was furious. Next morning, he called a meeting of the union, the Employees Committee and the section chiefs. With such short notice, and no indication of the purpose of the meeting, not everyone came. It was not reported whether Chingchai was present. Kovit, the president of the Employees Committee, was not present. At the meeting, Khun Iid was reported to have done all the talking—no-one else 'dared' (*klaa*) to speak. At the end, without consultation with Mr Suzuka, he took on himself the total decision and responsibility and gave Chingchai the sack on the spot.

Given that Chingchai's comments were not related to any contractual obligation, Khun Iid's anger suggests that his remarks offended the practice of *bun khun* and breached the relationship of client to patron. It also suggests that, in the eyes of Khun Iid at least, this was the basis of relations operating in the factory. His power rested in his position as majority owner and vice-president of the company, but his authority arose from his active role as patron for the employees. An accusation that he had betrayed those obligations was, in his view, unforgivable. This was not the view taken by the Committee of Labour Relations, to whom Chingchai and the remaining union executive appealed. After interviewing all the parties to the dispute and considering the case for several months, the Committee found that Chingchai had not breached any regulation. The company was ordered to pay him three months' severance pay, though not to reinstate him.

Death, then, disrupted the practical harmony that generally prevailed in the factory between the moral discourse of reciprocity and the emerging moral discourse of rights. In a sense, Chingchai's unwitting challenge forced the two into a confrontation in which the discourse of reciprocity continued to prevail. He himself became a direct casualty of the clash. But its ripples affected others as well. Vibun had been a close friend of Chingchai. He was also on the Employees

Committee and Chingchai and others blamed him for Chingchai's dismissal. This got to a point over the following weeks where Vibun avoided leaving the factory by himself at night for fear of being attacked.

Niroot was one of the union executive who supported Chingchai in his appeal to the Committee of Labour Relations. Even Khun Phadungcit thought that the company had been too severe in their treatment of Chingchai, though she qualified this view on the basis that she hadn't been there and therefore didn't know. Nopawan put the incident in its broader context of the reintroduction of martial law. In the hotbed of rumours that followed the coup, she had overheard friends of Chingchai saying that, before his sacking, Chingchai as secretary of the union had received a letter from the NARC, calling him to come and report on the union.

The situation was certainly complicated by its happening so soon after the coup and the imposition of martial law.

## In the shadow of the coup

Despite the employees' caution in getting directly involved in the politics of the three-year democratic period, there were repercussions of the coup in the factory. One was the curfew, when no-one was allowed in the streets between midnight and 6 am without official permission. There were others. A few days after the coup, a box was placed in each of the dormitories labelled 'Receptacle for Communist literature'. The box in the women's dormitory remained empty. The one in the men's dormitory scored a large pile of copies of *Prachachat*, one of the two liberal newspapers that were suppressed after the coup and whose editors were arrested. These 'subversive' materials were brought down in the middle of the night by those who felt they could be compromised by keeping them. The materials were subsequently taken away by the management and burnt. Relatives of the employees were no longer permitted to come freely to the dormitories but had to report to the office first. Nopawan pointed out that people did not like this but had to obey (*cheua fang, tham taan*). Two weeks before the coup, I had received permission from management to employ a translator, a Thammasat student, to assist me in my research. This permission was withdrawn after the coup.

The day after the coup, with a caretaker committee in charge of the union after the resignation of the executive, Wongkot, the original president, and Chingchai, the secretary, went to the Labour Department to clarify the situation concerning the proposed election. At that stage, there were 20 candidates for

15 positions. They were told that the election would have to be postponed. As well, no further union meetings could for the present be held although routine business could be attended to.

The new government did not repeal the *Labour Relations Act*, although it did suspend the right to strike and placed a temporary ban on political meetings of more than five people. As a result of the ban on meetings, even a scheduled meeting of the Family Planning Organisation of Thailand for factory staff was cancelled. Nevertheless, under these conditions, and because of the fact that it was registered, the trade union could legally continue. Five weeks after Wongkot and Chingchai's visit to the Labour Department, with permission from the Labour Department and the local police, the union elections were held. Representatives from other unions were invited to come as observers. A member of the Railway Union was there as the official representative of the Committee of Labour Relations, representatives came from two other textile unions, and two more. Others had been invited, but were unable to come.

Of the original 20 candidates, 17 had renominated; 307 of the 531 union members voted. This was even higher than the number who had voted under the more auspicious conditions of the first election. Of the new executive, one was also on the Employees Committee. After the coup, however, this link became of no significance as the Employees Committee, while remaining notionally active, effectively collapsed. None of the employees expressed any upset at its demise.

In contrast, the union resumed their regular meetings as soon as the government ban on meetings was lifted. This was a cause of some anxiety to Khun Thongying, who was not informed that members of the executive were meeting the Government's requirement of monthly reporting to the Labour Department and therefore worried that they were not doing so. As a result, he advised me not to attend union meetings in case there was a police raid, as I would have to accept the consequences if I were present. Niroot assured me that he, Mongolchai and Boongsongse took it in turns to report to the department, so I was not constrained to follow Khun Thongying's advice.

At the same time, the company accepted the continuing legitimacy of the union. In October it had accepted an application for leave from Mongolchai to attend a seminar in Manila of the World Council of Labour, a third-world organisation, and the Brotherhood of Asian Trade Unions (BATU). In December, Niroot requested permission, on behalf of the union, to organise training in labour issues for the employees. The company gave approval and five courses were held over the next few months. One was a three-week course on the labour law and labour relations, held at the factory and attended each evening by about 30 employees. Another, running over a fortnight, was on trade unions. Other Labour Department courses included a week's course on safety, and a fortnight on credit unions for which departmental representatives were invited by the union. The company also funded two factory representatives to go away for a weekend to a course on family planning, organised annually by the Labour Department under the auspices of the International Labour Organisation. When preparations were under way for the factory's tenth birthday celebrations in January, Khun Iid made the suggestion that the union invite the teachers from the seminars and this was done.

Jackson argues that Thailand is a society 'whose status as modern is at best ambiguous' and proposes a fundamental difference between Thai and Western forms of power and knowledge. On that basis, he suggests that the diverse crises of Thai modernity are productive not of a cultural convergence with the West but of novel forms of cultural difference and differences of understanding and meaning.[36] The factory was itself a hybrid, translating the experience of Western forms of industrialisation through Japanese practices. In the factory's first decade, it was this conjunction of Japanese and Western forms with Thai cultural understandings and practices that developed new ways for the employees to produce their own meanings and make their own moral choices in the novelty of their situation as urban industrial workers. They had available to them the moral discourses of *bun khun*, merit, and rights and drew on all of them. They also had available the practical conditions provided by the factory that satisfied many of their mundane material and social desires for a good life. On a day-to-day basis, they merged the diverse discourses into a practical routine of work and leisure activities. Their actions placed them in an agnostic but not rejecting position in relation to the Buddhist doctrine of *tham* or *dharma*, which teaches that social position is the consequence of merit. This agnosticism extended even to any recognition that the relationship of social position to merit is not rigidly predetermined, since merit itself is a matter of choice rather than an accident of birth.[37] In their practical view, the notion of merit from a past life had been transformed into luck in this one. Niroot thought that Khun Iid's children were lucky because their father was rich and that one could be rich by working very hard and spending one's money in the right way. In a similar way, employees saw their factory job as indicative of the possibility of choices that were not available in previous generations; their choice to work in the factory constituted them as agents in achieving a better life.

The move to establish an autonomous trade union grew out of an emerging recognition that achieving a better life was a collective as well as an individual project, that a good life was actively linked to the achievement of a good society. In this way, the employees forged their own links to the broader movement for change being undertaken after October 1973. Both movements demonstrated a

---

36   Jackson (2004: 351, 357).
37   Wilson (1959: 63).

fundamental shift arising out of modernising processes, from acquiescence in the status quo to varying but active participation in changing it. Both the activists more broadly and the factory employees in their own situation understood in different ways that social change was not something just happening to them, but that they themselves could be actors in shaping the process. This in itself was a transformation wrought by modernity. The union was not in its inception a necessary opposition to the patron–client relationships operating in the factory, but a novel move to redefine those traditional forms to suit a modern environment. It reflected the conditions produced after October 1973. The union represented a new interpretation and practice by the employees of the intersection of power, culture and meaning.[38] Despite incidents like Chingchai's sacking, when these new understandings clashed with the interpretation and practices arising from the past, the union did not come to grief in the same way that the radical movement did; even Chingchai had recourse to an appeals tribunal that required legal accountability by the company. Nor was the union dissolved as a result of the coup. It continued operating after the coup with ongoing support from its workforce. In this, too, it maintained links with the broader union movement in the country.

## And the aftermath

The NARC was not gentle with the labour movement. As well as banning strikes and political meetings, they organised raids on union offices and arrested a number of labour activists under martial law Order 22 as 'persons dangerous to society'. Other union leaders disappeared; some joined the students who fled to the jungle to join the communist insurgency. The National Labour Council, which it turned out was not registered with the Labour Department, was dissolved. Nevertheless, the NARC acted on advice from ISOC that the only way to neutralise labour was to affirm the labour law rather than abolish it. As a result, they invited its former president, Paisal Thavatchainant, to talks with them.[39] In the first weeks after the coup, Paisal and General Kriangsak, NARC Secretary-General, signed a three-point agreement. On 18 October, Admiral Sa-ngad, NARC Chairman, and General Kriangsak reaffirmed the NARC policy of upholding workers' rights to organise and bargain collectively, while suspending their right to strike.[40]

Kriangsak proved to be a critical player in the post-coup period. Despite the rhetoric of a return to stability, and the rigid enforcement of reactionary policies under Prime Minister Thanin, military factionalism remained an internally

38    Jackson (2004: 342).
39    Nations (1976: 67–8).
40    Morell and Chai-anan (1981: 201).

destabilising element. In October 1977, after a year of 'the Dark Ages of modern Thai politics', Sa-ngad and Kriangsak led a further internal coup. Kriangsak, installed as the new Prime Minister, expressed a program of moderation and a policy of reconciliation. He promised to hold new elections within a year; opened channels of communication with labour unions; invited such men as former New Force party leader Dr Krasae Chanawongse to advise him; ended Bangkok's curfew; and allowed more open expression of views in the press and on university campuses (though by no means endorsing freedom of speech).[41]

In 1978, he instigated the promulgation of a new constitution and over the next year gave an amnesty to those who had gone into the jungle after 6 October.[42] In February 1980, Kriangsak unwillingly but voluntarily resigned as Prime Minister and was replaced by General Prem Tinsulanonda, whose leadership provided the conditions for a period of political stability and economic growth. Despite two further attempted coups, Prem remained in power until 1988, through two elections and with the support of a range of civilian groups including that of former Prime Minister Kukrit Pramoj. He is generally credited as the person mainly responsible for defusing, if not resolving, the political tensions of the 1970s.

The period of General Prem's prime ministership is one of those defined by Chai-anan Samudavanija as a semi-democratic one, favouring a strong executive over the legislative branch.[43] The 1978 Constitution remained effective and Prem represented a moderately liberal regime, with student, labour and farmer groups allowed to organise on a restricted basis.[44] Early in his prime ministership, in 1980, his government formalised the amnesty for those who had joined the communists. Keyes points out that 'this amnesty became the foundation for a resurgence of democratic elements in Thai society'.[45]

But the promise of conditions that would allow a return to fully democratic government proved to be premature. On 23 February 1991,[46] General Suchinda Kraprayoon led a further military coup. When he installed himself as Prime Minister in April 1992, he provoked a level of popular protest that had not been repeated since the return of Thanom in 1976. The crisis that resulted led to a similar outcome: a massacre of unarmed demonstrators in what has become known as Black May. The area around the Democracy Monument was the scene of demonstrations, as it had been in 1973 and 1976. The site of the massacre was different: not Thammasat University but the Royal Hotel. The perpetrators were

---

41    ibid., p. 278.
42    ibid., pp. 279, 303.
43    Chai-anan (1992: 1).
44    Case (1995: 23).
45    Keyes (2006: 15).
46    A date that resonates not only in Thailand, but also, as we shall see, in Spain.

unarguably military troops supported by the Border Patrol Police. At 46 dead, the official number of those killed was demonstrably lower than the estimates of medical practitioners and others who helped the injured and dying and observed the dead. The reaction of the King recalled 1973 rather than 1976: in a poorly produced but unforgettable television appearance, the King publicly chastised both Suchinda and his highest-profile political opponent, General Chamlong Srimuang, and subsequently appointed a civilian prime minister.

The victims of the 1992 massacre have joined those of 1973 as publicly honoured heroes of democracy. Those of 1976 have remained anomalous in the national memory, and even in the memory of its protagonists. Thongchai Winichakul casts judgement on himself as well as on the events: 'Unlike the martyrdom at Tienanmin Square in China, or the 1988 event in Burma, which will be remembered because the ideals of those struggles remained unfulfilled, Thai radicalism has already proved to be a failure'.[47] He applies another writer's description of the 1965 bloodshed in Indonesia: 'the monument unbuilt, the story unspoken, is no more than an invisible inscription along history's silent edge, marking an official limit placed upon the past by the present'.[48] Others have argued that 6 October continues to be the source of a persistent crisis of authority of which Black May was the next symptom,[49] and that continues, with its most recent eruption in the 2006 coup and subsequent social and political upheavals.

However interpreted, 6 October 1976 cannot be seen in isolation from its counterparts of 1973 and 1992, and now the period leading up to and culminating in the violence of 2010, although it continues to stand apart, both in its shocking brutality and in the consequent shattering of faith, however misplaced that may have been, in a gentle and serene Thai identity. Shame led to silence and to a lingering reluctance to confront the meaning of 6 October.

Black May can itself be seen as an inevitable result of the national failure to address the fact of 1976 and to design institutions adequate for a modern industrial democracy. All three events represent an ongoing process of cultural politics, a 'struggle against ways of appealing to culture and history' that is used to legitimate relations of inequality.[50] In 1976, after their first tantalising taste of the possibilities of democracy, the demonstrators expressed resistance to a reappropriation of historical and cultural meaning by the military and other reactionary groups and to an authoritarian definition of a good society. They were savagely punished for their efforts.

---

47  Thongchai (2002: 278).
48  Steedly, quoted in ibid., p. 264.
49  Tanabe and Keyes (2002: 17).
50  Rosaldo in Garcia Canclini (1995: xiii).

For the factory employees, on the other hand, the novelty of political and social change generated by the 'democratic experiment' allowed them to produce their own notion of the good. This was both their response and their contribution to a developing modernity that was not achieved but was, at their historical moment, in a process of becoming.

# Postscript

The turbulent events from 2006 to 2010 make electrifyingly clear that the processes of modernisation and democratisation in Thailand remain incomplete, and that the events of 1973, 1976 and 1992 are precursor acts in an ongoing drama on which the curtain has yet to fall.[51] They also illustrate that the idea of democracy remains both a compelling and an elusive social imaginary for many Thais.

I have not returned to Thailand since 1990, but the accounts of the political upheavals since 2006 resonate all too strongly with those of the 1970s and identify them as the next acts in the crisis of modernity. I am indebted to subsequent analyses by contemporary scholars of the region to tease out both the continuities as well as the changes. To understand these, it is necessary to give a brief overview of the context for further violence and killings in 2009 and especially in 2010.

## Background to the emergence of the yellow shirts and red shirts: Politics, 1992–2010

The protests in Black May 1992 were triggered by yet another military coup, in 1991, and the military-dominated elections in March 1992. After the crisis, elections were held in September of the same year and returned a civilian government, though the military continued to dominate the Senate,[52] and to play an active role in politics. Change rather than stability, and constant allegations of corruption, remained as characteristics of government. Neither the 1992 government nor its successor after further elections in 1995 served its full term.[53] The administration of General Chavalit Yongchaiyut, having formed government after elections in 1996 from a coalition of multiple parties was, like its predecessors replaced in 1997 by a reconfigured coalition as part of the fallout from Thailand's economic collapse.

---

51   Pasuk and Baker (2010) describe Thailand's 2007 poll specifically in terms of *khon* or mask-play, which is a traditional Thai form of dance-drama.

52   Suchit (2004).

53   Thailand, Saphaphuthan Ratsadon (1996–2008).

Perhaps surprisingly, it was under this government that the 1997 Constitution, known as the people's constitution, came into force. It was intended to bring political corruption to an end by creating the processes for a stable parliamentary democracy with a strong, elected executive.[54]

In addition, all these elections continued to show the dominance that had emerged over previous decades of what Surin has dubbed 'a two-track politics [with] Bangkok on the one hand and the rural areas on the other'.[55] He goes on to say, 'the political significance of Bangkok is that in the past it set the direction of the political wind'.[56] This was reflected in the historical importance of the Democrat Party in Bangkok, but it began to change in the elections of 2001 and 2005.

In 2001, on the institutional processes created by the 1997 Constitution, the Thai Rak Thai party led by Thaksin Shinawatra won a massive victory, with only two seats short of an absolute majority.[57] In 2005, with an unprecedented 75 per cent turnout of voters, the party won 377 of 500 seats in the House of Representatives, becoming the first party ever to form a government alone. Thaksin became the first prime minister ever to win a second term.[58] His support came overwhelmingly from rural areas in the north and north-east and from urban workers. Thaksin himself came from the north, from Chiang Mai. 'Villagers felt that for the first time they had greater influence than the urban middle class or the military in determining the shape of government.'[59]

It was not to last. Accusations of corruption; a badly handled anti-drug campaign and repressive response to a Muslim insurgency in the south; the sale of the Shinawatra family's majority shares in Shin Corporation, a leading Thai telecommunications company, to a Singapore company, without any payment of capital gains tax on the massive profits; Thaksin's 'somewhat equivocal' relationship to Buddhism and tenuous relationship with the King were all factors that undermined his moral legitimacy.[60] In 2005, Chamlong Srimuang, who had been a popular leader in the 1992 protests and had originally backed the Thaksin government, had an open break with Thaksin. In February 2006, he joined the leadership of the anti-Thaksin People's Alliance for Democracy (PAD).[61]

---

54   Reynolds (2010: 1).
55   Surin (1992).
56   ibid., p. 46.
57   Pasuk and Baker (2010: 15).
58   Thailand, Saphaphuthan Ratsadon (1996–2008).
59   Keyes (2006: 18).
60   ibid., pp. 21, 23. Reynolds (2010: 1) makes a stronger statement about Thaksin's attitude to the monarchy: 'He was the first prime minister since the 1930s to challenge the monarchy openly, which he did by verbal and symbolic means that smacked of republicanism in the eyes of many Thai people.'
61   Keyes (2006: 19).

The PAD was formally established in early 2006 after Thaksin's sale of Shin Corporation, but it had developed informally from the media broadcasts of Sondhi Limthongkul. Sondhi, like Thaksin, had powerful media interests and had initially been an ally. Disenchanted, he became the public voice of criticism of the Government and leader of the PAD, or 'yellow shirts', whose supporters 'wear yellow, the colour for Monday, the day on which the present king was born'.[62] The yellow-shirt, anti-government demonstrations in late 2005 and especially in 2006 seriously destabilised the Government. In response, Thaksin announced the dissolution of Parliament in February 2006, and Thai Rak Thai again won a decisive victory in elections in April.[63] The Constitutional, Supreme and Administrative courts nullified these results in the same month.[64]

In the hiatus after the 2006 election, Thaksin agreed to remain as Prime Minister in a caretaker role until new elections could be held, but yellow-shirt protests continued. In September 2006, while Thaksin was out of the country, the army, led by General Sonthi Boonyaratglin, staged yet another successful coup.[65]

In May 2007, the Thai Rak Thai party was dissolved by the Constitutional Tribunal for malpractice at the nullified 2006 election and all members of the party's executive board were banned from politics for five years. Thaksin remained abroad, from where he continued to be very active. In July, key figures from Thai Rak Thai took over the People Power Party, which won the next election in December 2007.[66] The yellow shirts again took to the streets in protest, their most spectacular achievements being the seizure of Government House in May 2008, a blockade of the parliament complex in October that forced the Prime Minister and several others to climb over a fence to get out,[67] and the takeover and shutting down for more than a week of Bangkok's two international airports, Suvarnabhumi and Don Muang, in November.

Thaksin supporters also mobilised. Loosely formed as the United Front for Democracy against Dictatorship (UDD), they transformed into the 'red shirts'. After sporadic confrontations with the yellow shirts in Bangkok, but also in the regions, red-shirt rallies in Bangkok in April 2009 also turned into confrontations with the military. The subsequent violence was an ominous precursor of the events a year later, when red-shirt demonstrations resulted in another day that has become described as 'black': Black Saturday, on 10 April 2010, when 25 of those demonstrating near and around the Democracy Monument were killed and more than 800 were injured. As well as red shirts, the dying and injured

---

62  Reynolds (2010: 1).
63  This was not as decisive a victory as that in 2005, as the Democrats boycotted the election.
64  Keyes (2006: 24).
65  ibid., p. 25.
66  Pasuk and Baker (2010: 12).
67  Sian Powell, Police shot as Thai protest traps MPs, *The Australian*, 8 October 2008.

included four senior officers: a major general and three colonels.[68] Among the dead was a Japanese journalist, Hiro Muramoto, who worked for Reuters news agency.

The Democracy Monument was not the only site of major protest. Red-shirt demonstrations were also taking place in other parts of Bangkok, the most newsworthy being at Ratchaprasong in the heart of the city's commercial district where the protesters maintained their camp for nearly two months. What had started as an irritation, even if a significant one, ended in May with the military moving in, more dead, hundreds more injured, and Thailand's biggest shopping mall and other buildings in flames.

Thailand's democratic crisis did not end with the routing of the red shirts. Support for Thaksin, or at least for the popular will that he represents, remains strong. The divide between Bangkok and the north and north-east has deepened. In the elections in 2001, 2005, 2006, and even in 2007 after the coup, pro-Thaksin voters in the upper north and north-east 'were not only the less well-off but all ranks of society', indicating that the historical cultural identities of these areas, only incorporated into 'the Bangkok-focused Thai state in the nineteenth century', continue to matter.[69]

The 'unfairness' of the current social order remains:[70]

> The red shirt movement draws on deeply-held feelings that the current social order is unfair. In a society that official figures show is highly unequal in terms of income, wealth, land ownership and opportunity, the red shirts have increasingly proclaimed Thai society to be unfair, unequal and unjust…This makes for a movement that is detested and feared by an essentially Bangkok-based establishment.

In his absence, Thaksin was found guilty of corruption by the courts,[71] but his 'brand of populism and of upward mobility for the neglected masses' remains potent:[72] 'The reds have increasingly transcended Thaksin, and even eclipsed the UDD organisers in their commitment to political change and for the opportunities they glimpsed during the Thaksin years in 2001–2006.'

---

68    Richard Lloyd Parry, Shadowy 'third force' in Bangkok, *The Australian*, 19 April 2010.
69    Pasuk and Baker (2010: 32).
70    Hewison (2010: 14–15).
71    *The Independent*, 21 October 2008.
72    Thitinan (2010: 13).

Some commentators suggest that the most serious consequence of his ousting is a loss of faith in electoral democracy.[73] It is too early to judge whether or not that is true, or whether the events of 2010 represent one more act in an ongoing drama, or an end game.

## Connections between the acts

Some of the connections between these and earlier events are striking, not least the ongoing failure of the country to change 'a social and political order that has long been hierarchical and repressive'[74] and, as in the 1970s, to reconcile conflicting notions of a good society as a just society.

Reynolds highlights the symbolic significance of the Democracy Monument in this unfinished saga of periodic uprisings. Built to commemorate the first eruption in 1932, not of democracy but at least of the introduction of 'some democratic norms and practices'[75] and the end of the absolute monarchy, the Democracy Monument that has been at the heart of every subsequent rebellion is 'an unfinished monument built by a military government commemorating a constitution that has been written too often to remember in celebration of a democracy that was not yet in existence, let alone secure'.[76]

Nevertheless, the fact remains that the Democracy Monument continues to represent a deep desire for democracy, not just in Bangkok but also in the provinces, a desire further strengthened by each fleeting democratic experience.

To date, however, democracy remains in flux in the face of the power and influence that continue to be exercised by the military, specifically by the Royal Thai Army, and its stubborn commitment to acting as the guardian of the three traditional pillars of Thai society: Nation, Religion, King. It has also, since 1976, taken on itself the role of guardian of what it sees as an acceptable, that is, limited, democracy. As in the first 'democratic experiment' between 1973 and 1976, and despite the innovations of the 1997 People's Constitution, the Thaksin government ignored the need to establish strong democratic institutions that could be effective in the face of military hostility. The coup of 2006 was all too easy for the military to achieve.

The monarchy, too, continues to be invoked as central to stability and to the maintenance of traditional values. The yellow shirts of the People's Alliance for Democracy aligned them visibly with the values that its supporters see the monarchy as representing. Even though the King, now in his eighties

---

73   Walker and Farrelly (2010).
74   Hewison (2010: 14).
75   Suchit (2004).
76   Reynolds (2010: 3).

and ill, has refused to take part in recent events,[77] the monarchy as symbol remains potent and it appears that the Queen remains a powerful influence. In particular, the ties between the monarchy and the military continue: General Prem Tinsulanond is the Chairman of the Privy Council, the body set up to advise the King. Reports suggest that he is in strong alliance with the Queen.[78] Thaksin, during his caretaker premiership in 2006, engaged in a 'very public contention' with General Prem.[79] General Anupong Paochinda, who took over as Commander-in-Chief of the Royal Thai Army in 2007, is also reported to be closely connected to the Queen.[80]

More directly, the military's approach to Thaksin and his supporters provides a direct link to the events leading up to the coup in 1976. According to Pasuk and Baker, and based on internal documents:[81] 'The coup leaders believed Thaksin's populist politics represented a bid to seize the state and overthrow the monarchy—analogous to the communist insurgency of thirty years earlier— and hence the generals had a right and duty to deploy public money and public resources in opposition.'

They go on to cite a leaked document that held the transcript of a meeting held inside army headquarters on 21 September 2007 for General Sonthi Boonyaratglin, who had led the 2006 coup, to deliver a farewell speech:[82]

> Sonthi was preceded on the podium by the commander of the First Army who spoke about the abolition of the monarchy in the French and Russian revolutions, alluded to the Maoists' intention to remove the monarchy in Nepal, and reminded the audience of the army's success in defeating the Thai communists twenty years earlier...Populism, he went on, was simply a way to win over the people. Ordinary people who had been duped by populism were a 'red zone', the term for communist-dominated areas during the insurgency by the Communist Party.

The adoption of red shirts by Thaksin supporters, and their concentration in the north and north-east, very visually articulated these connections and intensified the dual image of a 'red zone'. As in the earlier anti-communist strategy, this time the Internal Security Operations Command (ISOC) targeted these regions and 'in the very last days of the government, the coup-appointed

---

77   In December 2008, the King for the first time did not give his traditional birthday speech. This was at the height of yellow-shirt protests and there had been anxious anticipation for him to give guidance and reassurance as he had in earlier times of turmoil. Nor did he give the birthday speech in 2009.

78   Freelander (2010).

79   Keyes (2006: 24).

80   Freelander (2010).

81   Pasuk and Baker (2010: 4).

82   ibid., p. 5.

parliament passed an Internal Security Act which clarified the powers of ISOC and created an ISOC structure reaching down into the provinces'.[83] The tactics used were very similar to those that had been used by the Village Scouts.

## Contrasts between the acts

Despite the deep roots of the most recent struggle, many things have changed since 1973 and continue to change. Economically, by the 1990s, Thailand 'achieved the transition from a poor, heavily rural backwater to a middle-income, semi-industrialised and globalised economy'.[84] Rural transformations have led to the emergence of middle-income peasants.[85] Globalisation has had an impact, most notably in the economic arena, including the 1997 economic crash and its subsequent recovery. It assisted Thaksin that this recovery picked up speed during the period of his first government.

The experience of a fully democratically elected government under Thaksin and the Thai Rak Thai party and its successors from 2001 points to 'a major deepening of participation in electoral politics among the mass of the population'.[86] Despite the coup, Thaksin's exile, and the dissolution of the Thai Rak Thai party, the results of the 2007 election gave a solid majority to its successor, the People Power Party, which everyone understood to be a Thaksin vehicle. This was at a level similar to that of Thai Rak Thai in 2001 and only narrowly short of an absolute majority.[87] In July 2011, the first general election held after the confrontations of 2010 was one of the most peaceful since the 1970s.[88] The new Prime Minister was Yingluck Shinawatra, Thaksin's youngest sister. With a 75 per cent voter turnout—the highest in history[89]—her Pheu Thai (For Thais) party gained an absolute majority, winning 265 of 500 seats.[90] This outcome reflected the continuing popular support for Thaksin, who has not returned from exile but continues to be a significant political influence. So too is the 'tiny but powerful royal–military–bureaucratic alliance', which still desires 'to return the country to an old model of "semi-democracy", in which the bureaucracy and military dominate politics under the auspices of the monarchy'.[91]

These dramas have taken place against the background of the King's illness and the looming succession. Holding the wealth of symbolic capital in his actual person, King Bhumipol's successor might have inherited at least some of it, but

83   ibid., p. 6.
84   Warr (2011: 4).
85   Walker (2012: 5).
86   Pasuk and Baker (2010: 33).
87   ibid., pp. 4, 33.
88   Prajak (2011: 7).
89   ibid., p. 8.
90   Baker (2011: 10).
91   Prajak (2011: 8).

will not. His successor will be his son, Vajiralongkorn, who is held in little esteem in the country, even in the face of the draconian lèse-majesté laws. These have not eased since the press's imposition of the Crown Prince's face in the mock student hangings at Thammasat University in 1976 sparked that coup. More immediately, Thaksin has publicly indicated that he sees Vajiralongkorn as good for democracy. In November 2009, he spoke from Cambodia of[92]

> a shining new age after the era of the ailing King…His remarks… suggest that he is placing hope in the man likely to accede to the throne, Crown Prince Maha Vajiralongkorn. 'He's not the king yet. He may not be shining (now)…But after he becomes the king, I'm confident that he can be shining…it's not his time yet. But when the time comes, I think he will be able to perform…The Crown Prince may not be as popular as His Majesty the King…[but] he had education abroad and he's young—I think he understands the modern world.'

Walker writes:[93]

> Thaksin's comments highlighted anxiety that a symbolically weak king will open up spaces in Thai political life where alternative forms of political authority can be asserted. For this reason I think that King Vajiralongkorn will be good for Thai democracy. Given his very limited stock of symbolic power he will be incapable of occupying a dominant position at the centre of the Thai polity. If he was younger, there may be potential for another long round of royal myth-making, but there are real questions about Vajiralongkorn's physical, intellectual or political capacity for that enterprise…The defence of the monarchy as a pre-eminent national institution is going through its death throes in Thailand.

There is also a question now as to how far the military might be prepared to go in defence of the monarchy. The evidence of a change of approach, and even of a 'deep rift',[94] within the army and its officer corps is tenuous at best and, as in the 1970s, the army has had previous experiences of 'young Turks' within its ranks. But it may be indicative that no coup followed the upheavals in 2010 or the election of the Yingluck government in 2011. Many of those in the leadership who were involved in the events of the 1970s and even in the 2006 coup are ageing or retired. Prem, like the King, is in his eighties. Sonthi, who led the 2006 coup, has been replaced. Personal support by the Queen continues to influence promotions. But this, too, is likely to change with the succession

---

92    Thaksin reform call stirs comeback fears, *The Australian*, 10 November 2009.
93    Walker (2010).
94    Freelander (2010).

to the King. Reynolds suggests that 'the conclusion seems inescapable that the Thai political system cannot be seriously reformed until the knot tying the army and the monarchy together is cut'.[95] It remains to be seen how that will play out.

## The future

With so much still in the balance, it would be foolhardy to attempt to predict the future direction of Thai politics or of its modernisation. There has been more recent acknowledgment, at least by scholars, of the ongoing reverberations of the 1976 coup and the failure of Thailand to heal those wounds or remedy the situations that gave rise to the protests. The fact that a fully democratically elected government can still be overthrown by the military in the twenty-first century demonstrates clearly that the country's democratic processes and institutions remain weak. The Bangkok establishment continues to hold economic and political power and to resist any attempt to share that. The monarchy remains the touchstone for 'deeply conservative conceptions of order, authority and morals'.[96] And bribery, corruption and violence continue to operate as a normal part of political activities.

Nevertheless—and it is a powerful nevertheless—the resilience of the red-shirt movement reinforced the potency of their rhetoric of fairness, equality and justice. They demand a just society:[97]

> Even if their rebellion is short-lived or defeated, the red shirts will not have contested the power of the establishment in vain. Their campaigns and protests have re-embedded ideas about fairness, equality and justice in the Thai political milieu in a manner that ensures that the ruling elite and, indeed, the monarchy can never again believe that Thailand is exclusively theirs.

Unlike the attempts of groups like the Farmers Federation after 1973 to gain the constructive attention and support of Bangkok for provincial regions, the red shirts made very clear that the provinces will no longer be silent and, as demonstrated in the 2011 election, that they have both the will and the right to participate in the benefits of modernisation. Like the Bang Khen factory workers in the 1970s, but very much more so, they have become politically aware and active in pursuing what they imagine as a good society and a good life. It is not possible to know whether they will now try to achieve this through violent or peaceful means. Thailand's crisis of modernity is as yet not over. We can only await the next act.

---

95  Reynolds (2010: 5).
96  Hewison (2010: 15).
97  ibid., p. 17.

# Part II. Tradition and transformation in a non-colonised state: Spain

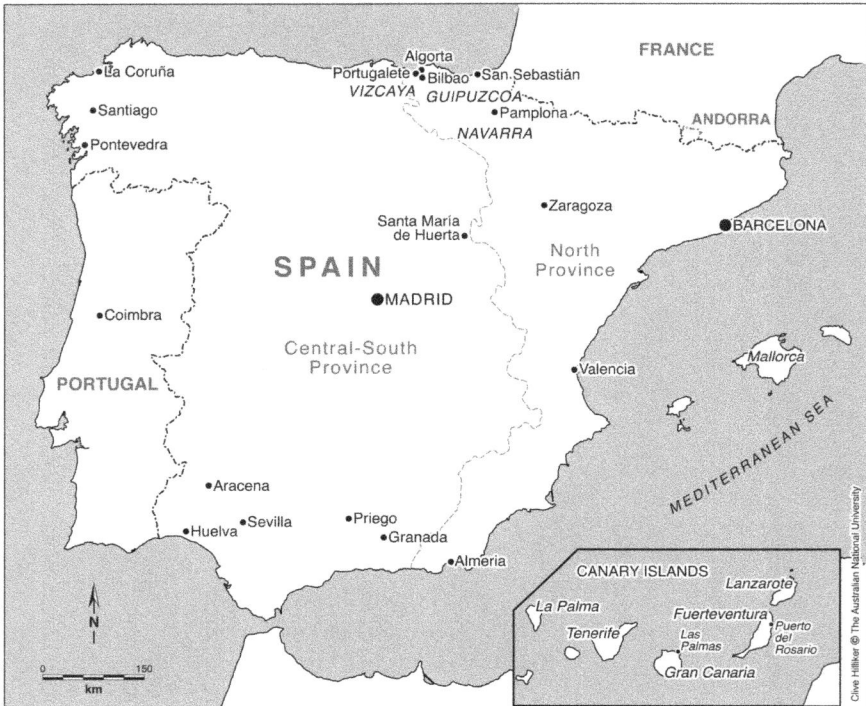

**Map 2. The Society of the Sacred Heart's Spanish provinces and their principal centres, 1982**

# 4. Old orders and new: The nuns as historical actors

For the nuns in Spain, the key event thrusting them into modernity came, perhaps surprisingly, not from awareness of social change or external political movements but from within the Catholic Church itself. This pivotal event was the holding of the Second Vatican Council (Vatican II, 1962–65). As Buddhist belief and practices in Thailand were historically linked to the monarchy and a conservative political regime, so a narrowly traditional Catholicism was used in Spain in the first half of the twentieth century to contain the forces of modernisation and to legitimise a largely feudal framework of social and political relations. The religious order to which the nuns belonged was implicated in these structures and, despite their experience of the Second Republic (proclaimed in 1931) and the Civil War (1936–39), it shaped the nuns' understanding of what constituted a good society. By their own accounts, Vatican II initiated their religious awakening and became the instrument of their political awakening. This happened at, and then combined with, the very moment of the rise of anti-Franco modernising social and political forces. Many of the nuns came to a view—and to act on that view—that a good society was impossible without social justice and its basis in human rights.

## Ethnographic continuities and discontinuities

We left Bangkok with our then twenty-month-old daughter in April 1977. At the time of my husband's posting to Spain at the beginning of 1981, we had three children. Madrid promised a hospitable environment for family and social life. It also challenged me to approach it ethnographically: a new culture, a new history, a new country experiencing modernisation after almost 40 years of dictatorship. The invitation was irresistible, because of, as well as despite, the serendipitous character of my being in Madrid rather than in some other place. I wanted to know Madrid and its people; I wanted to participate in their world, understand who they were and how they related to each other and to the outside world, to test the romance of the Spanish Civil War against the realities of people's experience then and now and of the legacy that remained for them. I wanted to gather the material from their everyday lives that would allow me to write another critical ethnography of a people in transition.

In an ideal world of consistency rather than of practical contingency, I would have built more directly on my Thai research and pursued my interest in labour relations. In real time and space, with three small children, no previous Spanish studies and no contacts in the industrial world, I decided against it. Instead, I made a judgement about the possible and moved to a topic in which I had extensive knowledge, experience and friendships: that of nuns.

# The first encounter

The first hint that I would find a political and social situation in Spain that was closer than I had expected to the one that we had encountered in Thailand came when we boarded the plane in Athens around breakfast time on 24 February 1981. On hearing that our final destination was Madrid, one of the Qantas crew commented that there had been a coup in Madrid on the day before. He didn't know the outcome; we had several anxious days in Rome and little access to English-language news. It was not until we arrived in Madrid that we learnt that the attempted coup had failed. We also learnt that, on 23 February, tanks rolled in the streets of Valencia under the direction of General Jaime Milans del Bosch. In Madrid, about 200 soldiers and members of the Guardia Civil (Civil Guard) stormed the Cortes, the lower house of the Spanish Parliament. They were led by an officer of the Guardia Civil, Colonel Antonio Tejero Molina. Firing automatic weapons, they took hostage the more than 300 Members of Parliament and held them for most of the next 24 hours. Convinced of the King's approval, Tejero called on him to make an announcement supporting the coup.

Comparisons between Thailand and Spain would have been vigorously rejected by most Spaniards. On the one occasion when I suggested the comparison to my friend Luz González, she was quite shocked and offended. It seemed to me then, however, as it does now, that the parallels were demonstrable. In perhaps equally informative ways, so, too, were the differences. Like the Thai coup of 1976 four and a half years before, 23 February also demonstrated contested ideas about the good and about what makes a good society. It involved the military, the paramilitary Guardia Civil, right-wing groups and the monarchy. Spain had experienced only five years of democracy—another 'democratic experiment'[1]— since the 36-year dictatorship of General Francisco Franco Bahamonde, who died in November 1975.

Unlike in Thailand, in Spain, the attempted coup of 1981—driven by many similar forces—did not succeed. Contrary to the expectations of the plotters, and many others, King Juan Carlos did not give his support. On the contrary, he actively opposed it and his opposition was the key to its failure. As soon as he was informed of the attack on the Cortes, he established a non-military administrative government base at the Zarzuela Palace and, using his position

---

1   Preston (2004: 459).

as Commander-in-Chief of the armed forces, contacted senior military officers to make clear that he did not support the coup and to demand their loyalty. At 1.15 am on 24 February, he made a nationwide televised broadcast from a mobile unit of RTVE, condemned the coup, and ordered its leaders to surrender. The tanks slowly withdrew from the streets of Valencia and, later that morning, Tejero released the parliamentarians. He was arrested, together with General Milans del Bosch and some others involved in the plot.[2]

As in Bangkok, I experienced the extraordinary events of these times through the response of ordinary Spaniards, their public insistence that they rejected a return to the authoritarian past and, whatever the problems, were committed to the peaceful implementation of a full democracy. We spent our first night in Madrid in a hotel in the centre of the city, overlooking the Plaza Colón and the massive demonstration of an estimated million and a half people who marched in support of democracy. A further million and a half marched in other cities across the country. Once again, it was raining, but this time the cold drizzle of a Madrid winter.

Pilar Duarte, one of the nuns who had grown up after the end of the Civil War, described her anxiety when she got back from her teaching day on the evening of 23 February and turned on the radio. What she heard was not the usual programs, but a news bulletin about the attack on the Parliament, followed exclusively by martial music. A small renegade unit had taken over the radio and television broadcasting studios (RTVE) at Prado del Rey and ordered that the station play only military music (although the RTVE Director-General managed to make these Baroque marches).[3] For Pilar, the news and the music signalled a return to the Franco years (*el Franquismo*). She was appalled. Her reaction was shared by many of her contemporaries.

Some of the older nuns had experienced the disruptions, often violent, of the Second Republic (1931–36) and the Civil War (1936–39) and had seen the Franco regime as the proper victory of the forces on the side of God over *los Rojos* (the Reds). For them, a return to the values and apparent stability of the dictatorship would have been welcomed. Among this group of nuns were two sisters of General Alfonso Armada Comyn, one of the central plotters in the failed 23 February coup. When Armada was condemned to a long prison sentence, an acquaintance commiserating with his sisters was assured that it was not the General about whom they worried. It was another brother, a Jesuit, who had rejected the conservative religious and social values of the family, lived in a

---

2   ibid., pp. 472–85.
3   ibid., p. 478.

working-class district of Madrid and wore ordinary clothes. The family always kept a priest's soutane hanging on the back of their front door so that, when he came to visit, he might dress in suitable clerical garb.

## Habit and habitus

The different reactions of these three women to the attempted coup offered only one aspect of the very contrasting lifestyles that had emerged in their Congregation over the previous decade. All the nuns whom I came to know had been trained in the certainties of the pre–Vatican II religious understanding of the world. They remembered a life of monastic orderliness and routine organised around religious rituals: rising at 5.20 am, washing in cold water before dressing in the very complicated religious habit; meditation for an hour from 6 am; chanting of Lauds, the first Divine Office of the day; the celebration of Mass. Private examination of conscience was twice a day, for 15 minutes before lunch and 15 minutes and in the evening. More Divine Office was chanted at set times throughout the day, the Angelus prayed three times, and the Rosary; meals as a time for public self-accusation of faults; regulated time for personal prayer. And silence as the norm, with the Greater Silence rung in at 9.15 pm. Teaching, principally in schools for daughters of the elite, and other duties were encompassed within this spiritual timetabling. Each community had a hierarchy of authority, and a Superior to whom unquestioning obedience was owed. This was the standard against which the nuns measured not only the different ways in which they subsequently chose to live their daily lives, but also the transformation for many of them in their understanding of the good, and of what it meant to live a good life. The different responses to the attempted coup reflected the very different meanings that these women had come to give to their lives.

General Armada's sisters continued to wear the religious habit, as they wished their Jesuit brother would do. They lived in traditional communities in the large convents belonging to the order, and, as they were no longer involved in teaching, followed an order of day dictated mainly by prayer and common religious observance. In each of these communities, one of the nuns was given the role of Superior by the Order's provincial governing team. On the other hand, Pilar Duarte shared a *piso* (apartment) with four other nuns in a working-class district of high unemployment in Madrid, taught in a local adult education centre dedicated especially to improving literacy skills, and assisted in the Centre for the Disabled. All five members of her community wore secular clothes that they bought themselves. Their daily routines were organised by work, involvement in the local parish, shared domestic responsibilities, and some informal time in the evenings when they tried to eat and spend time together.

They had no fixed common schedule of prayer or other religious rituals but undertook these as a personal responsibility. Nor was any of the group willing to be named or to accept a local Superior.

These striking differences in lifestyle were recent and represented the largely generational differences that shaped the nuns' various responses to Spain's convulsive encounter with modernity. They also represented changing and newly diverse notions among the nuns of the good, and of the meaning of their religious life in terms of it being a good life within 'the world', or a better life in opposition to 'the world'. These were questions that the nuns specifically confronted and articulated, at the international level of the Congregation, but also at the Provincial, community and personal levels. Carmen Vega, also working in an adult education centre and living in a small *piso* community but in a different Madrid neighbourhood, saw her religious life as one, but by no means the only, choice available to her as a Christian:

> We talk of Christian schools, Christian families, as though 'Christian' were an adjective. 'Christian' is a substantive. We are Christians *in* the schools, Christians *in* the family…The Christian is one who lives in different situations, whatever they may be. That is to say that, whatever the situation, the Christian transforms them or changes them by the way in which she or he lives them…The vow of chastity is a very functional vow in order to have a greater freedom.

This understanding of the religious life is close to Charles Taylor's identification of one of the key aspects of modernity, and of a secular idea of the good—that is, the affirmation of ordinary life and the rejection of spiritual hierarchy.[4] But Carmen Vega, like Pilar Duarte and many of their companions, had not entered the Congregation with this view. Nor did it represent the view of the nuns during the first century and more of their presence in Spain.

# The old order: History of the Society of the Sacred Heart in Spain

During this earlier period, the internal organisation of the Congregation, their relationship to the Roman Church and their form of education were all firmly hierarchical. Their view of the religious life was based on a Platonic and Augustinian separation of the temporal from the sacred order and of opposition between the spirit and the flesh, with religious life constituting a commitment to the spirit and a rejection of the flesh and, by association, of the world and of

---

4   Taylor (2003: 216–18).

worldly pleasures. This commitment to the spiritual and a consequent rejection of the world was defined in terms a lifelong fidelity to the three vows of poverty, chastity and obedience. Withdrawal from the world was actualised by life in convents based on a fourth vow, that of 'stability'. This vow confined the nuns to enclosure in a specific convent unless directed to move from there by their Superior. The religious habit, designed originally for simplicity, had become an elaborate costume suppressing individuality and femininity. Except in the classroom, and during scheduled breaks for recreation, silence was the norm, to be broken only when really necessary.

The nuns who arrived in Spain in the mid-nineteenth century were part of an international teaching order, the Society of the Sacred Heart, founded in France in 1800 for the education of girls. Members of the Society date its arrival in Spain from 1846 when the first permanent house was established in Sarria, near Barcelona. In fact, the first nuns had arrived in 1830, at the invitation of the Bishop of Gerona, who had offered them a house and whatever they needed.[5] The timing of such a venture could not, from the point of view of the nuns themselves, have been worse. Their arrival came towards the end of what Carr calls 'the ominous decade',[6] and of a long period of economic depression that had followed the War of Independence against Napoleon (1808–14).[7] The time of their stay (1830–36) coincided with one of the periods of crisis in a century defined by crisis, and with the radical laws of Prime Minister Juan Álvarez Mendizábal. These laws had resulted in the suppression of convents and monasteries, the exclaustration or expulsion of monks and nuns, and the appropriation (*desamortización*) of church and monastic lands. From the time of the Society's return to Spain 10 years later, in 1846, its alignment was with the Catholic bourgeoisie and, by extension, with the aristocracy. The first school was opened in 1848 in Sarria, to cater for the education of the daughters of wealthy Catholics who would otherwise have been sent to a Sacred Heart convent in France.

The second house, Chamartin de la Rosa, on the then outskirts of Madrid, was a gift of the Duke and Duchess of Pastrana in 1859. These patrons had already made a similar endowment to the Jesuits of a property opposite the nuns', and were also later responsible for the gift to the Society of their own palace in Madrid (Leganitos in 1886). The school at Leganitos was named St Dionysius after the Duchess, Doña Dionisia. The school had in fact opened two years earlier in a smaller house, also bestowed by the Duke and Duchess. On the death

---

5   Religiosas Del Sagrado Corazón de Jesús (1946: 8).
6   Carr (1983: 146).
7   Fontana (1974: 46).

of the Duke, however, the nuns moved to the ducal palace, and the Jesuits were invited by the Duchess to take over the nuns' previous house for their pastoral activities.

The Countess of Villanueva was the benefactress of the third house. This was a former monastery in Seville, with a reputedly miraculous statue of Our Lady of the Valley. The monastery had been one of those seized in the disentailments (*desamortización*) of 1834–37, and the buildings had been converted into numerous small flats for families. The gift to the nuns meant the displacement of these families: 'The cholera epidemic and the resistance of the ninety tenants, who were in no hurry at all to remove from the site, delayed until January, 1866, the definitive installation of the Mothers in Seville.'[8]

Other houses—in Zaragoza (1875), Bilbao (1876), Madrid (Caballero de Gracia, 1877), Barcelona (Diputación, 1888), Valencia (Godella, 1898), San Sebastian (1903), Palma de Mallorca (Son Españolet, 1902), Las Palmas, the provincial capital of the Canary Islands (1903), and so on—were purchased by the nuns. The emphasis was always on 'suitable'—that is, usually excellent—sites, and the pupils were drawn from families of the emerging wealthy middle class (*gente acomodada*) or the aristocracy. These classes also provided the young women who became the teachers (the choir nuns) for the Society. The poor were not forgotten; in accordance with the wishes of the foundress, poor schools were opened in association with each new foundation.[9] Indeed, at the time of the Spanish centenary in 1946, the number of girls who had received instruction in the free schools surpassed that of the fee-paying pupils. In one year (1906) this was as much as two and a half times as great (3346 compared with 1290). The quality of the education in the two kinds of school was, however, very different and the Society's reputation rested on its elite schools.

María Victoria (MariVí) Muñoz remembered one of the nuns who was a product of this time, a woman who had held the office of Provincial for many years, as

> a person who intimidated you. She gave you the impression that she carried a poster that said, '*Noli me tangere* [Don't touch me]'.[10] She kept her distance, but this was something that wasn't only a product of her training in the Sacred Heart as student and as religious, but also came from her aristocratic background. She was a great lady [*una gran Señora*] from her head to her toes.

---

8    Religiosas Del Sagrado Corazón de Jesús (1946: 27).
9    According to Susanna de Vries, Daisy Bates was a daygirl at the Order's poor school in Roscrea, Ireland. De Vries (2008) suggests that this is where she observed the behaviour and manners of the boarding pupils, over the wall and on occasional days when the two schools came together, and that this stood her in good stead when she first arrived in Australia.
10    The Latin Vulgate translation of the reported words of Jesus to Mary Magdalene in the garden after the Resurrection (John 20: 17).

Ana María Argaya, who had spent many years living the traditional religious life before overseeing the changes as part of the central governing body of the Society, made the point that one of the key changes had been that the nuns had moved from being *'les grandes dames du Sacré Coeur'* (the great ladies of the Sacred Heart) to being just anyone (*unas cualesquiera*). Marta de Vera, living in one of the more radical *piso* communities, commented that she could not understand why, since the changes, young women continued to enter the convent: 'For us it was part of the social environment…If I had to do it now, perhaps I wouldn't.'

Even within the general traditionalism and conservatism of the Society of the Sacred Heart internationally, the Spanish convents represented an extreme. Socorro Abel had entered the convent in France when she was thirty years old. She described her surprise on her return to Spain in 1962:

> I spent my novitiate and first years in France, and for me the change from the French religious life to the Spanish religious life was very great. *Very* great. For example, since I'd entered, I'd had a small professional autonomy within my own domain. No-one had told me how I ought to organise things in my professional work. And I'd never been disconnected from newspapers in France. In the novitiate on Sundays, we could read press cuttings; we couldn't read the whole newspaper because that was forbidden by Canon Law. But they did provide clippings that dealt with real situations, with political and social problems. And in France I was given a Bible; in Spain novices were not allowed to read the Bible. They were allowed to have the New Testament, but were not allowed to read the Old Testament. There wasn't even a Bible if you went looking for one!…And I'd read books of philosophy, even as a novice, that it wouldn't have occurred to anyone in Spain to read.

# Background: Early twentieth-century Spain

This contrast between a conservative Spain and a more liberal France was not confined to the nuns. Spain had flirted with modernity in the nineteenth and early twentieth centuries, but those forays had been sporadic and had stalled. The years 1923 to 1930 had seen the return of dictatorship under General Miguel Primo de Rivera. The dictatorship had had the support of the Bourbon King, Alfonso XIII. Even with the subsequent abdication of Alfonso XIII in 1931, the old order prevailed. Its characteristics had been 'monarchist, centralist,

Catholic, imbued with the values of empire and arms, and run by and largely for the social and economic elites'.[11] The declaration of the Second Republic promised a new order, and

> not merely a political system without a king. The Republic meant, for those who cheered its arrival, a democratic, civilian, secular order, in which the centre would have to be responsive to the periphery, and the top to the bottom. For those who were sceptical or hostile, it meant the abandonment of tradition, and a threat to stability, property and national unity.[12]

Moreover:

> No one expected the Republic to continue the church–state alliance that had existed between Catholicism and the crown. The separation of church and state and the introduction of religious freedom were inevitable concomitants of the historic turn to Republicanism. Many of the bishops feared something worse, namely an active attempt to secularise Spanish society and culture, and to limit the freedom of action of the church.

On the agenda of the Republic, too, were social and economic reforms, including the urgent issue of land reform, jobs, better working conditions, better education. This was in addition to attempting to curb the power of the church and the military. This democratic experiment lasted only five years, however, until the outbreak of civil war in July 1936, and suffered an even more bloody failure than the Thai 'democratic experiment' 40 years later.

There were three elections during this period: June 1931, November 1933 and February 1936. All the governments formed as a result of these elections were unstable coalitions. In 1931 and 1936, the largest number of seats was won by the Socialists (Partido Socialista Obrero Español or PSOE), but the party was not able to govern in its own right at any time. In view of the blanket term of *los Rojos* (the Reds) applied to them and to other left-wing groups by their opponents, then and later, it is notable that the Communist Party won only one seat in one of the elections, that of 1933,[13] although it did join the alliance of parties led by the Socialists that formed the Popular Front and won the 1936 election.[14] The two years following the 1933 elections came to be known as the *Bienio Negro* (the Black Period). The ambitious programs of the first Republican government had had only limited success. They were replaced by a right-wing

---

11    Lannon (2002: 17).
12    ibid., p. 17.
13    de Blaye (1976: 517–19).
14    Lannon (2002: 23).

coalition. Sporadic violence and growing unrest among both industrial and agricultural workers culminated in a revolt by Asturian miners in October 1934. In the subsequent pacification and repression, around 1000 workers were killed and thousands of political prisoners taken.[15] The elections of February 1936 were a last desperate attempt to save the Republic, but civil war was by then inevitable. Another brief eruption of modernity was once more stifled by the Civil War (1936–39) and the first repressive decades of *el Franquismo* (1939–75).

Together with the Anarchists, the Socialists and other Republicans, the Communists played a major part in the Civil War. With the exception of some of the nuns in Catalonia and the Basque Country, most of the nuns and their families identified with the Catholic right during the Second Republic and saw the Nationalist uprising against the government of the Republic as a godly crusade against *los Rojos* (the Reds). They were drawn into this political maelstrom by two main and historically related associations. One was the battle over the control of education. The other was the identification of the Society with the symbol of the Sacred Heart.

# Relationship of the nuns to Spanish political history

Until 1913, the struggle for the control of education had largely taken the indirect form of an attempt by the state to limit the development of religious orders. This attempt was vigorously, and mostly successfully, resisted by the Church. The success of the Church's resistance is reflected in the fact that this period had also seen the Society of the Sacred Heart more than double its schools, from nine in 1898 to 19 and a teachers' college by 1930. Moreover, the Church did not hesitate to invoke an extreme discourse that pitted secular against divine authority. To take just one of a myriad examples, against a proposed law in 1910 limiting religious associations, and by implication their involvement in education (the *Ley del Candado*), the hierarchy declared unequivocally in a public letter of protest to the King that the implementation of the law would imply mortal sin and excommunication.[16]

After the abdication of Alfonso XIII and the declaration of the Republic in 1931, the legislation of 1931–33 no longer approached the problem of the Church indirectly, but confronted head-on the question of control of education. The Constitution of 1931 contained a contentious provision, Article 26, which specifically prohibited religious orders from teaching. Nevertheless, the

---

15   ibid., pp. 21–2.
16   Iribarren (1974: 85–6).

prohibition was not instantly enforced, since the Government was not in an immediate position to replace the religious schools. These were granted a reprieve until the Law of Confessions and Religious Congregations of 1933, which, among other things, included an absolute, if ineffectual, prohibition of teaching by religious personnel. These laws, and the atmosphere of crisis in the Church that they provoked, finally dragged the nuns of the Society of the Sacred Heart into critical involvement with the political and social events from which they had previously stood back. These were the events that deeply affected the lives of the women of the Civil War generation and their work in the schools.

The most dramatic of these events took place on the fateful 11 May 1931, when the buildings at Chamartin—not only the school and the house of novitiate but also the provincial house—were among the convents burnt by mobs in an upsurge of anticlerical and antimonarchical violence. Eleven other buildings in Madrid were burnt on the same day. In the following days, the burnings spread to other parts of Spain: Valencia, Alicante, Murcia, Seville, Cadiz and especially Malaga.[17] The headquarters of the monarchist newspaper *ABC* were also burnt. Despite the ferocity, no-one died in the attacks.[18] With the burning of Chamartin went the provincial archives, so that written information from the period before the end of the Civil War is sketchy, but a number of the nuns remember it, in broad description and accidental detail.

The burning of Chamartin took place at about six in the evening. María Ángeles Martín-Barreda was there:

> I was in the novitiate, and on the 11th of May 1931, they came to burn Chamartin. We all had to leave. Mother Modet, the Provincial, and some of the novices—probably about 30—went to the house of the Countess... But she couldn't take so many; without postulants,[19] we were sixty. That night, I went to three different houses. In two, they refused me. In the end I went to the house of a relative. But there were some funny details. Those who'd got fat [in the novitiate] couldn't fit into their clothes. As for me, I'd always been fat, so they were all asking me for clothes.

Josefina Rodríguez remembered other details: 'The afternoon of the fire, the Provincial sent the novices to their families. The professed nuns[20] she told to go to the houses of the poor. But not one poor family would let them in.'

---

17  Garcia Villoslada (1979: 348).
18  Thomas (1977: 58–9).
19  The first stage of training after entering the convent was that of postulant. It normally lasted about six months, and postulants did not wear the religious habit. Novices did wear the habit, but with a white rather than a black veil.
20  'The professed' are those who have completed their training, taken their final vows and are full members of the Society of the Sacred Heart.

During the sacking of Chamartin, the statue of the Sacred Heart in the central courtyard was attacked and its right arm smashed. This was an early and lesser version of one of the most famous symbolic events at the beginning of the Civil War: the ritual execution by a Republican militia firing squad of the statue of the Sacred Heart at the *Cerro de los Ángeles* (the Hill of the Angels). In 1919, Spain had been officially consecrated to the Sacred Heart at this site by Alfonso XIII in a ceremony with clear political implications. The following eyewitness account of the event was given in her memoirs by the dissident and Republican Constancia de la Mora:[21]

> Later on in that spring of 1919 I went to another Spanish ceremony, this time with my grandfather, [Antonio Maura], then Prime Minister, and our entire family. King Alfonso was to dedicate a statue of the Sacred Heart—the occasion was so important that my grandmother appeared in public beside her husband for one of the few times of her life. We all motored to the *Cerro de los Ángeles* where stonemasons had erected the statue in the exact geographical centre of Spain near Madrid. My grandfather made a short speech and then King Alfonso, standing beside him, stepped forward and in his weak voice offered his country to the image of the Sacred Heart...
>
> The grave-faced noblemen, the Grandees, and all the other titles and their resplendent wives nodded solemnly as they heard the King of Spain pledge his subjects to the Church and the monarchy. The King lifted his hand to pull the veil covering the statue. The great crowd watching him stirred restlessly. Workmen bustled forward to assist. The fluttering white cover slipped off the stone to disclose the graven words: 'You will reign in Spain'.
>
> And then the crowd went mad with cheers. And the King and my grandfather and all the noblemen turned pale. For under the huge carved words was another slogan, roughly and hastily scratched on. In Spanish not nearly so elegant as the 'You will reign in Spain', were the words: 'You may think so, but it will not be true'.

Indeed, when the battlelines were irrevocably drawn during the Civil War, there was no doubt in people's minds as to whose side the Sacred Heart belonged; the symbol became reality. The destruction of the statue after the outbreak of war in July 1936 was a statement of fierce intent to fulfil that warning at the time of its dedication. It took several days, from 28 July until 7 August, to complete the destruction. The militia tried twice to dynamite the statue and then to topple it with the help of a tractor. They finally smashed it by hand with

---

21    de la Mora (1940: 32–4).

hammers. But the most memorable, and most remembered, of these events was the first: the shooting of the statue by a firing squad on 28 July.[22] So potent was this act of symbolic as well as actual destruction that the Franco government undertook the restoration of the sanctuary in the early years of their victory. In 1942, with the country still devastated by the effects of the Civil War, the Government made an appeal to the nation to transfigure the site, 'in view of the satanic attempt to convert the *Cerro de los Ángeles*—Hill of the Angels—into the *Cerro de los Rojos*: Hill of the Reds'. Instead it was to become 'another Mount Tabor, where the glory of Christ will appear in all the splendour of His Divine Presence, where His chosen disciples, the sons and daughters of Catholic Spain, will find light and strength, blessedness and peace, justice and charity'.[23]

The attack on the statue of the Sacred Heart in Chamartin, as well as on the convent and the school, must be read, therefore, as part of a wider battle over the symbols as well as the politics of the struggle between the new order represented by the Republic and the old order, ultimately led by Franco and the Nationalist rebels. There were of course other symbols. One was the flag. Within a fortnight of the abdication of Alfonso XIII, the new provisional government issued a decree announcing a new national flag and changing the tri-band red-yellow-red to the tricolour red-yellow-purple:

> The national uprising against tyranny, victorious since 14 April, has raised a sign invested by the understanding of the people with a double meaning: that of the hope of liberty and of its irrevocable triumph…A new era begins in Spanish life…The Republic protects all. So does the flag, which signifies peace, and the participation of all citizens under a regime of just laws. It signifies even more: the fact, new in the history of Spain, that the action of the State has no other motive than the interest of the country, nor any other basis than respect for conscience, liberty, and work.[24]

The old flag was made illegal. This caused severe problems for Dolores Suárez, who was eighteen and had not yet joined the Society of the Sacred Heart when the Second Republic was declared:

> They detained me, along with my brother and sister. We had a lamp—it was just an ornament—but the shade was crocheted in red and yellow thread. Because the Republic had declared the tricolour [illegal], they took me away. They took me first to the Security Department, and later to a convent near the Plaza de España that they had taken over to detain

---

22 Anibarro Espeso (1975: 44–54).
23 ibid., p. 131.
24 Decree of 27 April 1931.

people. It was very overcrowded with about 1400 people in the convent. I was there for three months. During the night, for about 12 hours, we didn't even have toilets.

For others, the possession of the old flag was a more intentional symbol of resistance. María Angustias de Heredia recalled the triumphant entry of Nationalist troops into Madrid on 28 March 1939:

> We had a maid at home, Antonia, and when the Republic arrived she went silly. She took off her uniform and left her hair loose. We couldn't do anything; though she did remain loyal. But when Franco arrived in Madrid, my mother had sewn a big flag—and the day that he arrived, she put it out on the balcony (the apartment was near Cibeles)—saying 'Welcome'. And she said: 'Long live Spain. Long live Christ the King. And you, Antonia, now you will go and tidy yourself and serve at table as God ordained.'

Many others in the Society of the Sacred Heart also welcomed the Nationalist victory and the possibility of a return to the ordered way of life that they had known before. The position of the nuns during the Second Republic is intimated in some of the few documents that survived the loss of the provincial archives in the burning of Chamartin in 1931. They are revealingly filed under the title 'Documents related to the Religious Persecution, 1931–36'. A number of these deal with the Congregation's association with Sociedad Anónima de Enseñanza Libre (SADEL: Limited Company for Freedom of Teaching), an organisation set up in 1933 under the auspices of the Catholic Association of Parents.[25] By transferring ownership of school properties to SADEL, the nuns were able to remain within the law and, at the same time, continue teaching. With these arrangements, the schools—by now numbering 17—on the whole continued to function, usually with the help of former students. By changing their title to *Academia*, doing away with a uniform for the students, and themselves dressing in secular clothes, a fairly normal routine was established. After her experience of seeking shelter outside Chamartin on the night it was burnt, María Ángeles Martín-Barreda was sent, with the rest of the novices, to Avigliana, in Italy:

> I returned to Spain in February 1933. That school year was normal, with the habit and everything, up till the end of the year. At the end of 1933 and the beginning of 1934, they founded SADEL…Under SADEL, they divided the house into two: the convent, that belonged to us, where we wore the habit and gave classes in religion and needlework; and the SADEL, where we wore secular clothes. We were employed by the SADEL, and only those who had qualifications [*título*] could teach. In

---

25   Report in *ABC*, 4 July 1933.

the last months before the war, we used to go out every night with the children to sleep in houses outside [*del pueblo*]. And look at the providence of God. The war broke out on the 17th July. The children had already gone on holidays. And there had been some teachers from the country who had come to make a retreat. They left on the last bus that left Madrid. After that it wouldn't have been possible to have returned to the villages.

Josefina Rodríguez had spent this time in Seville: 'In Seville, we had a secret door. We used to go through it into the school at eight in the morning. In the afternoon, we went back to the convent.' Even in the case of Chamartin, the school was reopened in the ruins within three months.

This dual existence lasted for the nuns until the outbreak of the Civil War in 1936. The war meant the closing of schools in Republican zones and the dispersal of communities. Some of the nuns, a group of 41, were detained or imprisoned for varying periods of up to several months, but none was executed. Josefina Rodríguez did not see this as something to be celebrated: 'We were one of the few religious orders without martyrs. We weren't worthy.' Josefina was not one of the 41 who had been detained or imprisoned; they were older and more senior nuns and are no longer alive. Others managed to reach Nationalist areas, or got to France or to Italy, though many lost fathers and brothers. The deserted convents were used in a number of different capacities: as hospitals, childcare centres, military barracks. The former ducal palace at Leganitos was in the front line of the siege in Madrid, and was virtually destroyed. Convents in the Nationalist zones rallied to the war effort, helped look after the wounded and opened their doors to religious from Republican areas.

With the Nationalist victory in 1939, the Society's schools were very quickly reopened, in a spirit expressed two decades later on the centenary of the founding of Chamartin: 'On Wednesday, 29 March 1939, Year of the Victory, was liberated Madrid, last bulwark of Marxism. And on 5 April, Chamartin renewed the thread of its history after three years of slavery beneath the powers of darkness. The imprint left by the enemy was apocalyptic, an infernal chaos.'[26]

In contrast with 'the imprint left by the enemy', the imprint left by the Franco years was a consolidation and growth of the work of the Society of the Sacred Heart. While much of the rest of the country suffered under the harsh repression of the regime, the Society opened 12 new schools or residences between 1939 and 1969, all with the same basic religious, political, social and educational orientations as before. Chamartin was rebuilt around the statue of the Sacred Heart that had survived the fire and the war with the loss of only its arm; and

---

26   *Mater Admirabilis* (Chamartin 1959b: 20).

the school of St Dionysius was reopened on a new site. At the centenary of Chamartin in 1959, one of the principal speakers was the former propagandist and Minister for Foreign Affairs Alberto Martín Artajo, who, even though he had fallen into personal disfavour with Franco,[27] was still publicly identified with the regime. His sister Carmen had been a nun in the Society, and his wife, his six sisters and his daughters were all educated in Sacred Heart schools.[28] At the same centenary celebrations, the Civil Order of Social Welfare (*Beneficencia*), the Cross of the First Class, was presented to the school by the Secretary of the Department of Social Welfare and Works, Antonio María Oriol. And students of the three schools in Madrid and some others made a pilgrimage of 'reparation' (*desagravio*) to the statue of the Sacred Heart at the *Cerro de los Ángeles*.[29]

There were a few exceptions among the nuns to the general adulation of Franco and his zealous reappropriation of Christian rhetoric and symbols. Marta Echave and Ana Garay came from separatist Basque families whose families were made to suffer bitterly after the war. Ángeles Alvárez's father was a captain in the army who was in Ciudad Real at the time of Franco's rebellion. Although sympathetic to the rebels' objectives, he regarded his oath of loyalty to the legally constituted government to be binding even when he did not agree with all its policies. He therefore fought on the Republican side in the Civil War. At the end of the war, he was imprisoned, tried by court martial and dismissed from the army. He lived in poverty and disgrace until an official reinstatement, sought by his family, in 1983. His daughter, like Marta Echave and Ana Garay, kept silent in her community.

# The Church's modernising moment: The impact of Vatican II

The first ripples of change began in 1962. In February, the Franco regime initiated a program for modernisation with its first 'plan of economic and social development'.[30] Two months earlier, on 25 December 1961, Pope John XXIII had announced the convocation of the Second Vatican Council—Vatican II—in order for the Catholic Church to engage with 'the modern world'.[31] For the nuns, Vatican II (1962–65) was the pivotal event that first provoked and then mediated their own experience of modernity. At the same time, even in these religious matters, the different generational responses were fundamentally shaped by the Civil War.

---

27  de Blaye (1976: 375).
28  Chamartin (1959a: 34).
29  ibid., pp. 36–7.
30  de Blaye (1976: 215).
31  Abbott (1966: 703).

Ana María Argaya, who was in Rome as a member of the order's governing body during Vatican II, commented: 'I was at the heart of the change, and I have to say that the changes came *solely* from the Council. Solely. There was no internal fuss…We knew that the young people felt very repressed…But the change came from obedience to the Council.'

This view was widely shared. MariVí Muñoz was in Rome from September 1966 to February 1967 for her period of Probation, the final stage for the nuns before they took their final vows. A decade later, she was deeply committed to the liberation theology that had emerged from Latin America. But she remembered this earlier time:

> In Probation, everything was very peaceful. I remember, and this is very funny: the Mother General called us together and told us that she was going to give us as the name of our Probation 'Unity in love', because in a moment when the Society was so divided—and I, I said to the person next to me, 'Why is it divided?' It's just—we had no idea of, of—as we used to be in Spain, so closed. The generations of Spaniards really, like champions of the faith, we knew nothing about trends, nothing about the Council, nothing at all. At least, we knew that there'd been a Council, certainly, but as for the documents, they'd come, but as there was no enthusiasm for anything new, well, we read them like a pious document and not like something that was going to change our lives.

Socorro Abel, a handsome woman in her fifties who lived in one of the small *piso* communities, made very clear that:

> Before the changes, the truth is that I, personally, never felt any need to change. That's to say that I've changed because others have pushed me. At least, they haven't pushed me, but it was others who had the idea, they were the pioneers and saw the changes that had to be made. When I saw them taking that step, how much that opened my eyes! And I said to myself that I also had to change. But I didn't initiate it.

This was the woman who had entered the order in France but had not felt 'uncomfortable' previously. Nevertheless:

> I changed from the religious habit at the beginning of the Seventies. As part of a course, I went three years running to Valladolid for the film festival. The first year, we all wore the habit; there were about 10 nuns. But to go to theatres in the city to see films, like *Isadora Duncan*, in the habit! We all agreed that we'd change it for the second year. Afterwards, in Madrid, where I was teaching in the school, I wore the habit to give classes, and then afterwards, straight away, I'd have to change it— everything, right down to underclothes—to go out. And trying to do

something normal with your hair after it had been covered for a week! I didn't know in which situation I was in disguise [*disfrazada*], in the habit or in secular dress.

When she did change from the religious habit, the first gift that her family gave her were earrings: 'part of women's clothing here, a custom'.

The radical nature of these changes for the nuns can only be measured by reminding ourselves about what had gone before. The reluctance to alternate between the habit and secular clothes in 1970 had a very different source from that for the nuns during the Republic. Now the change signified a dramatic shift in orientation arising from Vatican II, as the nuns grappled with the notion that their religious life was not principally about their own good, but about 'insertion' in the world. Having guided the Society through the first years of change, Ana María Argaya identified the key as

involvement [*la inserción*]; to choose and to want to live among men, in solidarity with them, living a normal life with people...The question of the habit relates to this involvement...The habit was a sign of separation from the world, indeed as a consecration to God, but a sign of separation from the world. Now we no longer want that separation from the world—the world in the sense used by Jesus: 'You shall not be of the world. You shall be *in* the world but not *of* the world'...If we're more involved, and want to be more involved, if we're going to go out into our neighbourhoods [*los barrios*], we have to wear normal clothes like everyone else.

## The Society's response

At first, the changes were gradual and took place in three main stages, each dependent upon a General Chapter of the Society of the Sacred Heart. The General Chapter is the principal official decision-making body for the Society and is held in accordance with the requirements of Canon Law that all recognised religious orders send representatives every six years to a general meeting. The General Chapters were held at the Society's central house in Rome.

The first of these was the regular six-yearly Chapter of 1964, and coincided with the Vatican Council itself. Having thrown open the windows of the Church, Pope John XXIII had died in June of the previous year and been succeeded by Paul VI. The work of the Council was not yet complete, and most of its documents had still to be finalised. But John XXIII had prepared a document for the opening of the Council that was issued in its first session. This was a *Message to Humanity*, and it set the tone and direction for what followed, both in the Church and for the nuns. For the Society, this was first reflected in the General Chapter of 1964. For the first time, some of what had seemed like immutable principles were questioned. Among these was the rule of enclosure which, along with the habit, had enforced the ideal of separation from the world. The representatives at the General Chapter made the bold decision that enclosure was to be suppressed. In order for this to be implemented, however, the nuns needed clarification of the canonical status of the vow of stability. Inquiries to the Sacred Congregation of Religious produced the surprising result that the vow of stability had no canonical foundation whatsoever for religious orders of the active life—those involved, for example, in teaching or nursing—and therefore no binding power at all. Instead of the major opposition that the nuns had feared, there was no official objection to the suppression of enclosure.

The formal suppression, however, did not have an immediate impact. It was left to the discretion of individual Provincials to implement it as they saw fit—and many did not see fit. Carmen Vega, who was a young nun in 1964, remembered 'Aurora [a former Provincial] told us that the great Chapter for change was 1964, even more than 1967…But the Provincials returned silent, silent [*calladas, calladas*]. Here, we knew nothing of all this.'

Socorro Abel added:

> But Aurora also told us about the situation when the Mexican Provincial was killed in a car accident just as she returned from Rome. Aurora was named as the new Provincial. She received a letter from [the Superior General] setting out what had been decided at the Chapter. Point one: we no longer have enclosure. Point two: but do not give too much importance to that, so that we do not lose the spirit of enclosure. Aurora's response was, how can we have the spirit of something that no longer exists?

Despite this general downplaying of the importance of the change, for some it had instant effect. Concha Jiménez was in Brazil:

> Because of enclosure, the nuns couldn't go to the shantytowns [*las fávolas*]. If there was a problem, they'd send one of the students, or one of the alumnae. When the Provincial came back from the Chapter of 1964, at seven o'clock in the evening she gave the news of the end of enclosure at seven in the evening. At 7.30 the nuns were in the shantytowns with the children.

The question of enclosure was closely related to another central theme of the 1964 Chapter—that of a specific commitment by the Society to the poor. This was qualitatively different from the practice of operating poor schools in conjunction with fee-paying schools that had been the custom up to that time. It was the Chapter of 1964, in fact, that directed the closure of those poor schools that still existed, as they did in Spain, on the grounds that such separation only served to perpetuate an unjust system based on inequality. Over the following years, all the poor schools were closed, and their students incorporated into the main schools, which adjusted their fee-paying systems accordingly.

Like Ana María Argaya, though in slightly different words, Rosario León, one of the older nuns who later became Provincial, identified the ending of enclosure and the commitment to the poor as the most important changes in bringing about the nuns' involvement with the world: 'It's one thing to know that there are poor people. It's another thing actually to see them.'

The 1964 Chapter, then, laid the foundations for the nuns to put into practice the connection between a good life, as focused on the pursuit of their own perfection, and a good society. The commitment to the poor was phrased in terms no longer of charity but of social justice. This impetus flowed into the deliberations of the extraordinary General Chapter of 1967, which, in the light of the full documentation of Vatican II, produced a definitive text for the Society. This was the *Orientaciones ad experimentum*, officially initiating three years of experimentation. It was in two main aspects—an emphasis on community and a commitment to education for social justice—that the *Orientaciones* envisaged the most profound change in the Society's direction.

The process culminated for the Society as a whole in the General Chapter of 1970. It was the 1970 Chapter that brought the nuns comprehensively into the world. Thirteen years later, Rosario León commented on the outcome of the Chapter:

> It continues to be the most studied, the most read, the most loved by us…It was when, in reality, we throbbed, we lived [the reality of the changes], with a great hope for community, a great hope to form small groups. The great changes—in life itself—have their roots in the Chapter of 1970.

As this comment suggests, the period after 1970 was one of energy, of rupture, of passionate commitment but also of resistance to change, and of conflict and confrontation. It was Rosario León who, when she was made Provincial in 1971 after spending a year working in Galicia, encouraged and facilitated the moves away from the traditional communities into *pisos* and alternative community work. When Ana María Argaya returned to Spain in the summer of 1971 after several years at the Society's central house in Rome and having presided over the 1970 Chapter, she was 'astounded. I saw such changes, in the way of living, of acting, of dressing—of everything; such very, very great changes that I was shocked'.

# The new order: Modernisation for the Society and for Spain

The three years of 'experimentation' coincided with a period of significant social change in Spain itself. This was the time when public opposition to the Franco regime was beginning to gather strength. As the nuns moved out to encounter the world, what they found was a society based on repression and inequality, with extensive poverty and underdevelopment. These were the conditions that the government technocrats were attempting to address in their 'plan of economic and social development', designed to cover the period 1964–67.[32] There followed a period of planned economic change and unplanned social stirrings brought about by the burgeoning of an 'economic miracle'. Some Spaniards began to enjoy prosperity after two decades of privation and repression. Others found their lives disrupted. There was a restructuring of industry and, for the first time, industrialisation was undertaken on a broad national base. This was accompanied by a process of economic modernisation.[33] The result was that Spain's economic base changed from a predominantly agricultural to an industrial one. By 1965, the factory was overtaking the farm as the leading employer of labour. Accompanying this change was a flight from the land. Between 1960 and 1975, five million people left the land for the industrial towns and the tourist regions.[34]

At the same time, Franco maintained strong central control and continued to suppress opposition and any moves to regional autonomy. The Civil War had been followed by widespread executions; an unknown number of Republican prisoners had died in constructing such monuments as the massive stone cross and monastery and the underground basilica of the Valley of the Fallen (*Valle de los Ca□dos*). But the regime was attempting to improve its international image and standing. The effort was without consistency. While tourism was becoming a serious industry, in 1962 the Communist Julián Grimau García was arrested and tortured. In 1963, despite international outrage, he was executed by firing squad. A few months later, two young anarchists were also tortured and executed, this time by the *garrotte vil*, an iron collar that slowly strangled them to death.[35] Repression continued in Catalonia and the Basque provinces, with the use of both languages forbidden. The year 1959 marked the birth of the violent resistance movement Euzkadi Ta Azkatasuna (ETA: Basque Homeland and Freedom).[36] Even Franco's home province of Galicia was denied any special recognition.

---

32   de Blaye (1976: 215).
33   Lieberman (1982: 7–8).
34   Harrison (1978: 150).
35   de Blaye (1976: 216–21).
36   ibid., p. 250.

For many of the nuns, what some referred to as their religious awakening was the very instrument of their political awakening. It was indeed the growing realisation of the political aspects of their commitment to social justice that marks perhaps the strongest difference between the women of the post–Civil War generation and many of the older nuns. Bourdieu suggests that central to the question of generational differences are different definitions of the impossible, the possible, and the probable:[37]

> Generation conflicts oppose not age-classes separated by natural properties, but habitus which have been produced by…conditions of existence which, in imposing different definitions of the impossible, the possible, and the probable, cause one group to experience as natural or reasonable practices or aspirations which another group finds unthinkable or scandalous, and vice versa.

For the older nuns, their experience of religious life, and of what they understood as a good life, had been forged in the deep traditions of the Church and the Society of the Sacred Heart and in the context of the Second Republic and the Civil War. The experience of the younger women of the traditional forms of religious life was direct and significant, but not as formative as that of the older nuns, and their knowledge of those critical historical events was at a distance. Their different definitions of the natural or reasonable were reflected in their different initial responses to the unthinkable, to what had seemed the impossibility of change, and to a very different concept of a good life and of a good society.

For a group of the older nuns, their first venture after the ending of enclosure was to the *Cerro de los Ángeles*. For many of the younger nuns, there began a questioning about aspects of what they had previously taken for granted. But habitus is not wholly definitive and the distinctions are not absolute. The questioning by the younger nuns opened the issues for some of the older nuns. For Rosario León, herself one of the Civil War generation, this kind of openness was a welcome novelty:

> That was when we began to criticise the hierarchy. I remember the first feeling, the first time—I still remember it—when I heard a serious criticism of the hierarchy. It was just—I'd never heard a criticism. Listen [whispering], I was forty-five years old, and I'd never heard a criticism of anything. And the first time that I saw, in a perfectly quiet way, a perfectly calm way, a criticism, based on the gospel, of the power of the Church, it was—I don't know…

Concha Varela had an equally embarrassing recollection:

---

37    Bourdieu (1979: 78).

Do you know what I did, my first year at university? I confused Luther with St Ignatius! I had the idea that Luther was such a monster, such a villain [*un bicho tan malo*], that when I read his text and commentaries, and they showed a man who was so intelligent, I said to myself that it had to be St Ignatius!

At a more material level, one of the questions asked as part of the new openness was about the geographical locations of the Society's schools: whether this aspect was, of itself, a denial of real commitment to the poor. Many struggled to reconcile a personal commitment to poverty with a life lived in enormous and often beautiful buildings, which ensured that they lacked for no material things. Many became acutely aware of the discrepancy between the siting of their schools and convents in affluent and predominantly urban areas when the critical social problems of the country were socially and geographically elsewhere.

# From dictatorship to democracy

In many ways, the personal histories of the nuns, especially of those of the post–Civil War generation, are part of a broader movement in which parts of the Spanish Church also became radicalised. A lead was taken in 1958–59 by two workers' organisations that were also Catholic Action groups: the Workers' Brotherhood of Catholic Action (Hermandad Obrera de Acción Católica, HOAC) and the Young Catholic Workers (Juventud Obrera Católica, JOC). HOAC provided the necessary shelter from which the far more radical—and illegal— Workers' Commissions were to emerge. In May 1960, a group of 339 priests from the Basque provinces and Navarre wrote a joint letter to their bishops denouncing police brutality and the complicity of the Church with the state. Dom Aureli Escarré, the 'red' Abbot of Montserrat, was forced into exile in 1965 as a result of his outspokenness against the repressiveness of the regime.[38] In Barcelona in May 1966, 130 priests and religious marched in silent protest against police maltreatment of a student.[39] The Bishop of Bilbao, Antonio Añoveros, consistently opposed the regime over its repressive policies towards the Basques. In retaliation, he was placed under house arrest in 1974 and an attempt was made to force him to leave the country.[40] This criticism of the regime was far from universal throughout the Spanish Church, but it was supported by the publication in 1961 of John XXIII's encyclical *Mater et Magistra* (*On Christianity and Social Progress*). The encyclical prefigured many of the issues dealt with by

---

38    de Blaye (1976: 242–4).
39    Fundación FOESSA (1976: 536).
40    Carr (1983: 737); Preston (2004: 290).

Vatican II and were taken up in the Council documents. They covered matters such as a just wage, balancing economic development and social progress, the demands of the common good, taxation, credit banks, and social responsibility.

Opposition to the regime came increasingly also, not just from pockets within the Church, but more broadly from across the country. The years between 1969, when Franco finally announced Prince Juan Carlos to be his successor as Head of State, and the death of *el Caudillo* (the Leader) at the end of 1975, were marked by strikes, demonstrations, arrests and banishments. The year 1970 began with strikes by 14 000 Asturian miners, 10 000 agricultural workers in the province of Jerez, 2600 shipyard workers in Cadiz, 3000 Basque metal workers, and 500 public transport workers in Las Palmas in the Canary Islands.[41] Some 817 strikes were officially recorded over the whole of 1970, despite strikes being illegal and strikers liable to prison sentences. Among these strikes was the first national day of action, called by the Workers' Commissions and involving a large number of workers—between 25 000 (the official estimate) and 50 000 (the commissions' estimate)—in Catalonia, the Basque Country, Madrid, Seville and Galicia.[42] 1970 was also the year of the Burgos trial: the trial of 16 Basque activists, including two priests, which unfolded as a trial of the regime.[43] In December 1973, a few days before Christmas, ETA carried out one of its most spectacular assassinations, that of the Prime Minister, Admiral Carrero Blanco. His car was blown up, as he returned from daily mass, by explosives buried beneath the Calle Claudio Coello. The force of the blast blew the car over the roof of the Jesuits' house on to a second-floor terrace in the next street. The explosion left a crater measuring 4 by 10 m.[44] In April 1974, the Portuguese dictatorship came to an end through peaceful revolution involving young military officers, an event that sent shock waves through the Spanish right.

Predictably, these events provoked a hardening of attitude by both the Government and the military. Other right-wing groups took fright, including the Falangists—the Spanish fascist party formed by José Antonio de Rivera in 1933—and those surrounding Franco's wife, Doña Carmen Polo y Martínez Valdés.[45] As Franco became increasingly frail and ill, there was much manoeuvring to entrench a hardline succession. This included an expectation that King Juan Carlos would cede effective power to the last Franco prime minister, Carlos Arias Navarro, and his cabinet. Arias's nickname from the Civil War was 'the Butcher of Malaga'.[46] Having stood in the shadow of Franco since he was a boy of eleven, the new King commanded some popularity but little respect. Santiago Carrillo,

---

41    de Blaye (1976: 272–3).
42    ibid., pp. 277–9.
43    ibid., pp. 281–323.
44    ibid., pp. 363–4; Preston (2004: 278).
45    Preston (2004: 284–8).
46    ibid., p. 277.

leader of the Spanish Communist Party, dubbed him 'Juan Carlos the Brief', a nickname that Carrillo himself was the first to reject in a remarkable speech recognising the King's crucial subsequent role in overseeing the transition from dictatorship to a constitutional monarchy and to democracy.[47]

The transition was far from smooth. Juan Carlos inherited a distrustful and distrusted prime minister. It was not until July 1976 that Arias finally resigned and the King was able to appoint his own choice for prime minister, Adolfo Suárez González. Although their partnership faced its own difficulties, the two men together steered the reforms necessary to achieve democracy. This included legislation in 1976 for the legalisation of political parties, with the initial exception of the Communist Party. Legalisation of the Communist Party came about in April 1977, when the Supreme Court ruled that there was nothing to prevent the inclusion of the Communist Party in the Register of Political Associations, causing outrage on the right. The year 1977 also saw the emergence of an allegedly Marxist-Leninist splinter group, Grupos de Resistencia Antifascista Primero de Octubre (GRAPO: Anti-Fascist Resistance Groups of the First of October), who engaged in violent acts of bombing and kidnapping. In January, right-wing groups murdered five people, four of whom were Communist labour lawyers, in an office of the Atocha district of Madrid. One of the murdered men was a cousin of a teacher at Chamartin.

On the same day as the Atocha massacre, a number of senior military officers met in Madrid to call for the resignation of the Government.[48] This meeting was just one of a number of attempts by the military over this second democratic experiment—el golpismo, the ongoing threat of a coup—to reinstall el Franquismo. Despite this very real and continuing threat, the first democratic elections were held in June 1977. Some 80 per cent of registered voters turned out to vote. The highest percentage went to Suárez's party, the Unión de Centro Democrática (UCD), and the next highest to the Socialist Party, the PSOE, under its leader, Felipe González. The Communist Party received 9.3 per cent of the vote.

In 1978, the Constitution drafted by the elected Cortes included Article 1(3), which stated that 'the political form of the Spanish State is a parliamentary democracy'. This reflected not just the view of the parliamentarians but also the direct commitment of King Juan Carlos to the consolidation of democracy.[49] The Constitution was ratified, first by the Chamber of Deputies and the Senate and, on 6 December, by a constitutional referendum. The only significant exception to this popular ratification was the Basque Country. But there had

---

47    ibid., p. 416.
48    ibid., pp. 380, 384.
49    ibid., pp. 400, 416–17.

been another unsuccessful attempt by the military to derail this process. One of the key plotters was Colonel Antonio Tejero Molina of the Civil Guard in what became known as *Operación Galaxia* after the Madrid café where the plotters met.[50] In March 1979, there were further general elections, in which Suárez's UCD again achieved the highest number of votes. Two years later, however, Suárez resigned. The party elected Leopoldo Calvo Sotelo—grandson of José Calvo Sotelo, whose murder had been the immediate excuse for the Nationalist rebellion in 1936—to replace Suárez as leader of the party and prime minister. In an act of delicious irony, it was while the Cortes was considering the Calvo Sotelo nomination that Tejero staged his attempted coup, on 23 February.

The failure of the coup, the active intervention of the King and the subsequent massive demonstration of people in support of democracy reflected the continuing stain on Spanish memory of the bloodshed during and after the Civil War. I hold dear the image of those demonstrators, my introduction to Spain, walking through the Madrid rain on a cold winter's night. An equally vivid image is one from 18 months later, on the eve of the general elections of 28 October. We went, along with thousands of others, to the rally in the grounds of the Complutense University of Madrid. Among other songs, Joan Manuel Serrat sang *Para la Libertad*—'for freedom, I bleed, I fight, I survive'—one of the poems of Miguel Hernández, who died as a Republican prisoner in a Nationalist jail in 1942. Because most Spaniards had a cigarette lighter, the sports arena came alight with tens of thousands of flames as the audience joined in the singing. In the elections the next day, the Socialist Party won an overwhelming majority, with 47.26 of the vote. For the first time, Spain had a democratically elected Socialist government and Felipe González became Prime Minister, a position he and the PSOE held through the next 14 years and three elections. The third Spanish attempt at democracy was successful and the ghosts of the Civil War were finally laid to rest.[51] Almost. With great honesty and generosity, Rosario León expressed the ambiguities of many of the nuns of her generation:

> I tell myself that I have to think with my head that socialism has to be a very good thing. But my own emotional character [*sensibilidad*] is of the old style. Sometimes, I can accept things with my head, but they don't feel good emotionally. Even today there are those of us who have lived certain things, with fearful horror. They came looking for my father. They were looking for him to kill him. And my mother said to him, 'Where you go, I will go'. That left us, poor things, moving from one place to another, one place to another, until the war ended.

Modernity, along with war, has its own costs.

---

50   ibid., p. 423.
51   Tremlett (2007) nevertheless makes clear that, in Spain, as in Thailand, there remains unfinished business. His book focuses on the exhumation, begun in 2000, of bodies buried in unmarked mass graves during the Spanish Civil War and the associated *pacto del olvido* (the pact of forgetting).

# 5. *'Quiero ser protagonista de mi vida'*: 'I want to be the main actor in my own life'

Pursuit of the principle of social justice after Vatican II took the form, for many of the nuns, of what they called *inserción*: involvement in the world, taking seriously the moral imperatives arising from the bond of common humanity. This process itself, in a reversal of that affecting the Thai factory workers, led to their redefining of what they understood as a good life. Central to this redefinition was a profound shift in their understanding of the relationship between the religious and the secular, brought about by a deeper engagement with social justice as human rights. In the process, the nuns' deeply personal understanding of the relationship between 'selfhood and the good, or…selfhood and morality',[1] underwent a transformation. After that, there could be no going back. These changes in traditional understanding and living proved too radical for some of the nuns and, ultimately, for the Roman Church itself. The return to conservatism under Pope John Paul II had repercussions for the Society of the Sacred Heart, exacerbating tensions within the Society and between the Society and Rome.

## Action

The chicken served by María Ángeles for the main meal of the day was made tender by its cooking with lemon and white wine. Unlike members of many others of the *piso* communities, her small community worked close enough to their apartment to come together from time to time for the midday meal. Socorro Abel taught in one of the Congregation's schools, but with flexible hours. Carmen Vega also taught, but in their local parish. María Ángeles herself undertook voluntary work in the parish. We sat around the circular table in what served as a dining room and chatted about the day's events and the plans for a new building to replace the creatively improvised ground-floor space that served as the parish church. The scene of comfortable domesticity—so different from the formal asceticism of their earlier years in the convent—delineated the ease with which these women had made the transition from the austerity of

---

1  Taylor (2003: 3).

a monastic religious ideal to an affirmation of ordinary life.[2] They had done this by shifting their understanding of the sacred and putting humanity at the centre of their lives.

This was a very different process from that of the Bang Khen factory workers. The links between the two groups exist only in the space created by modernity, and by modernity's demand that people recognise their common bond as human, and that they re-evaluate their past in relation to the present. The nuns with whom I worked in Spain were very actively engaged in that process.

In Spain in the early 1980s, the number of nuns in the Society was just under one thousand. They were divided into two administrative provinces: the North and the Centre-South. The North, which had some 450 members, included the geographical provinces or regions of Catalonia, the Basque Country, Navarre, Aragon, Valencia, Almeria and Mallorca. The Northern Province, like its regions of Catalonia and the Basque Country in relation to the rest of Spain, had a reputation for progressiveness in relation to its sister province of the Centre-South. This latter province, centred in Madrid, numbered around 500 members, and united the geographical provinces or regions of Madrid, Soria, Eastern Andalusia, Western Andalusia, Galicia, the Canary Islands and Portugal.

Living as I did in Madrid, my main, though not exclusive, focus was on the Centre-South Province, particularly the 19 residential units or communities in Madrid itself. Those living in Madrid accounted for almost half—240—of the numbers in the province as a whole. By the time of our arrival in February 1981, the nuns had experienced a decade of the Society's new directions. To some extent, therefore, the changes arising out of the General Chapters of 1964, 1967 and 1970 had been consolidated. Some of the nuns continued living in communities in their traditional convents, but in small rather than large communities. By 1981, there were seven communities in the Chamartin complex, four in the smallest community and 25 in the largest. Some of the nuns continued to wear the religious habit; many others did not. Some continued to teach in the Society's schools; others were involved in parish, diocesan or secular work. There were six *piso* communities. At the same time, the province was again experiencing considerable tension in the face of a growing reaction, from within and without, against the form and extent of the changes.

## Reaction

This reaction came from a number of quarters. One was a further General Chapter of the Society in 1976. This Chapter was seen by many as an opportunity to take

---

2  ibid., pp. 216–18.

stock, to stop and reflect on what had happened in the previous decade and the implications of this for a redefinition of the Society's own reality. Many in Madrid, however, saw the result as the beginning of a process of what they called 'involution'. Secondly, in 1978 the Polish Pope, John Paul II, had succeeded Paul VI's successor, John Paul I, whose brief papacy lasted a mere 33 days. John Paul II disapproved of many of the changes in women's religious orders since Vatican II, a disapproval that was expressed most immediately in his pressure for them to resume the religious habit and to return to living in traditional hierarchical communities. Thirdly, also in 1978, a new Provincial was appointed to the Centre-South Province. One of the post–Civil War generation, Dolores Álvarez Román was nevertheless committed to reasserting and reinforcing an institutional model for the province that would allow for more centralised control.

Her concern for the future of the province, and more broadly for the Society of the Sacred Heart as a whole, was not without foundation. This was made clear when the nuns met in Rome for the 1982 General Chapter. In that year, the General Chapter was called to finalise the new constitutions of the Society that had been required by the Vatican Council. Because of the internationality of the Society, communities do not come directly under diocesan jurisdiction, but they are subject to Rome. The new constitutions had to be submitted to the Vatican's Sacred Congregation for Religious if the Society was to continue as a juridically constituted apostolic body. The delegates to the Chapter met knowing that the Sacred Congregation would not ratify the constitutions if they did not contain explicit provisions to matters such as the habit, a local Superior for each community, and at least one formal hour of daily prayer.

When the delegates arrived in Rome they found that, for the first time in the recent history of women's religious orders in general, not just in the Society, the Sacred Congregation had appointed an observer to the Chapter. In fact, there were two observers, both priests. The first lasted only a matter of days, and aroused such hostility among the nuns that he voluntarily left and was replaced. The second proved a happier choice and, as the Chapter progressed, became a friend to many. Nevertheless, MariVí Muñoz, like the other delegates, was fully aware that

> this was a huge matter [*gordísima*]. It was as much as to say that the Sacred Congregation had thought: 'They're not sufficiently mature to form new constitutions, they don't have enough [true] spirit. We must supervise them'…Honestly, they really hate us terribly [*a muerte*]…As we say in Spain, they have us already judged. I think that because we were among the first who perhaps broke many things, that that created an appalling image [*imagen nefasta*] of us in the Sacred Congregation: terrible, frightful. The priest who did come to the Chapter finally told

us, after we'd become friends—in fact, he turned out to be a really good and delightful person—he confessed that, of course, he'd come with an idea of us, that we were, that we had no spirit, that religious life didn't matter to us at all, that we never prayed. That's the idea that they have of us. So of course he was very surprised when he saw that we prayed, that we had spirit, that we had very good warm and fraternal relations amongst ourselves; when he saw that we respected each other very much, [and] saw the cultural level—these things left him very impressed.

But of course—and this is the critical point—I think that many of the things that weren't discussed during the Chapter or that were accepted [were] with the understanding that we were in grave danger of dissolution. That's to say, that the Sacred Congregation—I don't know if the Church would actually dare to do it—but certainly, that they wouldn't approve the Constitutions, or that they'd do to us, for example, what they did to the Jesuits: impose on us a Superior General. I don't know, something dreadful—someone from Florence [an ultra-conservative community]! Or something like that—appalling. This was a condition that had enormous influence—including [with] the groups who'd arrived at the Chapter with a more critical attitude, from Latin America, for example. When they saw the situation, its effect was to make them say: 'Look out, we're at a very important point here, this is more serious than we thought, we can't make judgments.' Mind you, it united us very much, so that there was a kind of consensus not to create problems that were not, in the last analysis, fundamental, and in exchange, to leave the doors open. That's to say, let's pass over all those things that we wouldn't have passed over in another moment, that we would have done battle over, but, given the gravity of the situation, that they've sent an observer, we'll hold back.

The delegates also saw for themselves the personal cost to those who had been involved in the central government of the Society in Rome over the period since 1970. A number of the members of their General Council had become ill, and delegates to the 1982 Chapter saw Charo Galache, the Superior General, as under particular stress. This also influenced the deliberations of the delegates. They knew that John Paul II himself, on a number of occasions when he held an audience with nuns, had expressed his displeasure to the Superior General at the fact that these nuns of the Society no longer wore the religious habit. But people outside Rome had not realised the extent of the personal toll. MariVí Muñoz also commented:

The key to many things from the 1982 Chapter is the bad relation that we've had with the Sacred Congregation. It's just terrible, the persecution that Charo has suffered from them. It was a factor that had a lot of influence in making us tread carefully, to see Charo, whom everyone loved—I've never known anyone so universally loved as she was—under such pressure. We felt we couldn't put those in government in such a confrontationist position with the Sacred Congregation. We felt that if, without closing any doors, or at least, trying to make things broad enough...

The 1982 Chapter was also influenced by the wish to accommodate those in the Society itself who, far from embracing change, had been scandalised and alienated. For them, the changes had been a denial of authentic religious values; reinterpretation was not renewal but rejection. The convent in Florence represented the most extreme position. The Florence community had gone into what might be called a gradual schism from the rest of the Society in the years after the 1970 Chapter. In order to distance themselves entirely from developments in the Society, they appealed directly to the Sacred Congregation for Religious for individual juridical status. In an ironic counterpoint to the Society's own move to experimentation, the Sacred Congregation gave the Florence community permission to continue within the Society in a 'mode [régimen] of experimentation'. Further, in order to promote the traditions that they saw as essential, they had asked for permission to open a novitiate. This was consistently refused under Pope Paul VI, but was finally granted by John Paul II. In the event, they only had two novices: a German who left after a month, and an Italian. John Paul II's granting of this permission was indicative of the change for the worse in relations between the Society and the Vatican under this pope.

The developments in Florence had some repercussions in Spain. Two of the nuns from the Centre-South Province took refuge with the Florence community. On their return to Madrid, they asked for exclaustration from the province in order to depend directly on the Cardinal of Toledo. Two others afterwards joined them, and the four formed a community of their own. One of these was a widow who had entered the Society some years after her daughter had done so. The daughter was one of those who had left the Society during its period of most tumultuous change and had later married. Her mother blamed the Society for having 'ruined' (estropeado) her and chose to join the Toledo community as part of her continuing anger and hostility.

The status of exclaustration granted to the women in the Toledo community placed them outside the jurisdiction of the province but gave them the option of rejoining the Society if they ever so wished. It also meant that they continued to be nuns, with vows, but dependent upon the local bishop—in this case, the cardinal—rather than upon the Society. The province continued to support them by sending translation work from time to time, and by providing occasional material help. One of the Toledo community acted as secretary to the Cardinal-Archbishop of Toledo and Primate of Spain, Marcelo González Martín, who was regarded as one of the most conservative in the country. Along with many of his fellow bishops, he strongly opposed the legalisation of divorce undertaken by the Minister of Justice in the post–coup Calvo Sotelo government. This was the Social Democrat Francisco Fernández Ordóñez.[3] In response, González Martín forbade Fernández Ordóñez from taking his traditional place in the 1981 Corpus Christi procession. This annual procession itself represented the deep conservatism of Toledo. It was led by the widows and daughters of men who had been involved in the siege of the Toledo Alcázar (fortress) in the Civil War. This was a famous episode in which the Nationalists successfully held the Alcázar against much greater Republican forces. The relief of this siege was a great publicity coup for Franco, though it probably cost him the early conquest of Madrid.

# Practical transformations: From religious to political awakenings

In a sense, then, the 1982 General Chapter was the moment that marked most clearly for the nuns the culmination of the Society's own crisis of modernity. The documents of Vatican II were as revolutionary in their impact on them as Luther's *Wittenberg Theses* had been for the Church in the sixteenth century. Vatican II also created an analogous fracturing of the nuns' present from their past. It did so by transforming the meaning of 'the world' and the nuns' relationship to it. The Council's *Dogmatic Constitution on the Church* (*Lumen Gentium*: 'The Light of the World') placed the Church—bishops, clergy, religious and laity—at the service of the world, not at enmity with it. It redefined the Church as a pilgrim, not triumphant, Church, one that 'takes on the appearance of this passing world'.[4] It stressed service, not authority. In its section on religious women and men, the Constitution on the Church foreshadowed the later document dedicated specifically to the religious life (*Perfectae Caritatis*: 'Perfect Love'): 'Let no one think that by their consecration religious have become strangers to their fellow men or useless citizens of this earthly city', and it spoke of 'the work of building up this earthly city'.[5] The *Pastoral Constitution on the Church in the Modern World* (*Gaudium et Spes*: 'Joy and Hope') built on and made even more explicit these radical shifts: for the 'followers of Christ...nothing genuinely human fails to raise an echo in their hearts...This community realises

3   Preston (2004: 489).
4   Abbott (1966: *Lumen Gentium* VII, p. 48).
5   ibid., *Lumen Gentium* VI, p. 46.

that it is truly and intimately linked with mankind and its history'.[6] It shattered the justification for separation from the world and identified the task of the Church as scrutinising 'the signs of the times…We must therefore recognise and understand the world in which we live, its expectations, its longings, and its often dramatic characteristics' as 'mankind painstakingly searches for a better world'.[7] *Gaudium et Spes* committed all the members of the Church to social justice: 'it devolves on humanity to establish a political, social, and economic order which will to an ever better extent serve mankind and help individuals as well as groups to affirm and develop the dignity proper to them'.[8]

These were the transformations in the Church to which the Society of the Sacred Heart was responding in the 1967 and 1970 General Chapters and which suddenly offered the nuns a myriad new opportunities for their action. Pope John XXIII had thrown open the windows not only of the Church but also of its convents. Vatican II invited the nuns to inhabit a new moral space and to ask new questions about 'what is good or bad, what is worth doing and what not, what has meaning and importance and what is trivial and secondary'.[9] Different groups gave different answers, resulting in a previously unthinkable diversity. Those in Florence and Toledo rejected change and sought refuge in the stern traditions of the past; but with a traditionalism that, as Morris suggests in relation to Thailand, is itself a discourse, elaborated around the fear of tradition's loss.[10] The two Spanish provinces took seriously the process of experimentation. This began slowly.

## Beginnings and transformation

MariVí Muñoz described how change began for her as a young nun. It was a very unromantic encounter with the meaning of social justice within the Society itself, where the nuns were divided into two social classes: the choir nuns, who chanted the Divine Office every day and did the Society's teaching and other professional work, and the Sisters, who did the domestic chores. The 1964 Chapter had suppressed the formal division between the two groups. In practice, the distinction lingered:

> For me, my first spark was the summer of 1967. I read, and I remember it perfectly, imagine it, a journal that the Jesuits published. I remember some articles on the religious life, and on the involvement in social life

---

6   ibid., *Gaudium et Spes*, para. 1, p. 200.
7   ibid., *Gaudium et Spes*, para. 4, p. 203.
8   ibid., *Gaudium et Spes*, para. 9, p. 206.
9   Taylor (2003: 28).
10   Morris (2002: 71).

[*la inserción social*] of religious life. That opened up new horizons for me. I went to the Superior—a woman who was very open for those times— and said that I wanted to spend a summer in social work [*un verano social*], to look for an experience of work. She said to me, 'Very well. In the mornings, you can go to the kitchen, and in the afternoons, to the laundry.' It was wonderful, because it made me understand the life of the Sisters. I realised what it was like, the whole morning in the kitchen and the afternoon in the laundry. On the first day in the laundry, when I arrived, the whole room was covered in red water, and I said, 'What's this?' They told me that the washing machine had broken down and all the water from washing the [towelling] sanitary pads had come out. The first thing I had to do was clean it all up by hand.

Other changes from this period were more substantial. In 1967, a school was opened in Seville in a predominantly gypsy area (Torreblanca). In 1968, a small group moved at the invitation of the local parish priest to open a parish school in an outer industrial area of Madrid (Torrejón de Ardoz, then also an American base). Classes were held on the ground floor of an apartment block in which the nuns lived on a floor above. In the same year, a junior college (*Colegio Menor*) was opened in Santiago de Compostela as a residence for children coming to school from the villages of Galicia. In 1969, the former novitiate in Chamartin was turned into a residence for working women. In 1970, another junior college was opened, this time in Granada, again in a gypsy area (La Chana). There the nuns also used to go to the jail every Sunday with the wives of the prisoners, whom they also helped to find work or other means of support. In 1971, the more general move into *pisos* began: Hortaleza in Madrid and Zaidín in Granada, both dormitory or working-class suburbs. A childcare centre for working-class parents was set up in Vigo, in Galicia, and another junior college, with a primary school attached (Escuela-Hogar), in Priego, a village in the province of Cordoba. In 1972, a small group of four moved to one of the poorest areas in the Canary Islands, living in the pueblo of Castillo del Romeral in the south of the Great Canary Island and teaching in the state school. In 1973, a group of three nuns joined a mixed community in San Sebastian to work in a boys' reformatory. In 1975, the community from a university college (*Colegio Mayor*) in Madrid moved to Moratalaz, popularly referred to as a *barrio rojo* (a red or Communist neighbourhood). And in 1976 and 1977, other communities rented or bought flats in Madrid.

These were also, as we have seen, the last restless years of *el Franquismo*, with strikes, student protests and the emergence of other, though still illegal, forms of political activity. Such activities often occurred in the guise of social engagement. One such form was the Neighbourhood Associations (*Associaciones de Vecinos*).

Daniel Maldonado, elected in 1977 to the Senate as a Socialist representative in the first democratic elections after Franco's death, was one of those involved in setting up the Neighbourhood Associations in Granada:

> The Neighbourhood Associations grew up after the Law of Associations was passed in 1964. They began in parishes: a little sitting room for old men, with a TV, or where they could play cards. The first ones were set up in Bilbao, and we got copies of the statutes here in Granada. The first childcare centres were set up by these associations. It was in the Seventies that they became very politicised. Because political parties still hadn't been legalised, they used the Neighbourhood Associations as their platform.

Manu Negrín worked closely with Daniel Maldonado over this period:

> The Neighbourhood Associations began precisely in order to change society, to make people aware [*concientizar*] of injustice.[11] It's for that reason that I think a lot of the young nuns, the ones who were questioning, got involved in the associations, because they were responding to the gospel. All the people working in the associations were working for the same objectives. I was living in the girls' residence in La Chana, and I thought that to be a religious in a *barrio* either has meaning or doesn't have meaning. If it's to have meaning then it's only because you live the life of the people in the *barrio*. That's how I got involved in the Neighbourhood Association.
>
> In theory the associations had a certain legality, but in practice, no. The committee met every week, the association every fortnight or so. They had to send the agenda beforehand to the governor, or the mayor—I don't remember—with the date, the place, the time, and they couldn't change anything important afterwards. The police always came to supervise the meetings.
>
> What the associations tried to do was to improve the material and social conditions of the people. We began two childcare centres: one on another floor of the same building as the residence, and one other. They were begun to help mothers who had to go out to work. There are a lot of these, and there are a lot of gypsies in the *barrio*. We tried to help them by looking for work and getting them jobs.

As with MariVí Muñoz, however, Manu's romantic notions were quickly put to the test through her involvement:

---

11   This concept and educational process were elaborated in the work of Brazilian educator Paulo Freire.

One day I saw one of the gypsies, one of the mothers from the childcare centre, begging at the door of the church. I asked her why she was begging, and she told me she had no money. I said, 'Come to our house. You can clean the things we never have time to do—the windows, and the curtains—and we'll pay you.' 'How much?' she said. 'A thousand pesetas.' 'A thousand?! I can get 3000 begging. And on top of it all, I'd have to work!'

At the same time, in moving out of their big convents in the main urban centres, some of the nuns made the connection between the social and economic disadvantage of rural areas and the political struggle for autonomy. Mari Carmen Jiménez Delgado was later described by Rosario León as 'one of the most radical' of the nuns. Mari Carmen explained:

When I arrived in Galicia in 1971, I came up against the reality of extreme underdevelopment, at all levels. I'd asked to be sent to the overseas missions, but I came to understand that my true mission was in Galicia, a world that had been abandoned by so many religious. Simply, I felt a vocation; I felt a personal call to work with people in the rural areas.

Rosario León remembered: 'And Mari Carmen—I've seen her waving the flag of the most radical party in Galicia, surrounded by a circle of children and parents and other people from the region. That was giving people the service that they asked for.'

Perhaps the most dramatic initiative in these years was that in Castillo del Romeral, in the Canary Islands. For Paloma Morales, her experience there was 'a conversion' and she recounted it, and what it had meant, at length:

For me, what was fundamental was the Chapter of 1970. In 1970, I was sent to Las Palmas. I had a year in the school, as a class teacher. In the first Holy Week, two of us went to a pueblo in the south of the island. We got involved in a shanty settlement; we were in one of the shanties [*chábolas*]. For me, that was my major conversion. We stayed with a family, we had a room at the side, the roof was of that sort of paper, cartons, or paper of those bags of flour that has a very thick, strong paper. We had some mattresses, nothing else.

So there we were in Holy Week, in a shanty with some of the parents; we ate together, had dinner together, we spent time with the children, we prepared all the celebrations. They were wonderful days. Of course, there was no water, no toilets, no light, nothing. In the shanty we had nothing. And that really made me think a lot, really a lot, in actuality with how little it's possible to live. And those people, even within the exploitation to which they have to submit, when they have what is fundamental—that is, love—then they're happy. The settlement is only a quarter of an hour by road, 12 or 15 kilometres, from the hotels, the swimming pools, the lights. And I said to myself, 'We are educating the children of the exploiters.' And that's impossible, it's a contradiction, it can't be. I used to be happy and very committed when we were in the schools, with those other children; we didn't know any other reality. But as soon as I went out of the convent—that great castle—and encountered another reality, knew another kind of necessity; it's an irreversible process. So from that Holy Week, everything had to change. We made inquiries, talked with people. We found that in the Canaries in the south there's a great lack of schools, there are hardly any; teachers don't want to go the pueblos, they'd rather stay in the cities.

So we began to organise our papers. Everyone told us we were mad. Even in the legal office [*la Gestoría*], they said to us: 'What on earth are you getting involved in?' It's because the southern part of Las Palmas has the reputation of being very tough, very combative, aggressive. 'You'll be living like in a town of the wild west, with one gun to defend yourselves and the other to kill.' We arrived, four of us, on 20 August 1972.

Close by, there was a settlement that was linked to the pueblo, with really foul shanties, absolutely foul. There was no school there. They had to come into our school by public transport, even the very little ones. In the beginning, they let us use some old army huts, as a loan, but there came a moment when they said no. We had to ask for prefabs, those that they make in three months. Fine, very good, the local council would make them for us, no problem. Everything was fine, everyone happy. But it turned out that the council decided not to set them up in the settlement, but in Castillo, the nearby town. We went to the bishop, not the present one, the previous one, who was useless. We got together all the small landholders, all the tomato growers, and said, 'What are we going to do?' And of course, we were still in Franco's time, so that meetings were illegal. But we made a lot of fuss to the minister and to the civil governor, and to the mayor. But when the time came for school to begin, no prefabs. Right, we got together a big meeting, in the church in Castillo that's the only place big enough, as well as the fact that it was possible to meet without danger, because it was a church. We called the mayor, asking for an explanation as to why they'd made the decision not to build the prefabs, without consultation with the people. In case he was engaged, we wrote a letter. Everyone was at the meeting, all the children—and, of course, the children surrounded by all the police that it was possible to see on the island. We called the mayor. We waited an hour, two hours. Since we were in the church, we read bits of the gospel, we prayed psalms, we sang. It wasn't to try to sublimate the situation, but to see what, in this situation, Jesus would do. What were the rights that we had to defend? Without violence, without aggression, but they are rights that belong to us. So, what should we do? Right, go and look for the mayor. But the parents said, 'As we don't want violence, or to act by force, let's wait here another hour. If he doesn't come, we'll cut the highway, the traffic on the highway.' You can imagine it, the main tourist highway, in the tourist area. It was the parents who decided it: 'Come what may, our children come first.' Honestly, it made us tremble. These were new situations for us, totally new. But obviously, just because you're a nun, you can't stay safely at home. If you're with the people then you've got to go the whole way, no? In every situation.

Right, everything was organised for the big march to the highway. We knew that the mayor would come then, obviously. So we had to organise it very well. We had to think who would be arrested—so first, we were going to have the men on the outside, and the women and children in the middle, so they wouldn't be hurt. But then we thought, no, it's we who should protect the men, so they won't be arrested. So the women and children went on the outside; there were the people from three settlements there. We'd begun the meeting in the church at four o'clock, and waited till eight. The mayor lived about a quarter of an hour away. The mayor at that time was a man manipulated by the Count who owned all that part of the island. And people who lived on that land couldn't marry without the Count's permission; and this is only 10 years ago, they couldn't marry!

So off we went to the highway, singing as we walked. We had to walk two and a half kilometres, with the children as well. When we got to the highway, the police said, 'Please, break up this meeting'. Our spokespeople were Elena, the school principal, one of the priests and one of the parents. They said, 'No. We've come peacefully. What we want is to ask for a school. But we want the mayor to come. We think he ought to come, because we gave him plenty of warning. You must understand.' Of course, the Civil Guard and the police, they said, 'And if the mayor takes a long time coming?' One of the parents said, 'We're not in a hurry. Let's sit down here.' So we began to sit down on the highway. You can imagine it, with all the cars honking. When we were just about all sitting down, the mayor appeared, I don't know where from. He must have been waiting somewhere there, don't you think? To see just how far we were prepared to go.

So there he was. He said, 'Very well, here I am. And it's night already. Why don't we go to the church?' The church was on land that belonged to the Count. So we all went to the church. We were about 2000 people. The first thing that one of the parents said was, 'We want to talk to you. But please, what we don't want are the forces of public order. This is a matter between you and us. Be kind enough to leave, all the National Police, the Civil Guard, and the secret police.' Because of course, we didn't know which ones were secret police. But in the pueblo, everyone knows each other, and the schoolchildren were saying, 'This one doesn't belong to the pueblo, and this one'. So the children got rid of all those who didn't belong to the pueblo. It was perfectly plain that they were secret police—we could see the handcuffs in their pockets.

We closed the door, and there we were, with the mayor—and of course, it was all very emotional. We said, 'Señor Mayor, we want to know why you're not going to make the prefabs. We want a date, and we want it within three months'—we gave him three months, because they can make prefabs in two and a half—'and we want them in this pueblo.' 'Yes, yes, yes, yes, of course, of course, of course, of course. But obviously, I have to consult others.' 'You are the highest authority in the council, so you can agree. But let's have it in writing'—off they went to find a piece of paper—'We want to ask, first, that they'll build the school in the pueblo; second, that there will be no repercussions in any of the families who are here, that there'll be no repression. And thirdly, that we can leave here peacefully to return to the pueblo. We have two and a half kilometres to go, and it's dark.

'Yes, yes, yes, yes to everything.' And that's what happened: the mayor signed, the secretary signed—and the people, obviously, they knew that identity cards are very important, you always have to put your identity card number on everything—so they said to the mayor, 'Put your identity card number.' And that's how things turned out. We left it like that and went. When we got back to the pueblo—think of it, such a wonderful, beautiful thing—when we arrived at the pueblo, on both sides, there was a crowd of people clapping us. They were the labourers who hadn't been able to come with us. The next day, we went to school, and on every corner we saw the *Pair*—secret police—watching us. We had police for a month in the pueblo.

We cut the highway on the 14th of January. In three months, we had the prefabs. And we celebrated it properly, I assure you.

The aftermath of this incident, despite the (written) assurance of the mayor, was that two of the priests and the school principal, Elena, were fined. The people of the pueblo took responsibility for paying the fines, and collected the whole amount, some 600 000 pesetas (then about A$6000). The priests refused to pay the fine, but before all the due legal processes had been completed, Franco died. Paloma Morales narrated the denouement, when the Civil Guard arrived with the news that Elena would not be fined:

> This was funny. The Civil Guard arrived in the pueblo, but didn't know where we lived. They went to one of the houses and asked, 'Where is the school principal?' The woman answered, 'That depends. If you've come to fine her, I won't tell you where she is. You've got no right, after all she's done for us, how she's helped the children. Here we manage as best we can. So if it's something bad...' The police answered, 'Calm down, calm down, señora. It's good news.' 'Well,' she said, 'you tell it to me first so I can decide.'

## Obedience and subjectivity

By the time of Franco's death in 1975 and the General Chapter of 1976, the Spanish provinces looked very different from the uniformity and stability that, despite the disruptions of the Second Republic and the Civil War, had been their hallmarks for more than a century and a half. The plunge into 'the world' had brought the nuns categorically into contact with secularity and altered the balance between the secular and the religious. Prior to Vatican II, the Society's way of life had kept the secular firmly at bay. Static religious values and interpretations of the good dominated the nuns' view of the world. This domination was maintained in many ways, but perhaps most importantly by the exercise of the vow of obedience. The practice of obedience informed every aspect of the nuns' daily lives. In so doing, it maintained the sacred hierarchy of authority and subsumed the individual into the collective. Individuals constantly strove for subordination of the will, which was also the subordination of reason. They did this routinely from the time of communal rising at 5.20 am, as set down in the Rule, through the hour of meditation based on the Exercises of St Ignatius—whose *Rules* also contained much emphasis on the virtues of obedience over reason—until the final bell of the day sounded the 'greater silence' at 9.15 pm. Failures were subject to public self-accusation or, at selected times during the annual liturgical cycle, to public accusation by others. Penances were regulated and subject to permission from the Superior. Individuals resided and worked according to the 'obedience' they were given.

Such practices could only be maintained while the nuns remained cut off from the world and convents constituted true total institutions in Goffman's sense of the term.[12] The Society's commitment to *inserción* (involvement in the

---

12   Goffman (1962).

world) brought these practices, and much of the value attached to them, to an end. At the same time, *inserción* also brought about a number of fundamental reorientations. It removed the separation of the temporal from the sacred order. It reconciled the opposition between spirit and flesh. And it redefined the standpoint from which individuals interpreted the meaning of the good, shifting, in another echo of Luther's emphasis on individual conscience, from obedience to individual judgement and choice. This was within a context not of authority but of dialogue. In terms of agency, the individual subject moved from the margins to the centre, from a diffuse subjectivity to a centred one. This was as true for the nuns of Florence and Toledo as for those in the *barrio rojo* of Moratalaz; each asserted the centrality of her individual conscience and made her own decision in the face of what would previously have been unquestioning obedience to an unquestioned authority. Ironically, despite the apparent clinging to the past, the nuns in Florence and Toledo were in this sense even more fiercely modern than their sisters in the *piso* communities, though this is not a view that they themselves would have happily accepted.

The immediate consequences of these fundamental reorientations had been expressed in the rapid move to diversity in the Spanish provinces after the General Chapters of 1967 and especially of 1970. Everything was thrown into question. Concha Heredia was asked to reorganise even the program of training for the novices. She described that time:

> Everything was spring; everything was creativity. When the changes began, no-one knew what the novitiate should be. Everyone said to us, 'We know very well what it shouldn't be, but not what it should be'. From one point of view, I was very happy, because I love creating new things. They said to us in the 1970 Chapter, 'Do whatever you think best', and I thought that was marvellous.

## Obedience and the institution

But the 1970 Chapter also introduced an unavoidable tension between the concept of dialogue and the vow of obedience, between the autonomy of the individual subjects and the collective purposes of the institution, between the secular and the religious. For those who chose to stay in the Society—and many made the choice to leave over this period—religious interpretation remained central, but it did so as a source of meaning, not as an imposition. The 1976 Chapter revealed how quickly the tension had begun to be felt. Rosario León, despite her age—she was one of the Civil War generation—struggled with it already in 1971 when she was appointed as Provincial:

After a year, I couldn't go on. I couldn't because, for example, for me, giving what we used to call an obedience is something so contrary to my way of looking at things, so contrary to my own conscience, that, frankly, I had a very bad time in this. The work itself I enjoyed—making plans, organising projects—but the point of obedience has always been for me a point that, in this day and age, I don't see as many people see it. I don't see why, because you're the Provincial, you can say to me, 'Listen, leave this place and go to that'. I see it in dialogue and it's neither you nor I, but together, that we seek what God wants.

Very soon after, Concha Heredia, one of the post–Civil War generation, had similar problems with changing expectations for the novices:

I've never felt like a person who wanted to give formation to anybody, and I've always had a big problem with spiritual direction. I don't believe in spiritual direction—maybe it's because I don't know how to do it. I really only believe in relation. It seems to me that it's life that forms you.

But then everything began to develop. They began to talk a lot about the Mistress of Novices, and I began the fight against the idea of the Mistress of Novices. We had a meeting in Rome in 1975, and I could see that things were already changing. They were talking even more of the Mistress of Novices, and that was another thing altogether. I fought a lot there, but I realised that there was no point. There was a Frenchwoman there, very structured; we had great battles, we were the two who fought the most, but I realised that now there was a different option. She didn't believe at all in working in a team, she talked always about there having to be a person with the final say: she was the Mistress of Novices. I was very amused; they presented us with plans of formation that were so complicated—all with circles, all coming and going, everything was regulated, everything was down on paper. As for me, I said, 'I'm incapable of doing all this—I haven't prepared anything, I haven't presented anything—I don't know'. It seems to me that every person is a world and that the year of the novitiate is a lost year; for some people it's useless, they've been formed by other things, an important experience, or something else altogether. We had one novice who was experiencing a great crisis of faith. How could I read texts of the Mother Foundress to someone who didn't even know if she believed in God? It was impossible. And that case proves to me that life has got nothing to do with what is put down on paper. I have very little faith in papers.

By 1976, the shock sustained by the institution and individuals as a result of the proliferation of challenges and activities caused the voice of caution to emerge more strongly. Manu Negrín was one of the Spanish delegates to the

1976 General Chapter. She went reluctantly, having spent the previous six years living and working in the gypsy quarter of La Chana in Granada and with the increasingly politicised Neighbourhood Associations. She experienced the 1976 Chapter as one that 'did me much damage. The atmosphere of the Chapter seemed to me so different from the concrete reality of our work'. A year after her return from the Chapter, she was told by the then Provincial that she was to be moved to Galicia or Seville.

> I told her that I did *not* want to do that, that I would only go if she sent me a letter ordering me to do so, for the sake of obedience. But by the time the letter arrived, I had decided that there are more important things in life than obedience. I have to be the main player [*protagonista*] in my life, my only life.

She left the Society in order to be so. Others remained, but struggled increasingly to resist the growing pressure to re-subordinate their subjectivity to an authority that attempted to reinvoke sacred legitimacy. Quite a large number negotiated this satisfactorily. Others exercised passive resistance and ignored it. For some, it provoked a crisis. By 1982, of the seven *piso* communities in Madrid, there were two types, as described by Rosario León: 'those with the blessing of the provincials and those without that blessing'. To some extent, although not completely, the distinction was based on those who had agreed to choose a local Superior and those who refused. Other important factors were whether those in the community were engaged in work that also had the blessing of the provincials, and whether they participated in the broader activities of the province. And there remained a political dimension.

Vita Bandres lived in one of the *piso* communities that enjoyed provincial blessing. They were without a local Superior, but a number of them worked in a parish school that was run by the province. They also attended general meetings with other communities of the province, including the annual spiritual retreat. Vita, along with several others of the community, was one of the Civil War generation. The daily newspaper that the community continued to buy was the Catholic *Ya*. They also comfortably referred to themselves as *las derechas* (the right-wingers), as happened when all the copies of *Ya* were stolen from the local newspaper vendor during the election campaign in 1982. Vita complained, 'I had to buy *El Pa□s*, because all the copies of *Ya* had been stolen. They don't want us, *las derechas*, to read it.' At the same time, Vita was one of the most wholeheartedly resistant to the imposition of a local Superior. For her, after a decade of living and working in a *barrio* and a parish school, the return to relations of authority represented a return to her earlier self, a self who could choose as a private motto *'Disimular, sufrir, y callar, es a Jesús amar'* ('To conceal, to suffer, to be silent, This is to love Jesus'). She rejected both that motto and that previous self with horror.

In contrast, those who lived in the *barrio rojo* both refused to have a local Superior and undertook work that they, rather than the Provincial, judged important. Nor did they normally attend official provincial reunions or activities. They maintained contact with other like-minded individuals and communities, but they were seen by many as very marginalised. Their political position was also frowned upon by many; Rosario León took the comment of one of her community of the Civil War generation to refer to Moratalaz. The comment was made on the morning after the Socialist victory in the 1982 elections: 'Now those who voted for the Socialists will have to pay for it'.

# Balancing interpretations: The effects of the 1982 General Chapter

After the 1982 General Chapter, these communities, as well as the nuns more generally, waited nervously to hear the outcome. They knew that the Vatican's Sacred Congregation for Religious had imposed an official observer and wondered what that portended about the increasing conservatism of Rome under Pope John Paul II. And they had seen the new constitutions considered at the 1982 Chapter that had required Vatican approval. These began with an affirmation of obedience to the Pope. They also knew, however, that, whatever else might change, the Society would not try to impose a return to the religious habit; as Ana María Argaya pointed out, this was a practical judgement based on the knowledge that such a directive would lead to 'massive disobedience'. The accuracy of their fear was demonstrated during the Pope's visit to Spain later in 1982. Despite the Pope's well-publicised views on religious dress, and a directive from the Spanish hierarchy that all priests were to wear the soutane if they wished to participate in audiences with the Pope, none of the nuns who normally wore secular clothes was prepared to wear the habit. Only MariVí Muñoz made a concession, as she had been chosen to read the address of welcome on behalf of the Major Superiors of women's congregations; she wore a skirt instead of her usual jeans.

By 1982, the nuns had also experienced four years of increasingly centralised provincial government under Dolores Álvarez Román. They feared that the new constitutions would reverse the direction that had been established by Vatican II and the General Chapters of 1964, 1967 and 1970. To their relief, and despite the pressure from the Vatican, this did not happen. Tere Ibarurri's response was typical of many:

> It's acceptable. It seems a bit subservient to the Sacred Congregation in legal matters, and there are things like having fixed hours for prayer. As

for Superiors, as far as I'm concerned, all Superiors are bad. But in small communities like ours, it can be someone from outside. Still, in general, it's acceptable. The problem will be with those who will interpret them.

This was a far cry from the excitement generated in 1970, but it was also a measure of Tere's previous concern. It also suggests that by 1982, as with the country as a whole, the Society of the Sacred Heart's movement into modernity was irreversible. Individuals had changed to the extent to which they had absorbed and become part of the world of the new experiences to which they had been exposed. This did not prevent a resurgence of a more conservative interpretation and practice in the province, but it did define some limits.

Nevertheless, there continued to be anxiety about the way in which Dolores Álvarez Román appeared to be focusing on rationalising institutional matters, thereby reducing the level of creative improvisation and narrowing the choices made by individuals and by communities. She told a meeting of school principals that 'the option for the poor is an option for the Society, not for each individual'. She reorganised the various financial arrangements that had developed out of the period of experimentation, specifically in the *piso* communities, where the income that the community members earned had gone primarily to support the community and its work. Instead, a limit was placed on the amount to be kept by the communities, with the rest going to the province's 'community of goods'. Individual communities would have access to this, but only by going through official channels. Despite the low-key requirement of the new constitutions that communities could choose as Superior someone from outside their own community, Dolores continued to put pressure on communities to choose a local Superior. Despite their general acceptability to the provincials, Vita Bandres's community was threatened with a Superior every year. Inmaculada López, another of the older nuns, reported after a visit from Dolores:

We were telling her how well we get on without a Superior. Every person shares some of this responsibility, one person for spiritual matters, another for whatever. And she said that that was all very good, very good, and that as a reward for how good we were, she'd give us a Superior. After that, we've had a black cloud on the horizon, but no-one has said anything further. They wrote to me one summer and asked if I would be Superior. I wrote to them and said no. In the first place, it seemed to me disastrous to take this liberty of naming me without any consultation with the community; secondly, I didn't agree with the line of government being taken; and I felt no call to take on this kind of official position.

More immediately, Dolores returned to the practice of giving people their 'obedience'. Rosario León taught in the school at Chamartin but lived in one of the communities in the other large convent in Madrid. This was a choice that she had made herself some years earlier, after the experience of living in two different *piso* communities. She explained her reasons for this choice:

> In the *piso*, I was often tired in the evening and couldn't continue working like the rest of the community. They accepted this, but it made me feel like the señora of the house. But where I am now, the community is full of old nuns, older than I am, so I can help them out in different ways. What's more, I don't mind that they're conservative, because emotionally I still am of the old style in many ways too.

Her carefully worked out commitment to this community was shattered in five minutes over a lunch period in mid June 1983. We were chatting when Rosario was called out of the staffroom by Luisa Rodríguez, the regional representative on the provincial team, and given the obedience to change not only her work, but also her community. She returned stunned from this conversation:

> They've given me my obedience. In this way! In the corridor, in a free five minutes! My work is to change schools. But they also want to change my community! It's so totally unexpected, but—what can I say? That I don't want to change? That I'm perfectly happy where I am? They want to change me to one of the Chamartin communities. They say that I can help a lot there. But I don't know. The thing is, with the old nuns, I can respect them with my heart.

Rosario's experience was not an isolated one. A number of the other nuns were given their obedience in similar summary fashion, creating an atmosphere of extreme nervousness. As a result, Concha Varela committed herself by mistake to giving a course in the summer of 1983:

> Dolores called me a few days ago. When I answered the phone, she told me that she had a proposal for me. My hair stood on end! In this very dangerous period of obediences! When she only asked me to give a course in language to the young nuns, I was so relieved I said, 'Yes, yes, yes!' And I don't want to give it at all!

Nevertheless, this confrontation with the authorities, while an important constant in people's perception and experience, gives only a partial view of the situation by 1982. In the daily life of communities, especially of those in *pisos* and working outside the Society's projects, the weight of the provincials usually rested quite lightly. Indeed, the more marginal the community, the less their presence impinged on their mundane routines, and was in general reduced to the one formal visit the provincial made annually. Luisa Rodríguez, the regional representative, was welcomed, except in the 'dangerous period of the obediences'. She tried to visit each community every one to two months.

Other events also suggested that, in the wake of the 1982 General Chapter, most of the nuns had worked out their own terms for balancing the religious and the secular, the old and the new. They continued to negotiate their own terms for doing so, despite increasing pressure to return to a level of conformity that would be imposed through the vow of obedience. At a moment when people were seeking ways to maintain the diversity of chosen paths without overt confrontation, death became a powerful commentary on the concerns of the living.

## Death and transfiguration

Early in the summer vacation of 1983, Teresa Vigón, one of the nuns from the *piso* community of Torrejón de Ardoz that had been established in 1968, died in the intensive-care unit of a Madrid public hospital. The funeral rituals contained many of the elements of both continuity and change that characterised the contemporary experience of the nuns. Teresa had suffered a heart attack three days previously during a visit to one of the Congregation's long-established houses, Santa María de Huerta, in Soria. After her death, her body was moved to the side chapel of Chamartin. There, other nuns prayed beside her body throughout the whole day, just as they had always done in the case of deaths in the past. Some of these women came from the communities of Chamartin itself; many came from other communities in Madrid, especially from the smaller groups living in *pisos*.

Teresa's death had particular significance; it was the first death of one of the members of a *piso* community and therefore, for Carmen Vega, 'a moment for solidarity'. At this moment of sadness, the Society claimed its own; people turned for comfort to one of the places where the rituals of death, lovingly simplified as they were, could be performed with the beauty and grace that had always been marks of the ceremonial life of the Society of the Sacred Heart. The resting place for the body, the house of Chamartin itself, embodied the history of the nuns' presence in Spain as well as the challenges, the dilemmas and the changes of more recent years. The convent of Santa María de Huerta where the illness first occurred was also one of the grand houses of the Society, but had become a meeting place for women from many of the widely dispersed communities. Especially during the summer, Santa María de Huerta also offered a place for spiritual withdrawal and reflection at the end of a demanding teaching year. Involvement in those activities by the nuns who participated was a way of reaffirming their commitment, not just to their particular work and individual communities but also to their common membership in the Society.

At the same time, Teresa was one of those who had seized the opportunities for change after Vatican II. She was not typical of many of the members of the Society; she did not enter the convent until she was forty-three years old and already held a doctorate in physics. In other ways she was representative of the experiences of her generation. Her family, of five brothers and four sisters, was from Asturias. In 1932, the year after the declaration of the Second Republic, she enrolled in the University of Oviedo. During the years of the Civil War, she left Spain to live with her emigrant grandparents in Buenos Aires, thus avoiding the immediate horrors, though not the ideological conflicts, of those years. Her contact with the Society of the Sacred Heart came about subsequently when she was working as a section head at the Institute of Scientific Research in Madrid and was asked to supervise the thesis of one of the nuns of the Society. She entered the Congregation in 1955, at a time when the meaning and forms of religious life seemed immutable.

These included a career path that was normal for members of the Society at that time, both in Spain and elsewhere. After two and a half years in the novitiate at Chamartin—a time when the novices numbered as many as 100—she made her first vows in 1958. She moved then through another stage of religious training— the juniorate—to take charge of the studies in the juniorate itself and of classes in the school at Chamartin. She was later sent to teach at Pío XII, another school in Madrid belonging to the Society. All these moves were undertaken within a framework of obedience.

Within this general pattern of religious development and understanding, Teresa Vigón made her final vows of poverty, chastity, obedience and stability at the central house of the Society in Rome in 1963. This, as was customary, was after a six-month period of reflection and spiritual renewal—probation—shared with a group of young nuns of the Society from around the world. Her period in Rome coincided with the sessions of Vatican II, and Teresa and her fellow probationists knew the considerations of the bishops.

Teresa herself described the changes then occurring as 'turbulent' (*choquante*). Nevertheless, in 1972 she chose, with the approval of the provincial, to join the community of Torrejón de Ardoz, an industrial area of high unemployment and, at that time, an American base. She explained her reasons:

> It was work in the school in the *barrio*. But after a lot of hassles in planning a school, they took the site from us. This led to another situation and a moment of decision. Most of the community moved away, leaving only two of us. Eventually, others joined us and we are now five. At the beginning, we continued to give classes in Pío XII in the mornings. But after four or five years, they told us there that we would have to stay for the full day, so we resigned. Our struggle was for

evening classes for external students in Torrejón. Now we have them, from 5 till 10 pm…We began with morning classes with boys and girls who had completed EGB [Educación General Básica, the eight years of compulsory schooling] without graduating. But the school threw them into the street because there were no places for them to continue. In the evening, we ran literacy classes for adults. Our objective—in all of our work here—is to avoid people being marginalised.

Teresa's own desire to undertake a particular kind of work with marginalised young people had led her to an understanding of what she saw as her own special mission within the Society and within the Church, a mission that was embodied for her in her community and work in Torrejón. This was carried out within the structures, including the exercise of obedience, that continued to operate in the province. At the same time, her option for this place and this community involved a far more direct choice on her part than her earlier assignments to teach in Chamartin and Pío XII.

As well as the Adult Education Centre, of which Teresa was principal at the time of her death, members of the Torrejón community were involved in a number of other programs. The Adult Education Centre had previously been a work belonging to the Society but was no longer so. One of the community's other main responsibilities was a Special Education Centre. Queen Sofía officially opened its new building in 1983. The Special Education Centre was run mainly under the auspices of the Association of Parents of the Handicapped, with some involvement of the Ministry of Social Security. Teresa was involved as secretary of the centre. Her death, therefore, involved not just her own community and the other members of the province, but also people in the *barrio* with whom she had worked closely in her years in Torrejón. They held their own special Mass for her the day after her death.

I had visited the Torrejón community several times, talking, sharing meals and attending their places of work. I spent a morning watching Teresa teach maths to a class of children from the *barrio*. In Australia, I had been introduced to Cuisinere, a method using coloured rods of different lengths to teach mathematical concepts and skills to primary schoolchildren. I had been excited by its potential but disappointed at the failure by teachers to exploit it fully. Teresa used Cuisinere superlatively, and it was a revelation to observe the mathematical competence of the children.

The day after her death, I spent some time with the nuns who were keeping vigil beside Teresa's body. For many, including me, it was the first time they had seen one of their members laid out for burial without being clothed in the religious habit. Instead, Teresa's head and body were covered in a white shroud, leaving her face and one hand uncovered. Her hand was laid on her breast and held her crucifix of vows, an ongoing symbol, within the radical changes that had occurred, of the religious commitment that Teresa Vigón had made and maintained as a member of the Society of the Sacred Heart to the person of Jesus Christ.

The requiem Mass was held on the following day in the main Chamartin chapel. I joined the large congregation of family, friends, nuns and students for a ritual that expressed both continuity and change. As had been the case since the implementation of Vatican II's *Constitution on the Sacred Liturgy*, the Mass was in Spanish, not in Latin. Its basic form remained the same as it had been for centuries, though with greater participation by the congregation. But unlike the solemn rituals of earlier decades, there was no rehearsed choir intoning in Latin the stern warnings of the *Dies Irae*:

> Day of wrath and doom impending,
>
> Heaven and earth in ashes ending!

Instead, the whole congregation joined in the vernacular hymns, chosen by Teresa's community to reflect her own understanding of her religious commitment in the world. The Mass began with a hymn, 'We are a people on a journey' (*un pueblo que camina*); the last expressed the new meaning of the relationship between earth and heaven:

> Towards you, holy dwelling,
>
> towards you, land of the Saviour,
>
> pilgrims, travellers, we journey towards you.

Afterwards, I drove with Socorro Duarte and others to the Cemetery of San Justo for the burial. Originally, Chamartin had its own cemetery but that had long been closed and the Society owned plots in a number of different public cemeteries. In a simple ceremony, Teresa was buried in one of these. There were fewer nuns present at the burial than at the requiem mass; their presence marked their personal friendships with Teresa and their sorrow at her loss—'one of the really good ones'. Carmen Vega, who saw herself as 'not someone who cries easily. I cried'.

Teresa's death and burial not only combined the religious and the secular. They also made clear the extent to which the religious meaning of both, and of her life as a religious, had changed since she had entered the Society. She had shared the 'religious awakening' of others in the province in the wake of Vatican II. She had translated that religious awakening into a social and political awakening in her choice to join the Torrejón community and work. She had maintained the personal commitment to social justice that she shared with the rest of her community, as well as the internal democracy of the group: they were one of the *piso* communities who refused to appoint a local Superior. She explained on one of my visits to Torrejón:

> Our purpose in coming here was in order to live community life with a small group. But this ended up being not the most important thing of all. The most important thing of all—and this is incredibly important— was that the reality of the *barrio* took hold of us. It was the people who took hold of us, their problems. It was a political moment, with the Neighbourhood Associations [*Asociaciones de Vecinos*], before the death of Franco, and we became involved.

## Autonomy and modernity

As in the rest of the province, Teresa's journey to personal autonomy was inextricably joined with political developments in Spain, with the dictatorship of Franco, its opposition and its end, with the country's program for modernisation, and with the transition to democracy. The impetus for change had certainly come from within the Church, but its realisation was also political and secular. As with her sisters', Teresa's development as an autonomous subject did not happen in isolation. It took its place and shape in relation to others. Habermas suggests that subjectivity alone is not the key principle of modernity, but rather subjectivity in communication—what he calls communicative action.[13] He argues that the knowing self finds its place not in abstract consciousness but in mutual interaction and understanding.[14] The encounter of the subject with the other is fundamental; 'one is a self only among other selves'.[15] As Teresa made clear, the definitive change for her, as for many of the nuns, arose from her encounter with different others: the working class, the poor, the marginalised, but also with the politically active. As Teresa was changing, so too were the conditions of those others with whom she was engaged. The same can be said for Paloma Morales in Las Palmas, for Mari Carmen Jiménez Delgado in Galicia, for Manu Negrín in Granada. But it can also be said of those whose transformation was less obviously dramatic but no less fundamental: Rosario León with her openness to new challenges, Socorro Duarte in her willingness to recognise the need to change, Marta de Vera in her resistance to the re-emerging regime of obedience and of greater provincial control.

By 1983, it was no longer possible for these women to sacrifice their autonomy without challenging the core values that they had come to embrace, just as

---

13   Habermas (1981, 1987).
14   Habermas (2002: 295–7).
15   Taylor (2003: 35).

it was no longer possible for Spain to return to military rule or dictatorship. The worlds of the nuns and of Spain were no longer separate worlds, and the world had moved on. The failure of Tejero's attempted coup of 23 February 1981 had proved that the country was finally on an irreversible path to democracy and modernity. King Juan Carlos had used his position and his power to define the monarchy as modern rather than traditional and to ensure the transition to democracy. Spain's residual tensions remained, with nostalgia on the right for the certainties of the past, and ETA continuing its violent campaign for Basque independence. Sections of the military continued to work for the resuscitation of their coup, but in the years following 23 February most of the officer corps had shifted to what was known as the 'prudent sector'.[16] And of course older generals finally retired and died, including failed coup plotter General Jaime Milans del Bosch, who died in Madrid in 1997.

For the nuns, too, there remained tensions between the religious and the secular interpretations of the good. These were exacerbated by the conservatism of the Church under Pope John Paul II, and by the attempts under Dolores Álvarez Román as Provincial to reimpose a narrower religious meaning on the nuns' understanding of the good. But the attempt was based on the invocation of obedience in a form that required an unquestioning submission of personal autonomy and, for some, of individual conscience. For most, this was unacceptable. It was unacceptable because they saw it as once again attempting to divorce their understanding of the good from their commitment to achieving a good society. Their belief in the possibility of a good society was founded in their religious understanding of the world, but their vision was shaped by a secular understanding of social justice. For them, a good life was no longer possible if it did not include working for a good life also for the poor and the marginalised.

Perhaps the most important achievement for these women was to integrate consciously their striving for a good society with their search for spiritual perfection. In so doing, they gave a more complex meaning to one of the key criteria of modernity: that is, that modernity 'has to create its normativity out of itself'.[17] In drawing on their moral source, the nuns refused to make a distinction between their religious beliefs and their belief in social justice and in the fundamental bond of common humanity. They had inserted themselves into the secular world in order to make it sacred.

---

16    Preston (2004: 499).
17    Habermas (1990: 7).

# Part III. Colonised people and the nation-state: Aboriginal Australia

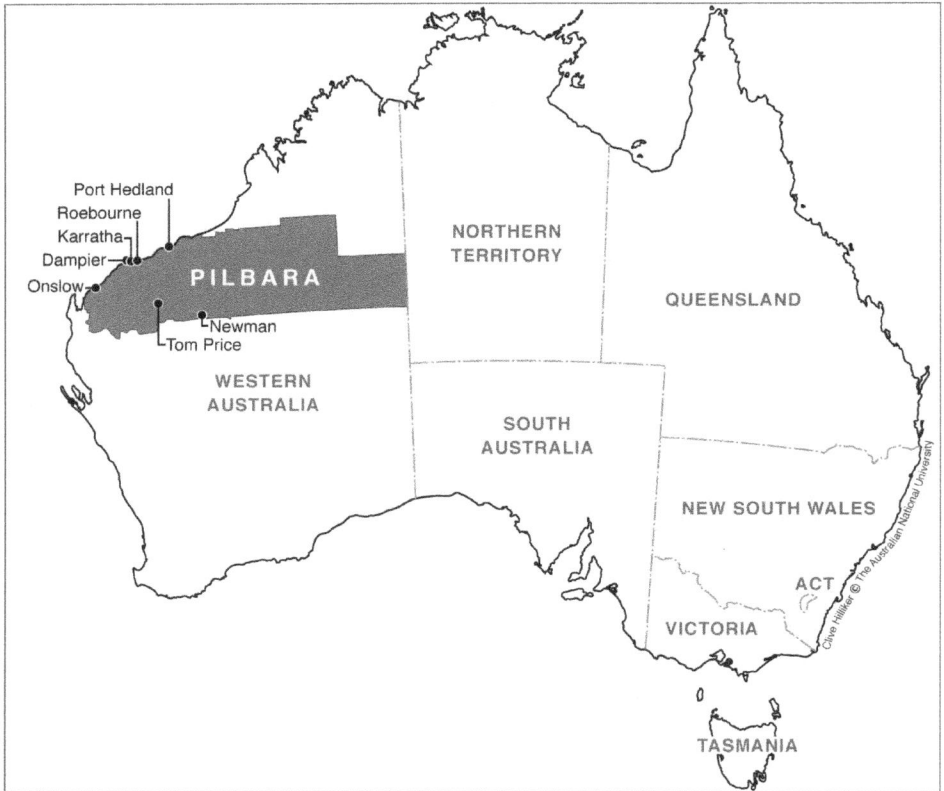

**Map 3. Australia and the Pilbara region**

# 6. Ordinary people enduring extraordinary things

For Indigenous people in Australia the encounter with modernity was produced by colonisation. This happened at different times in different parts of the country. In the Pilbara, in Western Australia, colonisation came relatively late, in the mid nineteenth century, and occurred in different stages. The pastoral industry was the first industry to be established in the region. It brought colonisation, but little modernisation. The beginning of inexorable modernisation and fragmenting of connections with the traditional past dates from the iron-ore mining boom of the 1960s. A defining experience of modernity for Pilbara Aboriginal people was marginalisation, encapsulated physically as well as socially in the town of Roebourne. A central struggle in the face of modernisation has been to maintain or re-create meaning, including what it means to have a good life, 'in the face of cultural devastation'.[1] Colonisation has meant that the meaning of a good life for Indigenous people is inextricably linked to their relationship with other Australians and to how that encapsulating group defines a good society.

## Colonisation as a vehicle of modernisation

On a humid Sunday morning in October 1987, I attended the weekly service at the Pilbara Aboriginal Church in Roebourne. The sermon was delivered by Yilbie Warrie, a senior Yindjibarndi law man and an elder in the church.[2] He presented to the congregation what he saw as the three symbols of modernisation for his people: a beer bottle, a packet of cigarettes and a can of Fanta soft drink. For him, all three were symbols of destruction and death—rampant alcoholism, wasted money and health, ravaging diabetes—and the social death arising from a loss of meaning in his people's lives. 'These,' Yilbie said, 'take our money, the kids not fed, make our people sick, die. We got a big problem. People down here drinking all the time. We tell people all the time, but nothing.' In a later public forum, he made the same point in different words: 'The Aboriginal people are now suffering. They are sick in the heart.'[3]

---

1   Lear (2008).
2   Yilbie, like a number of other Roebourne people named in this book, is now deceased. In Aboriginal custom in some parts of Australia, their names would not be used for a significant period. This is not formalised to the same extent in the Pilbara, although people often do avoid using a deceased person's name, depending on the context.
3   Johnston (1991: 1).

A few weeks before, my eldest daughter, then aged twelve, had gone with her class from the Roebourne Primary School for an end-of-term excursion to the beach close to the nearby mining town of Wickham. We had arrived in Roebourne well into the school year and she had only been at the school for a few weeks. She was therefore an outsider. As well, she was one of only three non-Aboriginal students in the class. In the way of children, her outsider status was interpreted in terms of the obvious differences, in this case, colour. When she and the other two non-Aboriginal children went to board the bus at the end of the day to come back to Roebourne, they were refused a place by the other children and told, 'This is a black bus. You shouldn't be on it.' They came home with one of the teachers.

In contrast, on another October day—as it happened, the eleventh anniversary of the 6 October massacre in Thailand—the three children and I were invited on a visit to two places outside Roebourne of particular significance to Yindjibarndi people. We went with Carol Lockyer, then an officer in the Department of Community Services and a Kuruma woman who had spent much of her life living and working in Roebourne. One of the places she took us to was Ngurrawaana, a small living area of social significance, set up in the 1980s on a lease granted by the Western Australian Government as part-compensation for the destruction of cultural sites by the building of the Harding Dam. Its aim was 'to establish an environment where Aboriginals can live without the influence of alcohol'.[4] We bumped along the 90 km of dusty pipeline road from Roebourne to Ngurrawaana. The area had been leased for 21 years by the WA Public Works Department to a group led by Yindjibarndi elder Woodley King.

Woodley was there to welcome us, as was another senior Yindjibarndi man, Allan Jacob. They took the time to show us not only the camp but also some of the surrounding country, Allan explaining to the children how the sap from one of the local trees made good cough medicine, Woodley showing us a termites' nest where they had successfully hunted an echidna. Both men talked about the importance of Ngurrawaana in allowing people to be on their own country, not just to get away from the grog, but also in order to maintain Yindjibarndi culture and law.

The second place we visited was central to that culture and law, for Yindjibarndi people, but also for other neighbouring groups who used to meet there for ceremonial and social purposes. This was the oasis of Millstream (*Ngarrari*) on the Fortescue River, the spine of Yindjibarndi country that rises back to the tableland and the Chichester Range. We picnicked with Carol in the shade of the paper bark and palm trees growing along the banks of the deep river, where the different language groups used to meet and feast. Millstream now forms part

---

4    Rules of the Ngurrawaana Group (Aboriginal Corporation) 1983, Objects of the Association, s. 6(a).

of the Millstream-Chichester National Park, but it remains of the highest sacred significance.[5] A written submission from a Roebourne group to the Seaman Aboriginal Land Inquiry in 1983 described it this way:[6] 'Our Law derives from the land itself and from certain objects and sites on the land. Our Law derives from the Millstream area and stretches throughout the Pilbara and into parts of the Kimberley.'

In addition, Woodley worried about the impact on the Millstream aquifer of the water that was being pumped out for the new mining towns. He lamented the government regulations that meant that Yindjibarndi had no special rights there, though he was glad his son could live there as a ranger for the Department of Conservation and Land Management (CALM) and have some responsibility for caring for his country.

These different incidents suggest that, for the Aboriginal people in and around Roebourne in the 1980s, modernity was crucially experienced in the first instance as alienation from their land, and an assault on the basic values and moral framework, deeply related to the land, by which they defined the good. Compounded by colonisation, modernity has also constituted the Other, at different times for both Aboriginal and non-Aboriginal people, in terms of race. This opposition was expressed in its simplest form by the children from the Roebourne Primary School. More radically, it was constructed from the beginning of colonisation by the process of colonisation itself.

# Constructing the Other: The first colonisation, 1866–1960

Colonisation came later to the Pilbara than to many other parts of Australia, including more southern regions of Western Australia. Remote as it was from the centres of settlement, it became of interest only in the second half of the nineteenth century. The first pastoralists arrived in 1864. The town of Roebourne was established in 1866 to service their needs. The site for Roebourne was chosen for two reasons: it was the only place in the area with a secure freshwater supply, and it was reasonably close to a suitable harbour at Cossack. The fresh water came from the Harding River, *Ngurin* to Ngarluma people on whose country the towns of both Roebourne and Cossack were built. It was therefore the coastal Ngarluma and the Yaburara, a possible Ngarluma subgroup and their

---

5   Seaman (1984: 71).
6   Mount Welcome Pastoral Company Proprietary Limited, 14 September 1983.

immediate neighbours on the Burrup Peninsula and adjacent islands, who bore the brunt of displacement and dispossession, and of introduced diseases, from this first wave of colonisation. Hasluck cites early reports:[7]

> One of the earliest reports of the first Resident Magistrate at Roebourne, in 1866…described how numbers of natives were dying from a disease and that their bodies were to be seen lying about the countryside. Another account declared that this 'smallpox' 'carried them off in hundreds if not thousands' and an early settler in the district, speaking in retrospect in after years, said, 'We lost one half of them through it'.

Ngarluma people were also among the first in the region to join other Aboriginal people used for the dangerous work of diving in the nascent but rapidly expanding pearling industry. By 1875, just a decade after the establishment of the two towns, 57 pearling vessels were licensed at Cossack and the number of Aboriginal divers employed by them, either voluntarily or by force, was 493.[8] Over the same decade, pastoral leases had been granted over most of Ngarluma land and, by the end of the nineteenth century, further inland over much of Yindjibarndi, Kuruma and Bunjima country. The permanent fresh water of Ngarrari was incorporated into Millstream Station as early as 1866. By 1868, within two years of the arrival of the first colonists, almost 1.2 million ha of land had been leased.[9]

# The pastoral industry

The establishment of stations, mainly for running sheep, nevertheless had a less destructive impact on local Aboriginal groups than other forms of settlement, for two main reasons. The first was that the stations were huge and unpopulated other than round the small area of the homestead, and all pastoral leases in Western Australia issued under the Land Regulations of 1864, and subsequently under other land regulations—the *Land Act 1898 (WA)* and the *Land Act 1933 (WA)*[10]—contained a reservation in favour of Aboriginal people. This allowed[11] 'full right to the Aboriginal natives of the said Colony at all times to enter upon

---

7   Hasluck (1970: 104).
8   de la Rue (1979: 77).
9   ibid., pp. 23, 24.
10   In fact, the *Land Act* of 1933 omitted this provision when first enacted. It was amended in 1934 to include the reservation by adding a subsection (2) to Section 106. This 'window' for pastoral leases without the reservation became an important issue when the courts came to decide on pastoral leases in native title claims in Western Australia, including in the Ngarluma Yindjibarndi claim that will be dealt with in Chapter 7.
11   Land Regulations 1882, 11th Schedule.

any unenclosed or enclosed but otherwise unimproved part of the [subject land] for the purpose of seeking their subsistence therefrom in their accustomed manner'.

The reservation meant that local groups could still have access to extensive areas of their country for hunting and foraging, and for meetings and ceremony. It did not mean that the early encounter between pastoralists and Aboriginal people was benign. Hasluck characterises it as marked for the European settlers by 'distrust, intolerance and determination that firm measures were essential'.[12] He supports this view by quoting Walter Padbury, who reached the mouth of the Harding River in 1863 and was granted one of the first pastoral leases in the area:[13] Padbury 'recounts that when he established his first station in the North-West, "my last words to Charlie Nairne (his manager) when I shook hands with him were, 'If you find the natives too troublesome you must shoot at them'"'.

In later years, his opinion reflected a fairly typical frontier history:[14]

> Let the Government have their resident magistrate and such police as they can afford in each district. But the pioneers and outside settlers must and will be the people to fight and subdue the natives, and the question is are we or the natives to be masters? And the sooner that question in each new district is settled, the less bloodshed there will be—the less expense and the greater security to property.

The second circumstance that made the establishment of stations a relatively benign form of settlement was that, in a region that they found isolated, uncertain and very difficult, many of the new settlers realised that, if they were to succeed, they would need the labour of the local Aboriginal people. Their knowledge of the country, their proximity and the government ban on the employment of convicts and ticket-of-leave men north of the Murchison River[15] persuaded the pastoralists to offer food, tobacco and medicine not only to potential workers but also to their extended family groups. In this way, the pastoral culture of the region developed, as elsewhere, with the pastoralists dependent on their Aboriginal workers and with the workers continuing to live with their own groups, maintaining their kin and social relations and obligations, and working on their own country. In the wet season, from around November to February, the quiet work time coincided with traditional ceremonial and social gatherings, and the Aboriginal workers were able to carry

---

12    Hasluck (1970: 177).
13    ibid., p. 178.
14    ibid., p. 178.
15    Biskup (1973: 18).

these out and fulfil their ceremonial and social obligations. For this second reason, too, the development of the pastoral industry in its first century was able to accommodate many aspects of traditional Aboriginal life.

By the 1980s, indeed, the time on the stations was seen by many of the older Roebourne people, as well as by older pastoralists, as something of a golden age— the good old days—when the local pastoralists and their Aboriginal workers and families knew each other, often grew up together and 'lived in harmony'. I spent time with Alice Smith, a senior Bunjima woman, sitting outside her house in the Village watching kids play in the yard. She remembered:

> You know, olden day, you used to have to say, I belong to Rocklea [Station]. I'm Bunjima…It was really good on the station, yeah. When you on the station you can do what you want to do. If you want to work, you know, you can work. If you want a day off, your day off you go down the river or wherever you want to go, hunting…When on the station, we can go where we want to go…That's what one of my family are trying to do at Rocklea now. All the Rocklea people, what they were talking, you know, they want to get that Rocklea Station so they can get all the old people back to their country, you know, where they come from. And settle down there…We all belong to Rocklea, see…We got a right to that country, all the cemetery there belong to the we fellas' family, you know, the people, they all there that we know.

Johnny Walker, a senior Yindjibarndi Law man who was born in 1926 on Tambrey Station on the tablelands, recounted to me: 'I turned out to be head stockman. Before they used to have big mobs, just giving them tucker and a few bob[16] a week…When I was the head stockman, we had about 15, 16 working on the station…I been on stations all my life.'

When I met him, Johnny was manager of the three stations near Roebourne— Mount Welcome, Woodbrook and Chirratta—that were owned by Roebourne's first Aboriginal organisation, Ieramugadu, through a shareholding in the Mount Welcome Pastoral Company. Part of the plan in buying the stations was to use them to train some of the young men in station work and give them the opportunity for involvement in the kind of work that their parents and grandparents had experienced.

While the earlier era of the pastoral industry in the West Pilbara wrought change, including the emergence of a population of mixed descent, it did not radically disrupt traditional life. Nor did it bring with it many aspects of modernisation for Aboriginal people. Instead, it was accompanied by practices that emphasised

---

16   Shillings in the pre-decimal currency.

for the colonists an opposition between them and Aboriginal people, especially those whom they defined as full-blood, entrenching Aboriginal people for them in the role, both imagined and actual, of the Other.

There were a number of dimensions to this process. One was political and legislative. Government developed a series of policies that gradually shifted from 'pacification' to protection. This took the form of the *Aborigines Protection Act* of 1896 and the establishment of the Aborigines Protection Board. Money was to be set aside for the benefit of Aborigines, but this was considered to be mainly for the distribution of relief from the depredations of contact in the form of rations and blankets.[17] In the eyes of the colonists by the end of the nineteenth century, the noble savage had become the poor bugger. Missions and reserves had been established that both conveniently removed Aboriginal people from the land and offered them refuge, though there was no mission presence in the Roebourne region. Even on the stations, where Aboriginal workers had become an integral part of the workforce, the custom of providing rations rather than wages, including rations to their extended families, allowed the pastoralists to see them in the role of dependants. Over 50 years, frontier hostility metamorphosed into paternalism.

Underlying the transformation was an unchanging assumption of innate superiority on the part of the colonists and—despite the friendships that developed among children growing up and playing together on the stations, or among station hands working together mustering, shearing, or in the dust of the stockyards—a sense of essential difference. For the colonists, fuelled by emerging ideas of social evolution, Aboriginal people from the beginning were Other. This was combined with the further colonial assumption of the right to take land and, in Padbury's words, to 'fight and subdue the natives' and to be masters, so that Aboriginal people were cast as the Other in a fixed opposition, justified in terms of racial superiority, between 'us' and 'them'. As Said argues in terms of the relationship between the Occident and the Orient, the relationship established by the colonisers with Aboriginal people was one 'of power, of domination, of varying degrees of a complex hegemony'.[18] The colonial way of knowing Aboriginal people was the product of the history of conquest that the colonists themselves had brought about.[19]

That this was not the way that Aboriginal people in the West Pilbara in the same period saw either themselves or the colonists is indicated paradoxically by their willingness both to do battle and to kill settlers and their stock and, later, to work to a limited extent with and for them. The colonial way of knowing Aboriginal

---

17  Hasluck (1970: 111).
18  Said (2003: 5).
19  Cf. ibid., pp. 4–5.

people was not initially the Aboriginal way of knowing the colonists. The latter arose inevitably out of the colonial encounter, but the colonial encounter did not define the Aboriginal social or moral universe. Instead of constructing a modality of 'otherness', based on a hierarchy of domination and subordination, many local Aboriginal people incorporated the newcomers into their social and moral landscape, firstly as enemy, then as a new group with whom ties of obligation and reciprocity were often developed.

Alice Smith, reflecting on what she had been told by the old people about those early days, saw it this way:

> You know, Aborigine people don't like white people when they first meet up. And they used to fight, kill one another. They shoot the Aborigine people and Aborigine people spear them. And next, they settle down now. When they settle down, Aborigine know this white skin, they got plenty food now, they find out, and to their country. When they like the white people, sent the wife, maybe one night to that person, whitefella, got a lot of food. In the morning they bring back lot of stores of flour and things. That's how all the half-caste children start off. One night friend, you know, they play the wife, Aborigine people, because they know whitefella's got plenty food coming from Perth or wherever they come from.

Woodley King, who was born at Millstream and worked on the stations for 30 years, saw the later situation a little differently: 'White people, they changing, some of them, you know. They like to sit down and talking with Aboriginal people and talking in the land. Different from old-time way. All friend together now. Very shy, you know, Aboriginal people never went near the white people.'

Coppin Dale, born on Croydon Station and a carrier of the Law for Ngarluma people, was in the Roebourne hospital, where I went to see him. He described the relationship: 'On stations, getting bit of bread, bit of meat. Before, when whites came, Aboriginal people and white like that [holding his index and middle fingers apart]. Now talk together, do things together. Don't pass each other in the street. Friendly now [his two fingers crossed].'

When Aboriginal workers led by Clancy McKenna, Dooley Bin Bin and non-Aboriginal activist Don McLeod walked off the stations further north and initiated their long-running strike in 1946 for better pay and conditions, Yindjibarndi and Ngarluma workers did not join in. Johnny Walker remembered:

> We watched, us mob, watched from Roebourne and up Wittenoom, up that way. We weren't involved in the strike. Only Port Hedland mob...I

mean, we all Aboriginal people, but we didn't join in with them. I dunno [if conditions were really bad], not where we were, might've been up that way. All right for us.

Some of the mob found other work that kept them on the country. Kuruma man Gordon Lockyer joined the Aboriginal Protection Board in 1953 and worked as a dogger, trapping dingoes all over surrounding stations until well into his retirement.[20]

The impact of colonisation on the peoples of the West Pilbara, then, brought change to their social relations and, with the introduction of exotic animals, to the landscape and to their economic environment. At the same time, the effects of this impact were experienced in different ways by different groups. If working on the stations allowed some groups to remain on their own country and maintain their traditional social and ceremonial practices, this was more the case for Yindjibarndi, Bunjima and other inland groups than it was for Ngarluma and other coastal people, although a few stations—including Mount Welcome, Woodbrook and Chirratta—were established on Ngarluma land. A group referred to as Yaburara, who may have been a northern Ngarluma group associated particularly with the Burrup Peninsula and surrounding islands, was effectively wiped out.[21] Ngarluma lost important parts of their country, including access to the fresh water of the lower reaches of the Harding River, when the towns of Roebourne and Cossack were built and expanded. Ngarluma people experienced colonisation much more directly as confrontation, loss and separation between themselves and the intruders. This separation was physically incorporated into the town's development.

## The town and the Old Reserve

Established initially to provide services for the pastoral industry, Roebourne also became the administrative centre of the region. At the turn of the century, it was firmly established as a non-Aboriginal town, with solidly built church, bank, courthouse, post office, hospital and three hotels. Cossack, too, linked by tramline to Roebourne in 1888, was a non-Aboriginal town, as was the new settlement of Point Samson where a jetty was built in 1903–04 to supplement the port facilities at Cossack where the harbour was beginning to silt up.[22] An early

---

20   Gordon Lockyer, in Rijavec and Solomon (2005: Biographies).
21   Gara (1983). This was also the court's finding in the native title determination *Daniel v State of Western Australia* [2003] FCA 666 (3 June 2003), paras 341, 352, 372–4, Appendix G. Paragraph 1478 of the judge's reasons states: 'It is common ground emerging from the submissions that there are no known living descendants of the Yaburara.' Despite this, a Yaburara and Mardudhunera people native title claim over adjacent land and waters remains extant.
22   de la Rue (1979: 60, 130); Gibson (1971: 55).

presence of Malays, Filipinos, Chinese, Timorese and later Japanese, brought to Roebourne and Cossack by the pearling industry, had all but disappeared by the early 1900s, though they, too, experienced the essentially European character of the towns. In Roebourne, they were segregated 'in their own shanty town situated to the west of the cemetery'.[23]

The only Aboriginal presence in Roebourne itself was in domestic service, on the annual race day, or in the court or jail. All prisoners were brought to Roebourne, the district's legal centre, for trial and, if found guilty, incarcerated in the local prison. Many of these were Aboriginal people from all over the West Pilbara, setting the pernicious framework for the law to define Aboriginal practices, and consequently Aboriginal people, as Other in terms of European hegemony and norms of behaviour. Colonisation on the frontier distorted one of the finest products of modernity, the rule of law, and turned it into an instrument of colonial repression. In 1904, for example, there were 72 Aboriginal prisoners in the jail, some aged as young as fourteen.[24] Aboriginal prisoners, often chained, were used as labour for the construction of public buildings and roads in Roebourne and Cossack, and for general tasks such as sweeping the town streets.[25]

These memories remain powerful for Roebourne people. In 1987, the Wickham Amateur Theatre Society staged a *son et lumière* at the old jail. The jail was built over several years, beginning in 1886, and using local stone, which, according to the background material provided for the performance, 'was easily available in a time when transport was very difficult and native labour was used to do any rough quarrying necessary'. There were two performances, representing the history of the region. To the disappointment of the organisers, they could get no Aboriginal people to take part, nor were there any in the audience for either performance. One of the men who did not attend explained later that it had been a mistake to use the old jail, it had too much bloody history and too many painful memories for people: 'Who wants to act the part of one of our old people, with a chain around our neck? Too much shame. I don't want to look at the past, reopen old wounds.'

A further separation between Aboriginal and non-Aboriginal people was incorporated into the physical layout of Roebourne itself. In the 1930s, an area outside Roebourne was designated for Aboriginal people to live. Over the years, people camped in a number of different sites, which, collectively, came to be known as the Old Reserve.[26] It was separated from the main town by the Harding

---

23   de la Rue (1979: 105–6, 107).
24   Juluwarlu Aboriginal Corporation (2004: 7), quoting John James Pond, Gaoler, Roebourne, to Commissioner Roth, 1904.
25   Gibson (1971: 56–7).
26   Michael Robinson, personal communication.

River. The separation was social as well as spatial; a curfew, in force well into the 1960s, formally excluded Aboriginal people from the town between 6 pm and 6 am. Regulations, announced in a notice at the entrance to the Reserve, required anyone living outside the Reserve to get a permit from the Department of Native Welfare before they could go there.

The population of the Reserve, initially used mainly by Ngarluma people, was swelled by Yindjibarndi and others from the 1940s till it became for a time the largest Native Reserve in Western Australia with around 300 people.[27] The housing provided did not match these numbers; in 1968, when the population fluctuated between 150 and 200, there was a mix of some 15 houses, the same number of huts, and additional tents and temporary bough shelters, together with three ablution blocks. Lighting connected to the town electricity supply was automatically switched off at 10 pm.[28]

The arrangements for schooling reinforced the practical separation of Aboriginal and non-Aboriginal people, further emphasising the racial opposition introduced by colonisation and incorporated into daily living in the town. Despite attempts by some of the older people, no school was opened on the Old Reserve and children from the Reserve or from the stations were not permitted to attend the school in Roebourne. Enrolment was available only to non-Aboriginal children or to the children of Aboriginal people who had been granted a certificate of citizenship under the *Natives (Citizenship Rights) Act 1944*.[29] One of the requirements of the certificate was to satisfy the magistrate that, for two years immediately preceding the date of application, the applicant had 'dissolved all tribal and native associations except with respect to lineal descendants or native relations of the first degree'.[30] In 1954, the Education Department stated its intention to allow children from the Reserve and from the stations to enrol. There was an outcry from the local non-Aboriginal parents. The result was that a separate primary school was established. Enrolments rose rapidly: 22 children in 1954, 45 in 1957, and 145 in 1959.[31] The only contact between the two schools was for sport on Fridays.[32] It was not until 1961 that a new, combined school for both Aboriginal and non-Aboriginal children was opened. Four years later a hostel, Weeriana, was built to offer accommodation to those Aboriginal children whose families lived away from the town.

Despite the indifferent conditions, and the uncomfortable proximity of different language groups, the Old Reserve was an Aboriginal space. It allowed people to

27    Johnston (1991: 285).
28    Gibson (1971: 26, 32).
29    Biskup (1973: 249).
30    ibid., p. 207.
31    Gibson (1971: 121).
32    Carol Lockyer, in Rijavec and Solomon (2005: Biographies).

live in their traditional family groupings and to maintain to some extent their customary social organisation. This was reflected in the mundane activities and interactions of every day, from eating to playing cards, but included also the ongoing exercise of authority in relation to Law by senior Law men and the performance of ceremony by those able to attend as and when necessary to fulfil the Law.[33] People coming in from the stations for supplies or, after Weeriana was opened, to drop off or collect their children at the beginning and end of school terms, stayed on the Reserve. With a decline in the pastoral industry in the 1960s, more of these families became permanent residents. Alice Smith described what happened for her family:

> I come to Roebourne in 1969. That's when I come from the station. We been 20 years out on the station working. My husband used to be contract fencing and building yards for the station, if the station want a yard or a fence. And he used to go round putting a fence up and that. And we come around Mulga Down way now, all round Mount Florence, Coolawanyah. And that's when I had the last one mine, when he was two years old I come down to Roebourne. Because my children was in the hostel then, and I asked my husband could I get a house in Roebourne and settle down with the kids, when the new hostel was built. So we come up, get a house in here then.

The time when Alice and her husband, Jack, settled in Roebourne coincided with a number of major changes in the region that, together, created the context in which modernisation for Roebourne Aboriginal people could be characterised by Yilbie Warrie in 1987 as grog, disease and death. These were the years that completed the alienation of traditional lands, thereby fracturing the relationship between present and past, and most deeply altering their customary social and moral framework. This was the time of the second colonisation.[34]

# Mining and modernisation: The second colonisation, 1965–1980

## Construction and urbanisation

The local experience of modernisation, and the 'big problem' referred to by Yilbie, came with the second colonisation. This second wave hit the region with

---

33  Rijavec and Solomon (2005); quoted in Juluwarlu Aboriginal Corporation (2004: 16).
34  I owe the reference to the beginning of the iron-ore boom of the 1960s as the second colonisation to Bob Hart, who lived and served in Roebourne as a Department of Community Welfare officer for some 15 years through the 1970s and 1980s.

the devastating force of one of the worst of the annual cyclones. The Pilbara is immensely rich in iron ore and other minerals. Small-scale mining had been established as early as the 1870s with copper and, later, gold. Local Aboriginal people themselves undertook sporadic alluvial mining—yandying—and were involved in the loading and carting of blue asbestos from Wittenoom through Roebourne to the coast.[35]

But when the Federal Government lifted its ban on the export of iron ore in 1961, the big mining companies and their construction workers moved in, many of them to the caravan park in Roebourne. Maureen Whitby, a non-Aboriginal woman who grew up in Roebourne, described what it was like:

> All of a sudden we were invaded by about 5000 men. It was just men everywhere. They were flying them in here for the Hamersley Iron railway line by the DC4 load, straight from Queensland. We never saw a TI [Thursday Islander] in our life before till all these black people started jumping off the aeroplane. They just flew them straight in because they're the best railway workers. And they built that Hamersley Iron one in record time.

Within a decade, 10 new towns, four new railways, hundreds of kilometres of roads and pipeline, and three new deepwater ports were constructed in the Pilbara generally. Three of the new towns—Dampier, Karratha and Wickham— were on Ngarluma country. Dampier, developed by Hamersley Iron, and Wickham, built a few years later by Cliffs Robe River on land excised from the Mount Welcome pastoral lease, were closed mining towns, with accommodation and services available only to company employees. Karratha, excised from Karratha Station, was established as an open town, but almost all its residents were non-Aboriginal.

The Victoria Hotel in Roebourne—the Vic—the only pub within a hundred-mile radius until the new towns were fully established,[36] boomed. An ABC program for *This Day Tonight* in 1972 reported:[37] 'The Victoria Hotel eighteen months ago employed three people behind the bar and struggled to sell forty barrels of beer a week. Now it has fifteen full time bar staff and its bulk beer sales put it among the top five hotels in the state.'

---

35   There has only recently been any attempt to assess the long-term impact of blue asbestos on these men, but also on the people who were then children, as the bags of asbestos were stored in an open area in Roebourne that children walked through, and often played in, on their way to and from school. In 2006, the National Health and Medical Research Council funded a program on the effects of asbestos exposure in Aboriginal people from Roebourne and Baryugal. Its chief investigator was Professor Richard Murray from James Cook University. In Roebourne, the project partnered with Mawarnkarra, the Aboriginal health service.

36   Johnston (1991: 287).

37   Rijavec and Solomon (2005).

This was in a town that the 1961 Census showed to have a population of 568 non-Aboriginal people. The number did not include the fluctuating population of the Old Reserve, as Aboriginal people were not counted in the census until after the Commonwealth referendum of 1967.

## Drinking rights

The impact of the rapidity and scale of these developments was compounded for local Aboriginal groups by a number of further changes. One of these concerned what Roebourne people refer to as drinking rights. Beginning in 1843,[38] it had been an offence under the *Licensing Act* for Aboriginal people in 'proclaimed areas' to supply or receive alcohol. This changed for the West Pilbara in November 1966 when a government proclamation removed the prohibition.[39] At the same time as the construction workers were inundating the Vic, Aboriginal people from the Old Reserve and from the stations were also permitted into the bars and to take alcohol away for the first time. The novelty of being able to share in an aspect of Australian life from which they had been legally excluded and that had come to represent equality proved overwhelming. Old man Coppin Dale gave his meaning to the experience: 'Why drink? Made the people happy. Have a few drinks, then start to talk.' For many, alcohol entered their understanding of a good life.

This was not how younger people growing up in Roebourne at this time saw the situation. Roger Solomon, son of a Ngarluma father and an Yindjibarndi mother, was twelve in the early stages of these changes. In his narration for the film *Exile and the Kingdom*, he described it this way:[40]

> Thousands of single men flooded in to build the railways and towns for Hamersley Iron, but Roebourne was not ready for the boom and couldn't cope with it. There were more construction workers living in Roebourne's caravan parks than in the town itself, and after work hundreds of them came to town to let off steam in the pub. Our community just fell apart, everything fell apart.

Even Alice Smith, who chose to move into Roebourne at this time, described it later to Commissioner Johnston during the Royal Commission into Aboriginal Deaths in Custody:[41]

> In 1969 Roebourne was just starting to get worse because of alcohol. The new towns started from 1960 up to now. The first was Dampier,

---

38   Brady (1998: 8).
39   Rowley (1972: 358–9).
40   Quoted in Juluwarlu Aboriginal Corporation (2004: 16).
41   Johnston (1991: 287).

the bad one for the Aborigine people. All the working people...used to come and drink here at this pub, Thursday Islander people, Yugoslav people and whatever. And the Aboriginal people started more and more to make friends with them, drinking with them, going in their cars, getting killed, all that started. All the Aboriginal people thought that was good, being with those people, drinking, going around in cars with them, girls especially. It was especially bad for the girls, more than the men. But the men got really drunk here, would go staggering away along the road and get hit by cars and pick fights with each other, things like that. Alcohol is the problem we've got...Even the new generation coming on. When they finish school they've got nothing to do because they haven't got work to go for...All they do is go drinking with their Mum and Dad down the street, getting drunk and some of them getting killed. It's the young people we are losing.

Another woman described the impact of alcohol as 'like [being] trapped in a big spider web'. Other women—although few wished to talk about this period—sometimes referred to these years as a time of fear, when as girls they were afraid to walk by themselves, even during the day, and they have stories of harassment and, in some instances, rape.[42] Roger Solomon mourned the many people of his generation who had been lost because of alcohol.[43]

Other people who had worked and lived on the stations were also affected. More Yindjibarndi and some Bunjima and Kuruma families moved onto the Old Reserve. For some, this was as early as the 1950s.[44] For others, it happened as work in the pastoral industry declined. This was a complex process, including as the result of drought and mechanisation, as well as an increasing unionisation of workers from which Aboriginal people were excluded. A permanent move off the stations and into Roebourne and other towns was accelerated after 1 December 1968, when the decision of the Commonwealth Conciliation and Arbitration Commission to award equal pay to Aboriginal pastoral workers, first in the Northern Territory and then by extension to the States, came into effect;[45] many pastoralists either refused or were unable to meet the necessary extra costs.

---

42  Edmunds (1989: 10).
43  Rijavec and Solomon (2005).
44  Michael Robinson, personal communication.
45  Rowley (1972b: Chs 14 and 15, especially pp. 345–8). The extension of the award from the Northern Territory to the States was made possible by the 1967 Referendum, which altered the Constitution to give the Commonwealth power to make laws for Aboriginal people (s. 51 [xxvi]).

# The Village

This move away from country represented not only a further dislocation for Yindjibarndi, as well as for those Ngarluma who had continued to work on the surrounding stations, and for the other groups. It also put increasing pressure on the already grossly inadequate housing in the Old Reserve. In an attempt to address these conditions, and the concerns of people living on the Reserve, the State Housing Commission (Homeswest) undertook sporadic consultations with people in 1973 about moving them into Roebourne itself. The move was fiercely opposed by the non-Aboriginal residents. One of them described how 'the whole town was up in arms opposing it and a committee was formed to oppose it'. The consultations came to an abrupt end when Cyclone Chloe wrought extensive damage to the Reserve housing at the beginning of 1975. The physical separation of Aboriginal and non-Aboriginal people experienced on the Reserve was replaced with the rapid relocation of Reserve families to 'the Village', the new Homeswest housing in the town. As had happened with Asian residents more than 70 years before, the Village was separated from the rest of the town by the cemetery.

This separation remained even when the administrative centre for the shire had moved to Karratha in 1971, as, over the next few years, did services and many of the non-Aboriginal people. Despite ongoing maintenance of the distinction between its Aboriginal and non-Aboriginal residents—government officers, health and hospital workers, police, hotel staff, shopkeepers—Roebourne was transformed in a very few years from a non-Aboriginal to a largely Aboriginal town, expanding the distinction to one between Roebourne and all the new towns in the shire. The new towns were for those working for the mining companies or involved in servicing them. The effective exclusion of local Aboriginal people from the extensive employment opened up in the region identified Roebourne as a welfare town. The region's minerals boom brought new industry, new employment, new towns and new ports. But not to local Aboriginal people.

At the same time, anecdotal accounts suggest that the move from the Old Reserve to the Village altered the informal living arrangements that had to some extent reflected the traditional relationships within and between different groups. The allocation of housing in the Village removed those choices. People were allocated according to Homeswest criteria that bore no relation to customary arrangements. Nor did the Village have the autonomy of the Reserve in terms of its being an effective Aboriginal space. Its greater proximity to the town, its incorporation as a bureaucratic entity, the greater visibility of its residents and their behaviours to the police meant a much more constant interaction with non-Aboriginal people and, more significantly, a much more regular intrusion of non-Aboriginal institutional processes and demands.

# Rupture

The second colonisation, therefore, while it arrived without the guns and chains of the first, nevertheless constituted an even greater assault on the lifestyle and on the traditional values and beliefs of Roebourne Aboriginal people. Their threshold experience of modernity was an experience of marginalisation. The advent of large-scale mining and urbanisation in the West Pilbara was, in a sense, a triumph of rationality, stripped through its assertion of power of any moral responsibility for its effects on the Aboriginal inhabitants. When Hamersley Iron began the development of its mines and of the towns of Dampier and Tom Price, there was no legislative requirement for them to concern themselves with anything outside the legality of the leases and permissions that they had been granted by the State Government. The first legislative protection in Western Australia for any Aboriginal sites as distinct from Aboriginal people, or land reserved for their use and benefit under the *Land Act 1933*, was the *Aboriginal Heritage Act* in 1972. This came too late to soften the impact of the first wave of development.

For the factory workers in Bangkok and the nuns in Spain, modernisation over this same period created a fracture between the present and the past, but access to a wide range of core cultural meanings remained available to them. Colonisation as experienced in Roebourne actively denied people their past by alienating them from their country. In so doing, it removed their economic base, as well as the source of their social and moral vision and practice. The consequence for Roebourne people was a distortion of the coherent connection between moral evaluation of the good and the social practices—embodied in family and kin, in deep knowledge of country, in subsistence activities, and ceremonial ritual—designed to express and promote a good life.

This raised for people the question of culture loss. Stuart Kirsch, examining the impact of nuclear testing by the United States in the Marshall Islands, comments:[46]

> Whereas local histories were once intimately associated with the landscape, the destruction of the places where these events occurred has prompted these communities to reformulate their narratives of the past in chronological terms...The notion of loss has two primary registers. It may refer to possession—to the objects or property for which one might claim rights or ownership...In other contexts...it is possible to speak of loss in relation to the notion of kinship and belonging rather than possession...

---

46   Kirsch (2001: 167–9).

> The dynamics of memory and forgetting, the entropic tendencies of ritual knowledge, and the incompleteness of the intergenerational transmission of knowledge all pose questions about the possibility of loss.

For people like Gordon Lockyer, who continued to travel his country as a dogger, this sense of loss was immediate. Open-cut mining followed the course of the Robe River, damaging the surrounding hills: 'these ghost hills that he could no longer show to his children and grandchildren, that belonged now only to the country of his mind'.[47] The huge mine at Mount Tom Price engulfed a rich deposit of red ochre that had been important not only for local ceremony, but also as an item of trade across the region.

Roebourne people also expressed their sense of loss in terms of loss of knowledge. They talked about this with reference to the passing away of the old people who held the knowledge, anxiety about and among the middle generation having only incomplete knowledge, and concern about learning more before it was too late and about passing knowledge on to the next generations. A Ngarluma woman recounted: 'I was brought up like white people. We was on the station. I don't know about the old ways. I'm Ngarluma, but I don't know my skin colour[48]...I think it's sad, not to know my culture, the old stories. I don't have this.'

In the period of rapid development from the 1960s, Roebourne people's dialogue with the past is complex and shifting. For many, especially in the early years, modernisation meant only loss: loss of country, loss of tradition, loss of knowledge, and often loss of family members because of alcohol. Nor did they find solace in modernity's orientation to the future, which seemed to demand a rejection of the past, with a promise of the break between present and past being reconstructed as 'forever new "new beginnings"...dismantling old structures and building new ones from scratch',[49] recapitulating 'the break brought about with the past as a continuous renewal'.[50] The responses in Roebourne—and also in Bangkok and Madrid—suggest that too drastic a break between present and past is experienced in the first instance by those whom it affects as breakdown, not renewal; that it shatters the base on which people have built their systems of meanings and values, leaving them without a framework:[51] 'A person without

---

47   Gordon Lockyer, in Rijavec and Solomon (2005: Biographies).
48   'Skin' is the colloquial term used throughout Australia to refer to a form of traditional social organisation of larger descent groups that allocates people on the basis of their parentage into sections or subsections. Central and West Pilbara people are organised into four skin groups or sections. An individual belongs to one of these subgroups, or skin groups, on the basis of descent through either father or mother. Skin groups determine many of the ways in which people relate to each other. In traditional law, this includes marriage.
49   Bauman in Bauman and Tester (2001: 72).
50   Habermas (2002: 7).
51   Subcomandante Insurgente Marcos, EZLN spokesman, quoted in *Zapatista*, [Documentary], Big Noise Films. Quoted in Rijavec (2005: 19).

a past does not exist…and has no future…A people without a history cannot advance…cannot exist as a people because in one way or another, the past is what makes you construct the present.'

## Continuity and innovation

Nevertheless, despite these drastic changes, they were played out in a particular cultural universe.[52] There were continuities to Aboriginal life, generally out of sight of the non-Aboriginal residents of the new towns and even in Roebourne itself. These continuities were low-key, an undercurrent, carried on in the interstices of daily living. Yindjibarndi people continued to carry out Law ceremonies at Millstream.[53] For others, there was a break of probably only two years, from 1969 to 1971. Ceremonies were performed, sometimes on the Old Reserve, often at bush meetings over the hot season, later at Woodbrook Station after it had been purchased for local groups, though never in the Village. They included initiation for boys. David Walker, one of the middle generation of Ngarluma leaders, explained in 1987:

> This is still important, the bush meeting; it takes place every year. Roebourne still takes a big part. Before, people used to stick to their own place. Now, they've opened up the ground, can go as friends. Man's one is at Christmas, or maybe in the August holidays. There was a big meeting in 1975 in Wittenoom, called by the parents of some boys. That opened it all up. People came from Jigalong, La Grange, from all around. When they come from other places, they do it the way the local people want. When we go to their place, we do it their way.
>
> The old people have passed it on. Now it's our generation, we've learnt it from them, we're teaching it to the young people.

At the same time, the Aboriginal way of life with its own independent culture and social practices could no longer be taken for granted, even by Aboriginal people themselves. One of the effects of colonisation was the 'self-consciousness of culture', but also its resistance to complete annihilation.[54] In the face of the assault of rapid change through the 1960s and 1970s, this was initially inchoate and adventitious. As David Walker indicated, even bush meetings had changed to take account of the new circumstances in which people found themselves.

There were new ways, too, in which people struggled to come to terms with the enormity of change and to make sense of their own place within it. This involved finding new meanings and new ways of acting, often in the form

---

52   Cf. Sahlins (2005: 52).
53   Michael Robinson, personal communication.
54   Sahlins (2005: 48).

of a reaction to the ubiquitousness of drinking. One expression was through Christianity, despite the previous absence of any established mission. In 1969, a group of senior men, both Ngarluma and Yindjibarndi, worked with Pastor Dave Stevens to establish the Pilbara Aboriginal Church. This was part of a Pentecostal denomination, the Apostolic Church of Australia. Its members felt no contradiction between traditional beliefs and those of Christianity. Woodley King explained that he saw 'Mingala' as both an ancestral being and the Christian God. Gordon Lockyer expressed this easy dualism: '*Burndud* [Law ceremony], given to Aboriginal people by God, Mingala. Our own God. But now we're Christians. Believe two ways. Good.'

The church became a vehicle for men and women to stop drinking; in Roebourne, as in many other Aboriginal communities, people came to make a distinction between being a drinker and being a Christian. It was a mainly Christian group who rejected the move to the Village and the easy availability of alcohol. They moved instead to the old shearers' quarters, the Woolshed, on Mount Welcome Station, about 3 km out of Roebourne. The first to use the old Woolshed buildings were Jacob Scroggins, a Ngarluma man, and his family. Renamed Cheeditha, it was begun as a dry community—no alcohol permitted—and continued under the leadership of Yilbie Warrie, Kenny Jerrold and Allan Jacobs. All three were leaders in the church. They were also senior Yindjibarndi Law men. And they, with others like Coppin Dale, were active in the establishment in 1973 of the Mount Welcome Pastoral Company, when the Mount Welcome and Chirratta stations were purchased (Woodbrook was added later), and, in 1974, of Ieramugadu Group Incorporated. Ieramugadu was the first legally incorporated Aboriginal organisation in Roebourne and the sole shareholder in the Mount Welcome Pastoral Company. Ieramugadu was also the partner in Hamersley Iron's first attempts to set up a program to provide employment for Roebourne Aboriginal people.

Women were involved in each of these initiatives. They also undertook others that they saw as allowing Aboriginal people to make their own place in the new order. A number of those who had previously worked on the stations became involved as Homemakers. This was an organisation that had begun in Roebourne at the time when people still lived on the Old Reserve. At the beginning, all its workers were non-Aboriginal women and their task was to provide family support to the Reserve community, and then to assist with the move to the Village.[55] They were then joined by Aboriginal women. One of these was Alice Smith:

---

55 Discussion with then long-term Roebourne resident Betty Connell, who had started as a Homemaker.

I got a little bit of a job for a while, just cleaning the shop. I was in the shop then, that 4-Square now. And then I got the Homemaker job. I was a Homemaker working in the Village then. And I got the licence, drive the car then. I was working eight years in Homemakers.

Funny thing happened with the Village. I thought, when they put the Village up, I thought they were going to be European and Aborigine people mixed up, y'know. But they done a very wrong thing. They let all the Aborigine people just living in the Village one side. And when I first come there and they was damaging, you know, everything finished, all our houses, and they don't know how to look after the houses. We had to teach them how to keep the house, and how to pay them bills and things like that. They were going good when they had a Homemaker working.

Over the same period, Wendy Hubert, an Yindjibarndi woman, joined the Health Workers program. She saw this as the first step in her ongoing activities in the community:

It was an education for me. I've seen a lot of things come and a lot of things change. I was raised in Onslow, went to school in Derby at the UAM [United Aboriginal Mission], I had two years in high school. The parents of the tribal children haven't been educated in the white people's way. We've got the power in the Aboriginal way but not the white-man way. We've got to be educated to get on that spot.

## Colonisation and surveillance

These early attempts by Roebourne people to take back some control and to engage with their changing world remained subject, however, and subjected to external forces of ongoing colonisation. One of the most visible of these was the police. To look at just one point over these years, in 1986, there were 10 police officers stationed in the town: two sergeants, six constables and two Aboriginal police aides. The total population of Roebourne was around 1700. The 1986 Census identified 786 of these as Aboriginal. This meant that there was one police officer for every 170 inhabitants, and one to every 79 Aboriginal residents. In the neighbouring company town of Wickham, there were four police officers for a population of some 2500 people, a ratio of one police officer to every 625 people, which the local sergeant-in-charge regarded as too high. In Karratha, there were 10 police for around 10 000 people: one for every 1000.[56]

---

56   Edmunds (1989: 96–7).

This level of police presence in Roebourne involved a degree of constant surveillance that effectively encompassed the whole Aboriginal population. Every year over this period some 2000 cases were brought before the magistrate. In 1984, 1975 adult charges and 169 children's charges were laid; in 1985, 1991 adult and 233 children's charges; in 1986, 2181 adult and 169 children's charges.[57] In Western Australia more generally, a census of prisoners during these years showed that, on a given day, one out of every 10 nineteen-year-old Aboriginal people in the State was in prison.[58] A study examining two periods in Roebourne in 1983 showed that virtually all of the people arrested in Roebourne were Aboriginal. The people arrested were reasonably young: 15 per cent under twenty years old and 56 per cent under thirty. Drunkenness and offences related to licensed premises accounted for more than three-quarters of the offences. The figures also showed a very high level of repeat offenders: 2.45 over three months.[59]

This was the context in which a fight took place outside the Victoria Hotel between police, who were off duty and had also been drinking, and a number of Aboriginal men on the night of 28 September 1983. By the end of the fight, five of the Aboriginal men had been arrested and were taken to the Roebourne police station. One of them was a young Yindjibarndi man, John Pat. The consequences were to prove devastating.

## Death of John Pat

Within an hour of being locked into one of the police station cells, John Pat was found dead. It was a month before his seventeenth birthday. A coronial inquest found that he had died of a closed head wound. The post-mortem examination also found 'many other injuries, including some significant injuries'[60] that extended to two broken ribs and a torn aorta, the major blood vessel leading from the heart.[61] John Pat's death, erupting out of the deepest fissure arising from colonisation in Australia, reverberated in the town, in the State, and eventually in the nation. It gave Roebourne national notoriety, with intense media focus on drunkenness, dysfunction and violence. But it also proved to be a critical culmination of 20—or indeed 120—years of dislocation in the region and of difference interpreted in terms of race; it was a moment of truth for the broader society in terms of its own claims as a good society.

---

57   ibid., p. 95.
58   Grabosky (1988: 89).
59   *Royal Commission into Aboriginal Deaths in Custody* 1990 Regional Research Papers COM/5, WA.
60   Johnston (1991: 11).
61   Grabosky (1988: 88).

These claims were tested when the coroner committed the five police officers—Constables Terence Holl, Steven Bordas, Ian Armitt, James Young and Aboriginal police aide Michael Walker—to stand trial in the Supreme Court of Western Australia for the manslaughter of John Pat. The trial was held in early 1984 in Karratha before a jury of all non-Aboriginal people. In May, the five police were acquitted and reinstated. None, except for Michael Walker, returned to duty in Roebourne, and he was transferred later to another town. Nevertheless, the fact of the trial—if not either the process or its outcome—was a muted signal that it was possible for the rule of law to be practised in support of Aboriginal people and not only as a tool of colonisation. The associated debate, at both State and national levels, invoked the language of rights and situated itself in the context of international law and standards.

Locally, the shire responded by building a community centre, a building generally referred to, because of its hexagonal shape, as the 50-cent hall, which was its sop to the lack of community and recreational facilities in the town. The WA Government set up a Special Cabinet Committee on Aboriginal/Police and Community Relations in 1984 and set out a three-stage program. The first stage was a study of Aboriginal/police relations in the Pilbara.[62] Its central aim was to formulate proposals for improving the working relationships between Aboriginal people and the police in the Pilbara, particularly with respect to Jigalong—another Aboriginal community—and Roebourne.[63] Stage two, the Roebourne Research Project, began in December 1986 and ran until mid 1987.[64] With coordination by community worker Gail Dawson, the team was made up of local Aboriginal people: Marion Cheedy, Nicole Cook, Cecil Parker, Sue Parker, Chrissie Tittums and Greg Tucker. The team worked closely with the new Sergeant-in-Charge, Ron Court.

Stage three was a review of the Roebourne project. The review observed:[65]

> Less than a quarter of the initiatives were directed at changing aspects of the law enforcement system…None of [the] six initiatives resulted in any real changes to the system. They were either blocked by some external agency, dropped through a lack of perceived demand, or politely listened to and then ignored.

> Therefore, any improvements in Aboriginal/police relations resulting from the project were the outcome of what happened to individual police and Aborigines rather than to changes in the system. Unfortunately this means there is a risk that when the current officers leave Roebourne the

---

62    Roberts et al. (1986).
63    ibid., p. 2.
64    Dawson (1987).
65    Jewell et al. (1988: 81).

benefits of the project will go with them. The Aboriginal community is aware of that prospect and is apprehensive about what a new set of police might bring.

Nevertheless, three months after the end of the Roebourne project, a serious attempt was made to bring changes to the law-enforcement system. After much campaigning by Aboriginal and other concerned groups both at the State level and nationally, and after a number of further deaths in custody in different parts of the country, the Commonwealth Government established the Royal Commission into Aboriginal Deaths in Custody. It was anticipated that the work of the Commission would take about twelve months. In the event, it took four years to examine the individual cases of the 99 Aboriginal and Torres Strait Islander people whom it found to have died in the nine years between 1 January 1980 and 31 May 1989 in the custody of prison, police, or juvenile detention institutions. The Commission's mandate was also broadened to look at the issues underlying these deaths.

Commissioner Elliott Johnston investigated the death of John Pat. He acknowledged that 'John Pat's death at the age of sixteen in the lockup of the Roebourne Police Station was one of the major catalysts behind national and international demands for a Royal Commission into Aboriginal deaths in custody'.[66] He sat in Roebourne for 35 days between March and May 1990, and took a further 15 days of evidence in Perth. Very early in his report, he pointed out that

> the jury who tried the issues in the trial of the officers necessarily were examining one aspect of the night's events. The only issue for them was whether they were satisfied beyond reasonable doubt that the five officers, or any one or more of them, unlawfully killed John Pat. The verdict of not guilty reflects the answer to that narrow question only.[67]

Commissioner Johnston went on to say:[68] 'The inquiry into the death of John Pat was the most lengthy of all the inquiries conducted by the Commission [there were more than 5000 pages of transcript] and one of the most factually contentious... The evidence was complex and generally marked by contradiction.'

Nevertheless, on the basis of that evidence, he did not 'accept Holl's evidence as to what happened in the bottleshop' (where the confrontation took place between Holl and Ashley James that sparked the fight). 'I cannot accept what he says happened outside the shop.'[69] The Commissioner also found that, when

66   Johnston (1991: 36).
67   ibid., p. 23.
68   ibid., p. 24.
69   ibid., p. 125.

the five arrested men were taken in vans to the police station, 'on any view of the evidence [the police] were guilty of lack of care'; that 'there was an absolute preponderance of police power at the time the prisoners were unloaded from the vans'; that 'it is nothing short of disgraceful that three of the five prisoners ended up on the ground'; that 'Holl was the main offender and that Bordas played a lesser role'.[70]

Commissioner Johnston recognised the grief occasioned in Roebourne by John Pat's death, but also by the Commission's hearings nearly seven years later. In his report, he quotes part of the statement from Mavis Pat, John Pat's mother:[71] 'When I heard about the Royal Commission…I used to wish it would come here…[But] I'm sick of the Royal Commission, it's taking a long time. I wish it to be over. I wish something to happen soon.'

For people in Roebourne, the wheels of the law ground very, very small, and intrusively at the day-to-day level, and very, very slowly beyond this, often losing the connection between cause and effect. What people saw as important was how they related to the police on a day-to-day basis. The Roebourne Research Project was immediate, and people had time for Sergeant Ron Court and his wife. The death of John Pat was too painful for it to be the focus of public anger among those who were related to him and for whom he was part of their social world. It was the fourth anniversary of his death soon after I arrived in Roebourne in 1987. I found that no-one wanted to talk about it. Most people, in common with traditional custom, avoided speaking his name. One man responded, 'That touches too deep. We don't want to talk about that boy.' Another couple commented, 'Ah, that was a terrible thing. But people don't want to talk about it any more. Of course they remember it, we never forget something like that. But what can we do? Mavis Pat, she got no money, no car, nothing. What can she do?' One of the new policemen in town responded:

> It's the media that's done it, drummed up all this business. I had a phone call just a couple of weeks ago…They'd heard, police under siege, carrying arms, because of the John Pat anniversary. All not true. Nothing happened all day. We sat out the front and had a barbecue.

Frank Rijavec, who had arrived in Roebourne with his partner, Noelene Harrison, a few months earlier than I had, proposing the idea of making a film with the community received a similar response:[72]

> Initially I proposed that the film hinge on the death of John Pat in police custody and examine the role of police in the town and the fraught

---

70    ibid., pp. 199, 202, 203.
71    ibid., p. 37.
72    Rijavec (2005: 7).

relationships between police and the community; that it be a tract about social justice. Community leaders I discussed the project with (including Alan Jacob, Roger Solomon, Woodley King, Violet Samson and David Daniels) made it clear that they were not interested in dragging their community over the same ground the mass media had been digging: the death of John Pat, relations between police and the community, dysfunction and substance abuse, etc. They set another direction.

The resulting documentary, *Exile and the Kingdom*, became a powerful statement by Roebourne people about how they saw the world in which they found themselves, what they saw as the important values, how they defined the good, and what they saw as essential to a good life for themselves and the next generations. This not only gave them a voice:[73]

> Ultimately the production, in collaboration with the community, of the documentary *Exile and the Kingdom*, from July 1987 through 1993, provided elders and the community with a radical contrast to the powerlessness and victimisation they felt at the hands of the media. It gave the community a voice in a way they had not before experienced.

It also reflected the growing confidence of people in setting out their own terms for a dialogue with modernity. Commissioner Johnston's report on the death of John Pat began with a statement from Yilbie Warrie:[74]

> Roebourne is a very significant place for Aboriginal people. This is a place where Aboriginal law was made for all Aboriginal people. The Aboriginal people are now suffering. They are sick in the heart. We need assistance to overcome the problems that have come since Europeans came here. We want the Royal Commission to help us with our ideas.

What this statement did not reflect, though the point was taken up later in the Commission's report, was the extent to which, even from the early 1980s, people in Roebourne had started to reconnect their present with their past, and with the meanings from the past that could allow them to deal better with the present and move into a different future.

A commentary on a different moment of disaster, that of the Blitz in London in 1940, when the familiar world was destroyed, can equally be applied to Roebourne people over the whole period, particularly that of the second colonisation:[75] 'People do what people have to do in the face of a disaster. They do what they can to get things back to normal. The strength of people was not understood…Ordinary people endure extraordinary things.'

---

73  ibid., p. 9.
74  Johnston (1991: 1).
75  *The Blitz: London's Firestorm*, ABC1 Television, 26 March 2006.

This is what people in Roebourne were doing through the 1980s as they began to recover from the assault of modernisation, from a basis described by Wendy Hubert: 'I reckon the tribal system is much better, if you've got the knowledge and the patience...We've got the power in the Aboriginal way...We got the power. We feel ourselves, we *feel* it. We feel it, and where does it come from?'

By 1990, this power was being exercised in diverse ways. One was a move towards putting in place joint management arrangements between Aboriginal people and national park management agencies. It arose from a discussion by the Aboriginal representatives at a Conservation and Land Management meeting held at Millstream in 1990 and was subsequently included in the Royal Commission's National Report as Recommendation 315.[76]

## Enduring extraordinary things: The strength of people

The first Aboriginal organisations in Roebourne set up to claim a legitimate place in their changing world were the Mount Welcome Pastoral Company and Ieramugadu. These were established in 1973 and 1974. They gave Ngarluma people legal access back to parts of their country and all Roebourne groups a place, Woodbrook, where ceremony could take place. Ieramugadu also played an active role in working with Hamersley Iron to develop a program to provide some employment opportunities for Roebourne people. More organisations began to be established in the early 1980s.

The Ngurin Resource Centre, named after the Aboriginal word for the Harding River (*Ngurin*) that runs through the town, was set up in 1985 in the wake of a controversy over the Harding Dam that I will look at in the next chapter. Wendy Hubert was its chair and it worked actively with the Aboriginal Sites Department of the WA Museum to protect Aboriginal sites in the area. Ngarluma leaders David Daniel and David Walker were both involved in this process and both accepted positions with the Museum. In the same year, Mawarnkarra, an Aboriginal Medical Service, was established. Woodley King was finally able to set up a community on Yindjibarndi land at Ngurrawaana. He did this with the help of two Sisters of Mercy from Perth, Sister Bernadine and Sister Bernadette, who, like the nuns in Spain, had embraced the possibility of change offered by Vatican II, and of Father John Gerharty, who organised an essential truck for the community through Catholic Relief. Violet Samson worked with others to organise the Gurra Bunjya cultural camp, known colloquially as the Kids Culture Camp, for young people. David Daniel, Roger Solomon and others set up the Ngarluma Yindjibarndi Dance Group.

Alice Smith reflected:

---

76   Lawrence (1996–97).

What we got, we started in Roebourne. When I first come to Roebourne, nothing was here, nothing belonged to the Aborigines. Aborigines had nothing, really nothing, no stations. Then we got Chirratta, Mount Welcome and Woodbrook, that's the first one, and Ieramugadu, that's the first one, alright? We started, and I started now, Aborigines started to work for welfare, work for my people in the Village...

You see this one now [the Village Hall]? We brought that here, we bring it up here. That's where the kindergarten used to be down at the river. Because we wanted that hall for the meetings for the people, you know, all the Village people...

And after, Cheeditha started, that one there. Aborigine people got that now. From that, we put in for this Mawarnkarra now. We had a meeting, in December, we tell all the people we want that Mawarnkarra Medical Service, so they got to come up here. And then Woodley King got some place up at Ngurrawaana. And we got Ngurin now. Lotta changes come after that...Everything change now, that's really good. Aborigine... know they got their place for themselves.

Alice's niece Eva Black, who was working as the education assistant at the Roebourne Primary School in 1987, had moved to Roebourne from Onslow in 1980. She commented, 'I really enjoy living up here, it's really good.' She was involved in the school's culture classes: 'When the kids tell the story, they usually tell it in Yindjibarndi. I write it down for them, in Yindjibarndi. We've got a dictionary now...And we've got Greg Tucker as our liaison officer.'

When I arrived in Roebourne in 1987, I came with reports echoing in my head about disaster, dysfunction, cultural loss and the received wisdom about the impact of colonisation on Aboriginal people having resulted in low self-esteem. That was not how I experienced the people whom I met there. There were certainly problems, and alcohol remained one of them. But I met people who were secure and confident. Woodley King made clear to me that I stood in a relationship to him of naive newcomer. I twice put myself in the position of being chastised by him. Both were on the basis of my erroneous acceptance of the view that time was not important for Aboriginal people. When I arrived late for an interview with him in Roebourne, he tapped his wristwatch and pointed out that I had not arrived at the agreed time. The second time was when I had arranged with him to go out to Ngurrawaana. I was late leaving Millstream with Carol Lockyer and the children and found very daunting the prospect of a further long drive along the pipeline road there and, more worryingly, back in the dark. We didn't go, and I found myself having to respond to Woodley's reprimand the next time we met with apologies and lame excuses.

As Alice Smith commented:

> Since I come here, I seen a change come for the white people. Also the white people getting good to the Aborigine people, you know, and some of the white people help them. But some of the white lady and the man, they still not right with the Aborigine people, because they different colour. I think they go by that. But we, Aborigine people, we know we all the same, doesn't matter what sort of colour you got, black or white. We all got the same blood. We're not different. All we different is the colour might be white, some of them black.

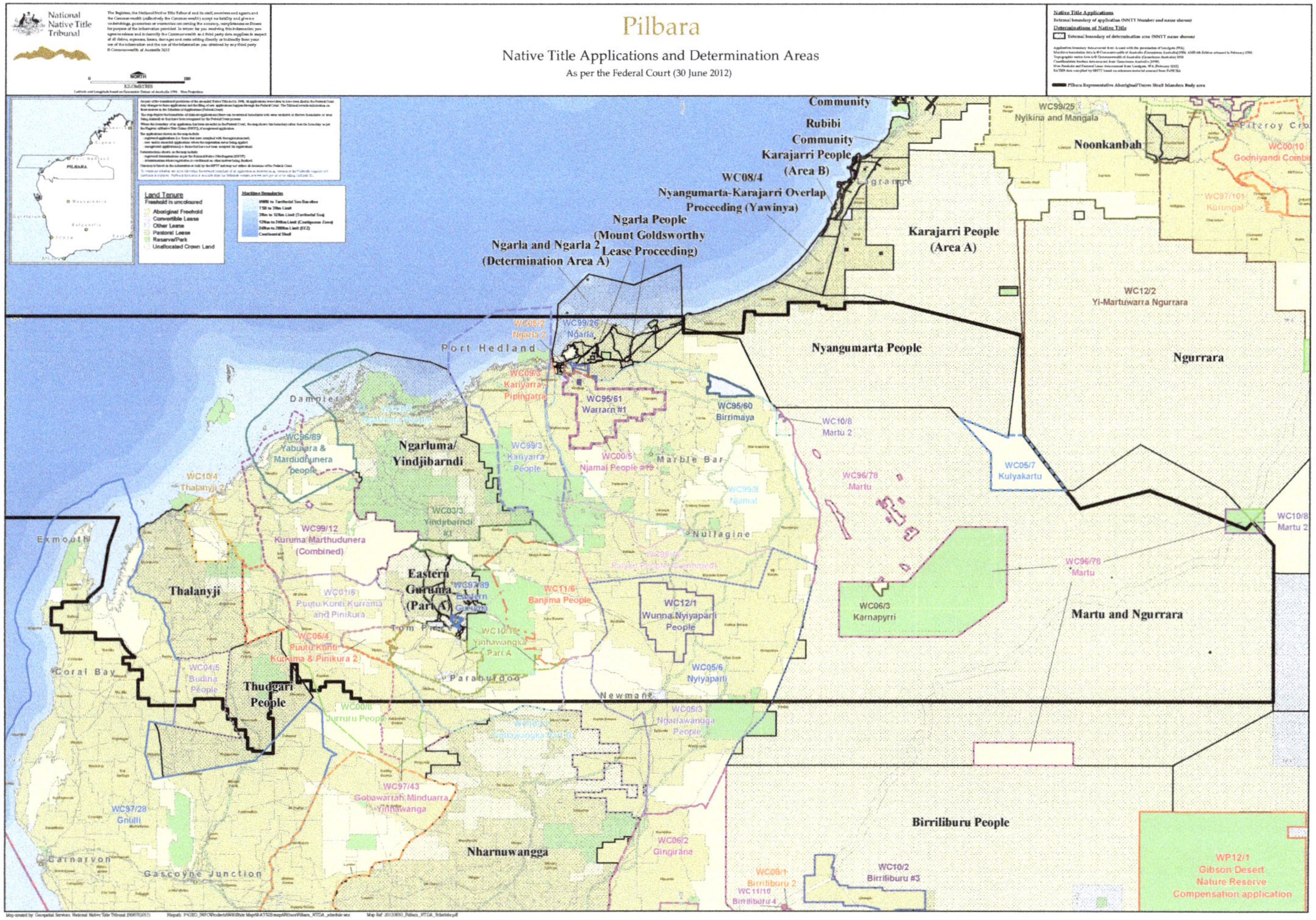

**Map 4. Pilbara native title applications and determination areas, 30 June, 2012**

Source: The National Native Title Tribunal (used with permission).

# 7. A winnin' battle

Pilbara Aboriginal people have had painful experiences of culture loss and, with that, stark challenges to their moral source, to their understanding of a good life, and to their grounding of a sense of a good life in the cultural practices previously constitutive for them of a good society. It took two decades for the beginnings of recovery from the shattering impact of the iron-ore boom of the 1960s. The basis of that recovery was twofold: a reassertion and reframing of the critical importance of country as a cultural and moral source; and the development of some legislative rights. In Western Australia, these came in the form of the *Aboriginal Heritage Act* in 1972. When these rights proved inadequate to stop the building of the Harding Dam, Aboriginal people turned to the Commonwealth's *Aboriginal and Torres Strait Islander Heritage (Interim Protection) Act 1984*. Although the dam and the Marandoo mine went ahead, the fight for country was the catalyst for political action.

The fight for country also brought Pilbara Aboriginal people into the wider discourse of land rights and, over time, of Indigenous rights. An event that changed the character of those rights in Australia and transformed the relationship between Indigenous and other Australians was the High Court's *Mabo* decision[1] and the subsequent Commonwealth *Native Title Act 1993*. Central to this transformation were both legal recognition of the traditional past as at least partly consistent with modernity, and a practical application to Indigenous Australians of the universal principles of human rights. Native title has not shielded Pilbara Aboriginal people from the ongoing impacts of resource development. Nor has it avoided internal conflicts. But it has made a major contribution to what Sahlins terms 'the indigenisation of modernity'.[2] And part of that process has been an ongoing process of redefining by Pilbara Aboriginal people themselves of what is meant by a good life in the intercultural context of modern Australia.

## Culture and the social imaginary

The experience of Roebourne and other Pilbara Aboriginal people in the first two decades of the second colonisation confronted them very directly with the question of culture loss. Displaced from their country, with much of that country legally alienated and, particularly once large-scale mining began, destroyed, it was simply impossible for people to carry out the full range of traditional

---

1  *Mabo v Queensland* [No. 2] (1992) 175 CLR 1.
2  Sahlins (2005: 47).

practices that had constituted their culture and moral and social universe. In his discussion of nuclear testing in the Marshall Islands by the United States, Kirsch makes the point that:[3]

> The severing of connections between people and place always entails loss…The alienation of land is of general concern for indigenous peoples…the loss of otherwise inalienable homelands can jeopardize not only the material conditions of survival, including subsistence practices, but also the requirements of social reproduction as embedded in kinship relations. Local knowledge and relations to place may be affected as well.

At the same time, a living culture does not exist outside the people who practise it. It is embodied in concrete domains, such as country, and expressed and reproduced in social and ritual practices. It also exists as a social imaginary, carried by individuals but shared with the others who make up their social world. Taylor links this to a sense of legitimacy:[4]

> By social imaginary, I mean…the ways people imagine their social existence, how they fit together with others, how things go on between them and their fellows, the expectations that are normally met, and the deeper normative notions and images that underlie these expectations… The social imaginary is that common understanding that makes possible common practices and a widely shared sense of legitimacy.

Taylor's social imaginary echoes key aspects of what would be called culture in anthropological terms but it is not synonymous. Culture, like the social imaginary, exists as ideas, but not solely as ideas. Inherent in the concept of culture is the recognition of the essential dimension of practice: of practical mastery and practical knowledge.[5] Culture is also tangible, in objects, clothing, art, adornment, organisation of space. We do culture perhaps even more than we think it, and we do it in real time. The possibility is always there of doing it differently as the environment in which we act changes through real time. It is in this sense that Sahlins can draw on West African writers and quote their view that 'culture is not only a heritage, it is a project';[6] Bauman can speak of culture as 'a permanent revolution of sorts' in a human world that is 'not-yet-accomplished';[7] Kirsch can suggest that loss 'may be integral…in that it permits

---

3   Kirsch (2001: 176, 177).
4   Taylor (2004: 23).
5   Bourdieu (1979: 4).
6   Sahlins (2005: 58).
7   Bauman in Bauman and Tester (2001: 32).

innovation and improvisation';[8] Peterson can observe that 'being able to buy kangaroo meat in the local store is likely to be one reason why desert people no long hold kangaroo increase ceremonies'.[9]

For Pilbara Aboriginal people, their social and cultural universe was not a closed one even before the advent of major development in the region in the 1960s. Their old people had been dealing with difference since at least the advent of the first settlers in 1866. Their practical worlds had changed, and they had changed them, accordingly. Their response to the modernisation that came with development was as people with their own history, and 'with their own cultural consciousness of themselves'.[10] Nevertheless, the extent and rapidity of change over those first two decades of the 1960s and 1970s shook that 'cultural consciousness of themselves', especially for the young people, and, with it, the authority of senior people in providing for the transmission of cultural knowledge and practice to the next generation. Modernisation destabilised the legitimacy of traditional values and practices and of their moral source. It offered tantalising alternative notions of the good, and of what constitutes a good life, including access to regular and substantial wages, without providing any effective means of realising them. Nor did it remove the racial division that meant that, even for those who did attempt to engage with the new system of work, there was little reward in the workplace. Early attempts by people like Ian Williams from Hamersley Iron and Carol Lockyer from Ieramugadu to provide employment foundered on the reluctance of others in the workforce, as one of the Hamersley supervisors explained:

> We had people actually working for us and living in the single quarters. Two or three at different stages. But they found it very hard to assimilate and I don't think they were really accepted by the workforce. I think the work situation wasn't so bad. It was the living afterwards. They were living in single quarters and the white men as I understand it didn't accept them into their cliques.[11]

---

8   Kirsch (2001: 170).
9   Peterson (2010: 251).
10  Sahlins (2005: 52).
11  In 1992, Hamersley Iron set up its Aboriginal Training and Liaison (ATAL) Unit in Dampier. Its first manager was Jeremy van de Bund. After a start that was cautious on both sides, ATAL gradually became a point of reference for local Aboriginal people in terms of Rio Tinto's engagement with them. In 1998 it won a Reconciliation Award.

# Practical transformations: Cultural concerns and political action

People did not find new meaning through the world of work. In the 1980s they began to do so by reasserting and reframing the central importance of country in the context of development, as development pushed them to political action. The catalyst was formal approval by the State Liberal government in August 1982 to build a dam on the Harding River.

The establishment of the new towns put increasing pressure on the scarce water supplies of the area. This was not helped by the nature of the towns. There was no attempt to adapt to the semi-arid environment; instead, they tried to reproduce the greener suburban environments of the south, with lavishly watered lawns and gardens. The initial source of water was the Millstream aquifer. Woodley King's anxiety about the depletion of this source and the dying back of the shallow-rooted paperbarks along its banks expressed the concerns of both Yindjibarndi and Ngarluma people generally. These concerns were more than environmental. The deep, permanent pools of Millstream were created by the great water snake, *Barrimirndi*.[12] David Daniels, a Ngarluma leader, talked about this at a workshop in 1985:[13]

> What Yilbie [Warrie] meant was the Millstream is special. We are the special people and you know we believe in the spirits, spirit of the land of ours. What Millstream means to us is not just the word of people... It's our tribal land, it's our home land, it's where our tribal laws started. And we are still carrying out our tribal laws till this day. That's how Millstream is very important to us.

There were additional worries extending to the whole of the Fortescue River. In 1975, the Public Works Department had produced a report outlining initial plans to build a dam on the Fortescue River, with preferred sites at Gregory Gorge or Dogger Gorge. These plans were discussed with alarm at the Pilbara Bush Meeting in July of the same year, making clear the importance of the whole of the Fortescue River area, not only to Yindjibarndi and Ngarluma, but also, with respect to the area around Gregory Gorge, to Kuruma people. As well as the strong opposition voiced at the Bush Meeting, the newly established Aboriginal Sites Department of the WA Museum was brought in to assess the archaeological and anthropological status of the area. Their report on archaeological and other sites of significance, together with a combination of technical, economic and environmental issues, resulted in the Public Works

---

12   Juluwarlu Aboriginal Corporation (2004: 1).
13   Daniels (1985: 36).

Department moving the dam proposal in 1981 to a stretch of the Harding River on Cooya Pooya Station. This was Ngarluma country, but responsibility for the site chosen was shared by Yindjibarndi people as part of a network of sites all along the Harding River valley interconnected with the Law and ceremonial life. An important rainmaking site (*thalu*) was situated right where the dam wall was planned. Its boss was an Yindjibarndi man, the rainmaker Long Mack. *Thalu* is an Yindjibarndi word. It refers to seasonal renewal or increase sites. Reynolds describes them:[14] '*Talu* are recognisable places where Aboriginal elders focus ritual action, activating or "taming and driving" spiritual forces. Usually associated with fertility and regeneration, *talu* may also be visited to bring drought, pestilence and discomfort to other people.'

The dam would flood the whole area and would destroy the rainmaking *thalu—bunggaliyarra*—and *nganirrina* (the tree in the moon)[15] in the earthworks necessary for its construction. There was also the further issue of the land around the dam that would be set aside under a special purpose lease as a catchment area, removing yet more land from access by Roebourne people.

These plans posed a painful dilemma for Aboriginal people in Roebourne and in the West Pilbara more generally. The need for an adequate water supply for the rapidly expanding population of the region made the building of a dam seem inevitable. Consequently, the destruction of sites was inevitable, regardless of which proposal was accepted. This forced people into the impossible position of being asked to make an assessment of the relative importance of differing sites, all of which formed part of an integral whole. At the Pilbara Bush Meeting, participants reluctantly agreed that it was the Fortescue that was of greater significance for Aboriginal groups in the region. When the Public Works Department made the recommendation to go ahead at Cooya Pooya, and Cabinet endorsed the recommendation in August 1982, it was left to Roebourne people to oppose it. This was a daunting task for people who had never previously mobilised to take concerted political action. But by this time they were able to draw on a number of new resources that provided them with a new basis for acting. One of these was the possible protection offered, after 1972, by the WA *Aboriginal Heritage Act*. The vehicle for this protection was the WA Museum's Aboriginal Sites Department, which, under a new Registrar, Michael Robinson, undertook serious research in consultation with local people. This was despite heavy commitments to carry out surveys in the Burrup Peninsula in the face of the establishment of yet another major resource development company, Woodside Petroleum Limited.

---

14  Reynolds (1989: 8).
15  Long Mack in Rijavec and Solomon (2005: Biographies).

Perhaps more importantly in the long run, people began to engage, tentatively at first, with the discourse of land rights that had emerged from the 1971 Gove case in the Northern Territory, when Yolgnu people had opposed the development of a bauxite mine by Nabalco.[16] The case had been lost, but it had led in the longer term to the passing by the Federal Government of the *Aboriginal Land Rights (Northern Territory) Act 1976*. By 1982, Aboriginal land rights were firmly on the national scene, even though they continued to be strongly contested by many other interests. Indigenous people across Australia were also making links with indigenous groups in other parts of the world, drawing on international law and the language of rights, especially as set out in the UN human rights regime.

In Roebourne, removed as it was from the centres of national political action, the process began slowly. In August 1982, the month of the Cabinet decision for the dam to go ahead on the Harding, Long Mack and Woodley King were in Perth. They took their concerns about the proposed dam to Michael Robinson at the Sites Department. They also went to visit Sisters Bernadine and Bernadette, then back in Perth, to explain the problem and enlist their support. In September, after further urgent investigation, the anthropologists presented their report on the importance of the area to the Aboriginal Cultural Material Committee of the WA Museum. In the end, however, the Museum Trustees—the people responsible under the Act—decided not to act on the recommendations made in the Sites Department's report. Work on the dam began. The only gesture to Roebourne people's concerns was the establishment by the Government of a working group to look at some form of compensation.

Early the following year, in April 1983, people held a large demonstration at the dam site with the support of the WA Aboriginal Legal Service. This was just two months after the Australian Labor Party under Brian Burke won government in Western Australia and a month after it won federal government under Bob Hawke. One of the first acts of the Hawke government was a proposal by the Minister for Aboriginal Affairs, Clyde Holding, to develop a national Aboriginal land rights policy. In the same month, March, the WA Government commissioned the Aboriginal Land Inquiry, to be carried out by Paul Seaman. He began his work in September 1983, the month of John Pat's death. It was also in 1983, however, that Long Mack died. Roebourne people associate his death directly with the destruction of country caused by the dam: 'He died of grief'.[17] Sister Bernadine made the same connection:

> The building of the dam was terrible. It was a shocking thing to do…I had a photo here, showing how Long Mack had come to Perth a couple

---

16   *Milirrpum v Nabalco Pty Ltd* (1971) 17 FLR 141.
17   Rijavec and Solomon (2005).

of years before, asking them not to touch that dam. Not to touch that particular place…When Long Mack got very ill, he came down to Perth, and he saw Bernadette and myself, and told us who to go to now in our dealings.

None of this slowed work on the dam. In July 1984, the Seaman Inquiry came to Roebourne. When the hearing began, in the middle of the dry season, 'the skies opened', as one of the witnesses described it, referring also to the unseasonal and eerie quality of the downpour. The general response of the Roebourne people present was that it was related to the damage done to the rainmaking site: 'See, Long Mack was right. He said this would happen.'

In his report, released in September of that year, Seaman included a number of statements by the witnesses who spoke to him. There were strong statements about the dam:[18]

> Yindjibarndi and Ngarluma meet there. It is at *Thalu* place…the old rainmakers came and the old people made rain. You have got to have a boomerang and throw it when you come out of the pool. We like our culture. When they break it they break everyone's feelings and we feel we have nothing. And how are we going to teach our young people. The old man said we have nothing and we want to teach our young people the Aboriginal way.

They were not to know, like Seaman himself and those who worked closely with him over an intensive year of listening to Aboriginal people all over the State, that the Government's proposed legislation would be defeated in the State's opposition-dominated upper house, the Legislative Assembly, in April 1985. This was after a concerted anti–land rights campaign over two periods in 1984 by the WA Chamber of Mines, supported by the then national mining industry umbrella organisation, the Australian Mining Industry Council. Burke's assessment that the Labor Party would lose a large number of seats in Western Australia at the next federal election if the Federal Government pursued its national land rights policy was also a key factor in the abandonment of that policy.

Nevertheless, during the course of this shifting debate, the Commonwealth passed its own *Aboriginal and Torres Strait Islander Heritage (Interim Protection) Act* in June 1984, a month before the Seaman Inquiry came to Roebourne. In the same month as the Inquiry hearings, July, Roebourne people lodged an application under the new Act to stop the dam. They did this after discussion with the Aboriginal Legal Service and others. Their application was the second one to be made under the new legislation. Roebourne moved again to the national

---

18   Seaman (1984: 52).

scene, this time not as a place of alcohol-fuelled violence and dysfunction, but as a place where people acted in defence of their culture. With 70 per cent of the dam construction completed, their application failed. The dam was opened in June 1985, 'with a silent protest from Aborigines', as reported in the *North West Telegraph* newspaper.[19]

At one level, then, the building of the dam represented yet another loss for Roebourne people and another instance of destruction. But David Daniels— himself a rainmaker looking after sites remaining on Cooya Pooya, Millstream and Sherlock stations—also saw it as a turning point:

> That dam really put the fight back into the people, even though they lost it. I told them there were sites that have to be protected. Before the dam, the people were just floating, didn't care about anything. But the dam made them realise the land was important. It gives us food. We have to make the sites work. Increase sites have to be made to work. Young people do go out; I'm teaching them. I always take five or six with me.

The State's compensation package provided some small gains: a 21-year lease for the land at Ngurrawaana, another small area of land near Millstream, and part salaries for two local people to be employed in site-related work. Both positions were taken up by Ngarluma men: David Daniels and David Walker. David Daniels made the further comment: 'Now we got some land. Before the Seventies we had nothing. Now we got something.'

In a crucial sense, the struggle over the Harding Dam can be seen as the first active collective engagement by Roebourne people with modernity. Their political action can be seen as a shift into the land rights discourse that, as for Indigenous peoples elsewhere, constitutes for them not a rejection of or a capitulation to, but a dialogue with, modernity. Modernisation was thrust upon them but, by becoming political actors, Roebourne people invoked the legal and political processes available to them as citizens of a democratic, secular society. The trial of the police officers for the manslaughter of John Pat could have suggested the possibility of protection for individuals under the rule of law. In the end it failed, although it did make clear that not even officers of the law are above the law. The struggle over the dam, as well as 'putting the fight back into people', gave some indication of the further possibilities for protection of country and sites that might be available, or could at least be sought, through other modern political and institutional processes.

In undertaking action to protect sites against destruction by the dam, for the first time Roebourne people consistently used the resources of the colonising, secular society in order to defend the sacred as the foundation and source

---

19   *North West Telegraph*, 5 June 1985.

of what they see as good and of what constitutes a good life for them. In the process, they reasserted the legitimacy of their moral evaluation of the good life and of the social practices necessary to express and promote a good life. In having to explain to the outside world the meaning of places such as Gregory's Gorge, Millstream, the Harding River, and the coherence of the belief system that underlies that meaning, they were very publicly expressing the value that they continued to place on their culture.

They were also setting out terms—their own alternative terms—by which country was to be valued, different from the economic terms that drive the industrial development of the region. They were affirming their own social imaginary and seeking a place for it in the modern world. They were initiating a local version of a project that Sahlins describes as 'the indigenisation of modernity':[20] 'What the self-consciousness of "culture" does signify, is the demand of different peoples for their own space within the world cultural order.'

In Roebourne, opposition to the construction of the dam gave notice of how people wanted to define their own space, even while pursuing programs for income generation, education, training and employment in the broader society.

The Harding Dam was not the only battle fought by Pilbara Aboriginal people over this decade. The dispute over Hamersley Iron's Marandoo mine in the Central Pilbara was also a key politicising event. The issue of destruction of sites by the mine was compounded by the siting of Hamersley Iron's mining lease in a national park. Karijini National Park includes traditional country of three main groups: Bunjima, Kuruma and Innawonga.[21] In 1989, these groups became involved in discussions with the then Department of Conservation and Land Management (CALM) about the possibility of joint management. As recounted by Slim Parker,[22] one of the key players then and later:

> In the course of this process the three groups established an umbrella organisation to monitor the park in an organised way and meet with CALM to work out the process of joint management...The organisation formed was the Karijini Aboriginal Corporation...The name Karijini is our Aboriginal word for a part of the Hamersley Ranges where our traditional land is situated.

The park area was also subject to a plethora of exploration and mining tenements mostly predating the proclamation of the park, most with Government Agreement

---

20  Sahlins (2005: 48).
21  A national park, under different names, had existed in the area since 1969 though the name was not formally changed to Karijini National Park until 1991.
22  Quoted in Olive (1997: 141–2).

Acts and all relating to iron ore.[23] Karijini Aboriginal Corporation, formed to deal with environmental issues, was in the front line to challenge the development of the Marandoo mine and the destruction of identified cultural sites when Hamersley Iron released the company's Environmental Review and Management Plan in 1992.[24] Once again, Western Australia's *Aboriginal Heritage Act* proved inadequate in providing protection; the company was granted consent under Section 18 of the Act and the Government then finalised legislation that excised the area from the park under the *Aboriginal Heritage (Marandoo) Act 1992*. The mine, like the Harding Dam, went ahead. Nevertheless, the recognition of native title by the High Court in the same year, 1992, was about to bring about dramatic change in the place of Indigenous people in Australia and to provide a new place of encounter between tradition and modernity.

# Practical transformations: Cultural concerns and legal action

In response to a bid by a different group—the Meriam people in the Torres Strait—to define indigenous space within the modern Australian legal and political system, the High Court of Australia gave its decision in *Mabo v Queensland [No. 2]* on 3 July 1992.[25] Their judgement held that the common law of Australia recognised native title, that is, that Aboriginal and Torres Strait Islander ownership of land and waters that predated colonisation could continue to exist and, where it did so, the common law could recognise those ongoing traditional rights and interests. The case itself was a claim by Eddie Mabo and others on behalf of the Meriam people to the island of Mer in the Torres Strait. The claim was based on Meriam ownership of the land and waters according to their traditional law and custom.

The judgement overturned the most basic tenet of landownership and title in Australia, that is, that the Crown gained ownership of all the land and waters at colonisation. This principle underlay not only the whole land-tenure system. It was also the basis on which Aboriginal land rights, in South Australia, the Northern Territory, New South Wales, Victoria and Queensland, had been granted by legislation; that is, that governments could choose to give certain lands and waters to Aboriginal people and the terms on which they would do so. The *Mabo* decision, for the first time, recognised that the Meriam people and, by extension, Torres Strait Islander and Aboriginal people generally had

---

23  Department of Conservation and Land Management (1999). Blue asbestos had been mined earlier, including by Lang Hancock before he moved to nearby Wittenoom Gorge in 1937.
24  Rio Tinto Iron Ore (2006: ix).
25  *Mabo v Queensland* [No. 2] (1992) 175 CLR 1.

owned country according to their own traditional laws and customs prior to colonisation, and that this ownership could have survived, as it did on the island of Mer.

The court also established some of the key limits of common-law recognition of native title: that the Crown had acquired sovereignty through colonisation; that it had to have been demonstrated that the Meriam people continued to practise their traditional laws and customs in relation to their land and waters and had done so without interruption; and that native title had not been 'extinguished' by subsequent valid grants of title, such as freehold title, to others.

For all its faults and limitations, the *Mabo* decision fundamentally changed the place of Indigenous people in Australia, in principle if not altogether in practice. It was not the first time that legal and land-tenure systems had provided for Aboriginal ownership of land to be based on the ongoing practice of traditional laws and customs; this was the tenet underlying the Northern Territory *Aboriginal Land Rights Act* and other land rights legislation in some States. But *Mabo* was the first time that the common law recognised that an Indigenous group was entitled, as against the whole of the world, to the possession, occupation, use, and enjoyment of its land and waters, not by grant of the Crown, but on the basis and under the conditions of its own traditional laws and customs. As a later High Court judgement observed:[26] 'Native title is neither an institution of the common law nor a form of common law tenure but it is recognised by the common law. There is, therefore, an intersection of traditional laws and customs with the common law.'

The *Mabo* decision constitutes acknowledgment by a rational, secular legal system of alternative systems of meaning. In so doing, the judges dared also both to draw explicitly on international law and to invoke moral values. Rationality embraced morality and brought Indigenous rights into line with human rights:[27]

> If it were permissible in past centuries to keep the common law in step with international law, it is imperative in today's world that the common law should neither be nor be seen to be frozen in an age of racial discrimination. The fiction by which the rights and interests of indigenous inhabitants in land were treated as non-existent was justified by a policy which has no place in the contemporary law of this country.

The judgement went on to say:[28] 'Aborigines were dispossessed of their land parcel by parcel, to make way for expanding colonial settlement. Their dispossession underwrote the development of the nation.'

---

26   *Fejo v Northern Territory* (1998) 156 ALR 721 at 46.
27   *Mabo v Queensland* [No. 2] (1992) 175 CLR 1, paras 41–2.
28   ibid., para. 82.

*Mabo*, like the common law itself, challenges the view that a definitive break with the past is essential to modernity, and that tradition stands separate from it and in stark contrast with it. It throws a different light on Habermas's recapitulation of 'the break brought about with the past' as a 'continuous renewal',[29] demonstrating that continuous renewal does not require a discounting of the past; rather, it must take account of the past in order to offer a solid base for the future. But it can also reinterpret the past, re-creating meaning and a moral vision grounded in the past—in this case, radically—offering alternative meanings as well as a new legitimacy. Central to this transformation was a practical application to Indigenous Australians of the universal principles of human rights.

The potentially radical implications of the recognition of native title were greeted with euphoria by Indigenous people and with dismay by governments, who saw the possibility of the land-tenure system collapsing in chaos. In the event, and over the following years, neither reaction proved to be justified. But the Federal Government moved to enact legislation to clarify the extent and limits of native title, to validate previous titles where possible, and to put in place a system to manage native title processes. After months of debate, fearmongering, discussion and consultation, including serious consultation with Indigenous people, the *Native Title Act* was passed a few days before Christmas in 1993. Its substantive provisions came into effect on 1 January 1994.

In addition to the recognition and protection of native title, and the validation of past grants, the Act provides for a future act regime by which determinations could be made as to whether future grants could be made or acts done over native title land and waters. In recognition that it would take time—though the drafters of the legislation had little idea how much time it would take—to come to a final determination, the Act provided for an interim registration process that gives registered native title applicants a limited but precious right to negotiate with the people who want to do anything on or to their land.[30]

In a mineral-rich area like the Pilbara, this provided altogether new possibilities, and a fundamental shift in the relationship between Aboriginal and non-Aboriginal people, to the alarm of many of the latter. It did not take Pilbara Aboriginal people and their advisers long to realise the importance and the possibilities of gaining recognition of their native title rights, thereby defining their own terms of participation more directly by moving from the periphery into the centre of future negotiations over proposed developments.

At the same time, the rush to application and registration of claims, and the need to define precise traditional group identities and boundaries, gave rise to

---

29   Habermas (2002: 7).
30   *Native Title Act 1993*, Division 3: Future Acts and Native Title.

a twofold response. One was to bring groups together in order to pursue joint objectives. The other was to precipitate the emergence of competing groups, in dispute over both boundaries and identities. At one level, such disputes reflect recurrent processes in traditional Aboriginal social life and the tension between what Sutton refers to as atomism and collectivism.[31] Peterson, Keen and Sansom also suggest that fission (the splitting of groups into smaller units) is a recurrent and therefore normalised process of Aboriginal life, reflecting in part the 'wide variety of links—through descent, adoption, marriage, conception, and so on— with other groups and country'.[32] Seasonal and demographic changes, as well as trading and ceremonial cycles, also played a part. However, another critical element now is the presence of modern resource development and Aboriginal people's desire both to protect country better and to ensure a maximum share of the benefits, both symbolic and material, for their group, their families, and themselves. On this basis, group and boundary definitions are fiercely, and strategically, disputed.

## Native title and collectivism

Both these processes, of collectivism and of atomism, were evident from the time of the passing of the *Native Title Act* at the end of 1993. The first Pilbara claim to be lodged was a joint one: the Ngarluma/Yindjibarndi application. The application was lodged by David Daniel,[33] James Solomon, Tim Kerr and Daisy Moses on behalf of Ngarluma people and by Bruce Monadee, Karrie Monadee, Woodley King, Yilbie Warrie and Kenny Jerrold on behalf of Yindjibarndi (then spelt Injibandi) people. John Pat's mother, Mavis Pat, was one of the Yindjibarndi claimant group and later gave oral evidence about how she had grown up on Mount Florence Station.[34]

The lodging of the application was just the first step in what was to prove a complex, difficult, often painful, and contested process that would be litigated and would last for more than 10 years. A number of the old people and other important claimants would pass away before a decision was finally reached on 2 May 2005.[35]

---

31   Sutton (2003: 85 ff.).

32   Edmunds (1995: 4); Peterson et al. (1977).

33   David Daniel and David Daniels are the same person.

34   *Daniel v State of Western Australia* [2003] FCA 666, paras 1246, 1259.

35   *National Native Title Tribunal, Native title determination summary, Daniel v State of Western Australia* [2005] FCA. The decision was of a single judge of the Federal Court. It was appealed on a number of grounds to the full Federal Court, which effectively upheld the decision of the single judge apart from his ruling of total extinguishment of native title on a number of pastoral leases; they found partial extinguishment instead. This finding supports the Wik principle of coexistence on pastoral leases (*Moses v State of Western Australia* [2007] FCAFC 78, and *Dale v Moses* [2007] FCAFC 82).

Many other Central and West Pilbara claims followed the Ngarluma/Yindjibarndi claim in those early, hopeful years— some 35 in 1995 and 1996[36]—many hastily, though not thoughtlessly, prepared and lodged. Only three of these in addition to Ngarluma/Yindjibarndi—Eastern Guruma, Ngarla and Thalanyji—have since been partly or wholly determined. Like Ngarluma/Yindjibarndi, all have taken more than 10 years. Unlike Ngarluma/Yindjibarndi, the determinations were finally achieved by the consent of all the parties rather than by litigation. A number of the other claims have since been modified, combined, or withdrawn, especially after the stringent amendments to the *Native Title Act* and in particular to the future act regime in 1998.

For groups wanting in particular to activate the right to negotiate processes in the shorter term, the rewards were to be more immediate. Initially, a significant number of claims were lodged as what were informally referred to as polygon claims. These were often small, irregularly shaped claims covering various mining tenements rather than the whole of a group's traditional country. Their aim was to protect that part of country subject to anticipated development. A very large polygon claim was the combined Bunjima, Niapali, Innawonga claim, lodged in mid 1996, to ensure access to the right to negotiate for all three groups over the proposed development of Hamersley Iron's Yandicoogina mine. The effectiveness of this combined approach made clear that the *Native Title Act*'s future act regime, with its right for registered claimants to negotiate with parties about developments on their land, had changed irrevocably the relationships between Pilbara Aboriginal groups and resource developers. On the one hand, responding to proposals for further development made constant demands on the native title claimants and their Native Title Representative Bodies in terms of time and energy. On the other, for the first time it gave Aboriginal people, in the Pilbara and elsewhere, a place at the negotiating table, and a place that was theirs not by courtesy but by right.

The Act also achieved a major change in the approach to Aboriginal people by the major resource companies. The leader in bringing about this change was CRA Limited, now Rio Tinto, of which Hamersley Iron was a part.[37]

---

36  I deal here only with some of the native title groups in the Central and West Pilbara, not with those such as the Martu and Nyangumarta, of the East Pilbara, both of which have also been determined after lengthy negotiations.

37  This view is supported by Fred Chaney (Rio Tinto Iron Ore 2006: 83): 'While being alive to the fact that nobody is perfect including Hamersley Iron or Rio, I think it's fair to say that they have been instrumental in achieving widespread cultural change in the mining industry.'

# Mining and modernisation

If the Harding Dam can be seen as the turning point for Roebourne people in their engagement with modernity, and Marandoo for Bunjima, Kuruma and Innawonga groups, then the same can be said for the *Native Title Act* in relation to mining companies to the extent that they finally accepted that Indigenous people remain part of the modern world and, more significantly, continue to have rights and interests in the land to which mining companies want access. Indigenous people can no longer be regarded as part of the past for mining and other resource companies; they are pivotal to their future.

This was wholly new in Australia. It was not that companies like Hamersley Iron had taken no account of Roebourne people previously. Once they were established in the region, they worked with Ieramugadu to put limited employment programs in place and gave some support to education programs. Robe River took on a small number of Aboriginal apprentices, one of whom, Brendan Cook, was their apprentice of the year in 1987. But these were very small gains for people who had been swept aside in the march of progress through the 1960s and 1970s. Moreover, the mining industry had played a very active role in opposing, first, the proposed Aboriginal land rights legislation in Western Australia in 1984. One of the most infamous of the Chamber of Mines' campaign advertisements was of a black hand building a wall of bricks across the whole northern half of the State, with a large sign attached to the wall: 'KEEP OUT. This land is under Aboriginal claim.' Then in the debate over the Commonwealth Native Title Bill in 1993, the industry had lobbied hard and extensively to limit the impact of native title in terms of retaining all their rights of access for exploration and mining, and argued that any mining or exploration grants should extinguish native title. They failed in the latter attempt. Their chagrin was apparent at midnight on 21 December 1993, when the Senate gave final agreement to the provisions of the Bill and the packed public galleries erupted in enthusiastic applause while, on the floor of the Senate, all but the opposition Senators stood and applauded in return. Many in the mining industry continued to sulk over the next year.

Then in March 1995, some nine months after he became the Managing Director of CRA Limited, Leon Davis made national headlines when he stated in a speech to the Securities Institute in Melbourne and Sydney that CRA welcomed the *Mabo* decision and accepted the central tenet of the *Native Title Act*. He made himself very clear:[38]

> Let me say this bluntly. CRA is satisfied with the central tenet of the *Native Title Act*. In CRA we believe that there are major opportunities

---

38    Davis (1995: 4).

for growth in outback Australia which will only be realised with the full co-operation of all interested parties. This Government initiative has laid the basis for better exploration access and thus increased the probability that the next decade will see a series of CRA operations developed in active partnership with Aboriginal people.

Davis had been in Bougainville in Papua New Guinea in 1989 when the CRA Panguna copper and gold mine had been closed down in the face of a secessionist movement that turned into a long-running civil war. He had learnt the lesson of what can happen when companies ignore or give an inadequate response to the rights and concerns of traditional landowners.

Past positions lingered, and CRA remained a party to the Ngarluma/Yindjibarndi native title litigation. Nevertheless, Davis moved swiftly to change things. As part of implementing the change, he established a new position of Vice-President, Aboriginal Relations, based in the company's head office in Melbourne, and appointed Paul Wand to the position.[39]

The CRA initiatives were echoed in the Australian Mining Industry Council. Their new President, Jerry Ellis, of BHP Petroleum, was quoted as confirming that the council 'handled its participation in the *Mabo* debate poorly':[40] 'We did get a bit out of control, I think, in the debate over land title issues and certainly we became ineffective. So we have decided to go back to some core values.'

In the Pilbara, the effects of this turnaround were first felt in the Yandicoogina negotiations; in March 1997, Hamersley and the Bunjima, Niapiali and Innawonga claimants signed the Yandicoogina Agreement (the Yandi Land Use Agreement). This was the first regional land-use agreement to be reached with a major resource company after the passing of the *Native Title Act*. Its lessons flowed on to Rio Tinto's dealings with Aboriginal people throughout the Pilbara.

Other companies also took heed. In 1999, for example, Woodside negotiated an agreement with Ngarluma and Yindjibarndi people to set up the Ngarluma and Yindjibarndi Foundation to create and operate 'initiatives for the social, cultural, economic, business and educational development' and 'the health and wellbeing of the Beneficiaries'.[41] Also in 1999, Robe River entered into an agreement with the Gobawarrah Minduarra Yinhawanga group over part of the West Angelas mine and the surrounding related infrastructure.[42]

---

39  Wand and Wilkie (2001: 6).
40  *Business Review Weekly*, 29 May 1995, p. 24.
41  Ngarluma and Yindjibarndi Foundation Constitution 2000.
42  This agreement was transferred to Rio Tinto in 2000, together with other Robe River agreements, when Rio Tinto took over North Limited, which had previously taken over Robe River.

BHP Billiton entered into negotiations for its proposed Area C mine with the same claimant groups that had constituted the Bunjima, Niaparli and Innawonga claim for Hamersley Iron's Yandicoogina agreement. By then, however, the groups had split and the Area C mining agreement is therefore made up of three separate agreements: Martu Idja Bunyjima native title claimants in December 2000; Innawonga Bunjima Niapaili native title claimants in June 2001; and Nyiyaparli claimants in relation to the powerline corridor to the mine. The split exemplifies two processes: one was the partial rationalisation of the initial polygon claim, with the Nyiyaparli group adjusting its boundaries and lodging its own country claim; the other was the process of atomisation.

## Native title and atomism

As already indicated, the impetus for the combining and splitting of groups arises within the traditional Aboriginal domain. From one point of view, disputes arise out of the removal of people from traditional country, the fragmentation of traditional networks of relations among neighbouring groups, and the deaths of old people who held the knowledge and the Law. This is one of the dimensions covered by the concept of culture loss. For Indigenous people, the issue of culture loss is as much about losing people as it is about losing access to traditional country.

From another perspective, the different combinations and separations represent the ongoing connection of people to their traditional country, even when they may no longer live there, and their deep concerns for country as their source of the good. Just as importantly, the lodging of separate claims can be seen as a vehicle for asserting legitimacy in the newly defined arena where traditional indigenous life engages with modernity and demands access to some of the goods from which they had been previously excluded. Overlapping claims also suggest that, for different individuals and groups, access to modern institutions offers an opportunity for personal and group gain, even at the expense of others.

The principles on which dissent developed among Pilbara Aboriginal groups are similar to those experienced by other native title claimant groups:[43]

> [They] are also the principles on which traditional relations operate, for example, questions of descent, of who has the right to speak, of who holds what knowledge and how that knowledge may be used. Particular disputes may be long-standing and deeply embedded, but often signal

---

43   Edmunds (1995: 2).

the importance of the matters at stake and the buoyancy of Aboriginal interests. Conflict, that is, is an indication of the continuing vigour of Aboriginal society, not of its breakdown.

In ways unanticipated by the framers of the *Native Title Act*, native title itself has become one more factor that has been added to the resources of Aboriginal political life[44] and part of the project of the indigenisation of modernity.[45] In the case of Pilbara claims, different accounts of descent also reflect a general characteristic of oral tradition: that is, that 'historical memory beyond two or three generations is blurred or forgotten'.[46] The different claims to the group affiliation of individuals from three or four generations back may not, of itself, indicate cultural loss but rather cultural memory.

At the same time, as Sutton suggests:[47] 'Where small landed groups belong to larger congeries, and also may overlap considerably in memberships and geographical scope, subgroups may pursue their interests rather atomically unless convinced that their interests are better served by some form of coalition.'

The coalition formed to negotiate the Yandicoogina agreement served the interests of the Nyiyaparli people well but it was always acknowledged that, once the agreement was reached, they would separate from the combined claim and lodge their own extended country claim east and southwards. They finalised this in 2005.

For the Bunjima and Innawonga groups in the combined claim, subgroup interests quickly emerged after the Gumala organisation, with its associated investment arm and trusts, was set up to manage the benefits from the Yandicoogina agreement. This management process, and the distribution of benefits, quickly became highly politicised. Disputes developed along family and subgroup lines. Without withdrawing from either the agreement or from Gumala, the Gobawarrah Minduarra Yinhawanga families split from the main Innawonga group and lodged a separate claim in mid 1997. This was to the south of the combined claim and covered part of the West Angelas proposed mine site and associated infrastructure corridors. A little more than a year later, the rest of the Innawonga group lodged their own separate claim, overlapping some, though not all, of the Gobawarrah Minduarra Yinhawanga claim and not including any of the West Angelas areas.

Bunjima also split into two subgroups: Bunjima and Martu Idja Bunjima. The split was along geographic as well as family lines, with the subgroups informally

---

44   ibid., p. 2.
45   Sahlins (2005: 48).
46   *Daniel v State of Western Australia* [2003] FCA 666, para. 365.
47   Sutton (2003: 85).

identified as Top End Bunjima, associated with the tablelands of the Hamersley Range, or Bottom End Bunjima, associated with the Fortescue River. When the Fortescue Bunjima—the Martu Idja Bunjima—lodged their separate claim in 1998, it overlapped the Bunjima part of the remaining Innawonga Bunjima claim. The overlap included the highly prospective Hope Downs 1 mining lease.

Both these disputes, as well as reflecting family and subgroup identities, also crystallised around particular forceful individuals. Some, like Slim Parker,[48] were veterans of the Marandoo battle and already canny in the ways of government and resource companies, as well as of Aboriginal politics. Others had gained their experience in the workplace, like Alice Smith's son Charles,[49] who emerged from working for BHP Billiton for nine years to lead the Yandicoogina and Area C negotiations and to be the first chair for Gumala.[50]

The Ngarluma group experienced a similar splitting. In mid 1997, five other claims overlapped parts of the Ngarluma/Yindjibarndi claim. Most of these were finally settled or withdrawn. One overlapping claim, however, was lodged in August 1996 by the Yaburara and Mardudhunera group. In the Federal Court hearings for the Ngarluma/Yindjibarndi claim, the court had to deal with the relationship between the Ngarluma and the Yaburara. The question was asked about whether any of the claimant families could identify as Yaburara, whether Yaburara were northern Ngarluma, or whether they existed as a group at all. The question was very relevant to the issue of traditional ownership of the Burrup Peninsula and whether the Peninsula was 'orphan country' to which Ngarluma claimed succession under traditional law, or whether it had always been Ngarluma country. This was a matter of concern to David Daniels even in 1987:

> The Burrup, there used to be Yaburara people. But [country is] always handed on. It's now being taken over by Ngarluma people. We were always related with Yaburara people. They were known by the old people as Yaburara Ngarluma. It's wrong that the Burrup belongs to nobody. We've had three dances there already.

In the end, the judge's findings were that[51]

> those of the second [Yaburara and Mardudhunera] applicants who claim to be Yaburara have not established that to be the case. The evidence

---

48   Martu Idja Bunjima.
49   Bunjima.
50   In 2011, what had been the separate and overlapping Martu Idja Bunjima and Bunjima claims were combined into a single Banjima People claim.
51   *Daniel v State of Western Australia* [2003] FCA 666, para. 352.

supports the view that the second applicants having a claim in the claim area claim as Mardudhunera. It should be noted, however, that they have by younger generation intermarriage strong links to the Yindjibarndi.

The existence of Mardudhunera people as a distinct group was not challenged. Throughout all the proceedings, the Ngarluma and Yindjibarndi claimants made clear that they regarded the families involved in the Yaburara and Mardudhunera claim as part of their own claimant group and that they were willing to accept them into the claim.

The same was true for the three families who lodged the Wong-Goo-TT-OO application in July 1998. Up to that time, they had been an acknowledged, and acknowledged themselves as, part of the Ngarluma group.[52] It was also accepted that the name Wong-Goo-TT-OO was not the name of any tribe or traditional landowning group but had been adopted for the purpose of submitting a separate application.[53] In the trial, Wilfred Hicks made the position of the Wong-Goo-TT-OO as a Ngarluma subgroup clear:[54]

> Wilfred Hicks claimed he had full rights in the core country of his claim area because he carried the law for that area. He had been 'overrun' by others such as the Yindjibarndi and had therefore not asserted his rights earlier. He claimed rights in the Ngurin [Harding] area through his grandfather. He said he was 'claiming as a Wong-Goo-TT-OO group of a Ngarluma person'.

The court's finding, upheld on appeal,[55] was that the Wong-Goo-TT-OO are not native title holders unless they are accepted as Ngarluma or Yindjibarndi.

At around 320 pages, Justice Nicholson's reasons, given in 2003, for the Ngarluma/Yindjibarndi judgement are lengthy and detailed, like many judgements in the native title process.[56] The determination was finally made two years later, on 2 May 2005. It was the first native title claim to be determined in the Pilbara. The judge handed it down in Roebourne, on the Old Reserve. David Daniels, who gave his name to the case and who had been a driving force in the development of the claim, did not live to join in the celebrations. Too many of the other representatives named in the original claim, as well as other claimants, had also passed away during the course of the proceedings.

---

52   ibid., para. 246.
53   ibid., paras 246, 354.
54   ibid., para. 1387.
55   *Moses v State of Western Australia* [2007] FCAFC 78 (7 June 2007).
56   Justice Nicholson's decision is among those giving comfort to those wishing for native title holders to enjoy the full benefits of the Mabo decision. In contrast, and because of its novelty, the legal implications of the recognition of native title have been examined exhaustively in the courts. With a few exceptions, notably the Wik determination, the courts have progressively narrowed the promise and potential of native title for Indigenous Australians.

David Daniels' wife, Tootsie Daniels, and James Solomon's son, Trevor Solomon, spoke on behalf of the claimant group in acknowledging the very important role played by them. 'They urged the younger people to remember them as role models, and to continue with the fight for land and recognition that they began over a decade ago.'[57]

Atomisation, however, continues. Before the Ngarluma/Yindjibarndi determination, all three of the registered native title claimant groups were involved in the very difficult two-year negotiations with the State Government and a number of companies over the Burrup Peninsula. Together with the surrounding Dampier Archipelago, the Burrup has one of the world's largest and most important collections of rock carvings or petroglyphs. The exact number of these is not known, but they are estimated to be in their thousands and many to date back thousands of years. Unlike the Yandicoogina negotiations, for the Burrup negotiations the three native title claimant groups did not combine though, in the end, all three signed the agreement in 2002[58] and the combined Murujuga Aboriginal Corporation was incorporated in 2006. The Corporation is to manage the benefits that flow from the agreement on behalf of the Ngarluma Yindjibarndi, Yaburara Mardudhunera and Wong-Goo-TT-OO people.

In practice, the logistics remained fraught; heritage clearances over the agreement area, for example, were often carried out twice, with the Wong-Goo-TT-OO insisting on their ongoing rights under the *Aboriginal Heritage Act* as 'a representative body of persons of Aboriginal descent [which] has an interest in a place or object to which this Act applies that is of traditional and current importance to it'.[59] Since their determination, disputes also emerged between the Ngarluma and Yindjibarndi groups, impeding access to their joint benefits for both.[60] And, in the Central Pilbara, the Bunjima and Martu Idja Bunjima dispute for a decade proved resistant to agreement. The claims were finally combined into a single new claim, Banjima People, in July 2011.

At the same time, the Bunjima and Innawonga joint claimants agreed in 2008 to the boundary that would be used to separate the Innawonga Bunjima claim into its separate country areas. And the two Innawonga groups have resolved their key differences. In 2010, a joint Yinhawanga claim was lodged over the area overlapped by the two previous claims.[61] Indeed, the transformation of Pilbara Aboriginal people through native title from affected observers to active participants has led increasingly to a culture of agreement-making rather

---

57   Government of Western Australia, Office of Native Title, *Newsletter* 2005(5), p. 1.
58   The Burrup and Maitland Industrial Estates Agreement Implementation Deed (the Burrup Agreement), 1 November 2002.
59   Section 9.
60   The Yindjibarndi group itself splintered in 2011 in response to proposals for mining and infrastructure development and related benefits by Fortescue Metals Group.
61   National Native Title Tribunal web site: <www.nntt.gov.au>, Publications, maps and research.

than of litigation. Yamatji Marlpa Aboriginal Corporation, the Native Title Representative Body, has played a key role in this development. So, too, have some of the major resource companies since 1996.

# Agreements as a negotiation of meanings between the old and the new

Agreements, along with native title itself, have become one of the intercultural arenas where Pilbara Aboriginal people are demanding attention, and forging new meanings for their traditional cultural beliefs and practices as they attempt to maintain them under the general pressure of modernisation and the particular and intense pressure of the latest resource boom. Companies have now to accommodate alternative meanings. The various agreement processes have turned out to be a test of the possibility of negotiating meaning between the old and the new in the context of a mediated modernity. They would not have happened without the native title process.

They have resulted in significant benefits for the claimant groups. They have also carried high costs for them, not least the constant and urgent demand for a response to developments by an increasing multitude of companies: the big ones, Rio Tinto, BHP Billiton, Woodside, Chevron; increasingly high-profile operators: Fortescue Metals, Sino Iron (joint-venture partner with Mineralogy); and the plethora of juniors. After the hiatus in 2007 and 2008 prompted by the global financial crisis, all returned to rapid expansion mode. Not all the resulting agreements are of high standard and the state has too often been absent from the scene.

Nevertheless, Rio Tinto, BHP Billiton and others have engaged in extensive and long-term negotiations with those native title groups affected by their operations and raised expectations—some possibly unrealistic—among the groups as to what is possible. In 2006, for example, Rio Tinto embarked on a coordinated and ambitious agreements project that included 10 of the 11 groups within its 'footprint'.[62]

This followed the publication in 2005 of a book by John Taylor and Ben Scambary, *Indigenous People and the Pilbara Mining Boom*, researched as part of an Australian Research Council linkage project between The Australian National University's Centre for Aboriginal Economic Policy Research and Rio Tinto. With its recent history of agreements, Rio Tinto expected to find that the

---

62    The eleventh group is the Eastern Guruma, with whom separate negotiations were already under way.

socioeconomic situation of Pilbara Aboriginal people had improved significantly over the previous two decades. The company was startled to find that this was not the case, and that there had been little or no improvement at all.

The authors summarise their conclusions:[63]

> It was noted that the number of agreements between mining companies and Indigenous community or regional organisations had grown substantially over the past two decades…However, research to date indicates that for a complex set of reasons, Indigenous economic status has changed little in recent decades—dependence on government remains high and the relative economic status of Indigenous people residing adjacent to major long-life mines is similar to that of Indigenous people elsewhere in regional and remote Australia.

The authors go on to give some reasons for this 'unexpected outcome':

> This situation of stasis partly reflects the limited capacity of Indigenous community organisations both to cope with the impacts of, and take advantage of, large-scale operations. On the other hand, it is also seen that such organisations and the people they represent may have ambivalent responses to the potential cultural assimilation implied by their increasing integration into a market economy and its monetisation of many aspects of social life.

Combined with the unwelcome reflections generated by the Taylor-Scambary report was the finalising, also in 2005, of a commercial agreement with Hancock Prospecting for a joint-venture development of Hope Downs mine. It was the urgency for Rio Tinto to develop Hope Downs, and the fact that it was covered by the various registered combined and overlapping native title claims, that was the main trigger for the development of the Rio Tinto Pilbara Agreements Project.

Working with the Native Title Representative Body, Yamatji Marlpa Aboriginal Corporation, agreements with seven of the groups were signed by the end of 2006. These were binding initial agreements, dealing with the company's need for clearance for development and, in return, providing substantial ongoing financial benefits to the groups. These agreements also included a commitment by the company to negotiate final agreements that would cover other matters such as employment and training, business development and contracting, cultural and environmental protection, and cultural awareness training.[64] In

---

63  Taylor and Scambary (2005: 1).
64  Litchfield (2009). Despite intensive negotiations over 2007 and 2008 and agreement on the key elements by the end of 2008, the process then limped on over the next two years. At the end of 2010, the stage-two agreements had not been finalised, suggesting that commercial urgency continues to play a key role in mobilising the company's attention and priorities.

addition, Rio Tinto proposed and successfully lobbied the Federal Government to fund a Connection Report Project that would allow Yamatji Marlpa to produce connection reports for all the claimant groups involved in the Agreements Project, including the Martu Idja Bunjima, as part of a broader Bunjima report.[65] The company also funded Yamatji Marlpa to engage consultants to work with the groups over several years to develop governance structures for the trusts that would manage the financial benefits from the agreements.

The results of this project remain to be seen but, with the financial benefits secured, the approach made a major contribution to the developing agreements culture and to the expansion of the intercultural space where the groups could assert what mattered to them and make clear that some meanings, whatever happened in practice, were non-negotiable. Also made clear in the process was that the Rio Tinto vision of regional governance, controversially embodied in the incorporation of Marnda Mia Proprietary Limited in early 2007, could only work if it was grounded in people's local rights and given local support.[66]

The processes involved in making agreements also provide more protection than does litigation or other adversarial options to those areas of traditional law and custom that people do not wish to reveal to outsiders: the specifically Aboriginal space that lies outside modernity and that is essential to the maintenance of a distinct Indigenous social imaginary. In engaging with the legal processes now available to them, which represent one of the avenues offered by modernity, Indigenous people are confronted with a decision about the extent to which they are prepared to subject their knowledge to external scrutiny and, by so doing, risk altering its social and cultural roles. The majority of Pilbara Aboriginal people made the choice to pursue their claim; in the long run, they saw it as their best way to protect and maintain the traditional bases for their values and practices, to pass on Law and culture to the next generations, and to do so under the conditions of modern life. Increasingly, they see agreements, including agreement about their native title claim itself, as the most effective avenue for achieving this.

At the same time as the attempts to maintain a distinct Indigenous space, modernisation has changed the lives of Indigenous people, drawing them

---

65  Connection reports are a requirement of the State Government. The Government assesses the reports as the basis of its agreement or otherwise to consent to rather than to litigate native title claims.

66  This issue had also arisen in the company's—then CRA's—approach to early negotiations over the Century Zinc mine in Queensland in 1996 and 1997. This had resulted in the Gulf Communities Agreement, reached with the State and the relevant native title groups after an earlier approach to deal with the matters on a regional level had failed. Marnda Mia was based on a loose coalition of native title groups, the Central Negotiating Committee, which came together in 2006 with the support of Yamatji Marlpa, the Native Title Representative Body, to deal with the Rio Tinto agreement negotiations. Its subsequent incorporation as Marnda Mia, with the support of Rio Tinto but without the support of Yamatji Marlpa, led to a troubled relationship between it and many of the native title groups who had previously been part of the Central Negotiating Committee.

increasingly beyond the local into regional and global arenas. Not least in this process has been the growing awareness by Indigenous groups, including Pilbara Aboriginal people, of international standards of human rights and, based on this, of Indigenous rights, an awareness based in international networks that has increasingly informed their local and regional politics,[67] and what they expect from agreements.

One of the transformations brought about by modernity, indeed, is the development of identity as Indigenous, as well as Aboriginal:[68]

> The term [indigenous] is relatively new, actively used for only the past few decades, yet it invokes people's sense of permanence and their ability to survive and stay close to their cultures and homelands despite almost insurmountable odds. With this paradox as its starting point, indigenous identity reveals itself to be a quintessentially modern phenomenon.

Pilbara Aboriginal people recognise their broader Indigenous identity, but that identity remains firmly grounded in their local domains. What remains at stake for Aboriginal people in the Pilbara generally is their interpretation of what constitutes the good and how they define a good life. The Pilbara experience suggests that people found their basis for action in reasserting the values grounded in traditional life and culture and in reaffirming these as their moral source. They did this through political action in the face of attempts to relegate their values and concerns to nostalgia for the past. They lost the battles over the Harding Dam and the Marandoo mine, but the *Mabo* decision offered legitimacy to their reasons for fighting them. It also, together with the *Native Title Act*, provided them with the first effective legal means to reposition themselves in relation to modern Australian society of which they are now part. The native title claims became an active reconstruction of a framework of meaning, offering the possibility of a coherent engagement with the broader society, and bringing the land, the Law, and ceremonial life out of the shadows to become potent not just for Pilbara Aboriginal people but also between them and those who had defined them as Other.

At the same time, native title has meant that that engagement has had to be negotiated in relation to the present and in a dialogue with modernity. As one of the Yindjibarndi native title holders commented, 'We always knew about our country. We didn't need to go to court to tell people about it.' But he also observed, 'Things in Roebourne are very different from what it was. A lot of positive things are happening.' To cite but a few, Roebourne is now home to a flourishing community of Aboriginal artists, with several centres providing

---

67    Niezen (2003).
68    ibid., pp. xi–xii.

work spaces and commercial opportunities.[69] Local Aboriginal artists figure increasingly in the Cossack [Acquisitive] Art Awards—which began in 1993 and have now become the richest Regional Acquisitive Art Award in Australia[70]—as well as in major exhibitions.

The Ngarluma Aboriginal Corporation is actively pursuing social improvement and commercial opportunities. The Ngarluma Aboriginal Sustainable Housing (NASH) development project in Roebourne is being undertaken jointly with government.[71] In 2012, stage one of the project for 100 housing lots was near completion.[72] The Yindjibarndi people have developed a successful media organisation, Juluwarlu, dedicated to the recording, preservation and maintenance of Yindjibarndi language and culture.[73] In the few years that it has been operating, Juluwarlu has undertaken live recording with people on country, developed an archive, and applied successfully to the Australian Broadcasting Authority for an open narrowcast television licence, one of only four such licences in Australia. It has established a media centre and mentors trainees who will receive a certificate in multimedia. Michael Woodley, Woodley King's grandson, sees operations such as Juluwarlu TV as 'adjusting to what society is now'. In 2004, the organisation prepared and published the booklet *Know the Song, Know the Country*, based on the film *Exile and the Kingdom*. In 2005, working with Frank Rijavec and Noelene Harrison from the original team, they released a DVD copy of *Exile and the Kingdom*, with extra material added. Their project, *Ngurra: Two Rivers*, involves the production of a video documentary about 'the Fortescue and the Lower Sherlock rivers that run through our minds, souls and hearts'.[74]

In other parts of the Pilbara, agreements with resource companies have resulted in substantial financial benefits being paid into relevant Aboriginal charitable and other trusts. Aboriginal contractors play an increasing role in resource and other projects. A few groups, such as the Eastern Guruma, have embarked on joint ventures with other companies.[75]

The dialogue continues to be uneven and unequal, questioning and calling to account various notions of the good, such as the monetisation of many aspects of social life, proffered as characteristic of modernity. Nevertheless, the involvement of the native title claimants in negotiations such as Yandicoogina, the Burrup,

---

69  BHP Billiton, Rio Tinto and Woodside all provide substantial financial and exhibition support.

70  <www.roebourne.wa.gov.au/CossackWinners>

71  *West Australian*, 25 May 2010.

72  Edmunds (2012: 162).

73  <www.juluwarlu.pilbara.net>

74  Juluwarlu Wangga, *Newsletter 2005* 1(1) (September): 1.

75  In 2009, Rio Tinto awarded a $200 million mining contract to a joint venture between the Eastern Guruma and mining services operator NRW (Rio Tinto media release, 18 December 2009, <http://www.riotinto.com/media/18435_media_releases_18844.asp>).

Hope Downs indicates that the distinction between these differing notions of the good is not absolute; nor are the domains inhabited by Indigenous and non-Indigenous Australians bounded and separate. Much of the development of native title is located in a profound collaboration between Indigenous and non-Indigenous individuals and groups.

At the same time, disjunctions between Indigenous and non-Indigenous understandings of what constitutes a good life and its sources, and resources, remain, and the engagement with modernity has generated often stark contradictions for Pilbara Aboriginal people, both internal and external. One of these is the question of culture loss, in terms of the need for culture to be practised as well as thought, now that yet another generation who lived on and knew the country intimately has passed away. Opposed to this is the sense of culture as not only a heritage but also a project,[76] Bauman's 'permanent revolution of sorts'.[77] In the Pilbara today, this means that the link between people and country remains a primary, though no longer the sole, connection or source of self. And new organisations, like those that emerged in the 1980s to counter the second colonisation, are becoming a nexus for the encounter between the old and the new.

In looking at the situation in the Pilbara today, I recognise the complexity and the challenges. But I am also reminded of the buoyant comment of an Aboriginal woman in another part of the country: 'It's a winnin' battle now. It used to be a losin' battle, but now it's a winnin' one.'

---

76   Sahlins (2005: 58).
77   Bauman and Tester (2001: 32).

# Part IV. Modernity and human rights

# 8. Durban 2001, the United Nations World Conference against Racism

The Durban NGO Forum and conference began with the high hopes of civil society and of nations that a conference held in the highly symbolic setting of post-Apartheid South Africa would bring new energy to the fight against racism and the more broadly ambitious agenda of racial discrimination, xenophobia and related intolerance. Instead, both the Forum and the conference degenerated into ugly confrontations between Palestinian supporters and Jewish representatives. One outcome was that a conference that in reality addressed a wide range of crucial social issues was reduced in the reporting and subsequent analyses to the single issue of anti-Semitism and expressed hostility to the state of Israel. Many saw this as a hijacking of the United Nations itself and an end to its legitimacy as the arbiter of universal human rights principles.

In terms of the discussion in this book, the NGO Forum and the conference covered many of the issues canvassed in the case studies and moved them into the international arena. The Durban conference tested, and came perilously close to jeopardising, the very human rights framework that provided the conditions for the ways in which each of the groups analysed in this book forged their specific encounters with modernity. At stake were fiercely contested notions of the good and of what constitutes the necessary conditions for a good society. In key areas, these questions remained unresolved. In the end, however, and in spite of the infamous reputation that has since attached to the conference, the official Durban documents did not qualify or limit the previously enshrined principles either of human rights or of respect for the bond of common humanity. These continue to provide a moral and political framework for ordinary people across the world, including many of us who participated in the NGO Forum, in striving to achieve a good life.

## The NGO Forum

It was spring in Durban when I arrived with a delegation of young people for the Non-Government Organisations (NGO) Forum that preceded the 2001 United Nations World Conference against Racism, Racial Discrimination, Xenophobia and Related Intolerance. The sun was shining over the Valley of 1000 Hills as our delegation was driven in the hotel bus to the site of the Forum at the Kingswood Cricket Stadium, and warmed us as we joined the thousands of other

NGO participants for the Forum's opening ceremony. The temporary stage in front of the grandstands and the white meeting tents spread throughout the stadium added to the festival atmosphere of creative improvisation.

Despite some earlier frustration about the number and extent of outstanding issues remaining after four regional conferences, five expert seminars and three sessions of the Preparatory Committee, the atmosphere was also one of energetic hope and warm recognition that, of all the countries where the Conference might have been held, South Africa stands as a symbol of the possibility of changing seemingly unchangeable racist divisions and practices. As UN Secretary-General, Kofi Annan, expressed it in his opening address to the Conference:[1]

> For decades the name of this country was synonymous with racism in its vilest form. But today, Mr. President, you and your fellow citizens have transformed its meaning – from a by-word for injustice and oppression, into a beacon of enlightenment and hope, not only for a troubled continent, but for the entire world.

> Where else, my friends, could we hold this conference? Who could teach us how to overcome racism, discrimination and intolerance, if not the people of this country? We salute you. We salute your leadership, Mr. President. We salute the heroic movement that you represent.

The point was also made in the welcoming speeches to the NGO Forum by both Mary Robinson, the UN Human Rights Commissioner, and Thabo Mbeki, the South African President. President Mbeki spoke from his experience as a South African:[2]

> We welcome you to the African continent, as victorious fellow combatants in the struggle that finally liquidated the system of colonialism and transformed the last and most stubborn domicile of white minority rule in Africa into a democratic country.

> We welcome you as comrades with whom we have combined, to form a world army of peoples united against racism, for the construction of a common universe of democracy, non-racism, non-sexism, human dignity for all and prosperity for all.

Nearly two weeks later, in her closing address to the Conference, the Conference President and South African Foreign Minister, Dr Nkozasana Dlamini Zuma,

---

1   World Conference against Racism, Racial Discrimination, Xenophobia and Related Intolerance, Opening address by UN Secretary-General, Kofi Annan, Durban, 31 August 2001, <www.racism.gov.za/substance/speeches/unopen.htm>
2   NGO Forum of the World Conference against Racism, Welcome address by President of South Africa, Thabo Mbeki, Durban, 28 August 2001, <www.racism.gov.za/substance/speeches/mbeki010828.htm>

also spoke of the meaning of having the Conference in South Africa, and bravely used the analogy offered by the renewal of spring to express hope at the end of what had proved to be a very difficult and often painful process:[3]

> At the end of this landmark and historic Conference, I think we will all agree that it was right that this conference was held and consensus reached on practical steps to be taken to push back the frontiers of Racism, Racial Discrimination, Xenophobia and Related Intolerance which are frighteningly on the rise in many parts of the world. I would imagine that we would also agree that it was proper that this conference should be held in South Africa, a country that has witnessed the most egregious form of institutionalised racism, yet rose to become a living testimony that racism can be defeated with the collective efforts of the international community...Like the blooming and blossoming flower in the spring, we have agreed on a fresh start and the new roadmap.

She went on to quote a poem written from the depths of Apartheid in the early 1970s by a South African poet:

> In closing, I want to refer to one of our finest poets, Wally Mongale Serote, who had these beautiful words to say in his work *Ofay-Watcher Looks Back:*
>
> 'I want to look at what happened;
>
> That done.
>
> As silent as the roots of plants pierce the soil
>
> I look at what happened
>
> Whether above the houses there is always either smoke or dust...
>
> I want to look at what happened,
>
> That done,
>
> As silent plants show the colour: green,
>
> I want to look at what happened,
>
> When houses make me ask: do people live there?
>
> As there is something wrong when I ask—is that man alive?

---

3   World Conference against Racism, Racial Discrimination, Xenophobia and Related Intolerance, Closing Statement by the President of the Conference, Durban, 7 September 2001, <www.racism.gov.za/substance/speeches/zumaclose.htm>

I want to look at what happened,

That done,

As silent as the life of a plant that makes you see it...

as silent as plants bloom and the eyes tell you: something has happened.'

She concluded: 'Something historic has indeed happened here today.'

Those two moments—the opening of the NGO Forum and the closing of the Conference—expressed the high ideals about what constitutes a good society as well a good international community. In between, the more ambiguous events of these encounters unfolded. In their confronting ambiguity, they demonstrated that even the agreed foundations for a good international order as set out in pivotal documents like the *Universal Declaration of Human Rights* are subject to differing and often incompatible meanings, and that a good society, like a good life, is an ongoing project, never a final accomplishment.

# Durban and the human rights imaginary

It has been suggested that the 1990s can be categorised as the decade of human rights, when human rights moved firmly to the centre of international discourse, representing a powerful moral charter for pursuing social change.[4] As part of the broader UN project, the Durban Conference was the culmination of a decade of World Conferences or Summits. Taken together, they set out and pursued a comprehensive and human rights-driven social agenda for the international community. In developing this social agenda, the United Nations aimed to confirm and further develop a range of standards that, collectively, would be internationally agreed as the principles and practical measures needed to implement a universal notion of the good and of the essential requirements for a good society and a good life. The Conference against Racism, like earlier Conferences and Summits, was designed to continue and build on the principles previously agreed to in the 1945 *Charter of the United Nations* and in the *International Bill of Human Rights*,[5] especially in the foundational document of the *Universal Declaration of Human Rights* (1948). Thabo Mbeki made the link explicit in his opening address to the NGO Forum:[6]

---

4   Wilson (2005: 6).

5   The International Bill of Human Rights consists of five documents: the *Universal Declaration of Human Rights*; the *International Covenant on Economic, Social and Cultural Rights*; the *International Covenant of Civil and Political Rights*; the *Optional Protocol on Civil and Political Rights*; and the *Second Optional Protocol to the International Covenant on Civil and Political Rights*, aiming at the abolition of the death penalty.

6   NGO Forum of the World Conference against Racism, Welcome address by President of South Africa, Thabo Mbeki, Durban, 28 August 2001, <www.racism.gov.za/substance/speeches/mbeki010828.htm>

Neither I nor anyone else can say anything more challenging and demanding than that all of us must act to ensure that the vision represented in the *Universal Declaration of Human Rights* is translated in our countries and throughout the world into a movement towards the universal achievement of these human rights. It is to define and to agree on the ways and means by which we can, practically, move all humanity towards the realisation of this goal that we meet here today, at this historic NGO Forum against Racism.

Both the UN Charter and the Universal Declaration place human rights at the centre of the moral and practical endeavour for nations to work together to ensure sufficient agreement 'to save succeeding generations from the scourge of war'.[7] The Preamble to the Charter states:

*We the Peoples of the United Nations Determined*

to save succeeding generations from the scourge of war, which twice in our lifetime has brought untold sorrow to mankind, and

to reaffirm faith in fundamental human rights, in the dignity and worth of the human person, in the equal rights of men and women and of nations large and small, and

to establish conditions under which justice and respect for the obligations arising from treaties and other sources of international law can be maintained, and

to promote social progress and better standards of life in larger freedom,

*And for these Ends*

to practise tolerance and live together in peace with one another as good neighbours, and

to unite our strength to maintain international peace and security, and

to employ international machinery for the promotion of the economic and social advancement of all peoples...

do hereby establish an international organisation to be known as the United Nations.

The purposes of the United Nations, set out in Article 1 of the Charter, include 'friendly relations among nations based on respect for the principle of equal

---

7  *Charter of the United Nations 1945*, Preamble.

rights and self-determination of peoples'[8] and 'respect for human rights and for fundamental freedoms for all without distinction as to race, sex, language, or religion'.[9]

The Preamble to the Universal Declaration begins: 'Whereas recognition of the inherent dignity and of the equal and inalienable rights of all members of the human family is the foundation of freedom, justice and peace in the world'; and states, in Article 1: 'All human beings are born free and equal in dignity and rights. They are endowed with reason and conscience and should act towards one another in a spirit of brotherhood.'

Together these documents, crafted in response to the terrible experience of war, distil a vision of the possibility of peace, based on the 'spirit of brotherhood'. In so doing, they embody a common understanding among nations of a 'moral order underlying the political—the idea of order as mutual benefit'.[10] This was not the first time that such an ideal had been expressed. But the UN documents were the first internationally ratified—that is, internationally agreed—documents setting out a moral order and framework and a common definition of human dignity and rights.

In contrast, *the Covenant of the League of Nations* (1920), dedicated like its successor, the United Nations, 'to promote international co-operation and to achieve international peace and security',[11] focused only on the obligations of nations and the organisation and procedures of the League itself and its members. The Covenant set out a legal, not a moral, framework.

The moral framework and order of the UN Charter and the *Universal Declaration of Human Rights* have humanity at their centre. Despite the enormous political, religious, cultural and geographic differences among the original 51 member states,[12] all of them subscribed to this understanding. Importantly, the UN Charter expresses a moral order that is not doctrinal or assumed to be external to humanity or ordained by a pre-existing moral—or religious—authority or source. On the contrary, the source of the moral order is humanity itself, a

---

8  ibid., cl. 2.
9  ibid., cl. 3.
10  Taylor (2002: 16).
11  *Covenant of the League of Nations 1920*, Preamble.
12  The original members of the United Nations were Argentina, Australia, Belgium, Bolivia, Brazil, Belarus, Canada, Chile, China, Colombia, Costa Rica, Cuba, Czechoslovakia, Denmark, Dominican Republic, Ecuador, Egypt, El Salvador, Ethiopia, France, Greece, Guatemala, Haiti, Honduras, India, Iran, Iraq, Lebanon, Liberia, Luxembourg, Mexico, Netherlands, New Zealand, Nicaragua, Norway, Panama, Paraguay, Peru, Philippines, Poland, Russian Federation, Saudi Arabia, South Africa, Syrian Arab Republic, Turkey, Ukraine, United Kingdom of Great Britain and Northern Ireland, United States of America, Uruguay, Venezuela and Yugoslavia.

humanity that is equal and common to all. It resides in 'the dignity and worth of the person'.[13] And this moral order is built through agreement, based on and resulting from what Habermas would call communicative action.[14]

The Charter's affirmation of 'faith in fundamental human rights' is then elaborated in the first of the United Nation's subsequent documents, the *Universal Declaration of Human Rights*. By 1948, with the addition of further member states to consider the adoption of the Universal Declaration, 48 states voted in favour, none against, and eight abstained. One of those which abstained was South Africa,[15] in the same year and six months after the National Party had won government and introduced their program of *apartheid* (separateness). The incompatibility between human rights and racism was inherent in the beginning. The Universal Declaration makes even more patent than the UN Charter that human rights are rights of the person, not of states, and that the moral order elaborated in the elucidation of fundamental rights and freedoms embodies a shared idea of the good that is 'the highest aspiration of the common people'.[16]

The rights set out in the Universal Declaration, and in the later Covenants and Protocols that contain the measures needed to implement these rights, are fundamental, but not absolute, insofar as they may be subject 'only to such limitations as are determined by law solely for the purpose of securing due recognition and respect for the rights and freedoms of others and of meeting the just requirements of morality, public order and the general welfare in a democratic society'.[17] Further, 'these rights and freedoms may in no case be exercised contrary to the purposes and principles of the United Nations',[18] nor be 'aimed at the destruction of any of the rights and freedoms set forth' in the Universal Declaration.[19] While not absolute, therefore, the *International Bill of Rights* nevertheless affirms that there are certain rights that may never be suspended or limited, even in emergency situations. These are the rights to life, to freedom from torture, to freedom from enslavement or servitude, to protection from imprisonment for debt, to freedom from retroactive penal laws, to recognition as a person before the law, and to freedom of thought, conscience and religion.[20]

Together, the UN Charter and the International Bill of Rights represent agreement—that has been achieved, not received—about a moral order that

---

13  *Charter of the United Nations 1945*, Preamble.
14  Habermas (1984, 1987).
15  UN High Commissioner for Human Rights (n.d.: 3); Wallach (2006: 115).
16  *Charter of the United Nations 1945*, Preamble.
17  *Universal Declaration of Human Rights*, cl. 29(2).
18  ibid., cl. 29(3).
19  ibid., cl. 30.
20  UN High Commissioner for Human Rights (n.d.: 6).

exists outside the individual person, but that is experienced by and through the individual person. This moral order is based on a shared idea of the good whose moral source and expression is the principle of respect for the common bond of humanity. The agents and subjects of this moral order are individuals who act in their primary role as moral agents, as well as being the subject of rights, and of justice.[21] At the same time, individuals are related to each other. All human individuals, without exception, share the bond of common humanity and, as the Universal Declaration affirms, 'are born free and equal in dignity and rights' and 'should act towards one another in a spirit of brotherhood'.[22]

Further, all human beings 'are endowed with reason and conscience'[23]—that is, with the twin faculties central to human be-ing and action. These are the faculties that allow individuals to have a vision of a rational order, to which the key is the idea of the good, and to make moral evaluations and act on the basis of that idea.[24] The UN Charter and International Bill of Rights express this moral order and the idea of the good in the language of rights, expressing what has been agreed to as universal moral norms[25] and giving meaning to those rights as the necessary basic conditions for a good life for all human beings.

Nevertheless, there is:[26]

> The invisible worm,
> That flies in the night,
> In the howling storm…
> And his dark secret love
> Does thy life destroy.

Expressed more prosaically by critics of the United Nations and its processes, the not-so-invisible worm destroying any potential of the United Nations is the enshrinement in its very constitution of the principle of national sovereignty. Unwittingly echoing the much earlier and brilliant satirical stories of Shirley Hazzard on the UN bureaucracy,[27] Douzinas is scathing:[28] 'Official thinking and action on human rights has been entrusted in the hands of triumphalist column writers, bored diplomats and rich international lawyers in New York and Geneva, people whose experience of human rights violations is confined to being served a bad bottle of wine.'

---

21 Rawls (1999).
22 *Universal Declaration of Human Rights*, cl. 1.
23 ibid., cl. 1.
24 Taylor (2003: 92–3).
25 ibid., p. 11.
26 'The Sick Rose', in Blake (1794).
27 Hazzard (2006 [1967]).
28 Douzinas (2000: 7).

He concludes that 'in the process, human rights have been turned from a discourse of rebellion and dissent into that of state legitimacy'. What element of truth may be in that—and certainly state politics continue to undermine the expressed ideals—Douzinas's assessment ignores the burgeoning of grassroots engagement with human rights:[29]

> The development of modern international and transnational human rights practices did occur in the late 1970s and early 1980s, particularly on the basis of the human rights struggles in Latin America and South Africa. It is by looking at these struggles and their relationship with the evolving international human rights protection systems and networks of human rights NGOs that one gets the richness of the contemporary human rights story contrary to overemphasizing the crossroads of international politics and human rights.

The case studies explored in earlier chapters of this book indicate that Douzinas's critique also ignores the impact of the human rights imaginary on people in their everyday lives. At the same time, in too many ways, Durban validated his identification of the paradox at the heart of the UN system:[30]

> Codification, from Justinian to the Code Napoleon, has always been the ultimate exercise of legislative sovereignty, the supreme expression of state power...The early declarations of rights helped bring into legitimate existence the sovereignty of the nation-state with its accompanying threats and risks for individual freedom. Something similar happened with the post-war expansion of international law into the human rights field. National sovereignty and non-intervention in the domestic affairs of states were the key principle on which the law was built, from the UN Charter to all important treaties.

## Durban and the human rights paradox

Any account of the remarkable shift in the international moral order expressed in the UN Charter and *International Bill of Rights* must, then, take into account this paradox if it is to reflect the antagonisms and anguish experienced in the course of reaching agreement on these or subsequent treaties and documents. In many ways, the processes involved in negotiating and, even more problematically, in implementing such agreement reflect the continuing struggle between conflicting notions of the good and of the sources and expression of moral legitimacy; of the relationship between the individual and the state and the extent and limits of

---

29   Rask Madsen (2002: 1).
30   Douzinas (2000: 118).

the power of the state; of self-interest and national interest; of strategic action in opposition to communicative action; and of vastly differing modernities and pre-modernities. The United Nations is a site of struggle. But it is the only forum to bring people together to deal with sensitive but critical issues of common concern, and to do so within the framework of human rights.[31] And the United Nations remains the only site also where states, numbering 192 in 2010,[32] continue to come together as equals under the purposes and principles of the UN Charter, to work—despite recurrent agonising failures—'to save succeeding generations from the scourge of war'.[33]

These conflicts and contradictions were played out in the decade of UN World Conferences and Summits. This was also the period in which NGOs, both international and national, became more directly involved and influential. In 1990, the UN began the decade with the World Summit for Children. Subsequently, World Conferences or Summits were held on Environment and Development (Rio, 1992), Human Rights (Vienna, 1993), Population and Development (Cairo, 1994), Social Development (Copenhagen, 1995), Women (Beijing, 1995), Habitat (1996), Food (1996), the Earth Summit (1997), Social Development and Beyond (2000), and Racism, Racial Discrimination, Xenophobia and Related Intolerance (Durban, 2001).[34]

Despite contention and difficulty, a majority of UN member states continued over the decade to reach at least some level of agreement on much of the social agenda encompassed in the Conferences. This included many highly charged issues such as, for example, family planning and reproductive rights (Cairo Programme of Action); Agenda 21, the Rio *Declaration on Environment and Development*; the Statement of Forest Principles; the UN Framework Convention on Climate Change and the UN Convention on Biological Diversity (Rio); and that women's rights are human rights (Beijing Declaration). Not all of the Conferences or Summits produced separate agreed Declarations; but all achieved one form or other of an agreed plan or program of action. These had then to be implemented at the national level. Many have not been, have been only partially implemented, or have been comprehensively violated. Nevertheless, the documents, and the

---

31 Nafis Sadik, former executive director of the UN Population Fund, Panel discussion organised by the Conference of NGOs (CONGO), Durban, 7 September 2001.

32 <www.un.org> At the time of writing, this number of UN members was out of a total of 243 entities considered to be countries. As well as the 102 UN member states, of whom the most recent is Timor-Leste, this includes a range of complex arrangements under international law and practice. In 1998, for example, the General Assembly granted Palestine some additional rights 'in its capacity as Observer' (Press release, GA/9427). The Vatican, in its capacity as the Holy See, has gone from self-invited status as a UN 'non-member permanent observer' in 1964 to ambiguous but powerful non-member State Permanent Observer in 2004. The rights it was granted by General Assembly Resolution 58/314 on *Participation of the Holy See in the Work of the United Nations* are greater than the additional rights accorded to Palestine and include taking precedence ahead of Palestine and any other accredited observers (Robertson 2010: 96–111).

33 *Charter of the United Nations 1945*, Preamble.

34 This is not the full sum of UN World Conferences; it covers only those held between 1990 and 2001.

various mechanisms established to monitor their application, have set agreed international standards that demand accountability and against which the performance of national practice continues to be measured.[35]

All the Conferences generated intense debate among both NGOs and national governments and between NGOs and governments. Anecdotal reports suggest that most, if not all, of the World Conferences, the preparatory meetings and their associated NGO Forums were difficult, unwieldy, intense, frustrating, often chaotic. NGOs have on most occasions, including in Durban, complained bitterly about the hours spent in queues, inaccessibility, exclusion, lack of information, and disappointing and unsatisfactory outcomes. Many of the Conferences teetered on the brink of collapse because of what appeared to be intractable disagreements between national governments. Nevertheless, for NGOs in particular, the participation in these processes as representatives of civil society has also been seen as an opportunity to develop strong international networks, to engage governments in developing ever more inclusive policies in the articulation and implementation of human rights, and to contribute actively to the processes of international agreement. And in the end none of the Conferences wound back the work of previous Conferences or lowered any standard that had been agreed to. Durban seems to have come closest, but drew back at the last moment. This in actuality became hours after the last moment, when the clock was literally stopped at midnight on the last scheduled day so that the desperate final negotiations could continue. Dr Dlamini Zuma acknowledged this in her closing address:

> Gathered at this conference, as Member States, we have at some time or another stood at the precipice. At each moment we stepped back and courageously dug deep into our strength and made a supreme effort to make the conference a success, that really it is. It was through the daring act of faith that sustained us through to the finish, because we must have said to ourselves that for the sake of posterity we must lay a firm foundation for the future of tolerance and harmonious co-existence that will be free from the cancer of racism. Indeed, we have found our way through the turbulent sea of events, at each point along the way, we had to respond creatively to both anticipated and unanticipated events.

---

35  The decision made by the General Assembly in 2006 (Resolution 60/251) to replace the Commission on Human Rights with the Human Rights Council was a way of demanding even greater accountability from member states (<http://www.ohchr.org/EN/HRBodies/HRC/Pages/AboutCouncil.aspx>). The Commission's history to date has been mixed, with membership sometimes including some of the worst human rights violators; but its establishment was an indication that these issues remain important to the international community.

# NGOs and failures of a shared human rights imaginary

Durban was affected by a number of key, and potentially destructive, issues. Some were divisive mainly at the intergovernmental level of the Conference. Others were elaborated and supported by the NGO Forum, but rejected by the Conference. These latter issues defined the limits of NGO influence on the Conference proceedings, marking the gap between the urgent inclusiveness of the concerns of civil society and the narrower interests of governments. This was the experience across each of the World Conferences, but was particularly the case in Durban, where the organisers of both the Conference and the Forum made a commitment to highlighting the voices of victims, many of them victims as a direct result of the policies and actions of governments.

One of the most contentious issues for the Conference government delegations was the question of slavery and reparations, referred to as issues of 'the past'. The crux of the debate was that African countries and countries with populations of African descendants wanted not only apologies for slavery from specific nations but also financial compensation to the victims of slavery and their descendants. This was fiercely resisted by countries like the United States and members of the European Union who could have been heavily implicated, although a number of developing countries suggested that reparations might take the form of debt forgiveness and developmental aid. In the final Declaration, the issue was dealt with by an acknowledgment that 'slavery and the slave trade are crimes against humanity' and that 'Africans and peoples of African descent, Asians and peoples of Asian descent and Indigenous peoples were victims of these acts and continue to be victims of their consequences'.[36] Unlike the Declaration from the NGO Forum,[37] in the Conference Declaration no reference to reparations was included.

A further issue for governments, and one that ultimately proved intractable, was intersectionality, generally referred to as 'the lists': that is, the identification by the Conference of the multiple bases of racism and discrimination and the interplay among them. The lists were elaborated around the intersection of the key bases of race, class and gender, but went beyond them to include other bases of discrimination. Most controversial amongst these was that of discrimination based on work and descent, specifically on caste. The Indian Government in particular argued strongly against the inclusion of any reference to caste. Pakistan alarmed both many other governments and NGOs by wishing to delete hard-won references to gender. In the end, and despite intensive efforts by

---

36 *World Conference against Racism, Racial Discrimination, Xenophobia and Related Intolerance Declaration* (2001), cl. 13.
37 ibid., cls 71–6.

Mexico which had been given the task of developing an acceptable formulation, the lists were not included in the final documents; but the references to gender did remain.

Despite its ultimate unwillingness to formalise the issue of intersectionality, the Conference—held in the splendid International Convention Centre several blocks from the Kingsmead Stadium—did provide space for personal stories. It hosted a series of lunchtime presentations under the banner of 'Voices Special Forum on Comparative Experiences of Racism'. These were popularly referred to as the 'Voices of Victims' sessions and gave minority groups a contained, but powerful, presence during the Conference. One presentation was given by Monica Morgan, a Yorta Yorta woman actively pursuing the Yorta Yorta native title claim in Victoria through the Australian court system. At the time, the Yorta Yorta people were in the process of appealing to the High Court from a decision of the Federal Court that their native title had been 'washed away by the tide of history'.[38] The High Court had not yet rejected the basis of their appeal by agreeing with the Federal Court that Yorta Yorta forebears had ceased to occupy their lands in accordance with traditional laws and customs. It would do so a year later.[39]

In contrast to the ordered calm of the Conference, seared but ultimately not shattered by the emotional issues that confronted it, the NGO Forum was dominated by the colour and noise of difference, and exposed to multiple expressions of pain. One of the most constant of these were the Dalit groups, the Untouchables from the Indian subcontinent, formally present for the first time at a World Conference NGO Forum. Their procession of drums and cymbals became part of the Forum's everyday background. Perhaps most poignant was a group of women from a coalition of community groups in Gauteng, the South African province north-west of Durban that includes both Johannesburg and Pretoria. It was reported that many of the more than 300 women were HIV positive.[40] When they arrived at the registration tent, they found that their registration fees had not been covered by the scholarships that they had applied for to the South African NGO Coalition (SANGOCO). SANGOCO was the organising body, together with the International Steering Committee (ISC), responsible for the Forum. For the next three days, and to the distress of other participants, the women camped in a train at a railway station outside Durban while SANGOCO 'looked into the situation'. Their entry into the Forum on its

---

38   Although these exact words are not used in the judgement, they reflect its general thrust and became a bitter descriptor for the judgement (*Members of the Yorta Yorta Aboriginal Community v the State of Victoria & Ors* [1997] 1181 FCA [29 October 1997]; *Members of the Yorta Yorta Aboriginal Community v State of Victoria* [Including Corrigendum dated 21 March 2001] [2001] FCA 45 [8 February 2001]).

39   *Members of the Yorta Yorta Aboriginal Community v Victoria* [2002] HCA 58 (12 December 2002).

40   *Human Rights Features*, Special print series for the World Conference against Racism 2001, Wednesday, 29 August 2001.

second-last day was a celebratory takeover of a panel on globalisation chaired by the then Aboriginal and Torres Strait Islander Social Justice Commissioner, Dr Bill Jonas. He warmly welcomed the singing and dancing women and handed the session over to them.

The NGO Declaration mentioned by name many of the other groups whose voices were heard during the Forum—Roma and Travellers, Tibetans, Jews, Palestinians, Cubans, Indigenous peoples—as well as many unable to participate, and was, indeed, exhaustive in its inclusiveness. This was recognised by Mary Robinson and others as one of the most important contributions of the NGO Forum. In summing up this aspect, Bishop Mvume Dandala, the South African presiding Methodist bishop, said:[41] 'In the conference, we have given time to people—to name the cause of their suffering and give them visibility. As a family of nations around the world, we can no longer say: We did not know.'

## Indigenous battles

Indigenous matters also became an issue of contention between the NGO Forum and the Conference. As in almost every meeting of Indigenous groups and governments under the auspices of the United Nations, they crystallised around what has been described as 'the battle of the "s"'[42] or 's-phobia'.[43] The 's' at stake either belongs, as Indigenous groups demand, to the term 'indigenous peoples' or not, which is the position taken by a number of states. The question reflects the critical importance of language in UN documents, not as a question of legal pedantry, but in this case, of rights:[44]

> Hanging upon the 's' is the question of whether indigenous peoples are the same 'peoples'—with an 's'—so prominent in the Charter of the United Nations (the preamble of which is formulated in the name of 'the Peoples of the United Nations'), and who therefore must be recognized as possessing all the rights that flow from that status, including the right to self-determination.

For national governments, including Australia and especially Canada, this raised the spectre of secession, loss of sovereignty and, given the location of many Indigenous peoples in remote but resource-rich areas, loss of resources. The question was critical particularly in the decade-long and unresolved negotiations

---

41   Bishop Mvume Dandala, panel discussion organised by the Conference of NGOs (CONGO), Durban, 7 September 2001.
42   Niezen (2003: 160–5).
43   *Human Rights Features*, Special print series for the World Conference against Racism 2001, Sunday, 2 September 2001.
44   Niezen (2003: 161).

on the UN *Draft Declaration on the Rights of Indigenous Peoples*.[45] This was the background to the contentious Article 27 in the Durban Conference's draft Declaration, which stated:

> The use of the term, 'indigenous peoples' in the World Conference… cannot be construed as having any implications as to the rights under international law. Any reference to the rights associated with the term 'indigenous peoples' is in the context of ongoing multilateral negotiations on texts that specifically deal with such rights, and is without prejudice to the outcome of those negotiations.

A number of the members of the NGO Forum's Indigenous Caucus were not novices to UN processes, but battle-scarred veterans of this long debate. Their experience was of the United Nations not principally as an 'unfathomable bureaucracy' but as facilitator of the 'original institutional space constituting a distinct social world' created through the regular meetings of the Working Group on Indigenous Populations.[46] In Durban, they used a number of avenues to campaign for the withdrawal of Article 27. Their press conference on the issue was held on the same day, the last day of the NGO Forum, as our *Tampa* press conference and information session[47] and gained rather more coverage. They ensured that Indigenous Caucus members had access to the treasured NGO passes permitting access to the Conference deliberations. They engaged in strategic lobbying of Conference delegates. Rigoberta Menchu, Nobel Peace Prize winner in 1992 'in recognition of her work for social justice and ethno-cultural reconciliation based on respect for the rights of indigenous peoples', addressed a Conference plenary session. Her challenge to the Conference was unequivocal:[48]

> Government representatives have negotiated, and are attempting to impose on us, paragraphs 26, 27, and 51 of the draft Declaration of this Conference, which not only ignore our desires and aspirations, but constitute a flagrant violation of the principle of universality and indivisibility of human rights, are racist [and] illegal…We demand the withdrawal of these paragraphs and their replacement with others that will guarantee the full and unrestricted recognition of the rights

---

45    On 13 September 2007, the UN General Assembly formally adopted the *Declaration on the Rights of Indigenous Peoples*. The battle of the 's' had been won. Australia was one of the countries that voted against its adoption. After the change of government later that year, Australia formally gave the Declaration its support (April 2009).

46    Niezen (2003: 4).

47    Discussed in Chapter 1.

48    World Conference against Racism, Racial Discrimination, Xenophobia and Related Intolerance, Plenary session, Durban, Tuesday, 4 September 2001. The translation from the original Spanish presentation is mine, and therefore not official.

of indigenous peoples…If this request is not accepted, we demand the removal of all reference to indigenous peoples in the Conference documents: our patience and our dignity are at stake.

For government delegations in Durban, however, the main debates were not around indigenous issues, and the offending paragraphs, though slightly altered, remained more or less intact. While fully recognising 'the rights of indigenous peoples consistent with the principles of sovereignty and territorial integrity of States',[49] the final Declaration made clear that 'the use of the term "indigenous peoples"…is in the context of, and without prejudice to the outcome of, ongoing international negotiations on texts that specifically deal with this issue, and cannot be construed as having any implications as to rights under international law'.[50] This remains unfinished business for Indigenous peoples, including Australian Indigenous people.

# 'Legalised anti-Semitism'[51]

None of these issues, however, had the potential to divide and derail both the NGO Forum and the Conference. That role was taken by the Israeli/Palestinian conflict. Its content was the competing claims of opposed communities in which 'the exchange of values, meanings and priorities' was 'profoundly antagonistic, conflictual and even incommensurable'.[52] Its effect was to call into question the possibility of invoking the same moral standard to negotiate an understanding of the good that would include both parties to the conflict.

The way in which this played out in the Conference was dramatic but not altogether unpredictable. In the NGO Forum, its expression was unanticipated, unseemly, and often shocking. Again, the focus was the wording in the two draft Declarations: that of the NGO Forum and, more importantly, of the Conference. The passion surrounding the wording reflected the struggle for legitimacy offered uniquely by recognition through the United Nations: moral acceptance by the community of nations of what can be called, in Habermassian terms, the validity claims of one side's truth against the other's.[53]

The centrality of this issue to the success of the Conference was flagged when reports began to circulate some weeks earlier that the United States might not attend. In a media briefing on 24 August, US President, George W. Bush, was

---

49   *World Conference against Racism, Racial Discrimination, Xenophobia and Related Intolerance Declaration,* para. 23.
50   ibid., para. 24.
51   Cotler (2010a).
52   Bhabha (1995: 2).
53   Habermas (1984: x–xi, 10–15).

reported as saying, 'We will have no representative there so long as they pick on Israel'.[54] This referred to the inclusion of proposed wording about Israel and Zionism in the draft Declaration as it stood at the end of the third session of the Preparatory Commission in August. The words remained bracketed, indicating that there had been no agreement on these parts of the text that referred to '[the practices of racial discrimination to which the Palestinians and the other inhabitants of the Arab territories occupied by Israel are subjected]',[55] and '[the emergence of racial and violent movements based on racism and discriminatory ideas, in particular, the Zionist movement which is based on racial superiority]'.[56]

When it seemed that the United States would attend, the question then was whether the delegation would be headed by the Secretary of State, Colin Powell. In the end, it was not, and both the United States and Israel withdrew from the Conference on the third day. The Conference bureau made an urgent announcement:

> The President of the Conference, Nkosazana Dlamini Zuma, convened a meeting of the bureau this evening to report on the withdrawal of two delegations from the Conference. The atmosphere of the meeting was one of determination to continue the work of the Conference, to build on the constructive work already done, and to bring the Conference to a successful end. Regret was expressed at the meeting at the withdrawal of the two delegations. At the same time, there were strong expressions of support for the Conference, its historic mission, and the importance of a successful outcome.

In her address to the plenary session on the following morning, Dr Dlamini Zuma commented that 'in creating a just and tolerant society, nothing is beyond discussion. It is essential to talk, negotiate, and to keep on doing so'. Mary Robinson at the same session 'regretted the decision by the United States and Israel to withdraw from the Durban meeting', but urged other delegations 'to persist in their endeavours for a ringing endorsement of tolerance and respect for human dignity'. Both women made the point that those who walked away would, in the end, be the losers. The withdrawal did, however, have a major impact on the Conference. Other delegations, including the European Union, Australia and Canada, reviewed their continuing participation on a day-by-day basis. Even on the last official day, the Conference remained, in the words of

54  *Human Rights Features*, Special print series for the World Conference against Racism 2001, Friday, 31 August 2001.
55  Preparatory Committee, Third session, Geneva, 30 July – 10 August 2001, *Draft Declaration*, para. 60.
56  ibid., para. 63.

one government delegate, 'on life-support' and it was a 'bruised' Dr Dlamini Zuma who presented her closing statement to the Conference after the frantic negotiations through the extra night and day finally reached consensus.[57]

The Declaration addressed the Middle East issues by recalling 'that the Holocaust must never be forgotten',[58] and by recognising 'with deep concern the increase in anti-Semitism and Islamophobia'.[59] Paragraph 61 expressed concern 'about the plight of the Palestinian people under foreign occupation' and recognised 'the inalienable right of the Palestinian people to self-determination and to the establishment of an independent State'. At the same time, it also recognised 'the right to security for all States in the region, including Israel'.

While the heat of the Conference debates took place behind closed doors, those at the NGO Forum were very public. The first intimation of the intrusiveness of the issue came at the NGO Forum opening ceremony, where a block of Palestinian groups and supporters shouted pro-Palestinian slogans through microphones over much of the proceedings. Once the Forum got under way, Palestinian representatives confronted Jewish representatives every day across one of the main general thoroughfares, which we came to refer to as the Gaza Strip. The confrontation was strident and occasionally erupted into physical violence, with the police called in on at least one occasion. There were many visible layers of anti-Jewish sentiment: a stall set up by the Arab Lawyers Union displayed anti-Jewish cartoons and sold copies of the notorious *The Protocols of the Elders of Zion*; at one session, a Jewish speaker was drowned out by shouts of 'Jew, Jew, Jew'. It was reported that the Jewish Caucus had been harassed to the point of choosing to meet outside the Forum venue at the Durban Jewish Club.

The confrontation was not without some rare lighter moments. Under the circumstances, few of us were prepared for the sight of a group of Orthodox Jewish men joining with Palestinian representatives and carrying signs: 'Authentic Rabbis oppose Israel', and 'Authentic Rabbis have always opposed Zionism and the State of Israel'.[60] Overall, however, the ubiquity of anti-Jewish action alienated many of the other NGO participants, who resisted the attempt to turn the Forum into a single-issue event and to impose a single and intransigent meaning that would exclude any possibility of rational communicative action.

These issues spilled over into the NGO Forum Declaration, already a highly vexed matter, although less vexed than it might have been had copies of the draft

---

57   Dlamini Zuma, interview with CNN, 8 September 2001.
58   *World Conference against Racism, Racial Discrimination, Xenophobia and Related Intolerance Declaration*, para. 57.
59   ibid., para. 59.
60   These 'Authentic Rabbis' belonged to a group, Neturei Karta, which refuses to recognise the State of Israel on the basis that 'the entire concept of a sovereign Jewish state is contrary to Jewish Law'. Neturei Karta International Jews United against Zionism web site, <www.nkusa.org>

been made adequately available. This was not the case. An outline of the draft Programme of Action was included in the kit that we received at registration. No copies of the full draft Declaration were ever provided. On the evening of the second-last day, some parts, in English only, were left at the back of the main tent.

The processes for adopting the documents were equally flawed. The plenary session to decide this, scheduled for the last morning of the Forum, had to be postponed until 6.30 pm that evening because of the difficulties of getting a full English text of the draft available for discussion.[61] As well, the procedures for adoption were not set out until the closing plenary session. Only then was it made clear that only caucuses—the formally registered representative bodies of particular groups—would be eligible to vote, and a list of the approved caucuses was circulated for the first time. As a result, and because the need to set up or belong to a caucus had never been specified, the first two hours were taken up with angry discussion about the proposed adoption procedures. A number of new caucuses (the exact number was never clear) were added on the spot to the 41 already approved. Because of other organisational muddles, some of us had never managed to locate our chosen caucus, and few caucuses had realised that they needed to develop an agreed position on the—non-available—draft.

Because of the lateness of the starting time, the plenary session continued until the early hours of the following morning. By that time a large number of delegates had left, some by attrition; others, including the Jewish Caucus and the Eastern and Central European Caucus, walked out in protest at the process.

A number of the caucuses subsequently circulated statements dissociating themselves from the documents on the basis of their inclusion of 'unacceptable concepts and language' and because 'the language of the chapter "Palestine" as well as the deliberate distortions made to the chapter "Anti-Semitism" is extremely intolerant, disrespectful and contrary to the very spirit of the World Conference'.[62] When the full version of the documents was finally made available—which was not until 3 September, two days after the official closing of the Forum—a significant number of international NGOs, including Amnesty International, Human Rights Watch and the Lawyers Committee for Human Rights, publicly dissociated themselves. The members of the Drafting Committee, after outlining, in an open letter to the NGO Forum,[63] the enormous difficulties under which they had worked on the NGO documents, stated that:

---

61  Even for the plenary session, there were not enough English copies for the several thousand delegates, and none in the other official languages of French and Spanish.

62  Eastern and Central European Caucus.

63  4 September 2001.

'We want to make it very clear that we, the members of the Drafting Committee, do not support any language in the NGO document that is racist or could be construed as racist.'

The Middle East issue also led to the unprecedented action by Mary Robinson of not commending the NGO documents in full to the Conference. This was because of their inclusion of clauses calling for 'the reinstitution of UN resolution 3379 determining the practices of Zionism as racist practices'[64] and

> the establishment of a war crimes tribunal to investigate and bring to justice those who may be guilty of war crimes, acts of genocide and ethnic cleansing and the crime of Apartheid which amount to crimes against humanity that have been or continue to be perpetrated in Israel and the Occupied Palestinian Territories.[65]

At the same time, Mrs Robinson agreed to attend an NGO briefing session on the last scheduled and fraught day of the Conference to explain her action. She outlined her position:[66]

> My position on the NGO documents: I did not reject them. I accepted them yesterday. But I am aware that the text contained provisions that were inappropriate and unhelpful—undermining what I was trying to do. I could not commend the documents to the conference delegates, which is what I usually do. This is the first time that I have not done this. What I have done is not to commend it in its entirety, but I have pointed out its useful parts…The conference has been very difficult. But it marks a great moment, and we will take these issues which are best represented in the NGO documents.

Although Mary Robinson did not formally commend the NGO documents to the Conference, Myrna Cunningham, a member of the International Steering Committee for the NGO Forum, presented them to the Conference plenary session on 5 September. Her presentation speech was an overview and summary of the documents and was, in the view of NGOs who heard it, unexceptional and, indeed, the kind of document that many had hoped and worked for. It contained none of the inflammatory language that made the formal NGO documents so

---

64  *NGO Declaration*, para. 419. UN Resolution 3379 was a resolution of the General Assembly passed in 1975 declaring that 'Zionism is a form of racism and racial discrimination'. This resolution was revoked by the General Assembly in 1991 (Resolution 46/86).
65  *NGO Declaration*, para. 420. The retention of references to Israel as an apartheid state in the NGO documents was with the support of a number of South African groups. This was to some extent the outcome of the military cooperation between Israel and the previous South African Apartheid governments.
66  7 September 2001.

controversial. Instead, it set out the key non-sectarian and inclusive issues on which general agreement had been indicated.[67] In her introduction, she commented:

> It has been a complex and difficult process, at times very hurtful. But we bring to you, today, the NGOs' outcome, the Declaration and Programme of Action, on the understanding that it reflects [the] regional processes, but the more important fact is that it reflects the diverse voices of victims of racism, racial discrimination, xenophobia and related intolerance.

## Divergent imaginaries

Like our *Tampa* information session and press conference outlined in Chapter 1, the NGO Forum can be seen as a clash of social imaginaries, all struggling for the recognition of their place in modernity, and disturbing any expectation of the sufficiency of rational goodwill. One imaginary constituted the Forum as a Habermassian public sphere, that space outside of formalised power where differences can be freely expressed and discussed among equals, where the potentially divisive and destructive consequences of conflict can be negotiated through rational debate, and where the practical focus and outcome would form an identification and mobilisation of the common good.[68] For others, the Forum also offered a legitimising space for a public performance of victimhood, a demand from the excluded to have their histories, and their understandings and actions, given common meaning; to be recognised and embraced within the common good. For yet others, the Forum was precisely a political arena, a site for the extension of incommensurable conflict in which there could be no rational debate and no common good, but only the defeat of one imaginary by a different one.

From another point of view, these divergent imaginaries were all mediated in Durban—as they were in each of the case studies examined in the book— through the secular concept of rights, and perhaps constituted more a clash within a range of possible alternative meanings for a modern social imaginary. Despite the differences, at the heart for all was an acceptance of a moral order articulated in terms of rights, and of the key principle set out in the *Universal*

---

67 It needs to be noted that there are at least two versions of Ms Cunningham's statement. The statement presented at the Conference plenary session and circulated at that time says only: 'The NGO's declaration affirms the right of the Palestinian people to self determination, statehood, independence and freedom and the right of the return as stipulated in UN Resolution 194.' The version subsequently available on web sites (for example, <www.hri.ca/racism/major/ngoplenary.shtml>, <http://wcar.alrc.net/mainfil.ph/statements/67/>) adds a further clause: 'And recognizes their situation as a new form of apartheid.' There is no explanation as to when, how, by whom, or on what authority this clause was added.

68 See Taylor (2004: 91).

*Declaration of Human Rights*—'All human beings are born free and equal in dignity and rights'[69]—a view expressed in different terms but with similar recognition by Alice Smith in Roebourne: 'We Aborigine people, we know we all the same, doesn't matter what sort of colour you got, black or white. We all got the same blood. We not different. All we different is the colour might be white, some of them black.'[70] At stake is how that principle is to be understood and translated in practice, within the distorting context of actual inequalities and the dialectics of power.

At the centre also, in a World Conference dedicated to tackling issues of 'racism, racial discrimination, xenophobia and related intolerance', was an intense encounter with the grim side of modernity—Weber's 'polar night of icy darkness' or 'iron cage'[71]—in which race, itself an imaginary produced by impositions of hegemonic power, has become the ultimate metaphor of the Other. The Conference, but the NGO Forum even more, was an attempt to redefine an oppositional relationship between us and the Other. It did not succeed, because of profound difficulties and a range of intransigencies. But it took an important step in delineating the scope of the problem, its sources, causes, and possible remedies.[72]

The aspiration of the NGO Forum, within its broader context of the World Conference, was to move away from a polarity of 'us/them' towards a mutual sense of 'both/and'. The accomplishment, of both the Forum and the Conference, fell very far short. At the same time, the Forum, more than the Conference, operated as a 'third space', 'the cutting edge of translation and negotiations, the in-between space'.[73] Bhabha's third space is a space outside the formal structures of competing cultural and historical traditions, a liminal space permitting a different encounter between, for example, the coloniser and the colonised, where the meanings of difference—but also of sameness and interdependence—can be acknowledged and renegotiated. In the process, this can become Franz Fanon's 'human world, that is a world of reciprocal recognitions',[74] a world that is relational.

In the words of Bishop Mvume Dandala in his reflections on the Conference:[75]

---

69  *Universal Declaration of Human Rights*, Article 1.
70  See Chapter 6.
71  Weber (1946: 128).
72  World Conference against Racism, Racial Discrimination, Xenophobia and Related Intolerance, Opening address by Mary Robinson, Durban, 31 August 2001.
73  Bhabha (1995: 38).
74  Referred to in Bhabha (1994: 8).
75  Bishop Mvume Dandala, panel discussion organised by the Conference of NGOs (CONGO), Durban, 7 September 2001.

This is not just a conference of victims. It is also one where both the victims and the perpetrators or descendants had the chance to dialogue. A large part of the world recognises the need for a robust dialogue if we are to end racism. But we have to recognise the problems of this conference in engaging in this kind of a dialogue. As well, the major democracies need to behave in ways that enhance belief in democracy. And we need to learn ways to engage in global dialogue...I am because you are, and you are because I am.

The third space 'represents the act of encounter which is always in a fluid state since it is always in a state of becoming and, hence, cannot be fixed into any stable final formulation'.[76] It is the space that comes between, 'meddling, interfering, interrupting and interpolating: making possible and making trouble, both at once'.[77] Combined with an identified principle of the equality of all participants, the third space is a place of formidable potential indeed. In Durban, the result was both possibility and trouble, with trouble having the greatest immediate impact.

# From Durban to the 'war on terror'

Three days after the close of the Conference, the 11 September attacks in New York and Washington initiated the 'war on terror' and, in the name of that war, on many aspects of the practice of human rights. Not even the right to freedom from torture has remained unchallenged in subsequent developments. Nor did the endorsement of the Conference documents by the UN General Assembly occur without disagreement. Although the adoption of the documents by the Conference on 8 September 2001 was by consensus, a number of countries had already left because of the unscheduled extra day; others, including Canada and Australia, made statements recording reservations. These covered a range of issues but were related particularly to the paragraphs on the Middle East.

When the various resolutions arising from the Conference were considered at the General Assembly meeting of March 2002, three draft resolutions were adopted by consensus. The fourth, the draft resolution on 'Comprehensive implementation of and follow-up to the World Conference against Racism, Racial Discrimination, Xenophobia and Related Intolerance'—the resolution, that is, that included the Durban Declaration and Programme of Action—was dealt with by vote. It was adopted by 134 votes, with two votes against—those of Israel and the United States—and two abstentions: Australia and Canada.[78] In

---

76  Bhabha (1994: 217).
77  Bhabha (1995: 9).
78  General Assembly Resolution A/RES/56/266.

statements to the assembly made in explanation of their position by the United States and Canada, both countries affirmed their strong commitment to the fight against racism and to the objectives of the Conference, but identified, as had Australia in its earlier reservation, 'unacceptable' references to the Middle East as the key reason for their objections. All four countries have maintained these positions in subsequent General Assembly resolutions on the Durban Declaration and Programme of Action.[79]

At the Conference's end, therefore, and subsequently, there remains a serious question about whether the outcome was worth the pain of the process, or whether the experience had been effectively one of disconnection and alienation.[80] The more important question is whether the failure of consensus about the key Durban documents represents a fracturing of the agreed universal moral order and framework set out in the UN Charter and Bill of Rights.

The UN Durban Review Conference on Racism (Durban II) held in Geneva in April 2009 did nothing to retrieve the badly sullied reputation of the earlier Conference. From many accounts, Durban II fared even worse than the original 2001 Conference. Once again, Israel and the United States did not participate. Nor did a number of other countries, this time including Australia. Others— the representatives of 23 states and organisations[81]—walked out during the keynote address to the participants by Iranian President, Mahmoud Ahmadinejad. Anti-Semitism, expressed in terms of an anti-Israel discourse, again dominated the process, sadly reflecting the continuing anti-Israel blocs that increasingly dominate UN General Assembly debates and even those of the newly constituted UN Human Rights Council. Cotler points out that 'in the first four years of its existence, the UN Human Rights Council has adopted 33 resolutions of condemnation. 26 of those resolutions, 80 per cent...single out one member state of the international community...Israel'.[82] The UN Human Rights Council has adopted no resolutions or investigative mandates 'for such human rights violator countries as China, Cuba, Libya, North Korea, Russia or Iran, to name but a few—all being listed on Freedom House's list of the 20 worst human rights abusers'.[83]

79  General Assembly Resolutions A/RES/57/195, 18 December 2002; A/RES/58/160, 22 December 2003.
80  Alfredo Sfeir Younis, panel discussion organised by the Conference of NGOs (CONGO), Durban, 7 September 2001.
81  Pogrund (2009: 1).
82  Cotler (2010a).
83  Cotler (2010b).

# The human rights imaginary as ongoing project

Despite the failures of Durban and the grim intensification since then of the Israeli/Palestinian and other ethnic, racial and religious conflicts, the World Conference against Racism did not attack the principles either of human rights or of respect for the bond of common humanity. On the contrary, all protagonists invoked those principles as the very basis of their dissensions. The level of disunity and confrontation was itself a measure of the profound difficulty of the practical implementation of those principles that the organisers of the NGO Forum and the Conference so bravely attempted to address. Delegations represented multiple modernities and resistant traditionalisms.

At the same time, the progress of negotiation of the documents, with the text being constantly revised on screen in the main Conference meeting room, was also a negotiation of culture. In this international forum, cultural difference as well as national interest was asserted. It was also subject to negotiation. As an anthropologist—although that was not the official capacity in which I was in Durban—I found it impossible to resist making the connections between the formal discourse of human rights as represented in the documents and the ways in which human rights are interpreted and experienced by particular groups. The concern of the anthropologist is human sociality and its cultural expression, and is therefore about rights at the level of social practice, human rights as embodied in social persons and embedded in social networks.[84] Paradoxically, Durban, like many other UN processes, demonstrated the vitality of culture as a framework for difference, as well as its malleability in negotiating those differences within a broader moral framework of common humanity.

The Durban Conference documents, for all their compromises and limitations, did not pull back from or undermine any previously agreed principles. What they do starkly illustrate is two things: first, that the meaning of those principles, and what they are seen to demand in practice, is subject to the particular circumstances and interpretations of different groups; and second, that agreement about those principles, and the universal moral order and framework that they support, is never final and can never be taken for granted. Particular cultural meanings can prove non-negotiable. The strategic interests of particular countries and groups, pursued through aggressive strategic action, will always have the capacity to—and do—destroy agreement. The urge to war remains often stronger than the desire for peace, and hatred is a powerful opponent to reason.

Nevertheless, the dialectic interaction between strategic and communicative action is central to all UN forums, including the World Conferences. UN member

---

84   Wilson and Mitchell (2003: 5, 8).

states and NGO delegations acted as participants in a—more or less—rational interaction, using language with the intention of reaching agreement. Part of that interaction required agreement concerning the reasonableness and the claimed validity of the range of utterances—negotiating points, national policies, strategic interests, and so on—that made up the content of the discussion. On many occasions, the mobilising of rationality was distorted by the mobilisation of interests, with the degree of conflict and cooperation varying with the given interest positions.[85] These different interests defined the debate and identified the limits—political, economic, cultural—beyond which individual governments, or indeed NGO delegations, were not prepared to go. They also offered areas of commonality on which agreement could be painstakingly reached.

The process of reaching agreement, although ultimately the responsibility of governments, involved an important dialogue between governments and NGOs that was to some extent reflected in final Conference documents. Even in Durban, despite its problems, the NGO Forum had some impact on the deliberations of the Conference and made a range of significant contributions to the drafting of the final Declaration and Programme of Action. Kofi Annan, the UN Secretary-General, recognised the critical role played by civil society; in an address to the Forum, he said:[86] 'No United Nations conference is complete without its NGO Forum. Gatherings like this are the best answer to our critics, and perhaps one of the best reasons for having UN conferences at all. So often it is you, the civil society activists, who breathe life into these events.'

The NGO Forum achieved proper and important agreements, a number of which were acknowledged by Mary Robinson, despite her reservations about the full text of the NGO documents. Most importantly, the Forum reaffirmed the fundamental principle that human rights are not negotiable. Secondly, the NGO documents list the bases of discrimination—something that was not achieved in the intergovernmental conference—and recognise their intersectionality. Thirdly, the World Conference against Racism NGO process provided perhaps the first international forum for many groups, such as Dalits and Roma, to make their voices heard and to be taken seriously. Fourthly, the Forum and NGO parallel events during the conference ensured that major international issues such as globalisation, migrants, refugees and asylum-seekers, and trafficking in people, especially women and children, remained firmly on the agenda. In summary, both events built on the NGO partnerships established through the UN conferences of the 1990s to strengthen the participation of civil society,

---

85    Habermas (1984: 99, 101).
86    Durban, 30 August 2001.

including its younger members,[87] in the 'robust' dialogue that is essential to the shaping of the new forms of organisation and action at the local, regional and national, as well as international, levels.

The Conference documents themselves support and develop the content of the universal moral order affirmed in the UN Charter and the *Universal Declaration of Human Rights*. As with all moral orders, breaches, including those being undertaken in the name of the 'war on terror', do not of themselves necessarily constitute a rejection of the moral order itself, or of the framework that allows a judgement about whether or not particular practices are acceptable in the terms of that order. They do, however, have the potential to undermine both the moral order and the framework, especially when the breaches are carried out in the name of an alternative moral order, whether religious, political or nihilist.

To date, and despite the massive changes to national borders over its history, particularly over the past 15 years, the United Nations offers legitimacy, albeit a fragile one, as the one truly international legal organisation dedicated to achieving international cooperation and to promoting the welfare of the people of the world. The United Nations has come under much criticism, from within and without, and from civil society as well as from governments. It has recorded many failures as well as achievements. The veto rights of the founding countries and permanent members of the Security Council all too often block decisions crucial to the United Nation's effectiveness in carrying out its mandate. Like all organisations, it could and must do better. But it can operate effectively only with the goodwill and good faith of all its members. Acts that defy its authority, such as the 2003 war against Iraq, place in jeopardy not only the organisation of the United Nations but also the human rights principles of which it remains the guardian and on which it is based.

Such acts call into question the practical implementation and universal applicability of the moral order and framework expressed in and through the United Nations. In a world still very much subject to the scourge of war, and to the rise of authoritarian alternative moral orders and social imaginaries, the United Nations, for all its multiple faults, remains the only medium for an expressed common understanding of the good, of what constitutes a good society, and of the necessary conditions for a good life. The world, whether expressed as the international community or experienced by people in our everyday lives, cannot afford its failure.

---

87   I have not dealt here with the Youth Summit that preceded both the NGO Forum and the Conference. It was the first time that the United Nations had organised such a summit. It was subject to many of the same pressures and problems as the NGO Forum but it provided a forum for young people, including our Human Rights Delegation, with their introduction to the processes of UN World Conferences.

# 9. Human rights and the promise of a good life

When the planes crashed into the World Trade Centre in New York on 11 September 2001, they threw into stark question the modern social imaginary and, with it, the fragile ascendancy of reason and of an international moral and legal framework articulated through the discourse and practice of human rights. These features of modernity were never absolute, as the history of the twentieth century had made brutally clear, and had been under escalating assault over the same period as 'the decade of human rights' in, among other places, Somalia, Bosnia, Rwanda, the Palestinian territories and Israel. Evil played its role, in shocking manifestations of hatred and cruelty, but was neither the cause nor the ultimate consequence. Nor were we witnessing a clash of civilisations,[1] although culture, and a plurality of certainties,[2] were factors. Rather, what was being played out, and continues to be played out, was a stark contest between opposing ideas of the good: whose good, what constitutes the good, what is the moral source of the good, what are the necessary conditions for a good life; or, in the case of some, a good death. The actions of those who carried out the attack, and the subsequent retaliations in the war in Afghanistan and then in Iraq, suggest that we have sacrificed the possibility of imagining or working together to achieve a common good. The invasion of Iraq in particular, carried out by the United States and its allies in defiance of the United Nations, puts at risk those very values of freedom and democracy in whose name the war was executed. The existence of the United States' detainment camp at Guantanamo Bay, removing detainees from any due legal process or protection under either international or national law, is a radical denial of the rule of law, of human rights, and of the underlying principle of respect for the bond of common humanity. Modernity, like Cronus, appears to be devouring its own children.

But this is to privilege 'the discretionary judgements of contemporary managers of the power of liberal states': the view from the top. Critical as that is, it leaves out 'the pivotal role of the democratic agency of ordinary citizens in making practical the ethics of human rights'.[3] It is this democratic agency of ordinary citizens and the agency of ordinary people that has been the focus of my book. I began with an account of the inquest into the deaths of two women, Nurjan Husseini and Fatimeh Husseini, and the circumstances of their families who were seeking asylum in Australia. Despite their bewildering initial brush with modernity, its complexities and its institutions, despite the draconian actions

---

1   Huntington (1993).
2   Phrase offered by Anne McMillan, personal communication.
3   Wallach (2005: 129).

of the Australian Government and even its offer to pay people to return to Afghanistan, Musa and his family, Sayed, their young witness, Ali Reza, and his brother maintained their choice to seek a better life in Australia. They were all finally recognised as refugees and now live in this country.

The interim period remained bleak. Although he was allowed to attend school, Reza was held under armed guard in a Perth motel for 11 months while immigration officials assessed his refugee application. In an interview published in *The Australian* newspaper, he was quoted as saying:[4]

> The motel was like a detention centre, it was prison for me. I was in the room and there were two officers there all the time watching me. Many times I was told I was taking very long showers and that Australia did not have enough water…but it was my only privacy. I would go in there and sit in the shower and think about the future. I decided to suicide, many times, but I thought about my family and that stopped me.

In 2004, he was granted a temporary protection visa and was finally able to live with his older brother. Later that same year, he was awarded a Rescue Medal by the Royal Life Saving Society for outstanding bravery for his attempts to save Nurjan Husseini.

After the inquest, Musa was sent back to detention on Nauru and Sayed to Christmas Island. Months later, Sayed was forcibly relocated to Nauru.

In May 2004, two and a half years after their rescue from the *Sumber Lestari*, Musa and his family and Sayed were officially recognised as refugees and released from detention on Nauru. Their next step was to gain Australian citizenship. Sayed expressed his desire for this goal in terms that Fatimeh is buried on Christmas Island.[5] For him, in spite of all that has happened, she is part of Australia and continues to evoke the dream of a better life that they had hoped to share.

# From 'bare life' to human rights

In becoming stateless persons, asylum-seekers and refugees are seen both by governments and by many humanitarian organisations as figures of 'bare life'.[6] Elaborating on the work of Hannah Arendt, Giorgio Agamben distinguishes bare life from political life. The critical distinction they both make is between the bare natural life (*zoe*) of humans simply as humans and the political life (*bios*)

---

4    18 October 2004.
5    Paul Toohey, Man overboard, *The Weekend Australian*, 12–13 July 2003.
6    Agamben (1998).

of the person as citizen. Their focus is on the break-up of the identity between man and citizen. Implicit in their argument is that a good life is only achievable by those who are citizens, since the Rights of Man only belong in the sphere of the nation-state:[7]

> The paradox…is that precisely the figure that should have incarnated the rights of man *par excellence*, the refugee, constitutes instead the radical crisis of this concept. 'The concept of the Rights of Man,' Arendt writes, 'based on the supposed existence of a human being as such, collapsed in ruins as soon as those who professed it found themselves for the first time before men who had truly lost every other specific quality and connection except for the mere fact of being humans.' In the nation-state, the so-called sacred and inalienable rights of man prove to be completely unprotected at the very moment it is no longer possible to characterise them as rights of the citizens of a state…The Rights of Man represent above all the original figure of the inscription of bare natural life in the legal-political order of the nation-state…Rights, that is, are attributable to *man* only in the degree to which he is the immediately vanishing presupposition (indeed, he must never appear simply as man) of the *citizen*.

This analysis would suggest that a bare life cannot become a good life, since a bare life is lived outside the law, outside politics; in a sense, outside society. For Agamben, the refugee 'unhinges the old trinity of state/nation/territory' and threatens not only 'the very foundations of the nation-state'[8] but also the possibility, at least in terms of Agamben's own argument, of achieving a good society. In this view, there is no substantive move from the limited Rights of Man to a concept of universal human rights that does not rely on a distinction between bare life and political life, or on the inclusion of individuals within any particular nation-state. And it ignores the possibility of an active rejection by refugees of a bad society that denies them the option of a good life and the driving desire to be accepted into a good society in order to achieve one.

The circumstances of the men in the dock in Fremantle, and of Musa's wife and children back on Nauru in indefinite detention, might seem to have borne out Agamben's view, with their rights, even their attendance at the memorial vigil to mark the first anniversary of the deaths of Musa's mother and Sayed's wife, denied by the government of a state of which they were not yet citizens. But this is only part of their story. Musa's and Sayed's lives in Afghanistan had been political lives of a sort, even under the limitations for Hazara people under the Taliban regime. But they were not just political lives. When they

---

7    Agamben (1995: 117).
8    ibid., pp. 117, 118.

became refugees, they also carried their own histories and their culture. Their rights were not just the Rights of Man discussed by Arendt and Agamben, but human rights as set out in the *International Bill of Human Rights* and elaborated with specific reference to refugees in the 1951 Refugee Convention.[9] Indeed, the Refugee Convention was one of the earliest UN declarations after the 1948 *Universal Declaration of Human Rights*, affirming the principle 'that human beings shall enjoy fundamental rights and freedoms without discrimination'.[10] The Convention makes clear that the rights of the refugee are precisely rights that do not depend on the status of citizen; they are not the rights of man as citizen. They are human rights dependent upon the mere fact of being humans.

For asylum-seekers arriving by boat after 11 September 2001, those rights were not honoured by the Australian Government. Their breach represents a weakening of the agreement that established international standards for the treatment of refugees and asylum-seekers. At the same time, those formal standards for rights were precisely what provided the critique by civil society of the Government's position. They also enabled the insistence on the application of rights under Australian law, through the Human Rights Council of Australia and others, that led to the holding of the inquest into the deaths of the two women; a small step, but one taken. Despite its undermining in recent years, particularly through the privileging of security and of the state of exception[11] in the so-called 'war on terror', the discourse of human rights remains a powerful legal as well as moral instrument. The case studies in the book suggest that it is also one of the key factors in transforming the experience of modernisation into an engagement with modernity.

# Human rights as a transforming discourse of modernity

## Thailand

In the struggle to develop new meanings during the period of the Thai 'democratic experiment' of 1973–76, the appeal to rights played a pivotal shaping role. For industrial workers and peasants, the advent of democracy after 14 October 1973 provided the first serious opportunity to assert rights, including the right to establish legal associations, in order to improve their conditions, protect and promote their interests, and as an avenue to a better life. The trade unions and the Farmers Federation became vehicles for linking people with the possibilities

---

9   *United Nations Convention relating to the Status of Refugees 1951.*
10   ibid., Preamble.
11   Agamben (2005).

offered by the implementation of rights and for pursuing those possibilities in practice. The events of 6 October 1976 made clear that such pursuit of rights within the context of democracy posed too great a threat to traditional values and practices. The new social imaginary remained at the level of ideas without being translated into sustainable practices or making sense of existing ones.[12]

For the Bang Khen factory workers, already experiencing working conditions that were superior to many others in the nation, this disjunction was less extreme. By deciding to seek employment in the factory, they had already exercised a choice to take advantage of the modernising processes starting to impinge on Thai society; but they encountered a workplace that did not demand a drastic rupture with their past, that integrated practices associated with merit (*bun*), obligations, reciprocity, gratitude, doing good. Making merit itself was a source of happiness, of feeling good, but even the work, monotonous and noisy as it was, allowed greater benefits such as 'more time to yourself'.[13] Nevertheless, their experience of modernisation was itself transforming, leading them to engage with the emerging moral discourse and practice of rights, expressed mainly as fairness. The establishment of their own trade union was a move to a form of communicative action, to explore through dialogue the possibility of a change from the patron–client hierarchy to relations based on equality rather than benevolence. The establishment of the trade union also represented an incipient recognition that achieving a better life is a collective as well as an individual project, that a good society is a desirable, indeed necessary, context for a good life. For the radical students, that link was essential but led to catastrophe. For the Bang Khen workers, engaging with modernisation meant a shift from acquiescence in traditional forms of social relations to a cautious participation in redefining traditional forms and practices within a changing modern environment.

The crises of 1976 and of Black May 1992, the more recent crisis surrounding the leadership of Prime Minister Thaksin Shinawatra and the associated violence, and the impending crisis around the succession to King Bhumipol: all suggest that Thailand has still not come fully to terms with modernity, that the country has yet to establish sufficiently strong and accountable democratic institutions. At the same time, inherent in these crises also are meanings that continue to draw on a customary order and moral framework that, in turn, reinforces those meanings underpinning particular notions of the good and of a good society. As Jackson suggests, the diverse crises of Thai modernity are productive not of a cultural convergence with the West but of novel forms of cultural difference

---

12    Taylor (2003: 2).
13    See Chapter 2.

and differences of understanding and meaning.[14] The transformation of the traditional Thai social imaginary, like Thai modernity itself, remains in a process of becoming.

## Spain

For the nuns in Spain, human rights also became central in the wake of the Second Vatican Council, though their focus was on working for rights for the disadvantaged. This was not the impulse to a charity towards the poor that was incorporated from the beginning into the life of their religious order but left unchallenged a social as well as a religious hierarchy. Their commitment to the practice of rights was to an egalitarian social justice. For them, the change was a direct result of a change in meanings: the reinterpretation of the relationship of the Church to the world brought about through Vatican II. Not only did the Vatican Council shift its gaze from heaven to earth and look for the 'signs of the times',[15] as well as for spiritual guidance. Its message was not confined to the faithful, or developed with the goal of conversion, but addressed to 'the whole of humanity'[16] in the spirit of Pope John XXIII's 'Message to Humanity' at the opening of the Council.

For the nuns, central to this shift in interpretation was what Taylor identifies as a key characteristic of modernity, that is, the affirmation of ordinary life. The corollary is the rejection of a spiritual hierarchy reflected in the distinction between religious and laity.[17] The nuns' response was to embrace involvement (*inserción*) in the world: they changed their religious habit for ordinary clothes; many moved out of their stately convents into ordinary housing (*pisos*); they sought new work in areas of disadvantage away from their elite schools; they engaged in the political struggles of the late Franco years. Their understanding of a good life became inextricably linked to the achievement of a good society, that religious life was not a better life, but a life dedicated to making a good life for others, and doing so firmly 'in this earthly city'.[18] In time, their very commitment to social justice and achieving rights brought many of them into conflict with a nervous authority, both in Madrid and in Rome. But their experience of modernity had also reoriented their understanding of obedience and shifted, in an echo of one of the generative moments of modernity, to the primacy of individual conscience. Having lived the changes, few were prepared to return to an unquestioning acceptance of traditional practices. While

---

14   Jackson (2004: 351, 357).
15   Abbott (1966: *Pastoral Constitution on the Church in the Modern World [Gaudium et spes]*, para. 4).
16   ibid., para. 2.
17   Taylor (2003: 216–18).
18   Abbott (1966: *Lumen Gentium* VI, p. 46).

retaining some links with a past that they saw as having ongoing meaning in their present, they did not see as negotiable the new moral space that they had come to inhabit.

At the same time, they recognised the ongoing tension between their religious and secular interpretations of the good. For a few, this was a terminal tension and drove them increasingly away from the Province and from the rest of the order. Others were prepared to accept it as a creative tension, not without pain, but one that required some flexibility as well as ingenuity in maintaining both autonomy and cordial relations with 'the provincials'. The religious bond, but a religious bond infused with reason, became their basis for communicative action, realised as a 'noncoercive intersubjectivity of mutual understanding and reciprocal recognition'.[19] The approach allowed them to engage in an ongoing dialogue within the Spanish Provinces, to reach sufficient consensus on a shared notion of the good while maintaining practical diversity, and to retain their imagined community[20] of the order as a whole.

## The Pilbara

For Aboriginal people in the Pilbara, struggles over the Harding Dam and the Marandoo mine became their defining encounters with the broader discourse and practice of land rights and, through that, of Indigenous rights and human rights. The pursuit of rights—through the fight against the dam, the Royal Commission into Aboriginal Deaths in Custody, the native title claims—became central to transforming their experience of modernisation as marginalisation to their own version of the indigenisation of modernity.[21]

This has not been a straightforward or simple process. The costs have been high, for both individuals and for communities. Communities have fragmented and different groups have sought to benefit from the new environment provided by native title in different, and often conflicting, ways. The court found that Ngarluma and Yindjibarndi people continued to hold native title over significant areas of their claim, but that the Wong-Goo-TT-OO claimants held native title only as part of the broader Ngarluma/Yindjibarndi group and not in their own right, and that the Yaburara/Mardudhunera families had no native title to the overlapping claim areas. Nevertheless, both Wong-Goo-TT-OO and Yaburara/Mardudhunera families continue as parties to the Burrup Agreement, which was concluded prior to the native title determination under the future act regime.

---

19    McCarthy, in the introduction to Habermas (1984: xvi).
20    Anderson (1983).
21    Sahlins (2005: 48).

This gives them ongoing status in the native title domain despite the court's decision against them, reinforcing ongoing resentment and disputes that would not have been resolved by any decision.

The original Bunjima native title group also split, as we saw, with the Martu Idja Bunjima lodging their own overlapping claim and taking both the benefits from their status as registered native title claimants as well as high-profile action in areas of joint cultural heritage concerns. In 2008, they were granted a special hearing of the Federal Court to take evidence about a site that would be demolished as part of the development of the Hope Downs mine.[22] They have taken the lead in the media over the impact of the dewatering from Hope Downs on Weeli Wolli Creek and the downstream Fortescue Marshes and Millstream. Their adoption of this leading role itself caused dissension with other groups who have traditional rights and responsibilities for both areas.

But underlying the articulation of rights has been an increasingly confident approach by Pilbara Aboriginal people to using the resources of the colonising society to defend their connection to country as their moral source of the good, and their traditional ways as legitimate and desirable components of a good life. By affirming their own social imaginary and its place in the modern world, they have moved from the margins into a dialogue with modernity. Such dialogue may be sporadic, episodic, fragmented, contested, but the terms are set at least in part by Pilbara Aboriginal people. This is not the sinister exclusion by the liberal state and 'scarring of indigenous alterity' argued by Povinelli and others.[23] Nor, on the evidence of the changes that have taken place in Roebourne since the Harding Dam controversy, or in the Pilbara more broadly since Marandoo and, more significantly, since the recognition of native title, is the notion of dialogue merely a mask for 'the political cunning and calculus of cultural recognition in settler modernity'.[24] To argue this is to reduce the complexities and ambiguities, as well as the pleasures, sorrows, and mundanities, of Aboriginal life in the Pilbara or elsewhere to the single and totalising dimension of relations of power. It is also to deny Pilbara Aboriginal people agency. As Habermas argues in his critique of Foucault, power operates but is not an inevitable component of reason nor the sole organising principle of social relations.[25] Rather, it is precisely along what he calls the 'seams between system and lifeworld' that new potentials for emancipation, resistance and withdrawal have and can develop.[26] We are back to Bhabha's third space: 'the cutting edge of translation and negotiations', the

---

22    French (2008: 1).
23    Povinelli (2002: 35–6).
24    ibid., p. 45.
25    Habermas (1987).
26    ibid., pp. 391–6, especially p. 395.

powerful 'in-between space'.[27] As suggested in Chapter 1, Habermas's work is a sustained investigation of the proposition that only in a society in which a general notion of reason can be invoked can we hope to sustain a good society.[28]

At the same time, Habermas is far from suggesting a model of social interaction based on harmony or the inevitable triumph of goodwill. On the contrary, he addresses the paradoxes of modernity, the uncoupling of system and lifeworld in which the lifeworld is subordinated to systemic constraints, and where crisis is also generated.[29] He identifies action that he calls 'communicative pathology'.[30] Ivison argues that the reliance on consensus itself is problematic:[31]

> The achievement of consensus is impossible and hence the ideal is fundamentally ambiguous. Any form of discursive consensus is at best only partial and transitory, since any rules or norms agreed to will always be subject to re-description and change given the dialogical contexts within which they were formed…Residues of misunderstanding, non-consensuality and injustice persist through the various mediums of communicative action which have gone into the construction of consensus. The gap between agreement and its application in practice is thus central and not peripheral to such a political sensibility.

He goes on to suggest:[32]

> We need to take the pluralization of public reason seriously, and aim for discursively legitimated forms of agreements that do not over-idealize consensus. I shall refer to such agreements as *discursive modi vivendi*: discursive because they emerge from the constellation of discourses and registers present in the public sphere at any given time, and subject to at least some kind of 'reflexive control' by competent actors; and *modi vivendi* because they are always provisional, open to contestation and by definition 'incompletely theorized'.

Pilbara Aboriginal people would probably support his view, although they would express it in different and more immediately practical terms like, 'We just feel it's nothing. We thought we was getting country back but a native title holder is the same as a claimant.' They have to live with the native title determination, the gap between that and its application in practice, and the consequences of the Burrup and other agreements. All remain contested within the community and Taylor and Scambary's investigations demonstrated that

---

27   Bhabha (1995: 38).
28   Seidman (1989: 1).
29   Habermas (1987: 153–97).
30   Habermas (2001: 130–70).
31   Ivison (2002: 73).
32   ibid., pp. 73–4.

Aboriginal people in the Pilbara generally were little better integrated into the regional economic and social life than they were before native title,[33] a finding that more recent research indicates may be in a process of change.[34]

But it is also true that, in the Pilbara as elsewhere in Australia, the native title process has mediated divergent social imaginaries and, through the concept and practice of rights, brought them into a sufficiently shared notion of the good, and of good action as mutual benefit. Rights, too, remain a project and not a final accomplishment.

## The United Nations as a 'third space'

As we saw in Chapter 8, it is also in their use of the United Nations as a third space, and in engaging in communicative action, that Indigenous people are developing further the scope of indigenous rights within the broader context of human rights. Niezen describes these processes:[35]

> Cultural differences have...defiantly entered the public sphere. They have been internationally politicized. Indigenous leaders from Asia, northern Europe, Africa, the Americas, and the South Pacific (including Australia, New Zealand, and the Pacific Islands) meet regularly in groups ranging in size from a dozen to several hundred to discuss the development of human rights standards for indigenous peoples... Indigenous internationalism is both a product of social convergence and an agent of it.

> The United Nations is well known as an unfathomable bureaucracy and, frighteningly, also as the arbiter of the world's important and usually bloody contests, but it is less recognized as a locus for village politics and for struggles between states and marginalized communities. In this new venture, in its regular meetings between Indigenous and state representatives, it has created an original institutional space constituting a distinct social world...The United Nations has thus become a new focal point of 'indigenism', a term I use to describe the international movement that aspires to promote and protect the rights of the world's 'first peoples'.

Members of the Indigenous NGO Caucus in Durban, including a number from Australia (though none from the Pilbara), exercised their familiarity with the UN system, resulting in a much more strategic contribution from them than

---

33  Taylor and Scambary (2005).
34  Edmunds (2012).
35  Niezen (2003: 3–4).

from other, more muddled or more belligerent groups. At the same time, neither the invocation of Indigenous rights in Durban as elsewhere nor the absence of any biological foundation blunted people's historical and personal experiences of racism. One of the sticking points in finalising the Conference documents that caused considerable surprise and no little consternation was the European Union's resistance to including any reference to 'race' in the documents. Under the circumstances, their action seemed almost laughable. Their explanation, however, was not. Despite the focus of the Conference on racism, their position was that race does not exist as a biological fact and references to race itself, as distinct from the social practice of racism, should not therefore be included in the documents. In the end, they bowed to the general consensus.

The European Union position highlighted that race is a metaphor. In the wake particularly of colonialism, it has become the ultimate metaphor for the Other. Racism, which inscribes difference as immutable, is its expression. The practice of racism therefore is not subject to dialogue, or communicative action, or renegotiation. It speaks always from a position of power and a will to dominate. It is a denial of the bond of common humanity. Racism is the product not only of colonialism, though colonialism has entrenched it in the modern landscape. Primo Levi talked about its roots and its extreme expression in the Nazi death camps (*Lager*):[36]

> Many people—many nations—can find themselves holding, more or less wittingly, that 'every stranger is an enemy'. For the most part this conviction lies deep down like some latent infection; it betrays itself only in random, disconnected acts, and does not lie at the base of a system of reason. But when this does come about, when the unspoken dogma becomes the major premises in a syllogism, then, at the end of the chain, there is the *Lager*. Here is a product of a conception of the world carried rigorously to its logical conclusion; so long as the conception subsists, the conclusion remains to threaten us.

This was the conclusion, along with 'the scourge of war', that the United Nations was established to prevent. This was the threat that the *Universal Declaration of Human Rights* set out to defeat with a clear recognition of our common humanity. The World Conference against Racism was one more attempt to tackle 'the sources, causes, forms and contemporary manifestations of racism, racial discrimination, xenophobia and related intolerance'.[37] The particular contribution of Durban to the elaboration of human rights was to go beyond a bald statement of cultural rights[38] to make explicit that difference

---

36   Levi (2001: 15).
37   World Conference against Racism, Theme 1.
38   *United Nations International Convention on Economic, Social and Cultural Rights 1966.*

itself is an intrinsic dimension of our common humanity. The NGO Forum in particular emphasised that 'the multiplicity of vantage points and worldviews in the public sphere is…not to be filtered or bracketed out, but recognized and accommodated'.[39]

Myrna Cunningham summarised this aspect of the NGO documents when she presented them to the Conference plenary session:[40] 'We recognize the richness of the diversity of cultures, languages, religions and people in the World and the potential within this diversity to create a World free of racism, racial discrimination, genocide, slavery, xenophobia and related intolerance.'

The Conference Declaration affirms the importance of 'tolerance and multiculturalism, which constitute the moral ground and inspiration for our world wide struggle against racism',[41] and includes acknowledgment of diversity:[42] 'We further affirm that all peoples and individuals constitute one human family, rich in diversity. They have contributed to the progress of civilizations and cultures that form the common heritage of humanity. Preservation and promotion of tolerance, pluralism and respect for diversity can produce more inclusive societies.'

Despite—or perhaps because of—the unexpected consequences of the encounter with difference,[43] Durban reaffirmed difference as part of being human, and openness to an equal other as key to recognition of the bond of common humanity. At the same time, the very phenomenon of racism that the World Conference was set up to tackle demonstrates that difference forges its own moral and political dilemmas. The patent conclusion, experienced but not formally acknowledged in Durban, is that conflict is as likely, or more likely, an outcome of difference as is its celebration. Conflict, too, is part of being human. Hence the need for strong institutions that transform human rights principles into practical and effective action.

## Conflict and human rights

Conflict has been an experience for the people in each of the case studies in this book. As Bauman and Williams point out:[44] 'The relationships between and within groups and individuals are the fundamental building blocks of a

---

39   Ivison (2002: 83).
40   Presentation on behalf of the International Steering Committee to the World Conference against Racism plenary session, Durban, 5 September 2001.
41   *World Conference against Racism, Racial Discrimination, Xenophobia and Related Intolerance Declaration* (2001), para. 5.
42   ibid., para. 6.
43   Ivison (2002: 89).
44   Bauman and Williams (2004: 4).

functioning society. They require maintenance and ongoing negotiation and re-negotiation…Disputes are a normal part of relationships and decision-making processes. All societies and individuals experience conflict and disputes.'

In now unfashionable, but tantalisingly useful, theoretical language, this might have been analysed in terms of the contradictions inherent in all societies and of their role in the dialectic. Bauman and Williams take the very practical course of reframing the response to conflict as one of conflict management rather than of conflict resolution. They go on to observe that 'all societies have a range of mechanisms for managing and dealing with disputes, and for bringing to account those whose disputes impact on the social cohesion and structure of the group or society as a whole'.[45] In a society in crisis, such as Thailand in 1973 and 1976 or Spain in the 1930s, the failure of the state to manage radical conflict produced by incommensurable social imaginaries erupted into violence. This was not, however—apart from the nuns who lived through the excesses of the Spanish Republic and the Civil War—how most of the people in the three studies experienced their own conflicts. In each case, even under the circumstances of rapid social change, or to some extent because of them, people had access to a range of procedures set up to manage conflict. Engagement with those procedures itself brought about change.

In the Bang Khen factory, the procedures were in some instances an exercise of authority: the dormitory supervisors dealt directly and usually expeditiously with disagreements and disputes among dormitory residents; Phii Iid took it upon himself to sack Chingchai for his perceived breach of the patron–client relationship. Other procedures—in particular, the trade union and the short-lived Employees Committee—were established on a model of negotiation and dialogue. Even in the case of Chingchai, and despite the military crackdown after 6 October, he and the trade union executive had a right of appeal to the external Committee of Labour Relations, a right that the factory management respected. Life in the factory went on as usual.

For the nuns, Vatican II's *Decree on the Appropriate Renewal of Religious Life* (*Perfectae Caritatis*) set in train an overturning of the unquestioning hierarchy of obedience that had in practice suppressed conflict. The Decree, reflecting the other Vatican Council documents and its whole orientation, revolutionised the governing structures and practices of their religious Order. The Council required 'an adjustment of the community to the changed conditions of the times'[46] and directed that 'the way in which communities are governed should

---

45   ibid.
46   Abbott (1966: *Decree on the Appropriate Renewal of Religious Life [Perfectae Caritatis]*, para. 2).

also be re-examined in the light of these same standards'. Constitutions and other directions and ceremonies were to be 'suitably revised', requiring 'the suppression of outmoded regulations.[47]

Subsequent General and Provincial Chapters of the Order set about implementing these changes, as we saw in earlier chapters. Not only was the Order's constitution revised, but also the nuns were no longer subjected every month to the reading of the *Letter of St Ignatius on the Virtue of Obedience*, which offered the example of 'Abbot John, who did not question whether what he was commanded was profitable or not, as when with such great labour he watered a dry stick throughout a year'.[48] And then there was the monk who obeyed his superior's order to plant cabbages upside down. Few of the women missed either Abbot John or the cabbages. Most responded by taking the changes further than, in the end, the Province felt it could sustain. Disagreements and disputes surfaced when obedience returned as an instrument of the provincial government after the appointment of a new provincial in Madrid in 1978 and the election of Pope John Paul II in the same year. Nevertheless, the nuns continued to engage in the processes of negotiation and dialogue that they had come to value as central to their idea of the good.

In the Pilbara, disputes such as that between families that had been internal to the groups prior to the passing of the *Native Title Act* became public through the lodging of overlapping claims. Bauman and Williams comment on the way in which conflict resolution has become 'universalised' using 'western legal paradigms'.[49] They argue that 'developing localised approaches to decision-making and dispute management that are responsive to the needs of Indigenous communities is essential' and point out that 'the approaches that are adopted can escalate or exacerbate fundamental pressures and tensions within Indigenous groups'.[50] Their particular focus is the native title process, which, in the case of the Pilbara, provided both the means and the resources for the formalisation of internal disputes and a process—not particularly adapted to local needs— for dealing with them. In that sense, native title became both a cause of and a channel for conflict. This remained true of the negotiations over the Burrup Peninsula and continues with other resource negotiations and agreements.

At the same time, the procedures involved—National Native Title Tribunal mediations, Federal Court hearings, agreement negotiations—all did more than manage the internal community disputes as well as conflict between the claimants and other parties. They also legitimated customary knowledge and practice within the broader context of modern Australia. The mediation

---

47  ibid., para. 3.
48  *To the Members of the Society in Portugal 1553 Letter on Perfect Obedience.*
49  Bauman and Williams (2004: 5).
50  ibid., p. 3.

conferences for the Ngarluma/Yindjibarndi claim were held in Roebourne. The claimants in general gave their evidence to the court on their own country, not in a formal courtroom. This way of taking evidence was permitted under the *Native Title Act*, allowing the court to 'take account of the cultural and customary concerns of Aboriginal peoples and Torres Strait Islanders'.[51] In the process, the conscious articulation of customary knowledge to meet the requirements of the procedures has effected change for the native title claimants and holders, but there has been change, too, in the Federal Court. Native title, as happened with Aboriginal Land Commissioners in the Northern Territory, has made common the image of judges conducting hearings in the open air. The caravan of four-wheel-drive vehicles has become a feature of native title as well as Northern Territory land-claim hearings. Attention to the weather is a new duty for the court. And being heard and taken seriously by non-Aboriginal Australia is a recent experience for people in Roebourne and the wider Pilbara.

## Conflict and culture

In each of the three case studies, people's approaches to dealing with conflict were culturally shaped as well as procedurally laid down by an external authority. Each of the three groups brought their own cultural expectations and meanings to both the disputes and their management. In each case, the 'living practice of negotiation and accommodation'[52] was carried out in a context of modernising social change, acting to transform those expectations and meanings and reinforcing Bauman's view of culture as both 'a permanent revolution of sorts' and 'a dialogical process of making sense with and through others'.[53] Even conflict, arising out of sameness as well as difference, has its part in this ongoing negotiation of culture, questioning knowledge, ideas, identity, practice, legitimacy, self-interests, agreements and their implementation. The transformation as well as transmission of culture by its inhabitants are part of people's actions and experience. The production of meaning is an ongoing and contested process. As a living process, and as we have seen throughout the book, the production of meaning involves both moral evaluation and rational judgement. It can re-imagine the meaning of the good and of a good life and it can, under certain circumstances, renegotiate the place of those interpretations in relation to different interpretations. Traditional meanings can crumble under this process, leading to alienation and anomie; but they can also provide a basis for people to act to come to terms with modernity.

---

51   *Native Title Act 1993*, s. 82(2).
52   Ivison (2002: 82).
53   Bauman in Bauman and Tester (2001: 32, 142).

In periods of rapid social change, the production of those 'webs of significance'[54] that people themselves continue to spin is also, when it encompasses a whole society, a process of transformation of their social imaginary. This is not a magical or an idealised process. It is carried out by individuals in the mundane and pragmatic compromises of their daily lives. Sometimes it takes place in the public sphere, and the effects may carry moral as well as practical weight. The book makes clear that particular individuals make a difference. It also makes clear the critical link between a good life and a good society. In the short term, all those in the three case studies experienced quite drastic public dislocations while their cultural framework permitted them to maintain private continuities. Their various responses to this disjunction underlie the emergence of three different experiences of modernisation and three different modernities. In these cases, modernisation has not led to cultural collapse. On the contrary, similar modernising—and now globalising—pressures have been themselves transformed in the encounter with three very different cultures and histories.

It is the concept of a humanity that is equal while culturally diverse that I set out to examine in this book. Using an anthropological approach, I have explored the experience of three different groups of people in order to identify how rapid social change, in the form of modernisation, has wrought change in traditionally held beliefs and practices. I also undertook to examine the propositions that concepts of the good and of a good life are human universals and that moral evaluation—morality—and the concept of the good are at the centre of human agency.[55] What the ethnographies allow has been the testing of a theoretical universalising against the lived experience of the different groups concerned. What they reveal is that the ways in which people hold and live their traditional beliefs and carry out their practices have also made the modernising process and its effects different in each case. The ethnographies place tradition and modernity, as well as religion and secular humanism, not in unforgiving opposition but as an interface, an ongoing and dynamic encounter—a dialectic—shaped by the complexities and idiosyncrasies of individual and group experiences, in which culture mediates the unfamiliar.

The studies, together with the briefer examination of the situation of a small group of asylum-seekers and of a UN World Conference, also elucidate that ideas of the good, and of the practical translation of those ideas into the experience of a good life, are culturally framed. Both generate action; they are at the centre of people's differing responses to modernisation and of the choices they continue to make between cultural continuity and change. Both are invoked by the people in the studies in making sense of their lives and of the directions in which they wish to move into the future. The shared action identified in

---

54    Geertz (1975: 5).
55    Taylor (2003).

the ethnographies is based on a shared notion of the good. Sometimes this has been reached through communicative action, negotiating agreement through a rational dialogue on what constitutes the good. Sometimes it has been a violent assertion of one idea of the good over others, in which the idea of the good is non-negotiable and antithetical to rational engagement.

In all the cases dealt with here, people have continued to act in response to and be acted upon by the demands of modernity. Modernity, the sibling of reason, is also child of the European Enlightenment and, as we have seen, also deeply flawed. Habermas, the strongest contemporary champion of modernity and the most incisive scourge of its critics, has sketched out a critical theory of modernity that analyses and accounts for its pathologies in a way that suggests a redirection rather than an abandonment of the project of the Enlightenment.[56]

The stories of the people in this book suggest that, whatever the ambivalence of responses, they act to create their own modernity: one that, Janus-faced, includes their own histories and cultures, that offers the promise of a good society, and, on those bases, also permits them to craft a new space. It is in that new space that they struggle to realise their own imaginary of a good life.

---

56   Habermas (1984: xl); McCarthy (1984: vi).

# References

Abbott, W. M. (ed.) 1966 *The Documents of Vatican II*. London & Dublin: Geoffrey Chapman.

Agamben, G. 1993 *The Coming Community*. Minneapolis: University of Minnesota Press.

—— 1995 We refugees. *Symposium* 49: 114–19.

—— 1998 *Homo Sacer: Sovereign Power and Bare Life*.

—— 2005 *State of Exception*. Chicago: University of Chicago Press.

Alston, P. 1994 Denial and neglect. In R. Reoch (ed.) *Human Rights. The New Consensus*. London: Regency Press in association with the United Nations High Commissioner for Refugees.

—— 1997 Neither fish nor fowl: The quest to define the role of the UN High Commissioner for Human Rights. *European Journal of International Law* 8(2): 321–36.

Altman, J. and M. Hinkson (eds) 2010 *Culture Crisis. Anthropology and Politics in Aboriginal Australia*. Sydney: UNSW Press.

Altman, J. and D. Martin (eds) 2009 *Power, culture, economy. Indigenous Australians and mining*. CAEPR Research Monograph No. 30. Canberra: Centre for Aboriginal Economic Policy Research, The Australian National University.

Anderson, B. 1977 Withdrawal symptoms: social and cultural aspects of the October 6 coup. *Bulletin of Concerned Asian Scholars* 9(3): 13–30.

—— 1983 *Imagined Communities. Reflections on the Origin and Spread of Nationalism*. London: Verso.

—— 1998 *The Spectre of Comparisons. Nationalism, Southeast Asia, and the World*. London & New York: Verso.

Anibarro Espeso, E. 1975 *Estampas del Cerro de los Ángeles: Tabor, Calvario, y Altar Mayor de España*. Madrid: Obra Nacional del Cerro de los Ángeles.

Ardener, S. (ed.) 1977 *Perceiving Women*. London: J. M. Dent & Sons Ltd.

Arendt, H. 1958 The Human Condition. Chicago: University of Chicago Press.

Artola, M. 1978 *Antiguo Régimen y revolución liberal*. Barcelona: Editorial Ariel.

Asia Pacific NGO Conference on Human Rights 1993 *Our Voice. Bangkok NGO Declaration on Human Rights*. Bangkok: Asian Cultural Forum on Development (ACFOD).

Baker, C. 2011 Elemental political conflict. *East Asia Forum Quarterly* 3(4) (October–December): 9–10.

Bauman, T. and R. Williams 2004 *The business of process. Research issues in managing Indigenous decision-making and disputes in land*. AIATSIS Research Discussion Paper No. 13. Canberra: Australian Institute of Aboriginal and Torres Strait Islander Studies.

Bauman, Z. 1973 *Culture as Praxis*. London & Boston: Routledge & Kegan Paul.

—— 2002 The fate of humanity in the post-Trinitarian world. *Journal of Human Rights* 1(3) (September): 283–303.

Bauman, Z. and K. Tester 2001 *Conversations with Zygmunt Bauman*. Cambridge: Polity Press.

Beevor, A. 1999 [1982] *The Spanish Civil War*. London: Cassell Military Paperbacks.

Bello, W., S. Cunningham and L. K. Poh 1998 *A Siamese Tragedy. Development and Disintegration in Modern Thailand*. London & New York: Zed Books.

Bhabha, H. K. 1994 *The Location of Culture*. London: Routledge.

—— 1995 Interview with W. J. T. Mitchell. *See* Mitchell, W. J. T.

Biskup, P. 1973 *Not Slaves, Not Citizens: The Aboriginal Problem in Western Australia*. St Lucia, Qld: University of Queensland Press.

Blake, W. 1794 *Songs of Innocence and of Experience*. London.

de Blaye, E. 1976 [1974] *Franco and the Politics of Spain*. Harmondsworth, Middlesex: Pelican Books.

Boonsanong Punyodyana 1969 Social structure, social system, and two levels of analysis: a Thai view. In H.-D. Evers (ed.) *Loosely Structured Social Systems. Thailand in Comparative Perspective*. New Haven, Conn.: Yale University Council on Southeast Asia Studies.

Bourdieu, P. 1979 [1977] *Outline of a Theory of Practice*. Cambridge: Cambridge University Press.

Bowie, K. A. 1997 *Rituals of National Loyalty. An Anthropology of the State and the Village Scout Movement in Thailand*. New York: Columbia University Press.

Brady, M. 1998 *The Grog Book: Strengthening Indigenous Community Action on Alcohol*. Canberra: Commonwealth Department of Health and Family Services.

Buber, M. 1970 [1923] *I and Thou*. New York: Scribner.

Bunnag, J. 1973 *Buddhist Monk, Buddhist Layman*. Cambridge: The University Press.

Callan, H. 1977 The premiss of dedication: notes towards an ethnography of diplomats' wives. In S. Ardener (ed.) *Perceiving Women*. London: J. M. Dent & Sons.

Callan, H. and S. Ardener (eds) 1984 *The Incorporated Wife*. London & Sydney: Croom Helm.

Camus, A. 2000 [1955] *The Myth of Sisyphus*. London: Penguin Books.

Carr, R. 1977 *The Spanish Tragedy*. London: Weidenfeld & Nicolson.

—— 1983 [1966] *Spain 1808–1975*. Oxford: Clarendon Press, Oxford History of Modern Europe.

Carr, R. and J. P. Fusi Aizpurua 1979 *Spain: Dictatorship to Democracy*. London: George Allen & Unwin.

Carvajal, J. G. M. and C. Corral 1976 *Relaciones de la Iglesia y el Estado*. Madrid: Facultad de Ciencias Políticas, Universidad Complutense, y Facultad de Derecho Canónico, Universidad Pontificia 'Comillas'.

Case, W. 1995 *Comparing regime continuity and change: Indonesia, Thailand and Malaysia*. Regime Change and Regime Maintenance in Asia and the Pacific Discussion Paper No. 15. Canberra: Department of Political and Social Change, Research School of Pacific and Asian Studies, The Australian National University.

Castells, J. M. 1973 *Las asociaciones religiosas en la España contemporánea: Un estudio jurídico-administrativo (1767–1965)*. Madrid: Taurus Ediciones, S.A.

Catalogue de La Société du Sacré Coeur de Jésus 1899–1982. Rome: Maison Mère.

Chai-anan Samudavanija 1992 Economic reform and institutional crisis, Thailand. *Economic Reform Today* 1992(3), <http://www.cipe.org/>

Chamartín, Colegio del Sagrado Corazón 1934–36 *Documentos referentes a la Persecución Religiosa*. Madrid: Archivos del Convento del Sagrado Corazón, Chamartín.

—— 1959a *Una Historia de Fuego. Memoria del Centenario 1859–1959*. Madrid: Chamartín.

—— 1959b *Mater Admirabilis*. Madrid: Chamartín, Revista Redactada por Antiguas Alumnas del Sagrado Corazón.

—— 1972–84 Official School Documents. Madrid.

—— 1985 *Mas lejos todavía*. Madrid: Novagraphic.

Charmot, F. 1953 *La Société du Sacré Coeur de Jésus*. Lyon: Lescuyer.

*Cien Años De Educación Cristiana. See* Religiosas Del Sagrado Corazón de Jesús.

de la Cierva, R. 1974 *Historia básica de la España actual (1800-1974)*. Barcelona: Editorial Planeta.

Clapham, A. 1994 Creating the High Commissioner for Human Rights: the outside story. *European Journal of International Law* 5(4): 556–68.

Clifford, J. 1988 *The Predicament of Culture. Twentieth Century Ethnography, Literature and Art*. Cambridge, Mass., & London: Harvard University Press.

Clifford, J. and G. Marcus (eds) 1986 *Writing Culture. The Poetics and Politics of Ethnography*. Berkeley & London: University of California Press.

Codina, V. 1969 *Teología de la vida religiosa*. Madrid: Editorial Razón y Fe.

—— 1972 *Nueva formulación de la vida religiosa*. Bilbao: Mensajero.

Codina, V. et al. 1981 *Análizar la Iglesia*. Madrid: Ediciones HOAC.

Comaroff, J. and J. Comaroff 1993 *Modernity and its Malcontents: Ritual and Power in Post-Colonial Africa*. Chicago: University of Chicago Press.

Comisión Episcopal de Enseñanza y Catequesis 1981a *Nota de la Comisión Episcopal de Enseñanza y Catequesis sobre los Acuerdos de la XXXIII Asamblea Plenaria de la Conferencia Episcopal Española acerca de Temas de Enseñanza. 24–29 noviembre 1980*. Madrid: Edice.

—— 1981b *Principios y normas legales reguladoras de la enseñanza de la religion y moral católicas en los centros escolares*. Madrid: Edice.

—— 1982 *Posición de los obispos sobre los problemas de la educación en la sociedad española actual*. Madrid: Edice.

Commonwealth of Australia 2002 *Report of the Senate Select Committee for An Inquiry into a Certain Maritime Incident*. Canberra: Commonwealth of Australia, <http_wopared.aph.gov.au_senate_committee_maritime_incident_cttee_report_report.pdf>

Confederación Española De Centros De Enseñanza (CECE) 1983 *Actualidad Docente*. Madrid: Confederación Española De Centros De Enseñanza.

CONFER 1980 *Guía de las Comunidades religiosas femeninas de España*. Madrid: Editorial Confer.

Conferencia Episcopal Española 1976 *Declaración sobre la Enseñanza*. Madrid: Ediciones Acción católica española.

—— 1982 *Totus Tuus. Visita pastoral de Juan Pablo II a España, 31 octubre – 9 noviembre 1982*. Madrid: Informe inédito elaborado por la Oficina de Información de la Conferencia Episcopal Española, con la colaboración de las Comisiones Episcopales y de la Oficina de Estadística y Sociología de la Iglesia.

Cotler, I. 2010a Anti-Semitism today: what we can do. B'nai B'rith 27th annual Anti-Defamation Commission Gandel Oration, 18 July 2010, <http://www.antidef.org.au/>

—— 2010b UN poisons its human rights mission. *The Australian*, 4 October 2010.

Daniels, D. 1985 Aboriginal rangers for Millstream National Park. In D. Smyth, P. Taylor and A. Willis (eds) *Aboriginal Ranger Training and Employment in Australia. Proceedings of the First National Workshop, July 1985*. Canberra: Australian National Parks and Wildlife Service.

Davis, L. 1995 New directions for CRA. Paper delivered to the Securities Institute of Australia, Melbourne & Sydney, March.

Dawson, G. 1987 Aboriginal/police relations: Roebourne Research Report, Special Government Committee on Aboriginal/Police and Community Relations. Unpublished paper. Perth.

Department of Conservation and Land Management 1999 *Karijini National Park Management Plan 1999–2009*. Perth: Department of Conservation and Land Management.

Department of Technical and Economic Cooperation 1974 *Thailand. Facts and Figures*. Bangkok: Office of the Prime Minister.

Donnelly, J. 2003 (2nd edn) *Universal Human Rights in Theory and Practice*. Ithaca, NY, & London: Cornell University Press.

Douzinas, C. 2000 *The End of Human Rights. Critical Legal Thought at the Turn of the Century*. Oxford: Hart Publishing.

Duocastella, R. 1969 La formación religiosa en los colegios de la Iglesia. *Educadores* XI(55): 775–90.

—— 1972 *Análisis de mentalidad y actitudes religiosas de tres parróquias de Madrid (Chamartín)*. Barcelona: Instituto de Sociología y Pastoral aplicada (ISPA), Multicopy.

Duocastella, R., J. A. Marcos-Alonso, et al. 1967 *Análisis sociológico del catolicismo español*. Barcelona: Editorial Nova Terra, Instituto de Sociología y Pastoral aplicada (ISPA).

Durán Herás, M. A. 1972 *El trabajo de la mujer en España*. Madrid: Editorial Tecnos.

—— 1982 Notas para el estudio de la Estructura Social de España en el siglo XVIII. In Ministerio de Cultura, Estudios sobre la Mujer (ed.) *Mujer y sociedad en España 1700–1975*. Madrid: Dirección general de Juventud y Promoción Socio-Cultural.

Edmunds, M. 1979 Patronage and politicization. A study of a Thai factory in the 1970s. Unpublished MA thesis. The Australian National University, Canberra.

—— 1986 But the greatest of these is chastity. A study of Spanish nuns. Unpublished PhD thesis. The Australian National University, Canberra.

—— 1989 *They Get Heaps. A Study of Attitudes in Roebourne*. Canberra: Aboriginal Studies Press.

—— 1994 *Claims to Knowledge, Claims to Country*. Canberra: Native Title Research Unit, Australian Institute of Aboriginal and Torres Strait Islander Studies.

—— 1995 *Conflict in native title claims*. Land, Rights, Laws: Issues of Native Title Issues Paper No. 7. Canberra: Native Title Research Unit, Australian Institute of Aboriginal and Torres Strait Islander Studies.

—— 2012 Commissioned papers. In B. Walker (ed.) *The Challenge, Conversation, Commissioned Papers and Regional Studies of Remote Australia*. Alice Springs, NT: Desert Knowledge remoteFOCUS, <http://www.desertknowledge.com.au>

Elliott, D. 1978 The socio-economic formation of modern Thailand. *Journal of Contemporary Asia* 8(1): 21–50.

Evers, H.-D. (ed.) 1969 *Loosely Structured Social Systems: Thailand in Comparative Perspective*. New Haven, Conn.: Yale University Council on Southeast Asia Studies.

—— (ed.) 1973 *Modernization in South East Asia*. Singapore: Oxford University Press.

Far Eastern Economic Review 1979 *Asia 1979 Yearbook*. Hong Kong: Far Eastern Economic Review.

Farrelly, N. and A. Walker 2009 Thailand's royal sub-plot thickens. *Inside Story*, 6 May, <http://inside.org.au/thailands-royal-sub-plot-thickens/print/>

FOESSA. See Fundación FOESSA.

Fontana, J. 1974 *La quiebra de la monarquía absoluta 1814–1820*. Barcelona: Editorial Ariel.

Frayn, M. 2000 (rev. edn) *Copenhagen*. London: Methuen.

Freelander 2010 The deep political crisis within the Royal Thai Army officer corps. *New Mandala*, 27 April, <http://www.asiapacific.anu.edu.au/newmandala/2010/>

Freire, P. 1972 *Pedagogy of the Oppressed*. Middlesex: Penguin Books.

French, R. 2008 Rolling a rock uphill? Native title and the myth of Sisyphus. Paper presented to the Judicial Conference of Australia National Colloquium, 10 October 2008, <http://www.hcourt.gov.au/publications_05.html>

Fundación FOESSA (Fomento de Estudios Sociales y Sociología Aplicada) 1967 *Informe sociológico sobre la situación social de Madrid 1966*. Madrid: Cáritas diocesana de Madrid-Álcala.

—— 1970 *Informe sociológico sobre la situación social de España*. (Colección FOESSA Vol. 4). Madrid: Euramerica.

—— 1972 *Síntesis del Informe sociológico sobre la situación social de España 1970*. Madrid: Euramerica.

—— 1976 *Estudios sociológicos sobre la situación social de España 1975*. Madrid: Euramerica.

—— 1978 *Síntesis actualizada del III Informe FOESSA*. Madrid: Euramerica.

—— 1983 *Informe sociológico sobre el cambio social en España. 1975–1983.* Madrid: Editorial Euramerica, S.A.

Gara, T. J. 1983 The Flying Foam Massacre. In M. Smith (ed.) *Archaeology at ANZAAS 1983.* Perth: Western Australian Museum.

Garcia Canclini, N. 1995 *Hybrid Cultures. Strategies for Entering and Leaving Modernity.* Minneapolis: University of Minnesota Press.

García Villoslada, R. (ed.) 1979 *La Iglesia en la España contemporánea 1808–1975. Historia de la Iglesia en España (Tomo V).* Madrid: B.A.C.

Geertz, C. 1975 *The Interpretation of Cultures.* London: Hutchinson & Co.

Gibson, J. 1971 The In-betweeners: a study of changing values and relationships in Roebourne, WA, with special reference to Aboriginal school children. Unpublished MA thesis. University of Western Australia, Perth.

Giddens, A. 1999 *Runaway World: How Globalisation is Reshaping Our Lives.* London: Profile Books.

Goffman, E. 1962 *Asylums.* Chicago: Aldine.

Gómez Molleda, M. D. 1966 *Los reformadores de la España contemporánea.* Madrid: C.S.I.C.

González-Carvajal Santabárbara, L. 1984 El compromiso cristiano. La Iglesia de los pobres. In J. Ruíz Giménez (ed.) *Iglesia, Estado y Sociedad en España.* Barcelona: Editorial Argos Vergara S.A.

González González, M. J. 1979 *La economía política del Franquismo 1940–1970.* Madrid: Editorial Tecnos.

Grabosky, P. N. 1988 Aboriginal deaths in custody: the case of John Pat. *Race and Class* 29(3) (January): 87–95.

Grayling, A. C. 2003 *What is Good? The Search for the Best Way to Live.* London: Weidenfeld & Nicolson.

Griffiths, B. 1996 The role of vocational students during the democracy period in Thailand. In B. Hunsaker, T. Mayer, B. Griffiths and R. Dayley *Loggers, Monks, Students, and Entrepreneurs: Four Essays on Thailand.* Illinois: Center for Southeast Asian Studies, Northern Illinois University.

Guerrero, J. M. 1967 *La vida religiosa en la Iglesia del Post-Concilio.* Bilbao: Mensajero.

—— (ed.) 1968 *Se Renuevan las Religiosas?* Madrid: Ediciones Studium.

—— (ed.) 1970 *La vida religiosa en el hoy de la Iglesia*. Bilbao: Mensajero.

Guerrero, J. M. and M. Rondet (eds) 1969 *El porvenir de la vida religiosa en el mundo secularizado*. Bilbao: Mensajero.

Guía De La Iglesia En España. *See* Oficina General de Información y Estadistica de la Iglesia en España.

Haas, M. R. 1964 *Thai–English Student's Dictionary*. Kuala Lumpur, London, Singapore: Oxford University Press.

Habermas, J. 1974 The public sphere: an encyclopedia article (1964). *New German Critique* 1(3): 49–55.

—— 1981 Modernity versus postmodernity. *New German Critique* 22 (Winter): 3–14.

—— 1982 A reply to my critics. In *Habermas. Critical Debates*. (Eds J. B. Thompson and D. Held.) London & Basingstoke: Macmillan.

—— 1984 [German text 1981] *The Theory of Communicative Action. Volume 1. Reason and the Rationalization of Society*. (Trans. T. McCarthy.) Boston: Beacon Press.

—— 1987 [German text 1981] *The Theory of Communicative Action. Volume 2. Lifeworld and System: A Critique of Functionalist Reason*. (Trans. T. McCarthy.) Cambridge: Polity Press.

—— 2001 [trans. German text 1984] *On the Pragmatics of Social Interaction. Preliminary Studies in the Theory of Communicative Action*. Cambridge, Mass.: The MIT Press.

—— 2002 [1987] *The Philosophical Discourse of Modernity*. Cambridge: Polity Press.

Hall, A. 1974 Patron–client relations. *Journal of Peasant Studies* 1(4): 506–9.

Hanks, L. M. 1962 Merit and power in the Thai social order. *American Anthropologist* 64(6): 1247–61.

—— 1975 The Thai social order as entourage and circle. In G. W. Skinner and A. T. Kirsch (eds) *Change and Persistence in Thai Society. Essays in Honor of Lauriston Sharp*. Ithaca, NY, & London: Cornell University Press.

Harrison, J. 1978 *An Economic History of Modern Spain*. Manchester: Manchester University Press.

Hasluck, P. 1970 (2nd edn) *Black Australians. A Survey of Native Policy in Western Australia 1829–1897*. Melbourne: Melbourne University Press.

Hazzard, S. 2006 [1967] *People in Glass Houses*. London: Virago Press.

Hewison, K. 2010 Rebellion, repression and the red shirts. *East Asia Forum Quarterly* 2(2) (April–June): 14–16.

Hill, M. and W. Montag (eds) 2000 *Masses, Classes, and the Public Sphere*. London & New York: Verso.

Ho, R. and E. C. Chapman (eds) 1973 *Studies of contemporary Thailand*. Research School of Pacific Studies, Department of Human Geography Publication HG/8 (1973). Canberra: The Australian National University.

Horkheimer, M. and T. Adorno 2002 [1947] *Dialectic of Enlightenment. Philosophical Fragments*. Stanford, Calif.: Stanford University Press.

Huntingdon, S. 1993 The clash of civilizations? *Foreign Affairs* 72(3) (Summer): 22–49.

Ingram, D. 1987 *Habermas and the Dialectic of Reason*. New Haven, Conn., & London: Yale University Press.

Ingram, J. C. 1971 (2nd edn) *Economic Changes in Thailand 1850–1970*. Stanford, Calif.: Stanford University Press.

Iribarren, J. (ed.) 1974 *Documentos colectivos del Episcopado español 1870–1974*. Madrid: B.A.C.

Ivison, D. 2002 *Postcolonial Liberalism*. Cambridge: Cambridge University Press.

Jackson, P. A. 2004 The tapestry of language and theory: reading Rosalind Morris on post-structuralism and Thai modernity. *South East Asia Research* 12(3): 337–77.

Jameson, F. 1992 *Postmodernism, or, The Cultural Logic of Late Capitalism*. London & New York: Verso.

Jameson, F. and M. Miyoshi (eds) 1998 *The Cultures of Globalization*. Durham, NC, & London: Duke University Press.

Jewell, T., L. Forrest and R. Chadbourne 1988 *Improving Aboriginal/Police Relations: The Roebourne Research Project*. Perth: Special Government Committee on Aboriginal/Police and Community Relations.

Johnston, E. 1991 *Report of the Inquiry into the Death of John Peter Pat*. Royal Commission into Aboriginal Deaths in Custody. Canberra: Australian Government Printer.

Juluwarlu Aboriginal Corporation 2004 *Know the Song, Know the Country*. Roebourne, WA: Juluwarlu Aboriginal Corporation.

Kaufman, H. K. 1960 *Bangkhuad. A Community Study in Thailand*. New York: J. J. Augustin.

Kellner, D. 1997 The Frankfurt School and British cultural studies: the missed articulation. Online at <http://www.gseis.ucla.edu/courses/ed253a/Mckellner/CSFS.html> [viewed 7 July 2003].

Kelly, M. (ed.) 1994 *Critique and Power. Recasting the Foucault/Habermas Debate*. Cambridge, Mass., & London: The MIT Press.

Keyes, C. 2006 *The destruction of a shrine to Brahma in Bangkok and the fall of Thaksin Shinawatra: the occult and the Thai coup in Thailand of September 2006*. Asia Research Institute Working Paper Series No. 80. Singapore: Asia Research Institute, <http://www.ari.nus.edu.sg>

Kikkawa, T. 1999 Strategies of Japanese corporations facing global competition: the cases of Sony and Toray. Online at <http://project.iss.u-tokyo.ac.jp/kikkawa/iss-6.pdf>

Kingshill, K. 1960 *Ku Daeng—The Red Tomb*. Chiang Mai: The Prince Royal's College.

Kirsch, A. T. 1975 Economy, polity, and religion in Thailand. In G. W. Skinner and A. T. Kirsch (eds) *Change and Persistence in Thai Society. Essays in Honor of Lauriston Sharp*. Ithaca, NY, & London: Cornell University Press.

Kirsch, S. 2001 Lost worlds: environmental disaster, 'culture loss', and the law. *Current Anthropology* 42(2): 167–98.

Klima, A. 2002 *The Funeral Casino. Meditation, Massacre, and Exchange with the Dead in Thailand*. Princeton, NJ, & Oxford: Princeton University Press.

Kruger, R. 2009 [1964] *The Devil's Discus. The Death of Ananda King of Siam*. Hong Kong: DMP Publications.

Lannon, F. 1975 Catholic Bilbao from restoration to republic: a selective study of educational institutions 1876–1931. Unpublished D.Phil. thesis. St Antony's College, Oxford.

—— 1979 The socio-political role of the Spanish Church: a case study. *Journal of Contemporary History* 14: 193–210.

—— 1982 Modern Spain: the project of a national Catholicism. In S. Mews (ed.) *Religion and National Identity*. Oxford: The University Press.

—— 1984 The Church's crusade against the Republic. In P. Preston (ed.) *Revolution and War in Spain 1931–1939*. London: Methuen.

—— 1987 *Privilege, Persecution, and Prophecy. The Catholic Church in Spain 1875–1975*. Oxford: Clarendon Press.

—— 2002 *The Spanish Civil War 1936–1939*. Oxford: Osprey Publishing, Essential Histories.

Lawrence, D. 1996–97 *Managing parks/managing 'country': joint management of Aboriginal owned protected areas in Australia*. Research Paper 2 1996-97. Canberra: Parliamentary Library.

Leach, E. 1954 *Political Systems of Highland Burma*. Cambridge, Mass.: Harvard University Press.

Lear, J. 2008 *Radical Hope: Ethics in the Face of Cultural Devastation*. Cambridge, Mass.: Harvard University Press.

Levi, P. 2001 [1979] *If This is a Man*. London: Abacus.

Levinas, E. 1979. *Totality and Infinity: An Essay on Exteriority*. Boston: Martinus Nijhoff.

Li, X. 1996 'Asian values' and the universality of human rights. *Report from the Institute for Philosophy and Public Policy* 16(2), <http://www.puaf.umd.edu/ippp>

Lieberman, S. 1982 *The Contemporary Spanish Economy: A Historical Perspective*. London: George Allen & Unwin.

Likhit Dhiravegin 1985 *Thai Politics: Selected Aspects of Development and Change*. Bangkok: Tri-Sciences Publishing House.

Litchfield, J. 2009 Rio Tinto Iron Ore's Pilbara native title negotiations. Presentation to the Native Title and Cultural Heritage 2009 Conference, Marriott Hotel, Brisbane, 27 October.

Mabry, B. D. 1977 The Thai labor movement. *Asian Survey* 17(10) (October).

McCargo, D. 1997 The politics of scandal: the case of the Thai press. In J. Stanyer and G. Stoker (eds) *Contemporary Political Studies (Proceedings of the Annual Conference of the Political Studies Association of the United Kingdom)*. *Volume 1*. Nottingham: Political Studies Association.

McCarthy, T. 1984 [1981] Introduction. In J. Habermas *The Theory of Communicative Action. Volume 1. Reason and the Rationalization of Society*. (Trans. T. McCarthy.) Boston: Beacon Press.

—— 2002 [1987] Introduction. In J. Habermas *The Philosophical Discourse of Modernity*. (Trans. F. Lawrence.) Cambridge, Mass.: The MIT Press.

Mallet, M. 1978 Causes and consequences of the October '76 coup. In A. Turton, J. Fast and M. Caldwell (eds) *Thailand. Roots of Conflict*. Nottingham: Spokesman.

Mares, P. 2002 (2nd edn) *Borderline*. Sydney: UNSW Press.

Marr, D. and M. Wilkinson 2003 *Dark Victory*. Crows Nest, NSW: Allen & Unwin.

*Mater Admirabilis* 1959. *See* under Chamartin 1959b.

May, R. J. and V. Selochan (eds) 2004 [1998] *The Military and Democracy in Asia and the Pacific*. Canberra: ANU E Press, <http://epress.anu.edu.au/mdap/mobile_devices/index.html>

Mauss, M. 1970 [1954] *The Gift. Forms and Functions of Exchange in Archaic Societies*. London: Cohen & West.

Miller, D. (ed.) 1995 *Worlds Apart. Modernity through the Prism of the Local*. London & New York: Routledge.

Milner, A. 1999 What's happened to Asian values. In D. Goodman and G. Segal (eds) *Towards Recovery in Pacific Asia*. London & New York: Routledge.

Mitchell, T. (ed.) 2000 *Questions of Modernity*. Minnesota & London: University of Minnesota Press.

Mitchell, W. J. T. 1995 Translator translated. Interview with cultural theorist Homi Bhabha. *Artforum* 33(7): 80–4, <http://prelectur.stanford.edu.lecturers/bhabha/interview.html>

de la Mora, C. 1940 *In Place of Splendour*. London: Michael Joseph Ltd.

Morell, D. L. 1977 Police power in Thailand. [Letter to the Editor.] *The New York Review of Books* 24(17) (27 October).

Morell, David and Chai-anan Samudavanija 1981 *Political conflict in Thailand*. Cambridge, Massachusetts: Oelgeschlage, Gunn & Hain, Publishers, Inc.

Morris, R. 2000 *In the Place of Origins. Modernity and its Mediums in Northern Thailand*. Durham, NC, & London: Duke University Press.

—— 2002 Crises of the modern in northern Thailand: ritual, tradition, and the new value of pastness. In S. Tanabe and C. F. Keyes (eds) *Cultural Crisis and Social Memory. Modernity and Identity in Thailand and Laos*. Honolulu: University of Hawai'i Press.

Nations, R. 1976 The first round to Bangkok. *Far Eastern Economic Review*, 12 November: 67–8.

Nelson, M. H. (ed.) 2001 *Thailand's New Politics. King Prajakhipok's Institute Yearbook 2001*. Bangkok: King Prajakhipok's Institute & White Lotus Press.

Niezen, R. 2003 *The Origins of Indigenism. Human Rights and the Politics of Identity*. Berkeley: University of California Press.

Noranit Setabutr 2003 The 1997 Constitution: the path of reform. Unpublished paper presented to the Thailand Update 2003 Conference, The Australian National University, Canberra.

Office of the High Commissioner on Human Rights 1993 *World Conference on Human Rights*, <http://www.unhchr.ch/html/menu5/wchr.htm> [viewed 5 March 2003].

Olive, N. 1997 *Karijini Mirlimirli*. Fremantle, WA: Fremantle Arts Centre Press.

Paisal Thaiwatchainant 1976 The labour movement in Thailand. Unpublished talk to the Foreign Correspondents' Club, Bangkok.

Pasuk Phongpaichit and C. Baker 2010 *The mask-play election: generals, politicians and voters at Thailand's 2007 poll*. Asia Research Institute Working Paper Series No. 144. Singapore: Asia Research Institute, <http://www.ari.nus.edu.sg>

Peterson, N. 2010 Other people's lives: secular assimilation, culture and ungovernability. In J. Altman and M. Hinkson (eds) *Culture Crisis. Anthropology and Politics in Aboriginal Australia*. Sydney: UNSW Press.

Peterson, N., I. Keen and B. Sansom 1977 Succession to land. Primary and secondary rights to Aboriginal estates. Submission to the Ranger Uranium Environmental Inquiry prepared on behalf of the Northern Land Council. Canberra: Commonwealth Government Joint Select Committee on Aboriginal Land Rights in the Northern Territory.

Piker, S. 1969 'Loose structure' and the analysis of Thai social organisation. In H.-D. Evers (ed.) *Loosely Structured Social Systems. Thailand in Comparative Perspective*. New Haven, Conn.: Yale University Council on Southeast Asia Studies.

Pogrund, B. 2009 Durban II, another opportunity missed. *The Guardian*, 24 April, <http://www.guardian.co.uk/commentisfree/2009/apr/24/Durban-racism-conference-ahmadinejad>

Povinelli, E. 2002 *The Cunning of Recognition: Indigenous Alterities and the Making of Australian Multiculturalism*. Durham, NC: Duke University Press.

Prajak Kongkirati 2011 Robust electoral politics, unstable democracy. *East Asia Forum Quarterly* 3(4) (October–December): 7–8.

Preston, P. 2004 *Juan Carlos. Steering Spain from Dictatorship to Democracy*. New York & London: W. W. Norton & Company.

Prizzia, R. and Narong Sinsawasdi 1974 *Thailand: Student Activism and Political Change*. Bangkok: Allied Printers.

Prudisan Jumbala 1973 *Patron–Client Relations, Entourage System and Development*. Bangkok: Thailand Information Centre.

Rask Madsen, M. 2002 If God is dead, then thank goodness for international law. A review of *The end of human rights* by Costas Douzinas (2000). *Journal of South Pacific Law* 6(2), <www.paclii.org.journals/fJSPL/vol06/14.shtml>

Rasmussen, D. M. 1990 *Reading Habermas*. Cambridge, Mass.: Basil Blackwell.

Rawls, J. 1999 [rev. edn] *A Theory of Justice*. Oxford: Oxford University Press.

Religiosas Del Sagrado Corazón de Jesús 1946 *Cien Años de educación cristiana*. Zaragoza: Librería general.

Reoch, R. (ed.) 1994 *Human Rights. The New Consensus*. London: Regency Press in association with the United Nations High Commissioner for Refugees.

Reynolds, C. J. 1987 *Thai Radical Discourse. The Real Face of Thai Feudalism Today*. Ithaca, NY: Southeast Asia Program, Cornell University.

—— (ed.) 2002 *National Identity and its Defenders. Thailand Today*. Chiang Mai: Silkworm Books.

—— 2010 Behind the Thai crisis. *Inside Story*, 20 April, <http://inside.org.au/behind-the-thai-crisis/>

Reynolds, R. 1989 *The West Pilbara Documentation Project*. Report prepared for the West Australian Heritage Committee, the Australian Heritage Commission, the Department of Conservation and Land Management, the Department of Employment and Training. Perth: Department of Aboriginal Sites, Western Australian Museum.

Rijavec, F. 2005 Sovereign voices: the redundancy of mass media; and moves towards routine and sovereign means of media production/distribution in Roebourne, Western Australia. *IM E-Journal of the National Academy of Screen and Sound* (1), <http://nass.murdoch.edu.au/nass_previous_issue_no1.htm>

Rijavec, F. and R. Solomon 2005 [1993] *Exile and the Kingdom*. DVD documentary. Roebourne, WA: Juluwarlu Aboriginal Corporation.

Rio Tinto Iron Ore 2006 *Breaking New Ground. Stories of Mining and the Aboriginal People of the Pilbara*. Perth: Rio Tinto Iron Ore.

Roberts, L., R. Chadbourne and R. Murray 1986 *Aboriginal/Police Relations in the Pilbara. A Study of Perceptions*. Perth: Special Government Committee on Aboriginal/Police and Community Relations.

Robertson, G. 2010 *The Case of the Pope*. Camberwell, Vic.: Penguin Books.

Rong Syamananda 1973 *A History of Thailand*. Bangkok: Chulalongkorn University.

Rose, D. B. 1994 Whose confidentiality? Whose intellectual property? In M. Edmunds (ed.) *Claims to Knowledge, Claims to Country*. Canberra: Native Title Research Unit, Australian Institute of Aboriginal and Torres Strait Islander Studies.

Ross, F. C. 2003a *Bearing Witness: Women and the Truth and Reconciliation Commission in South Africa*. Sterling, Va.: Pluto Press.

—— 2003b Using rights to measure wrongs: a case study of method and moral in the work of the South African Truth and Reconciliation Commission. In R. Ashby Wilson and J. P. Mitchell (eds) *Human Rights in Global Perspective. Anthropological Studies of Rights, Claims and Entitlements*. London & New York: Routledge.

Rowley, C. D. 1972a [1970] *Outcasts in White Australia*. Ringwood, Vic.: Penguin Books.

—— 1972b [1970] *The Remote Aborigines*. Ringwood, Vic.: Penguin Books.

van Roy, E. 1971 *Economic systems of Northern Thailand*. Ithaca: Cornell University Press.

de la Rue, K. 1979 *Pearl shells and pastures: the story of Cossack and Roebourne and their place in the history of the North West, from the earliest explorations to 1910*. Roebourne, Western Australia: Cossack Project Committee.

Sahlins, M. 1999 Two or three things that I know about culture. *Journal of the Royal Anthropological Institute* 5(3): 399–422.

—— 2005 On the anthropology of modernity, or, some triumphs of culture over despondency theory. In A. Hooper (ed.) *Culture and Sustainable Development in the Pacific*. Canberra: ANU E Press & Asia Pacific Press.

Said, E. 1993 *Culture and Imperialism*. London: Chatto & Windus.

—— 2003 [1978] *Orientalism*. London: Penguin Books.

Sarkar, N. K. 1975 *Industrial Structure of Greater Bangkok*. Bangkok: United Nations Asia Institute.

Saul, J. R. 1993 *Voltaire's Bastards. The Dictatorship of Reason in the West*. Toronto: Penguin Books.

Schregle, J. 1975 *Labor Law in Southeast Asia. Some Topical Issues*. Diliman, Quezon City: UP Law Centre, First Andres Bonifacio Annual Lecture Series.

Seaman, P. 1984 *Report on the Aboriginal Land Inquiry*. Perth: Government of Western Australia.

Seidman, S. (ed.) 1989 *Jürgen Habermas on Society and Politics. A Reader*. Boston: Beacon Press.

Sen, A. 1997 Human rights and Asian values: what Lee Kuan Yew and Le Peng don't understand about Asia. *The New Republic* 217(2–3), <http://www.sintercom.org/polinfo/polessays/sen.html>

Silcock, T. H. 1970 *The Economic Development of Thai Agriculture*. Canberra: Australian National University Press.

Skidmore, M. 2004 *Karaoke Fascism. Burma and the Politics of Fear*. Philadelphia: University of Pennsylvania Press.

Skinner, G. W. and A. T. Kirsch (eds) 1975 *Change and Persistence in Thai Society. Essays in Honor of Lauriston Sharp*. Ithaca, NY, & London: Cornell University Press.

Streckfuss, D. E. 1998 The poetics of subversion: civil liberty and lese-majeste in the modern Thai state. Unpublished D.Phil. dissertation. University of Wisconsin-Madison, Wisconsin.

Suchit Bunbongkarn 2004 [1998] The military and democracy in Thailand. In R. J. May and V. Selochan (eds) *The Military and Democracy in Asia and the Pacific*. Canberra: ANU E Press, <http://epress.anu.edu.au/mdap/mobile_devices/index.html>

Supachai Manusphaibool 1976 The role of the government and labour legislation in the development of Thailand's industrial relations system. Unpublished MSc dissertation. London School of Economics and Political Science, University of London, London.

Supachai Manusphaibool and Kanaengnid Tantigate (eds) 1977 *Foreign Management and Thai Industrial Relations System. Proceedings of the Industrial Relations Seminar, February 1, 1977*. Bangkok: Faculty of Economics, Chulalongkorn University.

Surin Maisrikrod 1992 *Thailand's two general elections in 1992: democracy sustained*. Research Notes and Discussion Papers No. 75. Singapore: Institute of Southeast Asian Studies.

Sutton, P. 2003 *Native Title in Australia. An Ethnographic Perspective*. Cambridge: Cambridge University Press.

Tambiah, S. J. 1968 The ideology of merit and the social correlates of Buddhism in a Thai village. In E. R. Leach (ed.) *Dialectic in Practical Religion*. Cambridge: Cambridge University Press.

—— 1970 *Buddhism and the Spirit Cults in North-East Thailand*. Cambridge: The University Press.

Tanabe, S. and C. F. Keyes (eds) 2002 *Cultural Crisis and Social Memory. Modernity and Identity in Thailand and Laos*. Honolulu: University of Hawai'i Press.

Taylor, C. 2002 Modern social imaginaries. *Public Culture* 14(1): 91–124.

—— 2003 [1989] *Sources of the Self*. Cambridge: Cambridge University Press.

—— 2004 *Modern Social Imaginaries*. Durham, NC, & London: Duke University Press, Public Planet Books.

Taylor, J. and B. Scambary 2005 *Indigenous people and the Pilbara mining boom*. CAEPR Research Monograph No. 25. Canberra: Centre for Aboriginal Economic Policy Research, The Australian National University.

Thailand, Saphaphuthan Ratsadon (House of Representatives) 1996–2008 Historical Archive of Parliamentary election results, <http://www.ipu.org/parline-e/reports/>

Thak Chaloemtiarana 1979 *Thailand: The Politics of Despotic Paternalism.* Bangkok: The Social Science Association of Thailand, Thai Khadi Institute, Thammasat University.

Thanet Arpornsuwan, Phichit Chongsathitwatana and Supachai Manusphaibool 1978 *The Trade Union Movement in Thailand.* Bangkok: Friedrich-Ebert-Stiftung, Federal Republic of Germany.

Thitinan Pongsudhirak 2010 The unstoppable red shirts. *East Asia Forum Quarterly* 2(2) (April–June): 13–14.

Thomas, H. 1977 [1961] *The Spanish Civil War.* Harmondsworth, UK: Penguin Books in association with Hamish Hamilton.

Thompson, J. B. and D. Held (eds) 1982 *Habermas. Critical Debates.* London & Basingstoke: Macmillan.

Thongchai Winichakul 1994 *Siam Mapped. A History of the Geo-Body of a Nation.* Honolulu: University of Hawai'i Press.

—— 2000 Siam's colonial conditions and the birth of Thai history. In A. Turton (ed.) *Civility and Savagery: Social Identity in Tai States.* Richmond, UK: Curzon.

—— 2002 Remembering/silencing the traumatic past: the ambivalent memories of the October 1976 massacre in Bangkok. In T. Shigeharu and C. F. Keyes (eds) *Cultural Crisis and Social Memory. Modernity and Identity in Thailand and Laos.* Honolulu: University of Hawai'i Press.

Tienchai Wongchaisuwan 1993 The political economy of Thailand: the Thai peripheral state, 1958–1988. Unpublished PhD dissertation. State University of New York at Binghamton, NY.

Toulmin, S. 1992 *Cosmopolis. The Hidden Agenda of Modernity.* Chicago: University of Chicago Press.

Tremlett, G. 2007 [2006] *Ghosts of Spain. Travels through a Country's Hidden Past.* London: Faber & Faber.

Turton, A. 1976 Northern Thai peasant society: twentieth century transformations in political and jural structures. *The Journal of Peasant Studies* 3(3): 104–42.

—— 1978 The current situation in the Thai countryside. In A. Turton, J. Fast and M. Caldwell (eds) *Thailand. Roots of Conflict*. Nottingham: Spokesman.

—— (ed.) 2000 *Civility and Savagery: Social Identity in Tai States*. Richmond, Surrey: Curzon.

Turton, A., J. Fast and M. Caldwell (eds) 1978 *Thailand. Roots of Conflict*. Nottingham: Spokesman.

United Nations High Commissioner for Human Rights n.d. *The International Bill of Human Rights*. Fact Sheet No. 2 (Rev. 1), <http://www.unhchr.ch/html/menu6/2/fs2.htm> [viewed 10 March 2004].

de Vries, S. 2008 *Desert queen: the many lives and loves of Daisy Bates*. Pymble, NSW: HarperCollins Publishers.

Walker, A. 2010 Why King Vajiralongkorn will be good for Thai democracy. *New Mandala*, 23 April, <http://asiapacific.anu.edu.au/newmandala/2010/04/23>

—— 2012 *Thailand's Political Peasants: Power in the Modern Rural Economy*. Madison, Wis.: University of Wisconsin Press.

Walker, A. and N. Farrelly 2010 Bangkok: how did it come to this? <http://inside.org.au/bangkok-how-did-it-come-to-this/>

Wallach, J. 2005 Human rights as an ethics of power. In R. A. Wilson (ed.) *Human Rights in the 'War on Terror'*. Cambridge: Cambridge University Press.

Wand, P. and J. Wilkie 2001 *South East Arnhem Land Collaborative Research Project: the origins in Rio Tinto*. South East Arnhem Land Collaborative Research Project (SEALCP) Working Paper Series No. 3. Wollongong, NSW: University of Wollongong.

Warr, P. 2011 A nation caught in the middle-income trap. *East Asia Forum Quarterly* 3(4) (October–December): 4–6.

Weber, M. 1946 Politics as a vocation. In *From Max Weber: Essays in Sociology*. (Trans and eds H. H. Gerth and C. Wright Mills.) New York: Oxford University Press. [Originally a speech at Munich University, 1918, published in 1919 by Duncker & Humblodt, Munich.]

—— 1985 *The Protestant Ethic and the Spirit of Capitalism*. London: Unwin Paperbacks.

White, S. K. (ed.) 1995 *The Cambridge Companion to Habermas*. Cambridge: Cambridge University Press.

Wijewardene, G. 1967 Some aspects of rural life in Thailand. In T. H. Silcock (ed.) *Thailand*. Canberra: Australian National University Press.

Wilson, D. A. 1959 *Thailand and Marxism*. Bangkok: Thailand Information Centre.

Wilson, R. A. 2005 *Human Rights in the 'War on Terror'*. Cambridge: Cambridge University Press.

Wilson, R. A. and J. P. Mitchell (eds) 2003 *Human Rights in Global Perspective. Anthropological Studies of Rights, Claims and Entitlements*. London & New York: Routledge.

Wright, A. 1977 *The Spanish Economy 1959–1976*. London: Macmillan.

# Index

www.ingramcontent.com/pod-product-compliance
Lightning Source LLC
Chambersburg PA
CBHW061243270326
41928CB00041B/3379

* 9 7 8 1 9 2 2 1 4 4 6 6 9 *